# Congress
## *and* Urban Problems

*A casebook on the legislative process*

# Congress
# *and* Urban Problems

FREDERIC N. CLEAVELAND
*and associates*

ROYCE HANSON

M. KENT JENNINGS

JOHN E. MOORE

JUDITH HEIMLICH PARRIS

RANDALL B. RIPLEY

THE BROOKINGS INSTITUTION
*Washington, D.C.*

THE BROOKINGS INSTITUTION is an independent organization devoted to nonpartisan research, education, and publication in economics, government, foreign policy, and the social sciences generally. Its principal purposes are to aid in the development of sound public policies and to promote public understanding of issues of national importance.

The Institution was founded on December 8, 1927, to merge the activities of the Institute for Government Research, founded in 1916, the Institute of Economics, founded in 1922, and the Robert Brookings Graduate School of Economics and Government, founded in 1924.

The general administration of the Institution is the responsibility of a self-perpetuating Board of Trustees. The trustees are likewise charged with maintaining the independence of the staff and fostering the most favorable conditions for creative research and education. The immediate direction of the policies, program, and staff of the Institution is vested in the President, assisted by an advisory council chosen from the staff of the Institution.

In publishing a study, the Institution presents it as a competent treatment of a subject worthy of public consideration. The interpretations and conclusions in such publications are those of the author or authors and do not purport to represent the views of the other staff members, officers, or trustees of the Brookings Institution.

# Foreword

THIS IS A BOOK ABOUT URBAN PROBLEMS—and about the United States Congress. It is a collection of legislative studies, each one focused upon an acute and perplexing problem associated with urban living and the efforts of Congress in the 1950's and 60's to cope with it. The central objective of each study is to analyze the complex political process through which Congress attempted to formulate policy and program to meet the problem. The collection as a whole has two important additional objectives: to explore the nature of urban problems as a field of national policy making; and to learn more about how Congress functions in this field.

Topics for the case studies were selected in part to further these research goals and in part opportunistically—two or three attractive subjects had to be abandoned in favor of others for want of a scholar available at the time to undertake them, or because essential data or sources proved inaccessible. The project's objectives required a series of cases that together would throw light on the shape and character of the urban affairs field, and individually would say something about the variety of problems, issues, and matters of concern that make it up. The alternative of focusing entirely on issues narrowly urban, like air pollution, was rejected to avoid the danger that case selection itself might suggest more structure and cohesion in urban affairs as a policy field than would otherwise appear. Instead, topics were included that focused upon both problems exclusively urban and those not exclusively urban but of acute concern to urban dwellers because of their high incidence in densely populated areas (juvenile delinquency, for example).

The legislative events analyzed in these studies occurred primarily dur-

ing the Eighty-sixth, Eighty-seventh, and Eighty-eighth Congresses, span-
ning in part three presidential administrations, from 1959 through 1964.
In most instances the policy issues under study had been before Congress
over a longer period of time, and they are likely to continue to require
congressional attention for years to come. No claim is made that these
seven studies cover the spectrum of congressional legislation for urban
areas, although they do suggest the range of city concerns that reach the
Congress. No study in the series gives central attention to housing, urban
renewal, the federal highway program, the "war on poverty," or government in the District of Columbia where Congress has served as city council. When cases are written on these subjects they will be important additions to this initial nucleus. This volume simply makes a beginning at
understanding the politics of what the authors believe is a newly emerging field of national policy making.

The case book is a product of Brookings' continuing research program
on the United States Congress. It follows Charles L. Clapp's *The
Congressman: His Work as He Sees It* (1963), Andrew Hacker's
*Congressional Districting: The Issue of Equal Representation* (1963,
revised 1964), Joseph P. Harris' *Congressional Control of Administration* (1964), and Randall B. Ripley's *Party Leadership and Legislation
in the House of Representatives* (1967).

The project was conceived by and carried out under the general direction of George A. Graham, then director of governmental studies at
Brookings. Planning began in 1963 under the leadership of Dean E.
Mann. Frederic N. Cleaveland assumed direction of the project in the
fall of 1963 when he joined the Brookings staff, on leave from the University of North Carolina. The seven studies were written by five political scientists on the staff of, or under contract with, the Brookings
Institution: Royce Hanson, Washington Center for Metropolitan
Studies; Judith Heimlich Parris, Brookings Institution; M. Kent Jennings, University of Michigan; John E. Moore, University of California
at Santa Barbara; and Randall B. Ripley, Ohio State University (at the
time on the Brookings staff). While no attempt was made to develop a
common research design, reasonable uniformity was ensured through discussions among researchers and extensive review of early drafts. Mr.
Cleaveland wrote the introductory and concluding chapters that provide
a setting for the studies and an assessment of what they reveal about
congressional policy making for urban affairs.

Each study was submitted for comment to a number of the participants in the events it described. Our special thanks go to these members of Congress and their staffs, executive agency officials, and representatives of interest groups who gave invaluable aid in ensuring that the cases portray complicated events accurately. We are also indebted to the respondents interviewed by each case researcher in developing his study; their cooperation and forthrightness were essential to the success of the project.

Mr. Ripley assisted Mr. Cleaveland in supervising the conduct of the case studies and in reading and revising the entire manuscript. Mr. James L. Sundquist of the Brookings staff also read and commented on the manuscript and helped to revise selected portions of it. Mrs. Ellen Joseph edited the volume, and Mrs. Helen B. Eisenhart prepared the index. Mrs. Elizabeth Patton served as secretary for the project, with assistance from Miss Deborah Bliss, Miss Barbara Maly, and Mrs. Sara Sklar. The contributions of all these people are gratefully acknowledged.

The Brookings Institution appreciates the support of the Ford Foundation that made the project possible.

The authors alone are responsible for the interpretations presented and the conclusions reached in this volume. They do not purport to represent the views of the trustees, the officers, or other staff members of the Brookings Institution or of the Ford Foundation.

KERMIT GORDON
*President*

*February 1969*
*Washington, D.C.*

# Contents

# Tables

FREDERIC N. CLEAVELAND

# Introduction

NO ASPECT OF CONTEMPORARY AMERICA offers more challenge to the policy maker and to the student of public affairs than the complexities of life in metropolitan areas. This is not surprising, for as a nation the United States is in the midst of galloping urbanization, nearing the point where three out of every four Americans are urban dwellers. Almost 90 percent of all future population growth in this country is expected to occur in spreading metropolitan belts scattered across the nation. Matching this explosive growth rate of the metropolis is the multiplication of problems created by, or aggravated by, rapid urbanization—social, economic, physical, and deeply human problems—many of which make new and critical demands upon government. The efforts of a federal system to cope with these demands in turn raise perplexing and significant issues for elected officials, for public administrators, and for voters at every level of government. Indeed, few would dispute the judgment of Walter Lippmann that "the problem of governing a great city . . . is by all odds the most important, the most pressing, and the most unavoidable, domestic problem we have to face."[1] In a real sense the welfare of the nation has come to depend upon its urban areas—upon how effectively they function, and upon the quality of living their inhabitants achieve.

Moreover, the increasing concern of the national government with problems of the metropolis is subtly changing the character of the American political system. Roscoe C. Martin, documenting the growing incidence of direct federal-city relationships, has concluded that we are evolving a new kind of federalism embracing three partners—nation, states,

[1] Walter Lippmann, "The Dog That Didn't Bark," *Washington Post*, Nov. 2, 1965.

and cities: "The expansion of the federal system from a two- to a three-way partnership stands as the principal incidental consequence of the growth of federal-city relationships. . . . What has emerged is an expanded system which reveals American federalism once more as a tough, resilient, flexible institution capable of adapting to conditions and complexities unforeseen by the founders."[2]

The involvement of the national government in the problems of urban areas has come about gradually and in piecemeal fashion, as the pragmatic activity of a government with vast fiscal resources responding to the needs of people caught in the dislocation of massive urbanization. And Congress has played a central role in the expansion of direct federal government relationships to cities. It has not always assumed the initiative—indeed the popular image portrays the legislature in the role of "reluctant dragon," responding to the leadership of a positive President and to the pressures of beleaguered local officials and aroused city dwellers. But wherever initiative has come from, Congress nevertheless has adopted statutes formulating basic policy to govern federal involvement in urban affairs; it has authorized programs and financed them through regular appropriations. Yet there has been no study of the part it has had and continues to have in strengthening the role of the cities in the federal system. This volume will aid in a fuller understanding of what Congress contributes to this evolutionary process.

There is an extensive body of contemporary professional literature on urbanization, on the growth patterns of metropolitan areas, on the many and varied problems of urban living, and on the equally varied governmental efforts to deal with these problems. This literature is the product of social scientists from several disciplines employing many different research methods and strategies. A continuous flow of urban studies has been financed by governmental agencies and private foundations, great and small, and encouraged by the proliferating metropolitan survey and action bodies and centers for urban research. Yet in all this scholarly attention one dimension of the field has largely been overlooked: urban problems as a subject of congressional politics.[3] This volume is intended to help fill this gap.

---

[2] Roscoe C. Martin, *The Cities and the Federal System* (Atherton Press, 1965), p. 175.

[3] One useful discussion of the subject is contained in Chapter 3, "Congress and Metropolitan Areas," of the book by Robert H. Connery and Richard H. Leach, *The Federal Government and Metropolitan Areas* (Harvard University Press, 1960).

## Some Underlying Assumptions

The broad objective of this group of studies is to contribute to a more comprehensive and realistic understanding of Congress and the dynamics of national policy making. Underlying and guiding the research projects are two assumptions about the nature of American politics and the processes of legislative policy making: first, that the structure and interaction of political forces do vary from one major field of public policy to another; and, second, that as a consequence the policy-making role of Congress and the behavior of congressional actors also vary in important ways from one policy sector to another. These assumptions need to be tested. To do so adequately will require systematic, in-depth explorations of Congress at work in a number of major fields of public policy. This series of studies in the area of urban problems represents a first step. It must be followed by research on congressional activity in other sectors before it can be determined whether significant differences distinguish the "politics" of congressional policy making in urban affairs from the "politics" of agricultural policy making, or the "politics" of fiscal policy making, and so on.

A third assumption underlying this research is that urban problems can appropriately be considered a distinct—though not isolated—field of public policy, with an identifiable structure, a predictable set of participants, and characteristic patterns of behavior by the congressmen, interest group leaders, executive agency officials, and others who are involved. While a full exploration of this assumption must also await comparison of urban affairs policy making with policy making in other sectors, these case studies were designed in the hope that they would furnish at least preliminary findings about urban problems as a field of public policy. In a direct sense, then, this third assumption represents an hypothesis to be examined in the immediate project.

Much about urban affairs severely complicates the job of defining it as a policy area for Congress. Since urban affairs involves many interests, as a policy field it will overlap and share concerns with other policy sectors. As a category for classifying proposed legislation, it must be conceived broadly. Yet the field might be defined so broadly as to include all the issues affecting urban dwellers, that is, people who happen to live in cities. Such a definition, in a largely urbanized society, would make urban affairs policy virtually coextensive with all domestic governmental policies. Other dangers confront an overly modest definition. The field might be defined as solely concerned with urban physical development, narrowing it to policy matters related to housing, slum clearance, urban renewal, and physical planning. But a policy sector so limited would exclude many of the problems weighing heavily today upon urban dwellers and their community leaders—problems of education, health, welfare, crime, and racial tensions—all of which exist to some extent in most settings but become acute in the cities.

Many recognized fields of public policy have a structure of generally accepted values, or are related to an institutional system or an identifiable profession or technology that help to resolve such troublesome questions of definition and scope.[4] Not so with urban problems as a policy field. It lacks a traditional structure of values and relationships. Indeed, the concept of urban affairs is new.

A perplexing conceptual issue arises because urban affairs as a policy field implies both the dimension of governmental function (urban development) and the dimension of geographic area (the city). Typically in American politics, fields of public policy have been visualized in terms of the clusters of values, objectives, and programs related to basic governmental functions alone, like education, law enforcement, or transportation. Executive agencies and legislative committees in federal, state, and local governments in the United States are for the most part organized in terms of these functions of government.[5] While major fields of policy so defined were once relatively discrete, however, they have become less so as urban concentration has grown, increasing the interdependence of modern living, accentuating old problems, and breeding new ones. Ef-

---

[4] The field of natural resources policy, for example, can be defined historically largely in terms of generally accepted values concerning the conservation of resources for public use and enjoyment. Education as a policy field draws structure and definition from the complex institutional systems society has developed to educate both young and adults. Public health as a policy sector derives cohesion, structure, and content from the health-related professions and their technologies.

[5] Congressional committee jurisdiction in both houses is organized functionally for the most part. The only real exceptions at the committee level are the two District of Columbia Committees with legislative responsibility for bills concerned with governing the District. At the subcommittee level, both the House and Senate Government Operations Committees have a subcommittee on intergovernmental relations focusing to some extent on areal concerns that cut across governmental functions. The Foreign Affairs and Foreign Relations Committees have subcommittee structures organized around world regions (Latin America, Africa, and so on).

forts to improve community health in socially decaying areas of the central city are surely part of urban affairs policy as well as part of public health policy, and perhaps welfare policy. Urban mass transportation problems create peculiar new requirements for solution not met by traditional transportation policy. Crime, delinquency and violence—long the concern of governmental policy makers—reappear in especially acute forms now as functions of the urban ghetto. Urbanism makes a difference, both as a cause of public problems and in necessitating coordination of remedial action. But a policy sector embodying an areal as well as a functional dimension complicates the classification of issues and presents legislators with difficult considerations.

Nonetheless, the concepts of urban environment, of community and neighborhood, are steadily becoming more salient in efforts to cope with the complex problems of mass society. Technological developments in professional fields like public health, social welfare, sanitary engineering, and urban and regional planning involve an increasing emphasis upon environmental considerations. Growing attention is being given to environmental factors in the diagnosis of delinquency, poverty, disease, and racial and ethnic tensions. It is evident that the areal dimension is growing in importance and in relevance, making a stronger and stronger case for the recognition of urban problems, or urban affairs, as a distinct policy sector.

Thus, reformulated for examination in the legislative problem studies, the third underlying assumption proposes that:

1. a growing body of problems, issues, and subjects requiring federal concern and action share a common element of urban-relatedness, either because they are uniquely associated with and part of the governmental function of fostering urban development, or because they are significantly more acute as problems or issues when occurring in an area of considerable population density;

2. these matters, although dispersed among the jurisdictions of several congressional committees, already provide a focus for some degree of patterned behavior among congressional, interest group, and executive agency actors—a focus, however, that is blurred by the traditional organization of the committees along the lines of separate governmental functions;

3. these matters have become sufficiently important nationally, sufficiently urgent in the large cities, and sufficiently coherent as a basis for policy formulation and action to warrant recognizing them as a category

of public policy—"urban affairs"—to be employed in assigning agency and congressional committee jurisdiction and in analyzing policy-making behavior.

## Some Suggestive Analytical Themes

If this volume is to be more than a collection of discrete case studies, and is to illuminate the dynamics of congressional policy making and the complex world of urban problems, the reader must apply a few modest tools of analysis. This section of the Introduction suggests some questions pertinent to such analysis. The questions are organized around three related themes that run through all the cases: the politics of congressional policy making for urban areas; urban affairs as a field of national policy; and the nature of urban interests and their representation.[6]

[6] Political scientist Theodore Lowi in "American Business, Public Policy, Case Studies, and Political Theory," *World Politics,* Vol. 16 (July 1964), pp. 677–715, has proposed a very different approach to analyzing case studies of domestic public policies. Although Professor Lowi also starts with the assumption that different types of policies have their own distinctive politics, he rejects the descriptive, subject-matter policy categories (e.g. agriculture policy, education policy, etc.) in favor of three broad classes defined in terms of the impact, or expected impact, of policies upon society. He proposes to classify every domestic public policy as either (a) distributive, or (b) regulatory, or (c) redistributive, each category having its characteristic political structure, style of decision making, and pattern of coalition building.

*Distributive policies* involve the giving away of some value (goods, resources, services) that is in near-inexhaustible supply through a kind of patronage process. The "pork barrel" approach of tariff legislation in the 1920's and the rivers and harbors bills illustrate distributive policy making. Coalition building is through log-rolling, a process congenial to a number of congressional committees.

*Regulatory policies* involve the application of general rules to individual cases, limiting one group for the benefit of competing interests, or expanding one group's opportunities at the expense of competitors (as in granting a television license). Thus the impact of the policies is broad, even though implementation is case by case. Regulatory politics are "balance of power" politics on the typical pressure-group model. Coalitions are unstable, regrouping as the balance of power changes.

*Redistributive policies* have a much wider impact than other policies, and involve interrelationships among large groups like social classes, the unemployed, property owners, etc. "Redistribution" signifies taking some value from one broad group for the benefit of another. The progressive income tax and welfare programs are examples. Coalitions in this arena tend to be large and highly stable, and they tend to engage in class-oriented, ideological politics.

Lowi's goal is an analytical approach capable of generating testable propositions and leading to a theory about public policies and the politics of policy making. Regardless

*The Politics of Congressional Policy Making for Urban Areas.* In examining this theme a variety of aspects can be analyzed. Three are focused on here because they may be particularly revealing in a search for patterns in congressional behavior and structure in the forming of policy. These three aspects are: legislative initiative; issue context (that is, the frames of reference legislators bring to bear upon urban issues); and congressional voting on the bills concerned with urban problems.

Legislative initiative in the sense employed here refers to both the contribution of ideas on policy and program and the provision of skilled judgment on tactics and parliamentary maneuver. Most bills that reach the floor involve a mixture of initiatives from several sources. What kind of mix of initiatives is typically present in bills on urban problems? Does policy and tactical leadership normally come from members of Congress and their staffs? From interest group professionals? From executive officials or White House staff? When a policy field encompasses problems calling for the application of complex technologies—as in the case of urban affairs—the knowledgeable professionals gathered to work together on a problem are another potentially important source of legislative initiative. Is there such a concentration of urban specialists located on Capitol Hill, perhaps attached to a congressional committee? Or in the Department of Housing and Urban Development? Or in the headquarters of one or another interest group? Patterns of legislative initiative may also reflect larger issues of national politics. What was the effect of divided government during the Eisenhower years—the President from one political party and the opposition party in control of the Congress? Did initiative patterns change with the transition from a Republican to a Democratic administration?

The issue context is another significant guide to congressional behavior in coping with urban problems. When a problem is presented to the Congress calling for legislative action, the way congressmen and senators perceive it—the frame of reference through which they view the problem and classify it for analysis—has much to do with how the bill is handled, with what attitudes and policy preferences are evoked, and consequently with policy outcomes. Thus, it is likely to make a significant difference whether a bill to strengthen the ability of local govern-

---

of the particular schemes scholars employ, however, congressmen, interest group leaders, politicians, and voters will of course continue to think and act in terms of familiar, descriptive policy fields. Accordingly, this project utilizes the more traditional subject-matter categorization of public policies.

ments to deal with civil disobedience is looked upon by members of Congress as a civil rights issue or simply as a matter of improving law enforcement. When a proposal is introduced and begins to move through the legislative mill, it is perceived as falling within a specified policy setting. This setting may help to determine the committees to which a bill is assigned; it may help to identify those executive agencies and interest groups that are presumed to have special insights, and those groups with significant stakes in the policy outcome. What the particular policy setting is thought to be will often furnish cues to congressmen and senators not directly involved in processing the bill, helping to guide their responses to the proposal. Therefore, examining the way issue contexts are defined for bills dealing with urban problems should reveal something about how congressmen go about legislating for urban areas. How do existing patterns of committee jurisdiction (typically based upon governmental functions) affect the way members perceive the issue context of urban bills? Are such bills often caught up in political questions unrelated to urban concerns? Does the intermingling of governmental function and areal considerations in urban affairs policy create special problems in defining issue contexts?

Voting patterns will also provide important clues to the dynamics of congressional behavior and the influences on that behavior. Standard interpretations of congressional behavior have concluded that political party is most often the decisive factor in determining how members vote.[7] However, because urban affairs issues embody a strong areal dimension, it might be expected that constituency influences are especially important here. Are congressmen from predominantly urban districts likely to vote for bills favored by urban interests regardless of the stand taken by their party's congressional leaders? Do the relative strengths of constituency and party vary with the particular kind of urban issue involved? For example, what is the effect when a substantial increase in federal spending is involved? How do congressional party leaders view bills on urban problems: do they consider it risky to take a party position on such bills because of the potentially strong influence of constituency? Do urban affairs bills tend to polarize members of Congress into two

[7] See, for example, David Truman's assessment of the impact of party in the House of Representatives: "The party label is clearly the single most reliable indicator of congressional voting behavior," although "it is admittedly somewhat less than perfect." David B. Truman, "The State Delegations and the Structure of Party Voting in the U.S. House of Representatives," *American Political Science Review,* Vol. 50 (December 1956), p. 1023.

groups—rural and urban—or is the division more complex, perhaps involving metropolitan interests, suburban and small city interests, and rural and town interests?

*Urban Affairs as a Field of National Policy.* Analysis of congressional policy making for urban areas may indicate whether recurring patterns of "urban affairs politics" are beginning to emerge. But the tough problems of defining that policy sector and determining its scope will still remain. It is perhaps useful at this stage to conceive of a policy continuum constructed along the dimension of "urban-relatedness" to serve as a guide in defining urban affairs as a policy field. All federal public policies of concern to urban dwellers could then be placed along this continuum. At one end would be placed public policies uniquely and distinctively urban; at the other end would be the policies that concern all members of a mass society, including urban dwellers, but that have no special urban relevance. Ranged along the spectrum between these two end points would be the great variety of federal policies that have some measurable urban dimension, without being distinctively or exclusively urban in character. Policies to cope with crime and narcotics control, with racial tensions and ethnic rivalries, with education in overcrowded schools, unemployment, unwed mothers, and abandoned children would all be located somewhere along the central portion of the continuum. Can such a continuum provide the basis for defining a field of urban affairs policy? Would such an analytical device aid members of Congress in developing appropriate issue contexts? Can it suggest ways to adapt the jurisdiction of congressional committees to facilitate the handling of legislation for urban areas?

*The Nature of Urban Interests and Their Representation.* In the highly pluralistic political system of twentieth-century America, the manner in which the interests of individuals and groups are expressed through organizational form and represented in the political process has a significant effect upon the structure of politics and the processes of policy making. In some recognized policy sectors like agriculture and labor, for example, relatively well-defined constituencies have emerged with stable organizations to articulate goals, translate them into public policy proposals, and represent these constituencies in the deliberations of the nation's policy makers. Are there well-defined urban constituencies? Have stable interest group organizations emerged in the urban field, broadly representative of urban dwellers? What kinds of interests do urban dwellers seem to have? Are they like producer interests? Consumer interests? Or some mixture? Do people who live in cities share widely recognized, common "urban" interests? Or are there potentially sharp conflicts between the interests of different segments of urban society? Are urban constituencies organized to reconcile any such conflicting interests? Do political parties play a role in representing urban dwellers? What effect does the nature of urban interests and of urban constituencies have upon congressional policy making in this area?

## The Political Context for Policy Making in Urban Affairs, 1955–64

The seven legislative problem studies that follow are all a part of the unfolding fabric of national policy of the 1950's and 60's. Each study is a kind of close-up, magnified picture of one small part of a much larger moving field. To place these events in proper perspective it is essential to see them continually against the background of the larger political setting.

*The Environment of National Politics.* The decade 1955–64 is a fascinating and perplexing period in which to explore national policy making in the United States. It was a time of ambiguous mandates from the electorate: the voters gave Republican candidate Dwight D. Eisenhower thumping majorities in 1952 and 1956, yet Republicans controlled the House and Senate during only two of his eight years in the White House, and then by a narrow margin. John F. Kennedy's election in 1960 was by the slimmest margin of any successful presidential candidate in this century. There was clear evidence in every election of increasing voter mobility across party lines. The editors of *Congressional Quarterly* noted in reviewing the politics of the postwar years "a willingness among the voters to support superior candidates of either party—candidates who represented, in large part, the domestic and foreign policy consensus of the postwar era."[8]

For President and Congress it was a time of divided government.

[8] Congressional Quarterly Service, *Congress and the Nation 1945–1964, A Review of Government and Politics in the Postwar Years* (1965), p. 1.

During six years one party controlled the legislative branch and the other the White House. Within the House of Representatives the division of strength between the parties was fairly even and the division of strength between liberals and conservatives still closer. In the Senate a similar balance between the parties continued through the Eighty-fourth and Eighty-fifth Congresses and then gave way in the election of 1958 to substantial gains by liberal Democratic forces. This change added another division, that between a liberal Senate and a more conservative House. This complex balancing of power made for a "politics of dead-center," placing an extra premium upon skillful legislative leadership from within Congress and from the White House if the policy-making machinery was to function effectively.

Shifts of voters across party lines in the metropolitan areas proved decisive in the outcome of presidential elections. Yet the impact of this increased voter mobility upon Congress was muted by the countervailing effect of seniority. Committee chairmen holding safe seats in the South or Middle West continued in power. New congressmen and senators elected by the votes of city and suburban dwellers simply took their places at the bottom of the seniority ladder, conscious of their vulnerability two to six years hence should their politically independent urban supporters again cross party lines.[9]

Foreign policy issues with major domestic political implications, like Sputnik, the U-2 incident, the Bay of Pigs, the Cuban missile crisis, and military involvement in Vietnam, dominated national policy making throughout the period. Economic recessions in 1957 and 1958 and again in 1960 provided ammunition both to sustain the Republican presidential vetoes preserving an economy drive, and to allow the Democrats in the campaign of 1960 to charge a slow-down in the rate of economic growth. From the Little Rock crisis in September 1957 to passage of the Civil Rights Act of 1964 the complex issues of Negro rights were before the Congress and the President almost continually in one form or another—school desegregation, voting rights, public accommodations, or employment opportunities. In the same way the agenda of every congressional session during this ten-year period was filled with domestic

[9] Editors of the *Congressional Quarterly* noted in their review of the postwar years: "The Congressional representatives least able to build up seniority, and thus the least likely to head committees, were those from the politically volatile suburbs and city fringe areas where the major new population movements—and many major problems—of the postwar era occurred." *Ibid.*, p. 2.

welfare and economic aid questions, revolving about proposals for area redevelopment, broadening social security benefits and unemployment compensation, raising the minimum wage, medical care for the aged, housing and urban renewal, federal aid to education, and grants-in-aid programs for water pollution control, community health facilities, and the like. Typically, the Eisenhower administration was more cautious than its Democratic successors in initiating, advocating, and supporting such proposals. The signs of economic recession in 1957–58 reinforced the administration's natural inclination toward fiscal conservatism. Thus by the time Democratic gains in the congressional election of 1958 had provided majorities able to pass some of this legislation, the President was ready to use his veto weapon repeatedly, and to work hard to garner enough conservative votes from both parties to sustain the vetoes. His success in the second session of the Eighty-sixth Congress was impressive.

John Kennedy's accession to the presidency in 1961 opened the way for passage of some of the proposals vetoed by President Eisenhower. Yet the uncertainty of Kennedy's electoral mandate, modest Republican congressional gains in the election of 1960, and a stand-off between the parties in the mid-term election of 1962 meant that the liberal-conservative balance shifted only slightly toward the liberal side. The shift was enough, however, to ensure first session passage by the Eighty-seventh Congress of such reintroduced bills as the depressed areas legislation, a comprehensive general housing package, a boost in the minimum wage to $1.25 per hour, extension of unemployment compensation, aid to dependent children of the unemployed, water pollution control, and juvenile delinquency legislation. But the administration was far from invincible on Capitol Hill, for during this same session it lost its bids for a new department of urban affairs, federal aid to education, and long-term Treasury financing of area redevelopment loans. The second session of the Eighty-seventh Congress and the first session of the Eighty-eighth brought a generally similar experience of mixed success and failure. From the President's point of view, a high point of his legislative achievements was the Nuclear Test Ban Treaty, negotiated and ratified in 1963. But congressional handling of foreign aid grew progressively tougher from 1961 to 1963, and the slow movement of tax reduction and civil rights bills through House committees reflected a hardening congressional position toward administration-sponsored measures, especially those involving spending. Perhaps the most vivid measure of congressional intransigence during 1963 was the snail's pace of appropriations bills through the two chambers: at the end of the first quarter of the new fiscal year only four out of twelve annual appropriations bills had cleared the Congress.

Then came President Kennedy's assassination on November 22, 1963. The second session of the Eighty-eighth Congress was a vastly different story; it was almost as if a massive logjam had been cleared. Whether as a memorial to John Kennedy or as a response to a master legislative tactician, Lyndon B. Johnson, or more likely both, the House and Senate achieved a truly remarkable legislative record in 1964. Every major legislative proposal submitted by the deceased President during his almost thirty-five months in office had been acted upon by the end of 1964. The list is staggering: a major civil rights act, significant tax reduction, the innovative antipoverty legislation, a sweeping federal pay raise bill, a foreign aid bill approved at close to the levels recommended by the administration, a major enlargment of the National Wilderness System, renewal of important programs like the National Defense Education Act and the Hill-Burton hospital construction program with broader financing assured, a grant program to support urban mass transportation, a permanent food stamp program, and eight of the twelve appropriations acts approved and on the President's desk by August 1964. The Eighty-eighth Congress indeed gave the Johnson-Kennedy program unprecedented legislative support.

Lyndon Johnson's landslide election victory in November 1964 ensured continuation of this strong support, for he carried into office with him a substantial liberal Democratic majority, capable of dominating both the House of Representatives and the Senate. As the ten-year period with which this book is concerned came to a close, the Eighty-ninth Congress was waiting in the wings, prepared to continue enacting into law measures that had languished before a divided Congress, in some cases for fifteen years or more.

*Federal Policy on Urban Development.* In the postwar period federal policies and programs to cope with urban problems have steadily become more important, gaining stature as part of the regular agenda for national policy making. Political party platforms include sections devoted to urban affairs. Presidents in their State of the Union messages to Congress concern themselves with urban problems. In no small measure the bellwether of this coming-of-age of urban affairs has been the transformation of federal policies on housing and slum clearance into a full-fledged program of community development. Since none of the legislative problem studies that follow is directly concerned with federal housing and urban renewal programs, a brief review of this policy evolution is presented here. This development is an important part of the contemporary political context for policy making in urban affairs, and of special relevance to this volume.

Before World War II the federal government's principal direct impact upon cities came through the depression-born programs in housing and the financing of home building. These activities focused primarily upon the objective of economic recovery through a strong construction industry, with better living conditions for disadvantaged groups a secondary concern. In 1949, after months of debate, Congress passed the Taft-Ellender-Wagner housing bill that added a third major goal, community development. This Housing Act of 1949 enlarged the public housing program and established a continuing slum clearance and redevelopment program. Five years later, in the Housing Act of 1954, Congress broadened the idea of slum removal, transforming it into the city planner's concept of urban renewal. This act provided all-out federal support for planned urban communities, authorizing grants for local planning assistance, and establishing standards for planning and plan-implementing machinery that communities would have to meet to receive urban renewal funds. This requirement of a "Workable Program for Community Improvement" represented a long step beyond urban redevelopment through slum clearance. In addition, under the 1954 act a separate Urban Renewal Administration was established in the Housing and Home Finance Agency.

During the decade this volume is especially concerned with, Congress several times enacted legislation expanding federal support for urban development—in 1955, 1956, 1959, 1961, and 1964. These laws enlarged the federal contribution to urban renewal and expanded the scope of the program itself, moving from what had essentially been a program for improving residential housing to one having the broad objectives of community renewal with increasing emphasis on rebuilding the central city. In addition Congress added more complete planning requirements and established a number of auxiliary programs, such as housing for the elderly, loans for public facility construction, loans and grants to assist development of urban mass transportation systems, grants to promote "city beautification" and help communities acquire permanent open space land, special programs for depressed areas, for housing displaced persons, and so on. Finally in 1965 Congress raised the Housing and Home Finance Agency to cabinet status as the Department of Housing and Urban Development.

The change in federal policy on urban development accomplished between 1954 and 1964 was dramatic, even revolutionary. Urban political sociologist Scott Greer puts it in these terms: "The older goal of increasing low-cost housing, of eliminating and preventing slums, is mixed with the newer goal of revitalizing the central city; to both has been added the more recent goal of creating the planned American city through the community renewal program."[10] Moreover, this evolution from slum removal through urban renewal to planned community development shifted the emphasis away from highly controversial public housing issues to new policies widely applauded by influential political forces with much greater access to Congress than public housing proponents could claim—big-city mayors, large-scale developers, and commercial and financial interests with important stakes in the downtown business districts of major cities. Greer highlights this changing support pattern:

> The Workable Program was never popular with most LPA [Local Public Authority] officials. Its emphasis upon housing and relocation together forced a commitment to public housing. Its emphasis on code enforcement led agencies into very complex and emotion-generating public policy. And, as housing became in many cities a problem chiefly among Negroes, support for housing programs in general dwindled. At the same time, other interests pressed for more concern with the problems of the central business district of the city. The central city mayors were worried about tax bases, for, as downtown property declined, shopping centers grew by leaps and bounds in the suburbs. The mayors pressed for general programs of city redevelopment and for smaller local contributions to the program. . . . To these interests was joined the steady pressure of those theorists who had always felt that urban renewal should be concerned with the entire urban structure, that slums and blight were merely symptoms of weakness in the general pattern.[11]

To complete this review of federal policy on urban development, the achievements of the Eighty-ninth Congress should briefly be noted, even though these additions to policy occurred in 1965 and 1966, after the period in which the legislative problem cases occurred. The Eighty-ninth Congress, elected with the Johnson sweep in 1964, passed major urban legislation in each session: the Housing and Urban Development Act of

[10] Scott Greer, *Urban Renewal and American Cities* (Bobbs-Merrill, 1965), p. 165.
[11] *Ibid.* pp. 27–28.

1965 in the first session, and the Demonstration Cities and Metropolitan Development Act of 1966 in the second session. The 1965 act included one significant policy innovation, the rent subsidy provision, designed to encourage private interests to invest more in housing for low income families by directly subsidizing rent payments. Thus, an eligible tenant would pay 25 percent of his income for rent and the Federal Housing Administration would pay monthly to the owner the difference between the tenant's payment and the market rental. The 1966 act authorized federal grants and technical assistance to cities to help them plan, develop, and carry out comprehensive "demonstration" programs for rebuilding or restoring entire blighted neighborhoods or sections by coordinated use of all available federal government aids, plus local private and public resources. The program called for massive new grant support, as well as an emphasis upon the coordination of various federal assistance efforts into a comprehensive whole for aiding a specific community.

*Interest Groups and Urban Affairs.* A final element of the environment for urban affairs policy making that deserves notice is interest group politics.[12] What kinds of interest groups are concerned with urban problems and what are their stakes in resolving these problems?

Business groups of national scope and broad interests, like the United States Chamber of Commerce and the National Association of Manufacturers, display only a secondary interest in urban problems. Typically, they derive their stand on federal policy regarding urban affairs from more general concerns for economy in government, for limiting the role of government at all levels, and for maintaining the traditional balance in the federal system. Producer interest groups play an active part whenever their special interests come into focus in congressional consideration of legislation on urban problems. Organizations like the Association of American Railroads or the National Association of Home Builders have long worked closely with congressional committees, their staffs, and related agencies in standard patterns of pressure group politics.

The role of organized labor, however, requires special comment. The behavior of large international unions reflects both a producer and a con-

---

[12] For another, more detailed treatment see Chapter 2, "Representation of Metropolitan Interests in Washington," in Connery and Leach, *The Federal Government and Metropolitan Areas.*

sumer orientation. These are mass membership organizations made up of urban dwellers, and their spokesmen often express consumer perspectives—concern for the quality of city life, for better housing, for recreation and open space, for a cleaner, healthier city. Also the labor movement has long advocated the increasing use of governmental authority to cope with problems of human need. Labor's support for more federal involvement in urban affairs, then, not only serves the desires of its members for better living conditions, but is also ideologically comfortable and consistent. Yet of course union labor speaks with many and often conflicting voices. Some unions have strong producer-like interests at stake in specific federal programs to cope with urban problems and will work energetically to win recognition and protection for these interests, even at the expense of the more general consumer interests of their membership.

The two organizations that appear to come the closest to representing urban interests across the board are the United States Conference of Mayors and the National League of Municipalities (or American Municipal Association, as it was known during the period covered by these studies). The Conference of Mayors speaks particularly for large cities and the League of Municipalities for towns and small and middle-size cities. The increasing commitment of federal resources to the solution of urban problems is testimony to the efforts of both these organizations. They are, however, spokesmen for local governments rather than direct representatives of city dwellers. Their orientation appears more like that of a producer interest than a consumer interest; the products their clients are engaged in producing are of course urban government and governmental services. Their priorities reflect the agenda of problems defined by city hall as targets for governmental action—and even at that high policy level of municipal government the perspective on urban problems is less than a whole view.

The Conference of Mayors and the League of Municipalities both maintain Washington-based staff members who carry on typical interest group functions. At times they work closely with staff from Capitol Hill and the executive agencies in drafting legislation. They testify before committees, urge action upon the President and Congress, supply congressional friends with facts and figures to support their case, and in all ways try to maintain and solidify the support they already have and, when the right opportunity presents itself, to pick up additional support.

Another type of group interested in urban affairs policy making is the professional association with special concern for urban problems. Almost every urban-related profession has its own association—social workers, sanitary engineers, city planners, transportation and traffic engineers, and so on. These groups display something of a producer interest; they tend to be concerned with the particular urban problems for which their skills and body of professional doctrine offer possible solutions. But they exhibit more than producer concerns; there is typically a professional ethic involved, expressed as a regard for the public interest and a commitment to employ the technology of their profession in the service of society. Also, these professionals often speak as employees of governments or as practitioners under contract to government. Despite claims to objectivity and expertise, these groups tend to regard the problems of urban life through the lenses of their profession, and, in so doing, often make an incomplete diagnosis of problems and of the public interest involved. Thus, the urban renewal specialist defines urban problems in terms of the causes and consequences of a blighted central city. He finds his solutions along the path of massive rebuilding of downtown slums through a mixture of public and private investment to recapture commercial vitality and tax paying properties. What happens to the dispossessed, their progressive alienation from the community, the effect of their relocation upon low income neighborhoods beyond the core city, all too often tend to be lumped together as "regrettable" costs of "progress" and "beautification." Yet such professional groups may hold a near monopoly over technical knowledge and skills that are often essential for resolving certain urban problems; and they do add another dimension to the representation of urban interests.

Still another type of interest group actively involved in certain urban issues is the "good government" or "do-gooder" lobby. The conservationist organizations that have staunchly and continually pressed for a stronger federal role in the control of water pollution illustrate the special character of this lobby. Typically the conservationist groups—the National Parks Association, the Wilderness Society, the National Wildlife Federation, the Izaak Walton League, and others—are nonprofit membership organizations, often led by wealthy, big-city easterners with a sportsman's interest in preserving natural beauty for the enjoyment of man, and a social conscience encouraging continued efforts for the public good, as they define it. In contrast to many other interest groups with important stakes in the resolution of urban problems, the conservationists and other "do-gooders" appear to represent the consumer interests on the urban scene, expressing concern for the amenities of life in the city.

With this brief characterization of the environment for congressional consideration of urban problems the reader is now ready for the legislative problem cases.

RANDALL B. RIPLEY

# Congress Champions
# Aid to Airports, 1958–59

ON MARCH 17, 1958 Democratic Senator A. S.
Mike Monroney of Oklahoma introduced S. 3502 into the Senate. The
bill provided for the expansion of an existing federal grants-in-aid program to publicly owned airports of all sizes. The program had been operating since 1946. But during almost its entire short history the executive
officials responsible for it and the members of the Senate and House interested in it had been at odds over a whole series of specific points. By
1958 the congressional proponents of a large aid program had become
convinced that the executive was going to kill the program unless Congress took new legislative action. The interested members of Congress, led
by Monroney and aided by a dozen interest groups, thus became engaged
in a legislative fight with the executive that was not fully concluded until
June 29 of the following year. It is the story of this combat that the present case study will relate.

This case deals with a situation in which Congress was extremely active. The strongest interest groups in the field of aviation were only tan-
gentially interested in the airport aid legislation. The less powerful but
more directly affected groups devoted most of their efforts to consulting
with and aiding the members of the Senate and House who were the
chief proponents of the legislation. They helped bolster the case of their
friends rather than directing their attention to persuading their enemies.
In the executive branch the friends of an expanded program were severely limited in the help they could offer senators and representatives. A
history of bitter division over this program haunted those who privately favored expanded aid and restrained their outward enthusiasm.

20

The top officials of the Commerce Department in 1958 and the Federal Aviation Agency (FAA) in 1959, as well as the White House and the Bureau of the Budget (BOB) in both years, opposed any expansion. Thus, with both the interest group and executive proponents of the legislation restrained, either by choice or by necessity, members of Congress interested in promoting the program could take the lead in mustering the support and votes needed. Almost inevitably this meant that senior members of the expert committees involved would be the most important congressional participants.

This case also involves a presidential veto. The power of the veto is demonstrated by what happened following it. It was particularly instrumental in mobilizing loyal party troops and promoting party warfare in Congress.

Finally, this case explores the way in which Congress considered one substantive area at the heart of federal-city relations. With minor exceptions the states have not entered the airport field. Airports are uniquely a city problem and the airports of the large urban areas are particularly visible and expensive. Before 1958 many of the battles over the federal aid to airports program had been fought along urban-rural lines.

Yet the debate over airport legislation in 1958 and 1959 was not cast in urban terms. Other points obscured many of the urban issues actually involved. In Congress even the strongest proponents of the program showed more concern for small airports for feeder lines and for general (noncommercial) aviation than they did for urban airports. They apparently felt that the support of rural and small town members of Congress was essential to the passage of legislation, and therefore the appeal was made to them. Also, in Congress in 1959 vigorous struggling between the two political parties defined the issues in terms of spending and a balanced budget rather than in terms of what was needed to improve the transportation network among the major urban areas of the country. The President and many of his chief advisers also thought primarily in terms of a balanced budget. Even those in the executive sympathetic to a substantial program were more concerned with the health of commercial aviation than with planning for transportation among major centers of population. This concern with commercial aviation permeated thinking in Congress as well. A few of the urban interest groups attempted to define the debate in terms of urban needs but their pleas attracted little attention. The most politically potent group in the aviation field represented commercial aviation and, though it had no primary interest in the airport aid program, this group's outlook prevailed in Congress and in the executive.

In short, the story that follows illustrates how an urban problem can be handled by almost all of the participants without much consideration of the truly urban issues. This does not mean that the urban needs will automatically be ignored, but it leaves a sizable opening for distortions to become entrenched in a federal program of aid.

## The Development of a Federal Interest in Civil Aviation

During the 1920's and 30's, the time that Mike Monroney had been a reporter and businessman in Oklahoma, the federal government began to show an interest in airports for civil aviation. Congress passed the Air Commerce Act in 1926, providing for federal aid to airways and air navigation facilities, but specifically excluding airport aid. In 1928 Congress authorized the government to lease public lands to local authorities for use as public airports. Until the beginning of the New Deal in 1933, however, the government had spent only a little over $1 million on civil airports. Between 1933 and 1941 it spent about $350 million. This aid was not part of a conscious program of airport development, though. It was instead a part of the antidepression effort and was successively administered by the Civil Works Administration, the Federal Emergency Relief Administration, and the Works Progress Administration.

In 1938, the year in which Monroney was first elected to the House of Representatives, Congress enacted the Civil Aeronautics Act. This law created the Civil Aeronautics Authority—split in 1940 into the independent Civil Aeronautics Board (CAB) and the Civil Aeronautics Administration (CAA) in the Commerce Department—with wide powers of regulation over air transport and a duty "to encourage and foster the development of civil aeronautics and air commerce in the United States, and to encourage the establishment of civil airways, landing areas, and other air navigation facilities." The act also gave the Aeronautics Authority the power "to acquire, establish, operate, and maintain, in whole or in part, air navigation facilities at and upon any municipally owned or other landing area approved for such installation, operation, or maintenance by the Administrator."

On the subject of airports alone the act required that the Civil Aeronautics Authority make a field survey of existing airports and then present to Congress "definite recommendations 1) as to whether the Federal Government should participate in the construction, improvement, development, operation or maintenance of a national system of airports, and 2) if Federal participation is recommended, the extent to which, and the manner in which, the Federal Government shall so participate." In complying with this section the Aeronautics Authority recommended that "Development and maintenance of an adequate system of airports . . . should be recognized in principle as a matter of national concern." Furthermore, "Such a system should be regarded, under certain conditions, as a proper object of Federal expenditure." The specific administrative recommendations were related to existing public works and work relief programs. The Civil Aeronautics Authority suggested that $100 million of such funds should be earmarked for airports and $25 million in additional funds should be appropriated for airport development. The report estimated as necessary a national system of 3,500 airports. The development needed to achieve this goal would cost about $500 million.

In 1940 Senator Pat McCarran, Democrat from Nevada, and Representative Clarence F. Lea, Democrat from California, introduced legislation authorizing $125 million for the development of landing areas. A subcommittee of the Senate Commerce Committee held two days of hearings on the bill but Congress did nothing further. In the fall of 1940, however, in a supplemental appropriations act, Congress gave to the administrator of civil aeronautics $40 million "for the construction, improvement, and repair of not to exceed two hundred and fifty public airports and other public landing areas." These 250 airports were to be "necessary for national defense" and the administrator's choices were to be approved by the secretaries of war, navy, and commerce.

During the war years, while Monroney was a member of the House Banking and Currency Committee, the CAA spent about $350 million for landing area development. At the end of the war, in accordance with the provisions of the Surplus Property Act of 1944, 500 airport facilities developed for defense purposes were given to various units of local government.

In June 1944 the House by resolution requested the secretary of commerce, acting through the CAA administrator, "to make a survey of the need for a system of airports and landing areas throughout the United States" including the number needed, their location, and cost. It also requested legislative recommendations. The secretary submitted his report five months later. The report envisioned a national network of 6,050 airports, the development and improvement of which would cost slightly over $1.25 billion. The secretary felt that the federal government should spend about half of that amount over a five- to ten-year period. The states or municipalities involved would provide the rest.

*The 1946 Airport Act.* Thus by the end of World War II the congressional and executive forces favoring systematic and extensive federal aid to airports were beginning to develop their ideas publicly. Several aviation and urban interest groups also joined in supporting a new federal program. Over 70 percent of the capital expenditures for civil airports in the United States before the end of the war had come from the federal government. However, much of this expenditure was for a large number of defense airfields in isolated spots. The restriction of commercial aviation and the ban on private aviation during the war also helped to produce what most knowledgeable persons felt to be serious gaps in the U.S. airport network in 1945.

The legislative process that resulted in the Federal Airport Act of 1946 began in March 1945 in the Senate Commerce Committee hearings on bills introduced by McCarran and Democratic Senator Josiah W. Bailey of North Carolina. It immediately became clear in these hearings that there was going to be almost no opposition to the program. Senator Bailey, the chairman of the committee, opened one day of the hearings by saying, "I am just going to suggest to those who talk to us today, you are just wasting your time and ours if you are arguing for this program. I think everybody in the country is for this program. . . ." There was also surprisingly little controversy over the amount necessary. No one thought a range of $400–$700 million over five to ten years unreasonable. Likewise, all agreed that a fifty-fifty matching provision was wise. Thus the debate quickly turned to the other details of the program.

Most disagreement revolved around two questions concerning the urban areas of the country. The first question was what size towns and what size airports should benefit. The representatives of the big cities felt that the program should be aimed at them. Those speaking for general aviation felt small airports should be the prime beneficiaries. The CAA officials testifying indicated that the core of the program would be aimed at small and middle-sized towns without adequate airports. The second question was what public agencies would be eligible for federal grants. The CAA and representatives of the state aviation agencies felt that all money should be channeled through the state agencies. Representatives of the cities insisted that the Civil Aeronautics Administration be able to make grants directly to sponsoring municipal agencies.

The Senate committee reported a bill calling for a five-year program of $500 million. Thirty-five percent of these funds would be available for an urban program, which involved the two largest classes of airports. These funds could be given directly to the municipalities as well as to the states. Sixty-five percent of the funds were for the three smallest classes of airports and had to be channeled through state agencies. The bill further provided that no project in the urban program could be undertaken "except upon . . . specific authorization by the Congress," on the rivers and harbors pattern. The state program was apportioned to the states half on the basis of area and half on the basis of population.

On the Senate floor the debate focused on the administrative pattern and also on the total money amount. Led by Republican Owen Brewster of Maine, those favoring an amendment channeling all funds through the states were successful. The economizers, led by Republican Robert A. Taft of Ohio, cut $125 million from the total funds authorized.

The House Committee on Interstate and Foreign Commerce held hearings in May and June of 1945. Again attention quickly centered on the administrative pattern. Extreme positions like that of the Association of American Railroads against all aid and that of the Personal Aircraft Council favoring an airport for every incorporated place in the United States (about 17,000 in number) were ignored. There were few comments on the amount of the program, the matching provisions, and the apportionment formula. Essentially the hearings provided an arena for the National Association of State Aviation Officials and its allies to debate with spokesmen for the cities (chiefly the American Municipal Association and the United States Conference of Mayors) and their allies. Mayor Fiorello H. La Guardia of New York, a former House member, gave effective testimony in both houses on behalf of the Conference of Mayors. The cities' position was supported by aviation trade groups, contractors, and the spokesman for the commercial airlines.

The committee bill as reported authorized a ten-year program of $700 million. It required matching funds from the local sponsors. Seventy-five percent of the funds were to be apportioned to the states on the basis of area and population and the administrator would be given the other 25 percent as a discretionary fund. Grants could be made directly to local sponsors unless state law required channeling through a state agency. On the House floor the committee leadership defeated efforts to cut $200 million from the program and to require channeling of the funds through the states.

The conference on the bill lasted for a number of months. The sticking point was the Brewster amendment passed by the Senate. The House delegation to the conference committee was in favor of the House provision. One Democratic senator, George L. Radcliffe of Maryland, refused to join his Democratic colleagues on the committee in supporting the House provision. Finally Radcliffe gave in and the conferees agreed to direct channeling of funds to cities, if state law did not provide otherwise. Both houses agreed to the conference report, after spirited debate in the Senate. President Harry S. Truman signed the bill into law on May 13, 1946.

This law authorized federal aid to publicly owned airports, on a fifty-fifty matching basis, in the amount of $520 million for a period of seven years. No more than $100 million could be appropriated in any single year. Three-quarters of the money was to be allocated to the states, one-half on the basis of area and one-half on the basis of population. One-quarter of it was to be distributed at the discretion of the administrator. Municipalities, as well as states, could apply for grants. The administrator had to prepare a national airport plan each year. This plan was to "specify, in terms of general location and type of development, the projects considered by the Administrator to be necessary to provide a system of public airports adequate to anticipate and meet the needs of civil aeronautics." Projects involving airports of the two largest classes had to receive specific congressional approval. The administrator was to submit all such proposed projects to Congress by April 30 of each year. Subsequent appropriations would be considered approval of the projects unless Congress objected by law or concurrent resolution.

*Subsequent Amendments.* Between 1947 and 1955 interest in the airport aid legislation remained alive. The Senate and House Interstate and Foreign Commerce Committees held nine separate hearings on proposed amendments. The Appropriations Committees acted each year to appropriate funds for the program. The executive became involved in various reexaminations of the program. Interest groups that had existed in 1945–46 continued their perusal of it. A new group representing the largest airports of the country, the Airport Operators Council, was organized in 1948. It spoke for the cities and counties operating most of these airports and was also concerned with the welfare of the commercial airlines that served them.

In 1947 Senator Brewster again championed the cause of the states (and rural areas) against the cities. As chairman of a subcommittee appointed specifically to consider one bill, he engineered committee approval for a bill requiring all airport aid money to be channeled through the states. The House took no action, however, and the bill never reached the Senate floor. Brewster was aided, of course, by the National Association of State Aviation Officials but was opposed by the Conference of Mayors and the Municipal Association.

In 1949 the House Subcommittee on Transportation considered bills that would increase the discretionary funds to 40 percent of the total and that would exempt airport projects costing less than $50,000 from the requirement of specific congressional approval. This second amendment passed both houses with little comment and was approved by the President in February 1950. Also in 1950, the year of Monroney's election to the Senate, Congress extended the expiration date of the original 1946 act by five years, making it a twelve-year program instead of a seven-year program. Congress wished to assure local sponsors of a continuing interest in the program and it also wished to allow time for the full $520 million authorization to be appropriated.

Beginning in 1948 the Department of Commerce took an increasingly dim view of the airport program. Thus the CAA and its Office of Airports were hampered in their support of a sizable program, although their inclusion of numerous rural and small airports in the national plan assured them of much support in Congress. In 1952 President Truman asked General James Doolittle and two others to serve as a temporary President's Airport Commission. He asked the commission to restudy "the Nation's policy on airport location and use." The commission reported in May 1952. Among other recommendations it specifically suggested that the program of federal aid to airports should be expanded.

When the administration of Dwight D. Eisenhower took office, however, the secretary of commerce, Sinclair Weeks, ordered a suspension of the airport program so that a new study of it could be made. Accordingly the Department of Commerce withdrew most of the pending budget (drawn up under Truman). The Bureau of the Budget requested no funds whatsoever for the airport program for fiscal 1954. Congress accordingly appropriated none. The undersecretary of commerce for transportation, Robert B. Murray, Jr., appointed an airport panel consisting of twelve men from various parts of the aviation industry to produce "a new look" at the national airport program. The panel contained no representatives of the Conference of Mayors or the Municipal Association. The twelve submitted their report early in 1954. The report recommended that the federal government should aid airports "to the extent that these airports serve the national interest," defined as "a demonstration of tangible aeronautical necessity in the area served"; and that terminal buildings should be excluded from eligibility, limiting aid to the landing areas themselves and some outside safety features.

The Department of Commerce requested and received a supplemental appropriation of $22 million for fiscal 1955. At the same time the department proposed to Congress three amendments to the Airport Act. The first would prohibit aid to airport terminal buildings. The second would increase the discretionary fund to 50 percent of the total. The third would allow aid only to airports meeting the "national interest" criteria defined as airports providing at least 3,000 emplaned passengers annually or having 30 based aircraft. This proposal would have limited the eligible airports in the country to 760. The department adopted these criteria administratively while waiting for legislative approval. Only administration spokesmen, the Airport Operators Council, and the Air Transport Association (spokesman for the commercial carriers) supported all of these proposals. Senators and representatives from states or districts that would suffer from the 30/3,000 provision were vocal in their opposition. Neither of the Interstate and Foreign Commerce Committees (with Monroney a freshman member of the Senate committee) reported any of the proposed amendments.

In January 1955 the budget indicated that the administration was still opposed to an already small airport aid program. It requested only $11 million for fiscal 1956. Congress raised this figure to $20 million.

By 1955 only $236 million of the original $520 million had actually been appropriated. Table 1 summarizes the shrinking interest in the program exhibited by the Department of Commerce, the Bureau of the Budget, and the Appropriations Committees as measured by the percentage of the annual CAA request for airport aid funds that each approved.

Congressional friends of federal airport aid decided to do something legislatively that would avoid the annual battle to save the program. In the Eighty-third Congress Monroney had been the second junior Democrat of the seven minority members of the Senate Interstate and Foreign Commerce Committee. The elections of 1954, coupled with the new

Table 1: *Action on CAA Airport Aid Requests, 1947–56*

| Fiscal year | CAA request (in millions) | Percentage allowed by Commerce | Percentage allowed by BOB | Percentage Congress appropriated |
|---|---|---|---|---|
| 1947 | $105.0 | 100 | 50 | 43 |
| 1948 | 85.0 | 100 | 76 | 38 |
| 1949 | 100.0 | 40 | 40 | 40 |
| 1950 | 100.0 | 40 | 40 | 39 |
| 1951 | 60.0 | 67 | 67 | 66 |
| 1952 | 27.5 | 100 | 87 | 68 |
| 1953 | 67.7 | 91 | 26 | 21 |
| 1954 | 29.9 | 7 | 0 | 0 |
| 1955 | 33.4 | 100 | 66 | 66 |
| 1956 | 41.5 | 75 | 27 | 48 |

committee assignments, left him as third senior Democrat of the eight majority members. The committee chairman, Democrat Warren G. Magnuson of Washington, created the Subcommittee on Aviation and appointed Monroney chairman. Thus in 1955 Monroney began to develop himself as the leading spokesman for and expert on aviation in Congress by taking the lead in enacting legislation abolishing the appropriations process for the airport aid program and instead giving the secretary of commerce the power to make contract obligations without reference to the Appropriations Committees. The new law set the contract authorization level at $42.5 million for fiscal 1956 (to supplement the $20 million already appropriated) and at $63 million for the subsequent three fiscal years ending June 30, 1959. It specifically made terminals eligible for aid, required that the national airport plan "include all types of airport development eligible for Federal Aid," and left the discretionary fund provisions unchanged. Thus Congress contradicted the administration and Commerce Department position on every major point. The 1955 act also repealed the section requiring specific approval of the largest projects. Congress had never used the veto power contained in the repealed section.

In reaching the decision to set airport aid at a $63 million annual figure, Congress was helped by a survey of airport needs jointly prepared by the Airport Operators Council (representing large urban airports), the National Association of State Aviation Officials (representing officials most interested in general aviation airports), and the American Association of Airport Executives (representing both large and small airports). This survey, based on questionnaire returns from airport operators, indicated that total development needs in the country were $468 million, $173 million of which were available in local funds. It further indicated that in fiscal years 1956 and 1957 the total need would be $370 million. The American Municipal Association organized an "Airport Crusade" in support of the new legislation.

Thus by 1955 the battle lines were substantially drawn for the succeeding years. The Department of Commerce, backed by the White House and the Bureau of the Budget, opposed a sizable program. Congress, backed by virtually all aviation interest groups, and given substantial support by some in the CAA, favored a large program. The struggles between 1945 and 1955 had finally determined many questions about the nature of the program. By 1955 it was clear that although Congress would allow a large percentage of the funds to go to airports in larger urban areas it would not allow a complete cessation of aid to small general aviation airports. Thus any program aimed solely at big airports or solely at airports that had scheduled airline service would be unacceptable on the Hill. By 1955 it was also clear that although the National Association of State Aviation Officials and a few others still favored a requirement channeling all money through the states, the direct federal-city relationship in the program was secure. The apportionment formula was never seriously questioned after 1946. Likewise, despite Commerce Department efforts, the provision for 25 percent of the money to be allocated to a discretionary fund seemed to be unchangeable. The fifty-fifty matching principle was generally unquestioned, although it could be altered for specific small items.

After the passage of the 1955 law, the projected increase in the size of planes and the numbers of planes, passengers, and private pilots dictated that local authorities would continue to need increasing amounts of money for airport construction, expansion, and improvement. Three principal questions about the federal government's role in this enterprise still attracted considerable attention. One was the always troublesome question of exactly how much aid should be given. Another was the question of how long the program should last. Finally, the question of aid to terminal buildings still remained.

*1955–57: A Second "New Look" at Airport Aid.* In the middle of the 1955 session of Congress one new study involving airport aid concluded and another one began. The finished study came from the Commission on Intergovernmental Relations in June 1955. This commission, which had been created by Congress in 1953, was headed by Meyer Kestnbaum and was charged with studying the whole range of federal-state-local relations and determining the proper role for the federal government. It recommended that airport aid be continued on the established basis, except for greater promotion of regional airports. It also suggested that Congress clarify its intent regarding the distribution of aid between larger and smaller airports. It felt that a reevaluation of the adequacy of the aid program should be undertaken and specifically asked for appropriations for at least two years in advance. A staff report to the commission, also published in June 1955, took the same positions in greater detail.

In May 1955 the director of the Bureau of the Budget, Rowland Hughes, wrote William B. Harding, a New York investment banker, asking that he head a small group to advise Hughes about whether "a study of long-range needs for aviation facilities and aids be undertaken," what the coverage of such a study should be, and how the study should be organized and conducted. Harding and six consultants reported on December 31, 1955. They indicated a long-range study was necessary and made specific comments about coverage and organization. Speaking through Fred Glass, a former aviation director for the Port of New York Authority and former official of the Airport Operators Council, they stated that:

> the responsibility for the financing of individual civil airports and the responsibility for their management and individual planning should remain at the local level. But the Federal Government must accept responsibility for overall planning of a national airport system as part of the national Aviation Facilities concept and for the programming of such additional funds, both direct and supplemental, as may need to be invested in airports in the national interest. Any other course of action could only lead to confusion and wasteful inadequacy.

In 1956 Congress again showed great interest in the airport program. Partially as a result of his cooperative attitude toward proponents of the $63 million bill in the 1955 hearings, Fred B. Lee, the CAA administrator since the beginning of the Eisenhower administration, was fired in the fall of 1955 by Secretary Weeks and the new undersecretary of commerce for transportation, Louis S. Rothschild. The acrimony surrounding this firing prompted Chairman Magnuson immediately to request the Aviation Subcommittee to investigate it. This the subcommittee did in early 1956 in hearings filled with bitter allegations. Monroney and some other members of the subcommittee used the hearings as a vehicle to point out the numerous shortcomings they saw in the Commerce Department's handling of the airport program.

Also in 1956 the Legal and Monetary Affairs Subcommittee of the House Committee on Government Operations held extensive hearings on the federal role in aviation. It pursued the lines of inquiry opened by the Harding report and thus gave some attention to airports and to the aid program. In its report the committee strongly criticized "the lack of aggressive leadership in the Department of Commerce" and "the lack of the executive branch's appreciation of the significance of civil aviation." Data on the program figured prominently in substantiating this charge.

Early in 1956 President Eisenhower appointed Edward P. Curtis to be his special assistant for aviation facilities planning. Curtis was a former air force officer and in 1956 was an Eastman Kodak executive. In his May 1957 final report to the President, the bulk of which dealt with recommendations for airways modernization and for organizations that subsequently were established as the Airways Modernization Board and the Federal Aviation Agency, Curtis also included four paragraphs on the financing of airports. He asserted that the primary responsibility rested with local governments. But he also recognized the national interest in an overall airport system and stated that the federal aid to airports program had made a valuable contribution. However, he thought that more and more airports would become financially self-sustaining. "Consistent with the progress toward self-sufficiency, the Federal Government should reasonably look forward to the eventual curtailment of direct financial participation in airport construction."

To implement the recommendations of this report the President on August 17, 1957 appointed Elwood R. (Pete) Quesada, a retired air force lieutenant general who for the previous seven years had been an executive for Olin-Mathieson and Lockheed, as his special assistant for aviation matters. Quesada also became chairman of the Airways Modernization Board, a new transitional organization created by legislation in 1957, and chairman of the Air Coordinating Committee. He replaced Undersecretary Rothschild in the latter job.

The patterns of conflict over the airport program thus were pronounced and strong by mid-1957. Congress, led by Monroney's subcommittee and supported by Democrat Oren Harris of Arkansas, chairman of the House Committee on Interstate and Foreign Commerce, championed the program. The most powerful aviation interest group, the Air

Transport Association, had come to espouse it, although never considering it to be of first importance. Other aviation interest groups, led chiefly by the Airport Operators Council, were more directly interested and offered active aid. General municipal groups, primarily the Municipal Association and the Conference of Mayors, could not give airports the same attention as larger programs, such as housing, but they were active in their support.

In the executive branch in mid-1957 the Commerce Department still controlled the program. The leading figure involved with it there was Louis Rothschild. A successful retail clothing businessman from Kansas City, Rothschild had been in government since 1953, after being a leading fund raiser for Eisenhower in Missouri in 1952. He had served on the Kansas City Planning Commission for seventeen years, acting as chairman for about half that time. He had become undersecretary for transportation early in 1955 and had fought the extension and expansion of the airport program then. Like Weeks, he disapproved of all grants-in-aid programs. His strongest beliefs about the relation of government to transportation were that industries should pay for services rendered by the government and that the government must stop or cut much of its spending in the transportation field. Rothschild essentially wanted to eliminate the airport program in a relatively short time. He was seconded by the Bureau of the Budget and publicly supported by Weeks, who asked that the program's contract authority be rescinded and replaced by normal appropriations of about $20 million annually.

The administrator of the Civil Aeronautics Administration in mid-1957 was James Pyle, who had spent his entire career in various phases of aviation since his college graduation in 1935. The head of the Office of Airports in the CAA was Herbert H. Howell, who was primarily interested in technical matters and was beginning to spend a large part of his time on choosing a second airport site in Washington, D.C. Pyle and Howell did not agree with the policy decisions made by Rothschild and Weeks, but they had no real alternative to acting in accord with them. Generally, CAA personnel working with the program wanted its retention, but were not vocal about their desires.

General Quesada, who had rapidly become the chief administration spokesman on aviation matters after his appointment to the three different aviation jobs, wanted the airport program reduced and terminal-free, but not entirely eliminated. Thus within the executive branch, as well as between the executive and Congress, the seeds were sown for prolonged and vicious warfare over airport aid. These seeds were to sprout in 1958 and 1959.

In addition to patterns of conflict over federal aid to airports, entrenched patterns of thought about this aid had also developed by mid-1957. With the exception of the Municipal Association and the Conference of Mayors no one talked about aid to airports as essentially aid to urban areas. And even these two groups invested most of their time and effort in areas other than airport aid. The rest of the participants—congressional, executive, and private—all conceived of the program as aid to civil aviation. Helping the development of cities as such was not considered one of its particular objectives. This civil aviation perspective, which was also Monroney's perspective, would continue to dominate discussion of the program in 1958 and 1959.


1958: Congress Proposes, the President Disposes

In the fall of 1957 the Commerce Department further enraged Monroney and the aviation interest groups. Despite an August 1957 memorandom from the director of the Office of Airports in the CAA to the regional administrators to the effect that they could receive requests from and plan projects with individual sponsors, the Commerce Department did not set a date by which requests for fiscal 1959 projects would have to be filed. Thus on October 18, 1957 the president of the Airport Operators Council wired Secretary Weeks that:

> Our members advise that Fiscal Year 1959 project requests under Federal Airport Program are not being requested by CAA because of lack of program announcement date which we understand can be made only by you. An early announcement of the 1959 program is vital to the construction and financing planning locally for completion of urgently needed airport facilities. The concern of our members is greatly increased by widely current reports to the effect that Commerce Department is recommending severance of Fiscal 1959 program from present four-year program.

Ten days later Weeks routinely acknowledged this telegram. On November 8 the manager of the Oklahoma City airport wrote Senator Monroney summarizing the impasse between the interest groups and the Commerce Department. He indicated that in addition to the Airport Operators Council, the American Municipal Association, the United States Conference of Mayors, the National Association of State Aviation

Officials, and the American Association of Airport Executives all were attempting to get information about the programming for fiscal 1959. Two representatives from each of these groups, he said, were to meet with Weeks in November.

This meeting was held on November 14 with Rothschild instead of Weeks. Rothschild informed his visitors that the administration was indeed reluctant to prepare an airport program for fiscal 1959. He indicated that if the groups would not press for an extension of the program past June 30, 1959, the Commerce Department might be willing to expedite the fiscal 1959 program. Furthermore, Rothschild indicated that the President's budgetary plans now called for national security spending as a top priority. Airports did not fit this category. Finally, Rothschild told the groups to review the exact financial requirements for airport development and to contact him later. This the groups agreed to do.

Two representatives of the Airport Operators Council, disgusted by this meeting, contacted the Air Force the next day to pinpoint its position on the national security aspects of the airport aid program. The Air Force replied by supporting the continuance of the program. The following Monday the chairman of the legislative committee of the Operators Council wrote General Quesada at the Airways Modernization Board that "If need be, our associations are prepared to go to the Congress for a Federal Airport Program. We have done it before over the opposition of Mr. Weeks and we feel we can do it again."

Within a month the Commerce Department announced February 1, 1958 as the due date for fiscal 1959 project applications. No further meetings between the Commerce Department and the aviation interest groups were necessary.

As the interest group pattern of support for new airport aid legislation began to emerge, E. Thomas Burnard, executive director of the Airport Operators Council, became the coordinator of group activities. While a law student at the University of Pennsylvania in 1939 Burnard had entered the government's civilian pilot training program. During the war he had been a naval officer working on liaison duty with the Army Air Force. After the war he had worked for nine years, until 1955, for the Air Transport Association. Since 1955 he had been executive director of the Operators Council. Thus he was familiar with the needs and concerns of the users of the airports from his Transport Association days and he was currently in the organization that had the greatest stake in a substantial aid program. Operators Council member airports, although few in number (3 percent of the U.S. total), required over half of the funds needed for airport development. They received virtually all of the biggest grants (twelve out of the thirteen that reached the maximum $1 million in fiscal 1958). Thus it was natural that the Operators Council would take the lead among the groups, and Burnard was well fitted for his task.

Five other groups in the "airport supplier" category aided the Operators Council. The Municipal Association and the Conference of Mayors, along with the National Association of County Officials, represented the cities and counties that operate most of the nation's public airports. These groups put the weight of the general urban lobby behind the drive for more airport legislation. The National Association of State Aviation Officials and the American Association of Airport Executives in large part represented smaller-scale airport suppliers than the Airport Operators Council. The Airport Executives had no Washington office. The State Aviation Officials had in the past been at odds with the other groups over the matter of exclusive state jurisdiction over federal grants, but by late 1957 had agreed to put aside this issue temporarily in the hope of getting an increased amount for the aid program.

Of the "airport user" groups the Air Transport Association was by far the most important politically. The Air Line Pilots Association, the Aircraft Owners and Pilots Association, the Association of Local and Territorial Airlines, and the National Business Aircraft Association all supported the proposed legislation, although with much smaller resources than the Transport Association. The Transport Association was the only user group with which Burnard maintained constant contact. Building on his 1955 experience Burnard realized two things: unanimity of the aviation groups was essential if legislation were to succeed; and the commercial spokesman (Air Transport) had substantially more political weight than all of the airport supplier groups combined. When congressmen, and even CAA officials, thought of aviation they tended to think of the commercial airlines—the health of aviation had largely come to mean their health.

The commercial airlines had a natural interest in the airport legislation. Better airports could help the airlines' business. The Transport Association was also eager to keep user charge provisions out of the legislation. Finally, it was especially concerned about the great amount of work needed if more than a few airports were to be ready for commercial jet traffic, which was scheduled to begin in early 1959. On January 8, 1958 the Transport Association presented a "jet symposium" to the members of the Senate Aviation Subcommittee. Two of the ten papers presented were on airports. Throughout subsequent testimony on the proposed legislation the Transport Association stressed the interrelationship of a continuing growth in aviation and a continuing federal role. Most of the group's legislative efforts during 1958, however, were devoted to the proposed federal aviation act.

One of Burnard's principal suggestions was for the interest groups to cooperate on another survey of airport needs, similar to the one conducted for the 1955 legislative struggle. The Association of State Officials, the Airport Executives, and the Operators Council therefore began in early November 1957 to compile the development requirements of American public airports. This was done by sending a questionnaire to all existing and proposed new public airports (about 3,000) asking them what was needed in the next four years and how much it would cost. The questionnaire also asked about available and anticipated local funds.

The results of the survey were compiled in December and showed a total need of slightly over $1 billion for the next four years with a little over $450 million not supplied by local funds. Burnard immediately showed these results to Monroney and to Oren Harris. The Board of Directors of the Operators Council met in January 1958 and invited Monroney, Harris, and Rothschild to attend in order to learn the survey results. In late January Burnard also sent copies of the survey to Thomas D. Finney, Jr., Monroney's administrative assistant since the fall of 1957, and to Chairman Magnuson. Thus the figures were well known before formal publication of them.

In late January Burnard was instrumental in persuading the other airport supplier associations to join the Operators Council in publishing an eight-page brochure entitled "The Federal Airport Program Should Be Extended." The Air Transport Association also helped finance the distribution of the brochure, although its name did not appear on it. The Conference of Mayors handled the business arrangements for the brochure.

Throughout the next sixteen months Burnard was the principal contact for the airport suppliers with both Congress and the executive. He helped write and rewrite much of the formal testimony they presented in 1958 and 1959 to the congressional committees.

*Congressional Initiative.* With this interest group activity as a prelude, the congressional advocates of the airport aid program began to stir. Alerted by the groups and by Monroney, Senator Magnuson on November 13 sent a telegram to Weeks expressing concern over the future of the program for fiscal 1959. As soon as the survey figures were complete and were made available to them, staff members on the Senate side set out to draft legislation extending the program beyond 1959 and also expanding it. Principally involved in this process were Tom Finney and Aviation Subcommittee staff members Robert Murphy and John Black, appointees of Democrat John O. Pastore of Rhode Island and Magnuson, respectively. The four-year length of the extension included in their draft came both from the 1955 legislation and from the time period covered by the interest group survey. The amount in the bill ($100 million annually plus an initial $75 million emergency fund aimed at jet transition problems) was derived from the 1946 legislative limit of $100 million on annual appropriations, the survey, and the Transport Association's jet symposium. The proposals were also related to an antirecession program sponsored by Senate Democrats, which included $2 billion for community facilities and housing.

Monroney did not introduce the $475 million airport bill until March 17, 1958. On January 13, 1958, however, Republican Senator Frederick Payne of Maine, a member of Monroney's subcommittee, introduced a bill extending the $63 million airport program for four years. On January 22 Magnuson announced that the Aviation Subcommittee would hold hearings. Finally, on March 20 Monroney announced that these hearings would begin on April 14. On March 27 Black, Murphy, and Burnard met to discuss the shape of the coming hearings.

Simultaneously with this activity on the airport aid legislation the Senate committee and all of the other participants were becoming increasingly busy with the legislation creating an independent Federal Aviation Agency. This in some ways overshadowed the airport legislation. On the House side the Interstate and Foreign Commerce Committee, which had never specialized in aviation on the Senate model, was further distracted from the airport legislation by the involvement of Chairman Harris in uncovering the story of Sherman Adams and Bernard Goldfine. Only one staff member on Harris's committee, Martin W. Cunningham, worked on the airport bill. Cunningham, an Oklahoman who had known Monroney at the University of Oklahoma, worked with some of the Senate staff people but had few contacts with interest group personnel. Two

House subcommittees of the Government Operations Committee, one on Legal and Monetary Affairs and one on Intergovernmental Relations, touched on airport aid in their more general investigations in 1958.

Thus, because of both position and interest, Mike Monroney became the leading congressional exponent of the four-year $475 million airport aid program. Monroney had had three years of experience as chairman of the subcommittee. He had had a long-standing interest in aviation, beginning during his days as a reporter in the 1920's. By 1958, after Monroney had spent twelve years in the House and seven years in the Senate, aviation had become his special niche in the Senate structure.

*Executive Response.* In December 1957 Percival F. Brundage, then director of the Bureau of the Budget, wrote to Secretary of Commerce Weeks indicating that his department should stretch out the programming and obligation of the remaining airport aid funds. He added an injunction against supporting any extension of the program. Thus Weeks's own feelings about the program were reinforced by the Bureau of the Budget. Weeks and Brundage agreed a few months later, for tactical reasons, that the program for fiscal 1959 should have a high level of obligations. But the basic antipathy on the part of both never wavered.

The Commerce Department gave less attention to the airport program in 1958 than to what became the Federal Aviation Act and the Transportation Act of that year. Undersecretary for Transportation Rothschild, while recognizing there might be some necessity for a small program concentrated on a few of the biggest airports making the transition to jet equipment, shared Weeks's opposition to airport aid and made this clear to the department. However, officials in the Civil Aeronautics Administration, which was in Rothschild's domain, favored the program and saw a need for the $100 million annual level. CAA Administrator Pyle argued this view with Rothschild. Not only did he see the proposed level as reasonable but he argued that unless the Commerce Department willingly shaped and directed the program, Congress would do so. For administrative reasons Pyle felt it unwise to allow Congress this kind of control. Pyle's views were known outside of the CAA and Commerce but he had no regular outlets for expressing them. Commerce did not allow the Civil Aeronautics Administration to handle its own congressional relations. Thus Pyle and his subordinates, although favorably disposed toward the program, had to back Commerce's anti-aid position in public.

Weeks finally announced the fiscal 1959 program on March 21. The program called for $63.5 million, the highest annual figure so far. Weeks felt that this high figure would take some of the steam out of the drive to extend and expand the program a year before it actually expired.

In March two persons entered jobs that were automatically involved in the airport aid fight of the next fifteen months. One was a new director of the Bureau of the Budget, Maurice H. Stans. The other was a new director of the Office of Airports in the CAA, George R. Borsari. Since his graduation from college in 1934 Borsari had worked in the airport field for the government, first in the Works Progress Administration and then in the Civil Aeronautics Authority. He had become friends with Pyle and was promoted over several people into the directorship. Borsari had worked intimately with the airport aid program since its beginning and felt strongly that it was valuable. He realized, however, that he could not speak publicly in opposition to the wishes of the department. Therefore, his position was that he could answer questions and present facts on airport needs but could not interpret those facts to take positions on questions that had to be decided politically. Nevertheless, since Monroney and others on the two congressional committees knew Borsari and knew his expertise in the field, they sent him numerous factual questions during the entire fight over the legislation. His answers provided much raw material for the proponents of the program in Congress.

In early April, with Senate hearings set for April 14, representatives from the general counsel's office in Commerce, Rothschild's office, and the CAA met to work out for Rothschild the testimony opposing Monroney's bill. A draft was ready by April 3. On April 9 Rothschild met with high officials from the White House and the Bureau of the Budget to complete plans for his testimony. It was agreed that Rothschild leave room for the possibility that an extension of airport aid might be considered later by the administration as part of an antirecession program.

Once the Commerce position was clear and was adopted by the administration the Bureau of the Budget played its normal role of coordinating the legislative positions of the various executive agencies that might be asked by Congress to comment on the proposed extension. The only agency that seemed unwilling at first to back Commerce was the Department of the Air Force but once the issues were explained, it agreed not to support Monroney's bill.

Relations between Commerce and Congress on this bill during 1958 were virtually nonexistent aside from formal testimony before committees. Nor were there many contacts between Commerce and the interest groups. Burnard talked with Rothschild in the spring of 1958 and representatives of the Airport Operators Council and the National Association of State Aviation Officials visited with Weeks in June. Neither visit made the slightest impression.

*Legislative Unanimity.* Monroney introduced S. 3502, the four-year $475 million bill, on March 17. It was cosponsored by three Democrats, Warren Magnuson, Richard Neuberger, and Ralph Yarborough, and by Frederick Payne. Payne's support was a major reason for the Republican acquiescence in the Senate. The subcommittee, whose members in addition to Monroney and Payne were Democrats George A. Smathers of Florida and Alan Bible of Nevada and Republican Andrew F. Schoeppel of Kansas, held hearings on the bill and on two others involving minor parts of the program from April 14 through April 17. Eighteen witnesses testified in person at the hearings. Eight came from the airport supplier groups, including representatives of cities, three came from the airport user groups, and only Rothschild testified for the administration. That the spokesmen for the big airports were the most numerous was natural: for fiscal years 1956–58 airports with commercial service had received 86 percent of the total grants. Medium and large hub airports (each handling over 0.25 percent of all enplaned passengers) alone received 55 percent of the total.

Rothschild, who was the only witness to oppose the bill, testified first. He and Monroney argued vigorously with each other. Rothschild insisted that airports were a matter of local responsibility and that "Airports have come a long way toward self-sufficiency." As had been agreed at the White House meeting he left room for administration support for airport aid as part of a public works program but he offered no details. His bluntest statement was that "We just have a pretty strong conviction that this is no longer the function of the Federal Government; that airports in general are becoming adequately able to develop enough income to meet their own requirements." He specifically argued against aid to terminal buildings. He also pointed to large and growing federal expenditures for airways (primarily navigation) development and suggested that this was enough federal aid to aviation.

Monroney countered by arguing the great need for improvements and the continuing interest of the federal government in those improvements. He insisted that without a federal aid program the government would have no right to regulate the placement of airports and make other regulations necessary for safety.

One of the most effective witnesses from the airport supplier groups was Mayor William B. Hartsfield of Atlanta, representing both the Municipal Association and the Conference of Mayors. He followed Rothschild and congratulated Monroney on his questioning of the Under Secretary. "Mr. Chairman, your interrogation was such that we almost felt we didn't need to make any further presentation." Hartsfield, who a year earlier had stressed airport development in Atlanta in his campaign for reelection, emphasized the great urban need for airports as contrasted with the shortage of local funds. Other supplier group representatives followed and the six-organization brochure, containing the survey figures, was printed in the record.

At one point the Airport Operators Council representative objected to the prohibition in the bill of funds for "parking lots, bars, cafes, or other space to be rented or leased by concessionaires." Monroney stated his reason for including the prohibition: "My legislative experience indicates we are liable to be in serious trouble. I understand the President just vetoed the rivers and harbors bill. The next strike is liable to be the highway bill. We don't wish this to be the third strike on the basis that we are putting too much money into cocktail bars and shopping centers."

The only agency supporting the bill in the hearings was the independent Civil Aeronautics Board. Monroney stressed the tie between CAB support of the legislation and safety requirements under CAB control.

After the Senate hearings there was no dissension in either the subcommittee or full committee of eight Democrats and seven Republicans, and on May 9 the committee unanimously approved S. 3502. Only Republican Senator Norris Cotton of New Hampshire indicated that he did not support the entire bill. His objection was limited to the $75 million emergency fund. On May 13 the committee reported the bill.

In the report the committee argued that:

> Airports are indeed an essential part of our aviation facilities and have a direct and valuable relation to our civilian and defense requirements. The amazing growth of our air commerce . . . has already taxed our airport facilities beyond present capacity. The advent of the jet age promises revolutionary benefits, but poses problems of airport planning and development which exceed the financial ability of local public taxes to go it alone. Airport capacity must be kept in balance with airway capacity.

The bill as reported spelled out even more precisely than the original draft what revenue-producing facilities would not be eligible for matching federal funds: passenger automobile parking facilities, "those parts of passenger or freight terminal buildings or other airport administrative buildings intended for use as bars, cocktail lounges, night clubs, theaters, private clubs, garages, hotel rooms, commercial offices, or gamerooms," or anything else "which, in the opinion of the Secretary, is not essential to the welfare and safety of those persons using airports for public aviation purposes."

In addition to the printed hearings and report each senator had available to him the printed record of the jet symposium given by the Air Transport Association. The brochure prepared by the six airport supplier groups had been sent to each senator in mid-April.

The bill reached the Senate floor on May 14. The Senate passed it by voice vote, without dissent. In the short debate preceding the vote Monroney stressed that the bill merely extended the use of a long-standing principle. He also stressed the features in the bill that would aid small general aviation airports.

The bill was referred to the House Interstate and Foreign Commerce Committee on May 15. Three days later Burnard cabled Chairman Harris from San Juan, Puerto Rico, asking for early hearings on the bill. From that time until late July when the hearings were actually held, the interested parties became increasingly worried that the other concerns of the committee—centering around Sherman Adams and Bernard Goldfine and complicated by internal committee troubles caused by Bernard Schwartz, a controversial subcommittee counsel—would prevent legislative action in the House before adjournment. The Airport Operators Council, the Municipal Association, and the Conference of Mayors all contacted Harris directly and asked members to contact him to urge the scheduling of hearings. The supplier groups also sent their brochure to all committee members in early June and to all House members in mid-July.

In the drive to assure hearings early enough to allow floor action Burnard talked with both Harris and Kenneth A. Roberts of Alabama, the ranking Democrat on the Transportation and Communications Subcommittee, of which Harris was also the chairman. Leo Seybold, a vice president of the Air Transport Association, even suggested that Harris allow Roberts to conduct the hearings. Harris refused this suggestion and indicated he would hold the hearings as soon as possible. Finally, on July 10

Harris wrote Burnard that "I fully appreciate the urgent need for extending the Federal Airport Act for another four years, and hope to find time in our very busy schedule to set this matter down for hearings within the next week or ten days. After which the Committee will attempt to clear this bill through executive sessions as expeditiously as possible. . . ."

The two-day hearings began before the Subcommittee on Transportation and Communications on July 22. In addition to Harris the subcommittee members were Democrats Roberts, Harley O. Staggers of West Virginia, Walter Rogers of Texas, Samuel N. Friedel of Maryland, John James Flynt, Jr., of Georgia, and Torbert H. Macdonald of Massachusetts; and Republicans Charles A. Wolverton of New Jersey, Joseph P. O'Hara of Minnesota, Robert Hale of Maine, William L. Springer of Illinois, Steven B. Derounian of New York, and J. Arthur Younger of California.

In March Republican Thor C. Tollefson of Washington had introduced the Monroney bill into the House. Democrats John J. McFall of California and John D. Dingell of Michigan, and Republican John B. Bennett of Michigan had all introduced bills similar to Payne's original proposal: a simple extension of the $63 million program for four years. The committee hearings focused, however, on S. 3502 as passed by the Senate.

Twenty witnesses appeared in person before the House subcommittee. Eight had testified previously in the Senate. There were seven witnesses from the supplier groups and three from the user groups. CAA Administrator Pyle accompanied Rothschild but the latter did virtually all of the talking for the executive position. The arguments produced in the hearings were mostly repetitions of those in the Senate hearings. Rothschild was again alone in opposing S. 3502. More doubts about the program were expressed here than in the Senate committee, however. Congressman Flynt, for example, stressed that individual airports could be self-sustaining and indicated that he certainly did not want to regard the program as permanent.

On August 8 the full committee approved a four-year extension of the program at the $100 million level. It retained the Senate language on bars, parking lots, and similar facilities. The committee struck the $75 million emergency fund from the bill. This was done as a result of Chairman Harris's judgment that the bill would have trouble passing the House otherwise. The committee filed its unanimous report on August

11. It argued that improved airports were indispensable parts of the national airways system. General aviation was stressed as well as the transition to the jet age. Defense and postal considerations were mentioned as necessitating continuing aid. No minority report was filed.

On the following day, August 12, mayors from seven of the largest cities and the representative of an eighth, along with the executive directors of the Municipal Association and the Conference of Mayors, met with Speaker of the House Sam Rayburn of Texas to urge the necessity of passing the bill and to impress him with the need for speed if the bill were not to be lost in the session-end shuffle. The Operators Council urged its members to write House members asking for speedy approval.

With adjournment in view at week's end Harris brought the bill to the floor on August 18 under suspension of the rules. This procedure allows only forty minutes of debate and requires a two-thirds majority for passage. In this limited time five Republicans questioned the bill, mainly because they objected to the suspension of the rules procedure for it or because they objected to continued bypassing of the annual appropriations process. No Republican member of the committee opposed the bill on the floor. At the end of the forty minutes the House passed the bill by a division vote of 152 to 42.

The following day, without debate or objection, the Senate concurred in the House amendment eliminating the emergency fund and the bill went to the President for signature. Congress adjourned five days later, on August 24.

*Presidential Veto.* On July 21, the day before the House hearings opened, Rothschild, Weeks, and Quesada met with officials from the White House and the Bureau of the Budget to determine administration strategy. The meeting agreed that Rothschild would continue his opposition to S. 3502 in the House hearings and that the Commerce Department, the Bureau of the Budget, and Quesada would unanimously recommend a veto if the bill passed the House. Those present also agreed that the veto message would hold out some hope of a small future program devoted entirely to solving problems of the transition to jet aircraft. Weeks and Quesada would be expected to determine if these limited needs could be met out of the authorization that did not expire until June 30, 1959, or if some additional funds should be recommended by the President in January 1959.

After passage of the bill on August 19 the Bureau of the Budget, following the normal procedure, requested agency opinions on the enrolled bill. General Quesada wrote a particularly influential memorandum to the bureau. This memo became the basis of the veto message drafted by the bureau for the President. Quesada used the language of the Curtis report in stressing that airports were a local responsibility. He wanted the federal government to view airport aid as an obligation that could be terminated in the future.

But Quesada was far less negative in his approach to the question of airport aid than the Commerce Department. He also recommended that the Federal Aviation Agency (the Federal Aviation Act had passed Congress and would be signed by the President on August 23) draft an alternative to the Monroney bill that would give airports aid on a reasonable basis and at a reasonable level of expenditure. This alternative would be sent to Congress early in the 1959 session.

Pyle made one last attempt to salvage the legislation by writing the general counsel of the Commerce Department that the CAA had no objection to the approval of S. 3502. He stressed that since the FAA would soon come into existence S. 3502 would involve no expenditures on the part of the Commerce Department. Weeks rejected Pyle's views and recommended a veto to the Bureau of the Budget.

Only one agency, the Civil Aeronautics Board, which was already on record in support of the Monroney bill, actively recommended approval. But, as agreed on in the July meeting, Quesada's Airways Modernization Board, the Commerce Department, and the Bureau of the Budget all recommended a veto. The Bureau of the Budget, as is customary, transmitted the views of all of the agencies to the White House for a final decision.

Unaccountably, it was only after the bill had passed Congress that the interest groups began to suspect the President might veto it. The Conference of Mayors urged its members on August 20 to send telegrams to the President asking for approval of the legislation. Burnard talked with Quesada during these last days of August but Quesada refused to discuss the enrolled bill. On August 27 representatives from the Airport Operators Council, the Municipal Association, the Conference of Mayors, and the Association of Airport Executives met with several Bureau of the Budget officials to press for approval of the legislation. On the same day the Operators Council told its membership by telegram that there is a "very strong possibility of Presidential veto."

That strong possibility became reality on September 2 when President

Eisenhower announced from Newport that he was not signing S. 3502. He issued a memorandum of disapproval on this date using language supplied largely by Quesada to stress the local nature of the responsibility for airport development. He noted that the federal contribution to airports had been large, and valuable, in the past. "Now, however, I am convinced that the time has come for the Federal Government to begin an orderly withdrawal from the airport grant program." "Orderly withdrawal" indicated the necessity of a transitional program "to provide aid to urgent airport projects which are essential to an adequate national aviation facilities system and which cannot be completed in any other way." The President promised that the administration would recommend such a transitional program at the next session of Congress.

Thus the President vetoed a bill that had come to him with virtually the unanimous support of Congress. Slow action in the House had allowed a pocket veto, with no chance to vote on overriding it. Quesada, Stans, and Weeks had convinced Eisenhower that the bill was a threat to budgetary sanity and that aid to terminals was being abused. The President's action came as a shock to Monroney and other congressional supporters, who had expected congressional unanimity to preclude the possibility of veto.

## 1959: The Acceptance of a Compromise

The President's veto of S. 3502 immediately produced statements of outrage and almost as immediately produced planning for airport legislation in the Eighty-sixth Congress, which would convene on January 7, 1959. On the day following the veto Monroney condemned the action on several grounds. "The President's veto of the Federal Aid to Airports Bill strikes a body blow to air safety. Not only does his action endanger a safe transition to the jet air age, but it also jeopardizes the investment of more than \$2 billion in these advanced types of airplanes already on order by commercial airlines." On September 24, speaking at the convention of the National Business Aircraft Association, Monroney announced that he would introduce a bill identical to S. 3502 at the beginning of the new Congress.

The interest groups also made public statements during the fall of 1958. The Conference of Mayors met the second week in September at Miami Beach and both Mayor Hartsfield and Mayor Robert F. Wagner of New York blasted the President's action. Pyle, speaking at the convention, offered a conventional defense of the administration's position. Hartsfield, in the discussion that followed Pyle's speech, indicated a desire to debate with him but Pyle declined to do so. The conference responded by endorsing a resolution favoring aid at the $100 million level. The Municipal Association congress met in Boston in early December and endorsed a regular program of $100 million annually coupled with a $75 million emergency fund.

Congressional proponents of the program also made public statements during the fall of 1958. Oren Harris spoke to the Aero Club of Washington in late November and endorsed an annual figure of $100 million. On December 8 the Democratic Advisory Council supported new airport legislation.

There were few new decisions about the legislation to be made. Monroney was committed to the same program and the interest groups were eager to aid him in passing it. The main decisions were strategic and were made in a variety of meetings throughout the fall.

Shortly after the veto representatives of the Airport Operators Council, the Conference of Mayors, and the Municipal Association went to see a White House official working on intergovernmental relations. They made no headway with him, however, and for the remainder of the fall the groups confined their activities to working with their friends.

On September 29 and 30 the Operators Council held an informal meeting of its membership in Tulsa to consider future action on the aid program. Monroney was invited and he attended some of the meetings. In their discussions the members worried that the administration's concern with large airports alone would be politically fatal to the program. Three members were opposed to further federal aid to terminals. Monroney emphasized the necessity of excluding shopping centers and similar facilities. He also indicated that the portions of the program aimed particularly at general aviation airports in small towns were politically wise and increased the chances of new legislation.

On November 18 representatives of the Operators Council, the Municipal Association, the State Officials, the County Officials, and the Airport Executives met at the Hay-Adams Hotel in Washington for three hours to discuss strategy. A representative from the Conference of Mayors was invited but could not attend. Those present were unanimous in supporting the reintroduction of the provisions in S. 3502. The consensus was that all interested parties should concentrate on getting a satisfactory money amount in 1959, and that action on proposed administrative changes should be deferred and handled in separate legislation. As one report of the meeting put it, there was agreement to "get what we can get, when we can get it." Support for the $75 million emergency fund was less general but it was felt that the fund "would at least provide a bargaining point." Burnard and A. B. McMullen of the National Association of State Aviation Officials were appointed to call on Monroney to discuss the emergency fund and future administrative amendments with him. There was no support for a meeting with Quesada, who had been named FAA administrator on September 30.

On December 18 Monroney wrote to Burnard informing him of final plans for the introduction of the airport bill, which was to become S. 1. He stated that hearings would be held in January.

Finally, just as Congress was convening in January Burnard proposed to the same six groups that had sponsored the printing of the airport brochure in 1958 that they finance the mailing of surplus copies of the brochure to all senators and representatives and to key members of the press. The groups agreed.

*Quesada's Position.* The Federal Aviation Act had transferred the powers of the secretary of commerce and the administrator of the Civil Aeronautics Administration to the administrator of the Federal Aviation Agency. The FAA officially came into being on November 1, 1958, although the CAA did not become part of it until December 31. Commerce immediately gave legislative responsibility for the coming year to Quesada and merely administered the airport aid program until the end of 1958.

James Pyle, the CAA administrator, agreed to become Quesada's deputy. The administrative structure of the FAA called for the Airport Office to be established on a division rather than a bureau level. This downgrading was thought to be in accord with the administration's de-emphasis of the airport program. George Borsari became the division chief. Quesada picked Daggett "Bud" Howard to be his general counsel. After a short time as a Wall Street lawyer, Howard had worked in various foreign aid jobs for the government from 1943 through 1947, when he began a five-year stint with the Civil Aeronautics Board. Since 1952 he had been the associate general counsel for civil aviation in the Department of the Air Force. He had come to Quesada's attention through the part he played in settling an airspace controversy between military and civilian aviation authorities.

The immediate task that Quesada faced was shaping an administration alternative to Monroney's airport bill for 1959. He soon came to regret the "orderly withdrawal" language he had supplied to the President. By "withdrawal" Quesada had never meant a termination of the program in the near future. But the more conservative elements in the administration, particularly the Bureau of the Budget, used "withdrawal" to mean termination within a few years. They advocated this position in discussions and communications with Quesada and his subordinates.

As early as September 22 Quesada wrote to Burnard that the administration was preparing legislation that would be an alternative to Monroney's proposals. The President, after many months of discussion with Weeks, Stans, and Quesada, had become committed to a small airport program that would get increasingly smaller with the passage of time. He also became dedicated to the elimination of aid for terminal buildings except for those portions that would be used for safety installations. He stated guidelines embodying these opinions in the veto message in September and again in the budget message of January 19, 1959. Quesada was certainly agreeable to working within these guidelines. Indeed, he had developed part of them himself. But he was anxious to avoid presenting a program that envisioned its own rapid elimination.

Before he could begin to hammer out the FAA airport proposal with the Bureau of the Budget, Quesada first had to debate some of the CAA personnel who would still be administering the program under the FAA. To facilitate this intra-agency debate Quesada on December 12 issued for agency and CAA consumption a statement on the extension of the airport aid program. In it Quesada indicated that the program expenditures should be as low as possible but should meet legitimate needs. He felt the legislation should emphasize the seventy or so airports that were preparing to handle jets. He argued that 50 percent of the money instead of 25 percent was needed in the discretionary fund. He advocated a "gate-to-gate" policy that would make the only legitimate expenditures in the program those for the landing field area itself. Facilities outside the gates of the fence surrounding the landing area—especially terminals—would be excluded from eligibility. Finally, Quesada specified the figures for the program: $12 million additional for fiscal 1959, and then $70 million for fiscal 1960, $60 million for fiscal 1961, $50 million for fiscal

1962, and $40 million for fiscal 1963—a total of $232 million. He explained that "The proposed funding level is selected to appeal to reasonable legislators and to oppose Senator Monroney's $437 million proposal with reasonable assurance of success. If the level is pitched too low . . . it will die in committee, and we have lost a chance to save $205 million."

Both Pyle and Borsari opposed the "gate-to-gate" policy. They also thought the proposed money amounts too low. They pointed to a just-completed survey of airport needs that the Civil Aeronautics Administration had begun in May 1958. This survey, based on figures developed by CAA district airport engineers and local airport officials, showed a need of almost $1.3 billion over the 1959–62 period. Quesada resented this survey, suspecting that it was a bureaucratic form of self-protection begun by those in the CAA who wanted to perpetuate the airport aid program. He felt that they could use it as a club to force support for a bigger bill from him. Borsari insisted, however, that he had begun the survey shortly after taking over the Office of Airports because he realized how little documentation of airport needs the CAA possessed. He even gave Rothschild credit for planting the germ of the survey by asking for hard information on airports only a week or two after Borsari had become director. Pyle concurred with Borsari that the survey was simply an attempt to transform vague speculations about airport needs to facts as hard as possible.

When the survey was finally published in late March 1959 as an integral part of the *National Airport Plan—1959* (a 500-page document), Quesada wrote a foreword discounting the relation of the survey to federal airport aid legislation:

> The statement of need included in this Plan should not be related to the need for Federal participation under the Federal Airport Act. Inclusion of an airport in the Plan does not necessarily represent ability, intent, or commitment on the part of the local community to proceed with development, nor should it be construed as a commitment of the Federal Government to participate financially in such development.

During these transitional months and into January Quesada had some difficulty in getting his Airports Division staff to understand and act upon his policies. Letters directly contrary to his stated policies would be drafted routinely and passed on to him for signature. This prompted Quesada to hold several meetings with the staff (about 100 persons) to tell them they could not continue encouraging local sponsors to apply for terminal aid and to rely on the federal government for large sums of money. He made clear that continued violations of these instructions could affect an employee's "career development." Borsari was glad that these meetings took place since he felt it was the best way for the new administrator to make his views known and felt. At the same time by encouraging the meetings Borsari could make clear to Quesada that although he disagreed with him he would be a loyal subordinate. Borsari stated his philosophy of service under both Rothschild and Quesada by saying that a man in his position had two choices: "Do it or quit." After making his policy preferences clear Quesada could depend on the loyal support of both Borsari and Pyle.

But Quesada's main problems within the administration did not come from those who thought his proposal too small. Rather he had to debate for several months with officials in the Bureau of the Budget who thought his proposals too large. In December 1958 CAA and BOB personnel met to work on legislative proposals. The CAA talked in terms almost twice as high as the bureau felt was justifiable. On December 10 Stans indicated to the FAA that further discussion would be needed before the administration's draft legislation would be ready to submit to Congress. He also indicated that the Bureau of the Budget would clear funds already authorized for the program only for projects inside the gates or related to safety.

After more consultation, and with Senate hearings slated to begin January 22, 1959, the Federal Aviation Agency and the Bureau of the Budget finally came to an agreement. The FAA formally submitted a draft bill to the bureau on January 19. This bill, which became S. 674, eliminated terminal aid and called for a program of $65 million in fiscal 1960, $55 million in fiscal 1961, $45 million in fiscal 1962, and $35 million in fiscal 1963—a total of $200 million. It also increased the discretionary fund to 50 percent of the total. Howard asked the bureau for speed in considering the bill. He wanted the administration to have an alternative with which to fight Monroney.

On January 20 bureau personnel met with Howard and Borsari to discuss the details of the draft bill. The bureau felt that the FAA justification for the program was shoddy and suggested improvements. These criticisms were summarized in a letter to Quesada on January 21, giving bureau clearance to the draft bill. Even in clearing the draft bill, the Bureau of the Budget made evident its desire to see the program terminate altogether in four years.

Quesada also faced the problem of creating some sort of viable relations with Congress. He had worked intimately with Congress in passing the Federal Aviation Act and, unlike the Commerce Department people, felt the necessity of personal relations with members of both houses outside of formal testimony. He had become friends with Monroney and while they disagreed on what was needed for airports they could, and did, talk freely about airport problems. Quesada understood that Monroney was committed to a $100 million annual program and Monroney understood that Quesada would advocate a smaller program.

The administrator realized it would be a delicate task to oppose the chairman's personal project in his first appearance before the Senate Aviation Subcommittee as head of the FAA. This helped him decide to handle the bulk of the congressional relations himself. He was aided by Howard and Borsari, John R. MacKenzie and Robert Williams of the FAA congressional liaison staff, and Bryce N. Harlow, Edward A. McCabe, and Jack Z. Anderson of the White House congressional liaison staff.

In approaching Congress Quesada favored the general strategy of stressing the merits of the arguments against the big bill and for the administration bill. The 1958 elections had produced an overwhelmingly Democratic Congress—64 to 34 in the Senate and 283 to 153 in the House—and there was little use in trying to bargain for individual votes. The arithmetic was too much against the FAA. Thus it was essential to mobilize the Republican strength as a hard core and then appeal to conservative Democrats through reasoned arguments, supplemented with ridicule of past abuses in the program.

Quesada also sought to make his difficult job with Congress somewhat easier by postponing the implementation of the gate-to-gate limits on the program until the 1959 legislative situation was clear. He felt that the 1955 example of legislative disaster after the implementation of new rules for grants by administrative action argued strongly for postponement of similar action in 1959.

One day before the Senate hearings opened Quesada finally had the administration position in the form of draft legislation. He was now ready to testify on a subject that had already become one of the most live political issues of 1959. The President, aided by the United States Chamber of Commerce, had launched a general campaign against governmental spending. He was clearly attempting to attach a "spender" label to the Democrats and thus make Congress wary about promoting new and expensive programs. The Democratic congressional leaders, on the other

hand, accepted the President's challenge and immediately began to promote three bills as test cases of whether the will of the President or the
will of the Democratic majorities in Congress would prevail. The bills
the leaders chose involved the expansion of the federal housing program,
the expansion of the airport program, and the establishment of federal
aid to depressed areas. The airport bill, with the politically attractive des-
ignation of S. 1, was the smallest of the three and apparently had the
widest base of support in Congress. It was therefore chosen by the Democratic leadership to be the first major legislation of the year.

*The Senate Fight.* On January 9, 1959 Senator Monroney and forty-
three cosponsors, including four Republicans, introduced S. 1. This bill
provided for $575 million over five years and was virtually identical to
S. 3502 from the previous session except for the addition of another
year. Monroney, in introducing the bill, emphasized that it was almost
identical to the bill passed unanimously the year before. He stated that
the bill "is designed to eliminate the present horse-and-buggy national
airport system and to make a wise investment in the future of aviation."
    On January 23, the second day of the hearings, Senator Schoeppel in-
troduced the administration bill, S. 674. His support was somewhat qualified: "The hearings now under way before the Aviation Subcommittee
may demonstrate that the best Federal Airport Act of 1959 is one merg-
ing features of the Administration bill and S. 1." S. 674 provided $200
million with 50 percent to be expended at the discretion of the administrator. It also provided that a grant could be made only if the administrator were satisfied "that the project is urgently required for and essential
to the development or establishment of an adequate national aviation facilities system."
    Throughout January the political tempo increased. On the opening
day of the hearings Monroney stated that S. 1 would be the first bill
passed by the Senate in the Eighty-sixth Congress, that it would be the
first bill vetoed by the President, and that it would be "the first Eisenhower veto ever to be overridden." Prior to Senate floor debate Lyndon B.
Johnson, then senator from Texas and the majority leader, referred to S.
1 as "Scalp No. 1."
    The executive was also aware of the political possibilities of the strug-
gle, and was eager to maintain a united front against the congressional
Democrats. The only agency threatening to support S. 1 was the independent CAB. It was finally persuaded to support the principle of airport aid in general without asking for an increased money amount.

At a news conference before the Senate floor debate the President spoke at length on S. 1. His opening statement at that conference was a denunciation of "reckless spending" with particular reference to the housing and airport bills.

> Now, in the airport bill, the airport bill of the Administration directs itself to one factor and one factor only: Improving the safety of flying whether it is in the air, take-off, or when you are arriving. It is not interested and does not interest itself in building a nice, lovely administration building and things that we would call, for the railroads, these depots. The Federal Government did not build the terminal for either the railroads or for the buses. I see no reason for doing it for the air terminals. . . .
>
> I think we should put our money into that [safety], and not into these things which are unnecessary, no matter how desirable they may seem to be to the locality. The locality ought to pay for those things, and the Government is certainly going to do its part to keep flying safe. . . .
>
> There are all sorts of places where the money is not needed, but it is needed for improved flying safety, and that is what I believe we should do.
>
> And, above all, let us remember, since we are doing necessary things, again we have the effect on budget and why should we cheapen dollars, and in the air field, in the airplane business, having higher rates, higher flying rates, and making everything more expensive, more expensive for the housewife and for you and for me and for everybody else. I am against it.

The President said in response to a question that he would promise neither to veto nor to approve the final legislation until he could study its exact provisions.

Monroney had announced publicly on January 16 that the hearings would begin January 22. The Commerce Committee was still in the process of organizing itself when the hearings began. Only three members of the Aviation Subcommittee remained from the previous session: Monroney, Smathers, and Schoeppel. For the hearings these three alone composed the subcommittee. Members of the full committee were invited to participate. Only Norris Cotton did so, however. The day after the hearings closed the decision was formally made to expand the subcommittee to eight. Accordingly three Democrats—Strom Thurmond of South Carolina, Clair Engle of California, and E. L. Bartlett of Alaska—and two Republicans—Cotton and Thruston B. Morton of Kentucky—were added. Thurmond took no part in the deliberations and withheld his judgment from the committee report. Cotton became ranking minority member.

In a newsletter to his constituents Cotton reported his views at the start of the hearings:

> All was quiet on the political front this week when the first guided missile

of the battle of the 86th Congress suddenly arrived. It exploded right under my seat, that of ranking Minority member of the Subcommittee on Aviation, to which I had been appointed only a few hours before. When the bomb burst, I was basking blissfully in that chair, happy that it will enable me to help New Hampshire get its full share of aid for airports, which can spell the difference between progress and stagnation for us. However, I hadn't bargained for action so soon and so hot.

At the three days of hearings thirty-two witnesses appeared in person. Quesada, accompanied by Pyle, presented the administration position. Fifteen witnesses from the airport supplier category appeared, including delegations from Los Angeles, Tulsa, and New Orleans. Mayor Hartsfield again appeared for both the Conference of Mayors and the Municipal Association. Five from the airport user category appeared. Only Quesada and Pyle supported the administration bill.

A large portion of the hearings was taken up by debate and discussion on the question of giving aid to terminals. The administration chose to make this issue as central as the question of annual money figures. Monroney had hoped to silence the question by including in S. 1 the prohibition against aid to bars, theaters, parking lots, and similar facilities. The administration pressed ahead, however, arguing that terminals should be paid for locally since they were matters of local pride and were not essential to safety but only to comfort. Quesada was eager to show abuses in the building of terminals in the past. About 25 to 30 percent of the program's money since 1946 had been spent on terminal projects.

Monroney agreed that safety was the primary consideration but argued that terminals had enough national importance to be left in the program. Smathers indicated he had doubts about terminal aid but would support S. 1 anyway. Cotton and Schoeppel were sympathetic to the administration's position on terminals.

During his testimony Quesada openly stated that "orderly withdrawal" did not mean termination. "As a practical matter I personally don't see the termination of a program providing for Federal aid to communities on the principle that the Federal Government must assume some obligation of meeting the needs of air commerce that the communities themselves physically cannot meet. I think that will be a continuing thing from now on out, as it is in other walks of life and other fields of endeavor." Monroney questioned this interpretation of the administration's intent. For obvious reasons he was eager to picture the administration as proposing rapid termination.

Monroney also asked the FAA administrator to cooperate by furnishing an updating of statistical data from the previous year. What Monroney wanted, and what Quesada supplied, was the data on the survey of airport needs conducted by the CAA in its waning months. This was not published until March 31 but Monroney received it on January 26.

Cotton and Schoeppel, the two active Republicans in the hearings, were only partially in accord with the administration's program. Both had favored the program in the past and Schoeppel was particularly concerned about general aviation and Cotton about feeder-line airports. Cotton, along with most of the witnesses, resented the "urgency" criterion in the administration bill, fearing that it would eliminate all but the biggest airports. Cotton agreed with the administration position on terminals although he announced that "I am by no means wedded to the administration bill as it is now presented."

The hearings ended January 26. By February 1 the subcommittee had agreed on a $565 million bill—cutting only $10 million from the discretionary fund. This cut was to offset uncommitted funds that would be left from the previous legislation on June 30, 1959. The final subcommittee meeting was held on February 3 and a perfunctory meeting of the full committee to review the bill and vote on it was held the following day. Thurmond did not vote. All other Democrats, except Frank J. Lausche of Ohio, voted for the bill and all Republicans, joined by Lausche, voted against it. Thus the committee ordered the bill reported by a 9 to 7 vote. A substitute measure simply extending the existing $63 million annual program for four years was defeated by the same margin.

In the printed report the majority asserted that the need for a continuing airport aid program was "almost self-evident." It cited the Kestnbaum, Curtis, and Doolittle reports and stressed defense and postal considerations. It also made clear that general aviation would not be ignored in the new bill. The emergency fund was defended precisely as a means for allocating a larger share of the regular $100 million annual amount to airports serving only feeder lines and general aviation. Terminal aid was defended "not only because of the universal recognition of the necessity for housing vital Federal functions at local public airports but also because of basic requirements of public health and safety which require the maintenance of appropriate facilities to accommodate our interstate and foreign traffic." The majority printed a table summarizing the FAA figures that showed a four-year airport development need of $1.3 billion.

The minority of seven also filed a report. They charged that S. 1 "ignores growing Federal responsibilities for navigational and safety aids; it overfinances the need, and it is fiscally reckless." They further argued that the "so-called need figures on which S. 1 relies are grossly inflated." As an alternative to S. 1 they proposed a four-year extension of the existing aid level of $63 million—a total of $252 million.

Thus the Republican senators were willing to support the administration in opposing S. 1 but they wanted no part of a program calling for gradually smaller amounts of aid. The absence of Senator Payne from the subcommittee was important in explaining the Republican willingness to agree even partially with the administration.

The Federal Aviation Agency, and especially Quesada and Howard, reacted strongly to this Republican coolness to the administration position. They informed the White House that the Republican senators were shirking their duty. Accordingly, Ed McCabe of the White House liaison staff talked with the Republican subcommittee members and told them of the agency's displeasure. Some mutual ill-will between the three senators and the FAA was bred in this way. At meetings with FAA officials the three senators on the subcommittee expressed some doubt about the wisdom of opposing S. 1 with amounts less than half as much. They felt that the "need survey" of the CAA-FAA might prove hard to reconcile with S. 674. Cotton voiced his doubts about the administration's airport position at a meeting of the Republican Policy Committee.

Quesada and Howard also felt that the staffing on the Republican side of the subcommittee was weak. In the main the only staff members working for the Republicans were John McElroy, a minority employee of the full committee; Jerry Kenny, legislative assistant to Senator Cotton; and Ernest Baynard, legislative assistant to Senator John Marshall Butler of Maryland. FAA-Republican staff relations were thus inevitably weak and unproductive.

Cotton, Schoeppel, and Morton met often during the few weeks between the hearings and the floor debate. Sometimes they were joined by FAA and White House officials and interested Republican senators from the full Commerce Committee. The FAA had numerous amendments they wished the senators to propose. For floor purposes the senators chose three—one for each—that they felt to be the most reasonable. It was made clear to the senators that the President would veto anything as large as S. 1, although exactly what would be acceptable was not described in detail. Senator Morton persuaded the minority to leave a strong attack on terminal aid out of the minority report. As he wrote to Foster Jones of the Louisville airport, an Airport Operators Council official,

Because of your persuasive arguments and because I am a political realist and know when I am licked, I will not personally push, introduce or speak for an amendment to deny Federal aid funds to terminal buildings. I have also been successful in eliminating any reference to this item in the Minority Report which will be filed tonight. I will also do my best to talk my colleagues on the Committee out of offering such an amendment.

The Operators Council, Conference of Mayors, and Municipal Association all sought the active help of members they hoped would be as persuasive as Jones.

The Senate debated S. 1 on February 6. At the outset Lyndon Johnson, in a move designed to produce at least the illusion of economy, offered an amendment reducing the bill from five years and $565 million to four years and $465 million. The Senate leadership had become concerned that the President's efforts to label Democrats as "reckless spenders" might succeed. Johnson told the committee leaders of this amendment on the floor and did not consult with them in time for it to be offered as a committee amendment. This procedure temporarily angered some of the majority members and staff. Nevertheless, the Senate adopted the amendment by voice vote.

Monroney, in opening the debate said that the issue posed by S. 1 was one of "continued support" as contrasted with "withdrawal." Monroney and Magnuson, seeking wide support, both stressed that the bill was not aimed solely at large cities. Monroney introduced the CAA survey and indicated surprise that the figures had not been much lower than the interest group figures the FAA had attacked—although there was, of course, a $200 million difference.

The Republicans concentrated on ridiculing the CAA-FAA survey, calling it "a letter to Santa Claus" and a "grab-bag." They tried to stress the advantages of an extension of the program at the $63 million level. They also attacked aid to terminals, arguing that the largest terminals were or could be self-supporting. Democratic Senator Joseph S. Clark of Pennsylvania, an ex-Mayor of Philadelphia, resented this attack on the biggest cities and replied to it.

Schoeppel offered the first Republican amendment, which extended the existing program for four years. He said he offered it in the spirit of compromise and on the basis of what had already succeeded. Monroney said it was a step backward. The Senate defeated it 53 to 35.

Cotton, for himself and five others, offered the gate-to-gate amendment prohibiting aid to terminals except for those parts containing air traffic control, weather, and communications facilities. Monroney insisted that federal aid to terminals saved money in the long run by providing space that the local airports gave to the government rent-free. The Senate defeated this amendment 53 to 33.

Finally, Morton offered an amendment reducing the annual program to $69.5 million for four years plus a $30 million discretionary fund—a total of $308 million. This figure, picked as a compromise, was offered by Morton because he wanted to see the program continued and felt the President might sign his substitute whereas he surely would veto S. 1. The Senate was little more receptive to this proposal, defeating it 48 to 37. After unanimously accepting one minor amendment the Senate then passed S. 1 intact, 63 to 22.

The most significant feature of the voting on these four roll calls was its party nature:

|  | Cut Program to $252 Million | Eliminate Terminal Aid | Cut Program to $308 Million | Final Passage of $465 Million |
|---|---|---|---|---|
| Democrats | 88% nay (51 of 58) | 91% nay (51 of 56) | 86% nay (47 of 55) | 91% aye (51 of 56) |
| Republicans | 93% aye (28 of 30) | 93% aye (28 of 30) | 97% aye (29 of 30) | 59% nay (17 of 29) |

Only Republican William Langer of North Dakota voted consistently with the Democrats in favor of S. 1 and against the Republican amendments. On final passage, however, both Republican senators from North Dakota, South Dakota, and Vermont and single Republican senators from Colorado, New Hampshire, New Jersey, New York, Pennsylvania, and Wisconsin joined the Democrats.

*The House Fight.* In the House, Chairman Harris introduced H.R. 1011 on January 7. This bill provided for $37 million additional for fiscal 1959 (to make a total of $100 million) and $100 million annually for the four succeeding years. On January 26 Republican John B. Bennett of Michigan introduced the administration proposal of $200 million spread in declining amounts over four years.

The Senate bill came to the House Interstate and Foreign Commerce Committee on February 7. Although there was a Subcommittee on Transportation and Communications (chaired now by John Bell Williams of Mississippi) Harris decided to handle the bill in full committee. By 1959, the beginning of his third year as chairman and his nineteenth year in the House, Harris had acquired a reputation for being a chairman who controlled his committee and who never lost a bill on the House floor because of his accurate "feel" for the temper of the House. Given the political importance of the airport bill, Harris did not send it to a subcommittee.

In the House hearings, held on February 9 and 10, thirty-seven persons testified. Seventeen came from the airport supplier category, four from the airport user category, and four from the executive. Sixteen of the witnesses had previously appeared before the Senate Aviation Subcommittee.

The intricacies of terminal aid were a principal topic of discussion in the House hearings. In part, terminal aid was seen as an urban problem. Some members were concerned about what would happen to projects already agreed on. Others thought it unfair to cities that had not yet applied for terminal aid to cut it off after helping competing cities. A delegation of seven from Los Angeles, led by the mayor, presented a case history of the development of the Los Angeles jet airport that was aimed partly at highlighting the necessity of terminal aid. Yet in the course of the hearings even Democratic members began to agree with Quesada that terminal building aid was unnecessary since it was not related to safety.

As the hearings progressed the FAA witnesses introduced a number of tables showing that even the airport funds currently available could not all be used. A number of committee members were impressed by the implications of these figures.

Quesada once again indicated that "orderly withdrawal" did not mean termination:

> To be very frank, I think that we have through error left the impression that orderly withdrawal carries with it termination and I tried to correct this in the Senate and I would like to correct it here. I bear the burden for this false impression. It was a mistake on our part. I will admit this. But when we say orderly withdrawal, we do not mean termination. I cannot foresee, certainly in my lifetime, that the Government would not have some role to play in this.

Quesada, in a letter to Harris printed in the record, also tried to discount the results of the CAA survey: "In arriving at these figures, the Civil Aeronautics Administration covered 3,321 airports in the United States and its Territories. The CAA conducted what can best be termed a speculative anticipation of the most utopian 1963 requirements of these 3,321 airports, with no basis for knowing the intent or the ability to perform on the part of the local communities."

Chairman Harris, feeling the tide running against his $437 million

proposal, and also keenly aware of the veto possibilities, stated the pragmatic situation to the president of the Association of Airport Executives
near the end of the second day of hearings: "Of course, you must also
recognize there is a practical situation here. . . . we are going to have
another problem of trying to get a bill through that we can get finally
approved. . . . down in the 1600 block of Pennsylvania Avenue or . . . by
a sufficient vote in Congress. I think that is a pretty important consideration that should be given attention. . . ."

Harris, in contrast to the Senate Democratic leaders, was also eager to
keep the bill from becoming a solely partisan dispute. "I regret the fact
that this whole thing has developed into more of a partisan position or
fight than anything else. I had hoped we would not have that, so far as a
program of this kind that is so important because, you know, we worked
hard and diligently to keep the partisan feeling out of it in the last 2
years." But on February 17, the day before the committee began executive sessions on the bill, the Republican Policy Committee endorsed the
administration's $200 million proposal. The partisan nature of the dis-
pute could not be altered.

The committee held executive sessions on the bill on February 18, 19,
24, 25, and 26. At the first meeting it rejected the administration bill,
with only one Democrat voting for it. At the second meeting Harris,
feeling the need to trim the bill in order to get it through the House,
offered several amendments. These kept the annual program essentially
at the existing level for fiscal 1959–61 and increased it to $75 million
for fiscal 1962 and 1963. The total figure called for was $363 million.
In addition Harris proposed to eliminate terminals "intended to produce
revenue." The committee of twenty-one Democrats and twelve Republicans adopted the money amendments. The question of terminal aid was
not reached at this meeting.

At the last three sessions the committee passed more amendments.
Bennett, assisted particularly by William Springer of Illinois, led the Republican drive for a smaller bill. At a meeting of the interested Republican committee members with FAA officials in Bennett's office on February 18 those present agreed that in committee the Republicans should
seek a $230 million program, with gradually diminishing amounts each
year. The Republicans were assisted by some Democrats, especially John
Bell Williams.

Bennett introduced the gate-to-gate terminal amendment and, after
substantial debate, it carried. Democrat Walter Rogers of Texas offered

an amendment cutting about $70 million more from the bill—approximately the amount that would have been spent on terminals. The committee finally agreed to a bill containing $297 million—$63 million a year plus a discretionary fund of $20 million for fiscal 1961, $15 million for fiscal 1962, and $10 million for fiscal 1963. Bennett wanted to cut another $40 million but the committee, by a vote of 14 to 12, reported the $297 million bill that barred terminal aid.

At the close of the last executive session, on February 26, Harris said he thought Monroney would be "unhappy" but indicated he would support all of the committee amendments on the floor. From the Senate side Monroney replied simply: "I fear it will meet considerable objection among the supporters of airport development in the Senate."

The committee filed its formal report on March 2. The majority used the same justification—even much of the same language—that the Senate majority had used. The terminal amendment was justified as money-saving although the majority also noted that the amendment would authorize grants to pay for up to 100 percent of the cost of providing space for federal agencies at airports.

Eleven of the twelve Republicans on the committee signed a minority report. They opposed H.R. 1011 because it was still "excessive in cost" and did not provide for an "orderly reduction in the cost of the program to reflect the diminishing requirement for Federal participation." The minority report also attacked the $1.3 billion CAA survey as unrealistic. Five members—four Republicans and Williams—submitted additional views, denouncing the "backdoor approach to the Treasury" that had been in the program since 1955 and was extended for four years by H.R. 1011.

Throughout early March FAA and White House personnel worked with House Republicans in order to plan strategy for the floor debate. The FAA wrote draft speeches for Minority Leader Charles Halleck of Indiana, Bennett, and Springer. Bennett requested that an amendment cutting the program to $255 million be drafted. On March 4 the Republican Policy Committee again discussed the airport bill. Eventually they reached a position in support of an administration amendment but remained undecided about what to do if the amendment were defeated.

The House adopted, on March 18, an open rule with two hours of debate for the consideration of H.R. 1011. The debate extended into the next day.

After general debate on the bill, which centered around the familiar arguments on both sides, Springer offered the administration's $200 million bill as a substitute. Curiously, at the same time he indicated that the whole airport aid program was aimed at the fifty largest cities in the country. "From a financial standpoint the average Member of the House has very little interest in the bill insofar as getting any dollars in his own district is concerned." Williams attacked the administration substitute primarily on the grounds that the provisions for increasing the discretionary amount to 50 percent of the funds would cut too many small airports from the program. Harris took this cue and said that the central issue in the vote on the Springer amendment was: "Are we going to throw overboard this formula for the allocation of funds for the construction of airports, that has existed since 1946, and give to an administrator of an agency, a bureau, twice as much to use at his discretion?" The House then rejected the administration bill by a teller vote of 181 to 144.

Democrat J. C. Davis of Georgia proposed an amendment also reducing the total program to $200 million—roughly $63 million in fiscal 1959 and $30 million in the following three years with the discretionary fund of $45 million left intact. After a short debate the House adopted this amendment 168 to 157 by teller. Williams offered an amendment to restore the program to an annual appropriations basis. Again after a short debate the House adopted the amendment, 169 to 154 by teller.

After the committee of the whole had risen Harris demanded roll calls on the two amendments that had passed. The House reversed itself and defeated the Davis amendment 214 to 194 and the Williams amendment 216 to 191. The House then passed the Harris bill, H.R. 1011, providing for $297 million over four years and prohibiting terminal aid, by a roll call vote of 272 to 134.

As in the Senate the roll call voting in the House proceeded along party lines:

|  | Cut Program to $200 Million | Restore Annual Appropriations Process | Final Passage of $297 Million |
|---|---|---|---|
| Democrats | 79% nay (209 of 266) | 80% nay (212 of 265) | 91% aye (242 of 267) |
| Republicans | 96% aye (137 of 142) | 97% aye (138 of 142) | 78% nay (109 of 139) |

The roll calls also reveal a rural-urban split in the support for the airport legislation. Despite the attempts to attract nonurban representatives by using some of the funds for small and general aviation airports, the

Table 2: *House Voting in Support of H.R. 1011, March 19, 1959, by Party and Rural-Urban Nature of Constituency*[a]

| Constituency | Number of Representatives | Cut program to $200 million (percentage nay) | Restore annual appropriations process (percentage nay) | Final passage of $297 million (percentage aye) |
|---|---|---|---|---|
| *Democrats* | *283* | | | |
| Rural | 74 | 68 | 61 | 80 |
| Small-town | 65 | 70 | 75 | 90 |
| Mid-urban | 50 | 76 | 89 | 91 |
| Metropolitan | 94 | 90 | 93 | 99 |
| *Republicans* | *152* | | | |
| Rural | 15 | 0 | 0 | 15 |
| Small-town | 44 | 0 | 0 | 15 |
| Mid-urban | 43 | 2 | 5 | 27 |
| Metropolitan | 50 | 8 | 4 | 24 |

a The categories used are defined in the *Congressional Quarterly Almanac, 1956*, p. 788.

more urban the district the more likely the representative was to take a pro-aid position. This generalization is true for both parties. Table 2, which uses a four-fold classification of districts ranging from rural to metropolitan, summarizes these voting figures.

*Conference and Compromise.* On April 20 the Senate took up the House amendments to the airport bill in order to ask for a conference committee and appoint conferees. Monroney, Magnuson, Smathers, Schoeppel, and Cotton were named as the Senate conferees. The House named its conferees on April 29: Democrats Harris, Williams, Roberts, and Peter F. Mack, Jr., of Illinois, and Republicans Bennett, Springer, and Alvin R. Bush of Pennsylvania. Bennett did not sign the conference report, although there is no indication in the *Record* that he resigned from the committee.

The conferees met five times between May 26 and June 11. They never came close to final agreement. At the first two meetings the negotiations, carried on almost exclusively by Monroney and Harris, reached agreement that the compromise should not exceed the Eisenhower budgetary figure of $65 million for the first year. Monroney proposed a total figure of $363 million. There was agreement on the House language on the discretionary fund. At the third meeting Monroney indicated that the absolute minimum figure that he would accept was $341 million. Harris insisted that he would not go over the House figure of $297 million.

The question of terminal aid also presented problems. Monroney wanted terminals left eligible. Again Harris did not wish to move from the House position that terminals should be excluded. Monroney was willing to adopt the House position if the money amount could be agreed on. After the June 2 meeting both the Municipal Association and the Conference of Mayors alerted their members to the possibility that only "hardship" cases would merit any further terminal aid. "Hardships" existed where local indebtedness had already been incurred on the basis of prospective federal matching funds, where architectural and engineering plans had been completed and approved by the FAA, or where funds already invested might be jeopardized if the programmed work could not be completed without federal funds.

Finally, by June 11 the conferees agreed to differ and report S. 1 in disagreement. At the same time they informally agreed simply to extend the existing program for two years. They could not formally report this agreement, however, since both bills had covered four years.

The possibility of a simple two-year extension had been mentioned by Tom Finney of Monroney's staff in a phone conversation with Burnard as early as April 8. Monroney, after becoming certain that Harris would not yield in conference, decided that rather than agree to what he considered an inadequate program ($297 million) for four years it would be better to extend the existing program for as short a time as possible and then try for a bigger program in another session. Two years was the most attractive time period for this extension because it would carry the program beyond the end of Eisenhower's presidency and Monroney was, of course, hopeful that a Democrat sympathetic to airport aid would succeed Eisenhower. Two years also gave some of the needed advance planning time to the municipalities submitting fund requests.

The rules of the two houses dictated that Monroney take S. 1 back to the Senate and move the acceptance of the two-year extension as a substitute for the existing text of the bill. This he did on June 15. After explaining the details of the disagreement in conference he summed up his feelings about the proposed substitute:

> I think this is the best we can do under the circumstances. . . . It will permit us to take another look at this problem prior to fiscal year 1962, at which time we will be in a much better position to appraise the needs for meeting the impact of the jet age and would permit us to legislate much more wisely, and with a better understanding on the part of the occupant of the White

House, than if we tried to write a 4-year program now in order to meet the administration's views on what is good for those years ahead for which it has no responsibility whatsoever. We are forced, by the approaching expiration of the law in 2 weeks, to follow the old adage: "Half a loaf is better than no bread." It is better to have something on the books, to continue a vitally needed airport program, than to have no legislation at all. . . . By making this an extension for only the next 2 years, at the end of that time we properly anticipate that President Eisenhower will have retired and will be able to use his hand on a mashie or a niblick instead of a veto pen. We know we can come back later, when we have a President who realizes civil aviation is here to stay, and can enact an adequate bill to meet the tremendous impact on airports forced upon us by the jet air age.

During this debate, at the insistence of the FAA, Senate Minority Leader Everett McKinley Dirksen of Illinois offered another amendment to remove terminals from eligibility. In support of the amendment Dirksen said, "I do not know what the President will do. But I do know that he laid down a hard concept and said, 'We are responsible for the safety of the individual from portal to portal: from the time he walks into the plane until when he leaves it. That is where we stop.' " After a short debate the Senate rejected the amendment, despite the veto threat, by a 54 to 27 vote. Then by 71 to 11 it adopted the two-year substitute. The vote on the amendment again shows a party-line division. The vote on final passage was the only bipartisan vote in the nine occurring in the two houses in 1959.

|  | Eliminate Terminal Aid | Final Passage of 2-Year Extension |
|---|---|---|
| Democrats | 96% nay (51 of 53) | 100% aye (54) |
| Republicans | 89% aye (25 of 28) | 39% nay (11 of 28) |

On June 17 the House discussed the substitute that the Senate had passed as S. 1 two days before. Harris moved to concur in the Senate amendment with one additional amendment. His amendment included language giving the administrator of the FAA additional discretion in refusing aid to terminal projects. Halleck indicated his eagerness to restore the former House language specifically prohibiting such aid but the parliamentary situation disallowed such an amendment. In the course of the short debate Harris gave his version of the conference committee meetings, stressing the disagreement over terminals more than the disagreement over money amounts. He also explained the complex parliamentary situation to the House. The House by a standing vote of 164 to 37 adopted the compromise version of S. 1, with Harris's amendment on terminals.

Later the same day the Senate considered S. 1 with the House amendment. Debate was almost nonexistent. Monroney, anxious finally to pass a bill, no longer wanted to argue: "Nearly as I can tell, the language is practically identical with the language I proposed in the anticocktail lounge provision. Perhaps the minority leader and others may prefer it. I am happy to accept it, because I do not think it will make any difference. I think the Senate could well support the action of the House, and send the bill to the White House with the hope that it will not be vetoed." The Senate concurred in the House amendment by voice vote.

*Presidential Acceptance.* The President was happy with the final result obtained from Congress on S. 1. To show his appreciation he had the Republican members of both committees to the White House for cocktails.

The Bureau of the Budget went through its normal process of soliciting agency opinions on the enrolled bill. No agency recommended a veto although several, including the FAA and the bureau itself, asked that a signing statement be issued on the day of approval. Quesada wrote that he felt Congress had departed from its original position to a greater degree than had the executive. He was obviously pleased with the results, although he wanted a signing statement in order to stress certain executive positions on the program. Stans agreed with Quesada in urging that a strong signing statement be issued.

Finally, on June 29 the story of airport aid legislation in 1958–59 came to a close when the President signed S. 1. The signing statement followed the general lines suggested by the FAA. The President praised the section of the bill making specific terminal items ineligible for aid, and added:

> The bill is not as conclusive, however, with respect to those parts of airport buildings intended for any other use. Federal money may be committed for their construction if, in the opinion of the Federal Aviation Administrator, they are essential for the safety, convenience or comfort of persons using airports for public aviation purposes. The dimensions of this latitude accorded the Administrator are supplied by the debate on this bill and by the whole history of this legislation. Thus viewed, the Administrator's discretion is very broad.

## Epilogue and Concluding Comments

During the remainder of Quesada's tenure as FAA administrator (until Eisenhower left office in 1961) he used his discretion to deny any new aid to terminal buildings. He made this position public in a statement on July 9, 1959. He and Monroney maintained cordial relations and worked together on a number of important matters affecting aviation. Monroney respected Quesada and took his own defeat on the airport legislation in 1959 with good grace.

As Monroney had hoped, a Democrat became President in 1961 and Congress again considered airport legislation. The administration requested a five-year program of $75 million annually. What finally emerged was a $75 million annual program for three years. This time, however, John Bell Williams was successful in his drive to return the program to annual appropriations.

The 1958–59 struggle was only one episode in the history of legislation that had already produced several major struggles and would produce more. The 1958–59 battle was fought in partisan terms. Party feeling ran high. Yet in some ways this partisan conflict was the prelude to greater consensus on what was desirable in a federal aid to airports program. A relatively high degree of substantive agreement was in evidence in both 1961 and 1963–64 when Congress again extended the program.

The classic description of American legislative politics, which assumes that legislation is passed by coalitions of powerful members of Congress, bureaucrats, and lobbyists with similar interests, appears at first glance to fit this case. Here there were members of Congress such as Monroney, members of the executive such as Pyle and Borsari, and interest group representatives such as Burnard who all favored the same general ends. But a deeper probing of the facts reveals that the classic pattern was operating only with gross distortions. The pattern as generally understood requires that the three elements—members of Congress, bureaucrats, and lobbyists—all be powerful and work together closely and effectively. Here, however, the executive officials favoring the program were passive and silenced by internal considerations. The interest groups were neither powerful nor creative. Their main function was to provide congressional friends of the program with information on airport needs and wants. In Congress a single senator, one not high in the Senate hierarchy, was the chief moving force behind the legislation. The model is too simple to explain what happened in this case.

The additional factor operating with pervasive effectiveness in 1959 was partisanship. The President's veto of the 1958 bill mobilized the partisan loyalties of the Republican members of both houses in Congress. Democrats attempted to reply in kind by making the airport bill a partisan matter of the highest importance. Whatever the reason—southern Democratic defections, the 1959 economy campaign of the President, or the inherent power of the presidency—the party battle ended as a qualified victory for the Republican President. Accordingly, most Republicans at that time felt that airports had been treated well. Most Democrats at that time felt that airports were doomed to be neglected until a Democrat occupied the White House.

The federal aid to airports program by 1958 was aimed centrally but not exclusively at urban areas. In the past it had produced some of the usual debates between those from the big city and those from the small towns and rural areas. But in 1958–59 most of the discussion was couched in terms of what was good for or needed by civil aviation. In order to build a broad base of support, legislation was produced offering something to every size town. Yet, despite the lack of debate based on a clash of urban interests with rural interests, the analysis of the House voting in 1959 shows there was an underlying pattern of conflict that to some extent pitted urban legislators against rural and small-town legislators.

Since the participants considered the legislation not in terms of urban interests but in terms of economy, partisanship, rural and small-town airports, and civil aviation, the question arises of who, if anyone, effectively represented the cities. The necessities of politics internal to the Senate and even more to the House suggest that, in general, cities must look to the executive or to influential interest groups for programs specifically tailored to their problems. But in this case Congress appeared in the unusual role of the most effective champion of urban interests—even though the congressional proponents of the program did not focus on developing cities and aiding their transportation needs.

The executive was in part divided over how it viewed the aid to airports program. The President was apparently convinced that this was chiefly a budgetary issue and that economy was the most important victory to be won. The Bureau of the Budget—acting in its normal capacity of staff arm to the President—both shaped and reflected his view. Thus the main impact of the bureau's legislative clearance function in this struggle was to stress the need for a small program with prospects of rapid termination. The bureau also engaged in its usual activity of questioning and probing agency justifications for programs in order to assure that the most convincing justification was finally made public and presented to Congress.

In 1958 the Commerce Department had no use for the airport aid program on ideological grounds of opposition to grants-in-aid. But in 1959 Quesada and the FAA did support a program, although one much smaller than Monroney desired. Almost all of the smaller amount would have gone to medium-sized and large cities. Quesada also thought in terms of the health of civil aviation but he made fewer concessions to the rural participants in the program than did the congressional sponsors of the larger money amounts.

The interest groups here did not speak too loudly for urban interests. The Conference of Mayors and the Municipal Association framed their arguments in terms of city needs but were not willing to devote much political muscle to the airport program. The Airport Operators Council was representative of urban areas but was also greatly concerned with civil aviation. Burnard's desire to prompt Air Transport Association activity in support of the airport aid legislation led to a relative downgrading of the urban interests and a relative upgrading of the civil aviation interests. The two interests are not radically divorced but the difference in emphasis was visible and important.

None of the major participants in 1958–59 had a clear concept of the urban interest in federal aid to airport development. They felt that the politically relevant arguments must be based on other grounds. Thus an urban problem received attention without the participants directly facing the urban issues. This case therefore poses the question of whether, given the American political system, urban problems can ever be defined in their own terms or whether they are inevitably destined to be overshadowed by other lines of argument and controversy.

M. KENT JENNINGS

# Legislative Politics
# and Water Pollution Control,
# 1956–61

An ADEQUATE SUPPLY of usable fresh water is an obvious necessity for any nation. Pollution can reduce that supply drastically and unnecessarily. Estimates made by the U.S. Public Health Service (PHS) portray in billions of gallons per day the changing nature of water supply and demand in the United States:

|                   | 1900 | 1920  | 1940  | 1950  | 1960  | 1970  | 1980  |
|-------------------|------|-------|-------|-------|-------|-------|-------|
| Municipal         | 3.0  | 6.0   | 10.1  | 14.1  | 22.0  | 27.0  | 37.2  |
| Industrial        | 15.0 | 27.2  | 52.0  | 84.0  | 159.9 | 218.3 | 394.2 |
| Agricultural      | 22.2 | 58.4  | 74.1  | 104.6 | 141.0 | 165.9 | 165.7 |
| Total Demand      | 40.2 | 91.6  | 136.4 | 202.7 | 322.7 | 411.2 | 597.1 |
| Dependable Supply | 95.0 | 125.0 | 245.0 | 270.0 | 315.0 | 395.0 | 515.0 |

The problem is even more serious than these figures suggest for in some areas of the country and during certain parts of the year there is a great imbalance between the available water and the need. In this situation the reuse of water becomes critically important. Over certain periods, for example, water from the Ohio River is used on an average of 3.7 times as the river winds its 1,000 mile course. "Dirty" or otherwise unsuitable water cannot be used for many purposes, especially for consumption by urban dwellers. Streams and rivers in earlier decades had the opportunity to purify themselves by natural means. Now the heavy incidence of wastes and the changing nature of these wastes require expensive artificial cleansing of the waters.

72

The problem of pollution can be documented by many kinds of "horror" statistics. Perhaps a more telling demonstration of the problem, however, lies in the impact of polluted water on people's everyday lives: towns and cities where the stench and ugliness of contaminated water cannot be ignored; beaches and rivers closed to recreational use; commercial and sports fishermen frustrated by the declining quality and quantity of the catch; and sudsy water pouring out of water taps in homes across the land.

Congressional consideration of water pollution has reflected rising concern since the early 1950's. From 1955 onward congressional debate has ceased to focus on whether there is a pollution problem; this has become an accepted fact. Issues for debate have since concerned ways to deal with pollution and, more particularly, the extent and nature of the federal government's role in pollution control.

Water pollution is not exclusively an urban problem. Conservation and purification measures are equally appropriate in the cities and in the country. Nevertheless the problem is often most visible in urban areas where industrial wastes or municipal sewage are primary pollutants and the results are evident to large numbers of citizens. With population growth and increasing urbanization, municipal use of water in the United States has expanded tremendously—from three billion gallons per day in 1900 to twenty-two billion in 1960, as the table above shows. Industrial usage has increased at an even faster pace; and most industrial users are located in urban areas. Good water supply is important to many industries, and many of the newer industries—the most rapidly expanding—are among the heaviest consumers of water. Adequate quantity and quality of water are significant elements in the competition among communities to attract new industry, and badly polluted streams and underground water sources are poor inducements in this competition. But municipalities most damaged by pollution may not themselves be offenders. A community that treats its sewage adequately before discharging it into a river may be threatened by another community further upstream pouring untreated waste into the same river, or by nearby industrial polluters over whom it has little or no control. Historically, the threatened community has had no effective recourse except to install expensive treatment facilities sufficient to make the water usable. Understandably, municipalities in this situation have strong preferences for locating authority over pollution control "above" the level of local government.

The 1956 Water Pollution Control Act

The first national legislative attack on water pollution was the Water Pollution Control Act of 1948, sponsored by Democratic Senator Alben W. Barkley of Kentucky and Republican Senator Robert A. Taft of Ohio. Although it represented a major breakthrough in terms of federal recognition of a national problem, it provided relatively little aid, control, or enforcement. The act declared that pollution was best dealt with at the local level. It recognized, however, the need for federal assistance to local and state governments. Thus the Public Health Service was to coordinate research, provide technical information, and—when asked by the affected states—provide limited enforcement over interstate waters. The act also provided for individual project loans of up to $250,000 at 2 percent interest to cover up to one-third of the total cost of a project. Congress, however, made only token appropriations, which declined from a high of $3 million in 1950 to less than $1 million in 1955. Consequently these loans, though a key part of the legislation, were not available to help local communities.

The 1948 act nevertheless established a foundation upon which subsequent legislation could be constructed. Furthermore, Robert Taft's key role in its enactment was symbolically important in convincing some Republicans that federal legislation in this field was legitimate. Similarly, the venerable Alben Barkley's role was not forgotten by Democratic proponents in subsequent years.

When the 1948 act expired in 1956 another major step was taken with passage of a new law containing major grants, research, and enforcement provisions. The bill (S. 890) passed the Senate on June 17, 1955. Sponsored by Republican Edward Martin of Pennsylvania and cosponsored by California's two Republican senators, Thomas H. Kuchel and William F. Knowland, it had the blessing of the Eisenhower administration. As introduced it was a vigorous, far-reaching proposal. However, Democrat Robert S. Kerr of Oklahoma, the chairman of the Public Works Committee's Subcommittee on Flood Control—Rivers and Harbors, voiced skepticism over an extensive federal commitment. He was willing to report only a relatively weak version of the bill.

Once in the House S. 890 became the property of Democrat John A. Blatnik of Minnesota, chairman of the Subcommittee on Rivers and Harbors of the Committee on Public Works. In ensuing years he was to become the principal architect of water pollution control legislation. Elected to Congress in 1946, Blatnik was a liberal and loyal to Democratic administrations. Water supply problems were minimal in his Eighth District along the Canadian border, and pollution less common than in most other sections of the nation, but Blatnik had an interest in the subject derived from two sources. First, he was a conservationist, joining an academic background in natural science and mathematics with practical experience in the Civilian Conservation Corps during the Depression. Second, as a member of the Rivers and Harbors Subcommittee, he was impressed with the filth and pollution he saw during his travels throughout the country. These exposures led him to believe that a crash program was necessary to rescue the nation from pollution.

Another factor prompted Blatnik to assume a leadership role. Congressmen generally make their mark in the House by establishing themselves as specialists in a substantive legislative area. Blatnik's record, while respectable, was not particularly notable prior to 1955, when he became chairman of the Rivers and Harbors Subcommittee. With knowledge, interest, and now power he was anxious to lead the way in new pollution control legislation.

Blatnik viewed the modified version of S. 890 as little more than a slight expansion of the 1948 act, which was to expire June 30, 1956. He wanted much stronger legislation to emerge from his subcommittee and the House. While he and several others had sponsored bills in the House, hearings had not yet been held. To consider S. 890 and the House bills Blatnik scheduled only one day of committee hearings in the summer of 1955, feeling that chances for success would be better the following year. The full Public Works Committee reported an amended version of S. 890 on July 26, 1955, but the House took no action on the measure until January 23, 1956, when it was recommitted to the committee by unanimous consent.

During a two-month lull following the recommittal Blatnik made preparations to hold hearings and build support for a modified bill on the subject (H.R. 9540). Its major innovation was a provision for grants-in-aid to help local communities build sewage disposal plants. While the pattern for grants-in-aid was well established in other fields, the idea had never been officially offered as part of a water pollution control program. The nearest parallel was the loan provision in the 1948 act, which had been inoperative for lack of appropriations.

Blatnik, with advisers from his office staff, the Public Works Committee, and the Public Health Service, first revised the Senate bill, strengthening the federal government's responsibility to encourage states and localities to control their pollution. He then instructed Jerome N. Sonosky, one of his legislative assistants, to draft a new section providing financial aid to municipalities so that they would have the resources for purification and control. Sonosky, who was Blatnik's primary congressional aide in pollution control matters—although Blatnik drew heavily on other staff members as well—secured help from an attorney in the general counsel's office of the Department of Health, Education, and Welfare (HEW), an official of the American Municipal Association, and a legislative counsel from the House of Representatives. They drafted the new section in one day, but left out the actual dollar amounts. Blatnik set the annual figure at $100 million on the basis of estimates by health officials that roughly $500 million in construction outlays were needed annually over the coming ten years. At least 50 percent of the funds were to go to municipalities of 125,000 or under. This stipulation was predicated on the belief that smaller towns and cities were having the most difficulty in financing adequate disposal facilities.

Public hearings were held March 12–15, 1956. Strongest support for the legislation came from conservationist groups and some municipal officials. Representatives of the American Municipal Association pleaded especially for the construction grants and for making greater sums available for metropolitan projects. General opposition emerged from some industries, and Eisenhower administration officials protested the construction grants. Most state health officers and water control organizations and officials also opposed the grants, although some support emerged even here. The state officials generally favored most other provisions, including the federal enforcement sections. The latter had largely been written by Milton P. Adams, executive secretary of the Michigan Water Resources Commission, and Dr. Daniel Bergsma, state health officer of New Jersey. Informal clearance with other state officials tempered opposition from the states.

In the executive sessions that followed the public hearings Blatnik's strategy threw the opposition off balance. The Republicans were chiefly opposed to the grants-in-aid provisions of H.R. 9540, and their preoccupation with this section tended to divert their attention from the enforcement provisions. The chairman called for a vote on each major section, but saved the grants-in-aid provisions until the end, rather than presenting them in proper order, and the Republicans, holding their fire until the grants section was introduced, allowed the enforcement provisions to slip by without much objection.

Discussion of the aid proposals was heated. In anticipation of Senate objections Blatnik had reduced the grants from $100 million to $50 million annually with a $500 million total for ten years. He observed that this amounted to splitting the difference between the Senate version with no grant provisions and his original $100 million. But conservative Republicans branded this provision as another step down the road to socialism. They claimed that the grants would take away local initiative and control, and that with increasing federal involvement the states and localities would more and more become puppets of the national government. Despite the Democratic majority, Blatnik had to overcome some Democratic skepticism to ensure the favorable outcome.

As reported out of committee on May 21, H.R. 9540 was in essence a Blatnik measure. The minority report confined itself to an attack on the grants-in-aid provisions and did not even mention the enforcement section. Modest though it was, the enforcement section did give the federal government more authority to deal with the pollutors of interstate waters through conferences, hearings, and—when all else failed—legal suits. This section laid a basis for future establishment of federal sanctions, which experts considered essential for an effective control program.

The roll call votes occurred in the House on June 13. The first came on a motion to recommit the bill, introduced by Republican J. Harry McGregor of Ohio, who had signed the minority report. If the bill survived this motion, chances were high that it would pass. The House rejected recommittal by a highly partisan vote of 213 to 165, with 79 percent of the present and voting Republicans for it and 88 percent of the Democrats opposed. Following defeat of the recommittal motion, final passage of the bill came easily on a vote of 338 to 31, with Republicans casting 26 of the 31 negative votes.

Senator Kerr reluctantly agreed to a conference report that contained most of the House provisions. The report was agreed to by both chambers on June 27, and President Dwight D. Eisenhower signed the bill into law (P.L. 660) on July 9. Although he noted his disapproval of certain parts of it (grants-in-aid particularly), he felt the legislation dealt with "an urgent national problem."

This 1956 act:

A. Required the Public Health Service to assist states in preparing comprehensive programs for the elimination and reduction of pollution of interstate waters and their tributaries.

B. Authorized the promotion of interstate cooperation in solving pollution problems.

C. Authorized expanded research in pollution control by the Public Health Service.

D. Authorized grants of $3 million annually in matching funds to state and interstate agencies to assist in developing comprehensive water pollution control programs.

E. Authorized $500 million for ten years for matching grants to help localities construct sewage disposal plants, with a limit of $50 million per year. Allocations were limited to 30 percent of project cost or $250,000, whichever was less. Fifty percent of the funds were to go to municipalities of 125,000 or less.

F. Established a Water Pollution Control Advisory Board, consisting of the surgeon general or his designee, and nine members appointed by the President, none of whom could be federal employees.

G. Made provision for enforcing the antipollution rules by authorizing the surgeon general to call a conference of officials when he "had reason to believe" pollution of interstate waters was occurring, and to recommend remedial action after the conference. If no action occurred within six months after the recommendation, the secretary of HEW could call a public hearing in the state where the pollution originated and require remedial action after this hearing. If the pollutor took no action within six months, the secretary upon request from the offending or the offended state could request the attorney general of the United States to bring suit against the offender.

With a moderately strong law and a new grants program on the books, the next question was how effectively and vigorously the Eisenhower administration would carry them out. The administration indicated a lack of enthusiasm when the Bureau of the Budget froze the funds appropriated for the program for several months before making them available to HEW and the Public Health Service.

The appropriation process revealed that the program had its enemies in Congress as well. The grants section of the act was a tempting target to budget cutters because it was a new program. On April 4, 1957, when the House was considering the HEW appropriations, Democrat O. C. Fisher of Texas offered an amendment to delete the $50 million authorization for the coming fiscal year. The Democratic floor leadership alerted its forces, and the motion was defeated by the relatively narrow margin of 185 to 231. Again the partisan difference was marked: 84 percent of the Democrats voted against deletion, while 77 percent of the Republicans favored it.

## A Showcase Hearing, 1958

The following year, 1958, brought a new twist in the Eisenhower administration's attack upon the grants program for pollution control. A recurrent theme throughout the Eisenhower years—ever since the appointment of the Commission on Intergovernmental Relations in 1953 —was that some federal grants programs should be remanded to the states and that further expansion or new programs should be discouraged. To emphasize this theme President Eisenhower had challenged the Governors' Conference to join with him in creating a Joint Federal-State Action Committee to determine which, if any, federal grants-in-aid programs might properly be turned over to the states. Composed of seven representatives of the executive branch appointed by the President and ten governors appointed by the chairman of the Governors' Conference, the committee issued its "Progress Report No. 1" on December 1, 1957.

The report asked the President to discontinue the grants program for pollution control, recommending that the states assume the financial support of treatment facilities and other antipollution measures. The committee offered an inducement to the states:

> The Joint Federal-State Action Committee believes that the local telephone service tax is a logical revenue source for State and local governments. It recommends, therefore, that the Federal tax on local telephone service be changed so as to provide 40-percent tax credit to those States enacting a 4-percent local telephone tax, not counting taxes already levied prior to the adoption of the credit device. This would mean that the Federal liability under the local telephone-service tax would be discharged to the extent of 40 percent for any taxpayer paying this amount of tax to his State government. At the end of 5 years the Federal levy should be reduced 4 percentage points automatically.

The tax rebate scheme was not specifically tied to the discontinuation of the construction grants program (or any of the other programs affected by the committee's report), but the clear and unavoidable implication was that the states should use such new revenues to help support construction efforts within their own boundaries.

President Eisenhower's budget message of 1958 discussed the recommendations of the Joint Federal-State Action Committee and noted:

> While this budget recommends continuation of this program at the 1958 level, it is expected that by the end of 1959 the Federal Government and the States will have had an opportunity to act on the recommendation of the Joint Federal-State Action Committee that the States assume this function entirely. Therefore, it is anticipated that no funds will be included in the 1960 budget for this purpose, should this recommendation be accepted as practicable by the Congress.

On May 14 the President specifically requested Congress to discontinue the grants provision. Thus what was originally legislated as a ten-year program of grants ($50 million per year) would be cut short after approximately three years of operation.

Blatnik, of course, was incensed by these developments. He was not alone in his feelings. In fact there appeared little likelihood that the Democratic Congress would accept the telephone tax rebate scheme. In the House, for example, the Subcommittee on Intergovenmental Relations of the Committee on Government Operations gave it a critical and uncomplimentary reception. In some respects Blatnik and other supporters of P.L. 660 had little to fear, for it hardly seemed likely that the construction program would be eliminated if the tax rebate scheme were disallowed, as it surely would be.

At the same time the situation offered opportunities for them to solidify their position since the weaknesses of the tax rebate plan made it an easy target for ridicule. Blatnik and his supporters made much of the inequities of the plan, especially its lack of any assurance that the additional revenues would be used for antipollution programs. On February 24 he entered in the *Congressional Record* a stinging criticism of the proposals, setting forth the accomplishments of the grants section of the law. This and subsequent speeches were quoted and requoted by other opposition forces in and out of Congress.

The record of the construction grants program was persuasive, even if one disagreed with the concept of federal support. Awards for the construction of sewage treatment works had gone from about $200 million in 1955 to well over $300 million in both 1956 and 1957. The program had proved popular in the states and localities. Some state officials and organizations that had opposed it on the grounds that it would discourage construction outlays—the Association of State and Territorial Health Officers, for example—now felt that the grants were stimulating construction and were essential for further progress.

Blatnik sought to attract further support by introducing major legislation amending P.L. 660. This move made it possible to hold hearings that could be scheduled, conducted, and publicized so as to keep the situation in hand and perhaps turn it to good advantage. One of his close associates said, "We had no intention of trying to push H.R. 11714 [the new Blatnik bill] through the House, let alone the Senate. This was a ripe opportunity for Blatnik and his allies to show certain people both inside and outside Congress that he could get a strong bill out of the Public Works Committee if he wanted to. The hearings also served the purpose of giving more publicity to water pollution control and pointing out the incredible position of the Administration."

Because the administration was trying to remove the grants section of P.L. 660, Blatnik concentrated his attention on this section in preparing the new bill. H.R. 11714 specifically authorized an increase in the annual grants funds from $50 million to $100 million, with an aggregate total of $1 billion (the figures he had advocated in 1956); raised the amount of any one grant to a possible high of $500,000; permitted municipalities to band together in joint projects without penalty in loss of grants; and permitted the reallocation of any state's unobligated funds to other states having projects awaiting funds.

The hearings occurred on May 20, 21, and 22. By design the great majority of witnesses were friendly. Officials from HEW and the Public Health Service found the situation embarrassing. While the department was somewhat less than eager to see the program discontinued, its spokesmen could not go on record as opposing the President's recommendation.

Elliot L. Richardson, assistant secretary for legislation, and Gordon E. McCallum, chief of the Water Supply and Water Pollution Control Division in the Public Health Service, had an unenviable task when they appeared before the subcommittee on May 20. Despite aggressive questioning by Blatnik and others, Richardson maintained the official position that the department agreed with the President and the Joint Federal-State Action Committee that the program should revert to the states. Still, the department's judgment was that the grants had accelerated construction:

BLATNIK: "Mr. Richardson . . . can you make any comment as to whether or not the existing grant program in Public Law 660 . . . has stimulated and increased and encouraged the construction of water-pollution-control facilities?"

RICHARDSON: "We have no conclusive evidence on the matter, Mr. Chairman, but judging by the dollar volume and number of projects for construction of waste-treatment facilities that were undertaken before this program was initiated, and the number that have been undertaken since then, and the total amounts of those, it would follow that the program has had a stimulatory effect."

In addition to forcing HEW officials to admit that the grants had increased construction efforts, Blatnik used the hearings as an opportunity to scold the department publicly:

> I will be very frank that I just cannot understand how the Department that knows this problem better than anyone else can come in here saying that this program which has been going on for a year and a half with a very successful record of accomplishment and a very high level of local participation for every dollar of Federal contribution, should be turned back to the States, how you can recommend we go back to the situation of leaving this in the hands of the States and localities. They have always had it in their hands before this and it has given rise to this national problem of pollution in the first place.

Significantly, Blatnik was careful in this declaration and in others not to condemn the PHS in particular or the Water Supply and Water Pollution Control personnel within the service. His attacks were on the higher level because there was strong support in parts of the PHS for the grants program, and Blatnik had allies he did not wish to alienate.

The hearings served their purpose. They had gained valuable publicity for the program, secured support from previous doubters, and brought to light information on the apparent success of the grants. Additionally, they had served notice on the Eisenhower administration and Republicans in Congress that Blatnik now had the votes to bring out of committee practically as strong a bill as he wanted. It seemed likely that when he was ready to move he could secure House approval of further amendments to the Water Pollution Control Act.

## The Stalemate of 1959–60

In 1959–60 a direct confrontation occurred between the heavily Democratic Eighty-sixth Congress and the Eisenhower administration. Congress, where the Democrats held 283 of the 435 seats in the House and 64 of the 98 seats in the Senate, passed more liberal water pollution control legislation; the President vetoed it; and Congress failed to override the veto.

*Group Support and Opposition.* As the 1959 proceedings got under way Blatnik could count on a number of supporters and opponents for expanded water pollution control legislation. In Congress he had secured strong backing from several fellow Democratic committee members, particularly Robert E. Jones of Alabama, Clifford Davis of Tennessee, Frank E. Smith of Mississippi, Frank M. Clark of Pennsylvania, Kenneth J. Gray of Illinois, Ed Edmondson of Oklahoma, James C. Wright, Jr., of Texas, and Harold T. Johnson of California. According to Blatnik the only Republican committee member who gave him much assistance throughout the period under study was Edwin B. Dooley of New York. Blatnik also had allies in the Senate where he had made personal efforts to sell his ideas for an expanded program. Senator Kerr was now beginning to espouse a stronger program than he had favored in 1955–56. In addition fellow Democrats from Minnesota, Hubert H. Humphrey and Eugene J. McCarthy, were potential allies, and McCarthy was on the Senate Committee on Public Works. By this time, too, Blatnik had the House leadership with him—water pollution control legislation had come to be recognized as his bailiwick.

Outside Congress a number of interest groups could be counted upon to supply advice on drafting legislation and planning strategy, give favorable public testimony, and use what resources they had to obtain favorable votes. Foremost among Blatnik's supporters were conservationist groups, including the Wildlife Management Institute, the National Wildlife Federation, the Izaak Walton League, and the Sport Fishing Institute; other related organizations such as the National Parks Association, the Wilderness Society, and the National Audubon Society; and two general organizations, the National Resource Council of America, a clearinghouse for most conservation bodies, and the Citizens Committee on Natural Resources, the only registered lobbying group among the conservation organizations. (To protect their public image and to avoid threatening their tax-exempt status, most of the conservationist groups have not registered as lobbies.)

From the 1955–56 period onward the conservationists channeled most of their efforts through Blatnik and the House rather than through Kerr and the Senate. Blatnik was more receptive, shared many of their conservationist perspectives, and saw them as a source of legislative support. Furthermore the conservationists had substantive disagreements with Kerr, and some had a personal aversion to him. Their better rapport with Blatnik helped determine their legislative tactics.

Other interest groups on which Blatnik could probably depend were the American Municipal Association and various municipal leagues throughout the country. The Municipal Association often prompted mayors of cities and towns to become interested in legislation. Its Washington staff felt that the pollution legislation, especially the construction grants section, was primarily a small-town program, and therefore felt more obliged to support the Blatnik proposal than did the United States Conference of Mayors, a predominantly big-city organization. The association had progressed in its views on water pollution control legislation from a rather weak posture to a strong commitment by 1960.

As of 1959 Blatnik could also count on the active support of the American Federation of Labor-Congress of Industrial Organizations (AFL-CIO). Prior to this time the union organization had always gone on record in favor of the Blatnik legislation, but had not vigorously pursued the cause. In the 1959–61 period the organization became more intimately involved, and by 1961 John Curran, a Washington legislative representative for the AFL-CIO, had become one of Blatnik's confidants.

Other interest groups had large stakes in pollution control legislation. The various associations of state health officers, sanitary engineers, and water resource agencies were active participants in the evolution of the legislation. They were not always allies, but by 1959 the great majority had come to support the construction grants, program grants, expanded research facilities, and other features. In fact, the nine-member Water Pollution Control Advisory Board—appointed by the President and including some leading state personnel—went on record in December 1958 as opposing the tax rebate scheme. Chairman Milton Adams was reminded by the press that the President supported the idea. "He's been ill-advised," Adams replied. In contrast to the conservationist groups, however, Blatnik usually had to persuade and cajole the organizations of state officials. They tended to be especially reticent on the matter of strengthened federal enforcement and they were jealous of the prerogatives of the states. Even though they often disagreed with him, Blatnik drew heavily on the counsel of three state officers: Milton Adams; David Lee, state sanitary engineer of the Florida State Board of Health; and Vivian Whitfield, chairman of the North Carolina State Stream Sanitation Committee.

Within the executive branch Blatnik could not count on open support for any far-reaching changes he might have in mind for the 1959 legislation. The Eisenhower administration, though interested in combatting pollution, clearly opposed the principle of the construction grants and would probably frown upon extensive broadening of the federal government's power in abating pollution. On the other hand, officials of HEW and the PHS were not intractable; many held views closer to Blatnik's position than to those of the White House and the Bureau of the Budget. It seemed likely they would not fight vigorously against any but the most extreme proposals. And at the operational level in the PHS Bureau of State Services, home of the water pollution control program, he could expect tacit support and collaboration.

Blatnik's office enjoyed good relations with the chief of the Water Supply and Water Pollution Division, Gordon McCallum. But the primary working relationship was with Murray Stein, head of the division's enforcement activities, and by 1961 the assistant chief. He was the idea man for Blatnik's legislative proposals. A lawyer by training, Stein had been associated with the water pollution program since the 1948 legislation. His special concern was enforcement and abatement activities. Blatnik, calling him the "blocking fullback" for the program, singled him out for praise at the 1961 committee hearings: ". . . perhaps no one single individual has done more, first to consult and confer with the different groups involved having a deep interest in this legislation, and, secondly, in handling delicate Federal-State relationships in the fields of enforcement, interstate compacts, and State legislation and administration."

Frequently opposing Blatnik—though by no means opposed to federal legislation per se—were the Republicans on the committee and in the House as a whole. By 1959 William C. Cramer of Florida had emerged as the primary antagonist in the committee and on the floor. While not antipathetic to a certain amount of federal activity in water pollution control, Cramer was nevertheless a consistent opponent of Blatnik's more far-reaching proposals. As noted previously, Blatnik relied little on Republicans of the Public Works Committee. Cramer later contended the committee could have written better legislation if Blatnik had been more cooperative. "Blatnik has always held me at arm's length," complained Cramer, "and the Democrats have never allowed us to have enough staff aid to do some of our own work."

Outside Congress the primary opposition came from certain business and industrial organizations and private firms. The National Association of Manufacturers and the American Paper and Pulp Association could be counted on to testify at public hearings against strong legislation. They consistently favored Senator Kerr's less expansive proposals if they had to make a choice between House and Senate versions. The United

States Chamber of Commerce was not a proponent of strong legislation, but made only modest efforts to oppose it.

Certainly the official position of the Eisenhower administration would be a key factor in any legislative struggle, determining the unity of the Republican opposition in the House. In addition there was the possibility of a presidential veto if Congress passed too strong a bill. Estimating how strong a bill the President might accept was the key decision to be made.

*The 1959 Proposals.* Blatnik and his supporters were heartened by the heavy Democratic gains in the 1958 congressional elections. Proponents of expanded pollution control legislation seemed to hold an advantageous position. It was now possible to assess the operation of the Water Pollution Control Act of 1956 over a period of two full years. Grants-in-aid for construction of sewage treatment plants had become the single most visible part of the program, and had attracted many proponents as well as antagonists. A strong case could be made that the grants had exerted a profound effect on pollution control efforts. During the two years, sewage construction works had nearly doubled. While the average for construction in the five-year period preceding the legislation was $222 million annually, every subsequent year had shown a marked increase: by 1958 an estimated $400 million in contracts were awarded. Thirty-five states had achieved their highest all-time levels of construction. One-third of the projects constructed in 1958 had received federal grants.

Nevertheless, Blatnik argued—with considerable statistical support from the PHS and the Conference of State Sanitary Engineers—that needs were still outstripping the aid provided by the program. In his new bill (H.R. 3610), drafted largely by his aide, Jerry Sonosky, he proposed a series of amendments designed to meet these needs. The major changes were those contained in H.R. 11714 of the previous Congress: an increase in federal grants for plant construction to $100 million annually, an increase in the limit on individual grants to $500,000, permission for municipalities to join in building treatment works without losing grant funds, and authorization for the reallocation of unused funds.

The bill also proposed an administrative reorganization that had not been included in the 1958 bill. It called for the establishment within HEW of an Office of Water Pollution Control directly responsible to the secretary and headed by a commissioner with a deputy commissioner and two assistant commissioners. Organizationally the program was then the province of the Water Supply and Pollution Control Division of the Bureau of State Services within the Public Health Service of the department—a hierarchical position that hardly reflected the magnitude of its responsibilities and the level of its expenditures.

In 1959 Blatnik and his allies were serious in attempting to produce new, progressive legislation. At the same time they were doubtful whether a bill with these innovations could escape a presidential veto. In all likelihood a veto could not be overridden. Nevertheless they were willing to take this risk.

There were two chief incentives for pressing vigorously. By forcing the administration's hand the legislation would be firmly imprinted with a Democratic stamp. Although Democrats had provided legislative leadership for the water pollution program since 1956, in hearings and floor debates the Republicans often took credit for its initiation. A presidential veto would clearly cast the Republicans as villains and the Democrats as heroes in the cause, and would establish an appealing campaign issue for 1960.

A second incentive was that a prospective veto would bring considerable publicity to the program. Proponents believed that grass roots support was vital to expanded legislation and especially to action on state and local levels. Blatnik was gratified when the League of Women Voters adopted water pollution control as a subject of national study by its membership. The mass media often gave attention to the subject, too. But Blatnik wanted still more publicity. He and his colleagues felt that they were laying the groundwork for later action—presumably in 1961 with a Democratic President to accompany a Democratic Congress.

Administration officials, not surprisingly, opposed the bill's innovations. HEW Secretary Arthur S. Flemming made a personal appearance at the spring hearings. He took the position that the federal government should pursue the enforcement provisions of the existing act with vigor, and should engage in the research and other support activities embodied in the program. He contended, however, that the grants program should be gradually eliminated. He also pleaded against an Office of Water Pollution Control. Blatnik commented: "Never in my years of experience on this committee have I heard a witness so clearly and effectively stating the case in which I believe, and which I have tried to set forth with far less persuasiveness, and then have the rug completely pulled out from under us on the last page of your statement. I must say it is most effectively done."

The Budget Bureau and the White House continued to support the rebate on the federal telephone tax. As in 1958, the absence of any guarantee that the rebates would be used for pollution control activities, and the unlikelihood that the Democratic Congress would adopt the proposal, made this alternative unrealistic.

The bill reported from the committee April 23 endorsed what Blatnik proposed, with one major exception: the reorganization proposals were deleted. HEW had elevated the program to divisional status earlier in the month, thus weakening the case for change. Except for strong support from the conservationists, the proposal had not drawn much favorable comment. The state organizations of health officers, sanitary engineers, and water control agencies, virtually all of which now favored the financial aspects of the bill, were either neutral or mildly negative toward the administrative changes. They feared that their access at the federal level would be altered or hampered in any reorganization. They also feared possible sanctions. The PHS had friends, allies, and other political resources both in the field and in Washington. To espouse a reorganization that would strip it of one of its programs was perhaps to risk retaliation or deprivation in other program areas. In view of this lack of support, the amendment was withdrawn in committee. Instead of prescribing reorganization, the bill instructed the secretary of HEW to submit to Congress plans for administrative changes for the program.

Eleven Republican members of the full House Public Works Committee issued a minority report objecting to the grants provisions and stating their intention to seek an amendment requiring states to match federal grants dollar for dollar beginning in fiscal 1963. In floor debate on June 4 they moved the amendment, which was defeated 130 to 60. On June 9 they moved that the bill be recommitted with instructions to amend it to require the matching provision. The motion lost 240 to 156, with Democrats voting 227 to 29 against and Republicans 127 to 13 in favor. On final passage the vote was 255 to 143, with Democrats favoring passage (228 to 28) and Republicans opposing it (115 to 27).

Action now shifted to the Senate where Senator Kerr presided over the fate of H.R. 3610. Hubert Humphrey and Eugene McCarthy had introduced S. 805 as the companion measure. Kerr was not pushing a bill of his own. Brief hearings were held on the two bills on July 23. They covered little new ground, but revealed Kerr's commitment to the matching grants idea, which he had been unenthusiastic about in 1956. As he told a Budget Bureau official: "As far as I am concerned, the words commending this program and sharing in the approval of the approach, and then limiting that approval to encouraging the States to go forward with it and pay for it doesn't make any sense to me, and I don't think it does to you." Kerr's changed attitude was partly a function of anger at the administration's continuing attacks on the program. He also believed (correctly) that HEW officials supporting the administration's position did not personally agree with it. His comments to Assistant Secretary Richardson are revealing:

> Well, Mr. Richardson, I want to tell you publicly that I have great respect for you. I have observed you before committees on which I have served for many years and you have always been forthright, able and sincere in your presentation. I don't want to ask you any questions, but I just want to say publicly that I sincerely sympathize with you when I find you in the posture of going through a pantomime such as that in which you are now compelled to be a public actor.

The Senate Public Works Committee produced an amended H.R. 3610 that differed little from the House version. The major changes reduced the $100 million annual grants total to $80 million; limited the total federal share for any one project to $400,000 instead of $500,000; deleted provisions for application of the Davis-Bacon Act (which guaranteed prevailing wage rates on federally aided projects); and removed the instructions to the secretary of HEW to submit to Congress a written report on plans for administrative changes for the program. Again the Senate committee proved less adventurous than its House counterpart.

On September 9 the Senate held one of its few roll call votes on water pollution control legislation, apparently because the President's strong position encouraged Senate Republicans to press for it. The measure passed easily—61 to 27— with the Democrats voting 48 to 8 in favor, and the Republicans 19 to 13 in opposition.

Congress was nearing adjournment. Allowing time for a conference, House and Senate supporters of the legislation calculated that it might not reach Eisenhower in time to prevent a pocket veto. Therefore, they decided to delay action until Congress reconvened in 1960.

When the conference committee convened in February the result was, as customary, an exercise in compromise. Inasmuch as the House wanted $100 million annually and the Senate $80 million, the natural final figure was $90 million. Similarly, since the House had voted for a

$500,000 maximum on any single project and the Senate $400,000, the compromise was $450,000. The Davis-Bacon application was restored, and the provision for an organizational plan from the secretary of HEW was dropped. Voice votes passed the conference report in the House on February 9 and in the Senate on February 15, and the bill went to the President.

*The Eisenhower Veto.* As expected, the President vetoed the bill on the basis of his conviction that the government's role in domestic affairs should be limited. The action was also consistent with the view held by Eisenhower and his White House aides that the budget should be kept down in the months before the coming national election.

The veto message was drafted in Secretary Flemming's office. What made the situation ironic was that Flemming himself and many HEW and PHS personnel, especially those in the Water Supply and Pollution Control Division, favored an expanded program. They wanted H.R. 3610 or something akin to it to be enacted. But, as one participant put it, "They couldn't get through to Ike." The message was signed on February 22 and delivered to the House the following day. It declared:

> Because water pollution is a uniquely local blight, primary responsibility for solving the problem lies not with the Federal Government but rather must be assumed and exercised, as it has been, by State and local governments. This being so, the defects of H.R. 3610 are apparent. By holding forth the promise of a large-scale program of long-term Federal support, it would tempt municipalities to delay essential water pollution abatement efforts while they waited for Federal funds.

The message went on to contend that "The Federal Government can help, but it should stimulate State and local action rather than provide excuses for inaction, which an expanded program under H.R. 3610 would do." The President indicated four appropriate steps. Three involved provisions already contained in the Control Act of 1956: modest federal support for the state administration of control programs, research and technical assistance, and enforcement action on interstate waters (here the administration proposed to strengthen the government's hand). The fourth step called for a national conference on water pollution to be held in December. The conference was to ". . . provide a forum in which all concerned can confront and better appreciate their mutual responsibility for solving this pressing problem."

On February 25 the House attempted to override this veto, the first of the 1960 session. Since this was a contest between parties, the Democratic leadership took responsibility for the attempt although Blatnik, as floor manager of the bill, was actively involved. There was feverish activity on both sides of the aisle. Republican leaders corralled possible dissidents with the argument that they "couldn't let the President down on this one." By the same token the Democratic leadership urged their members to show solidarity; it would be a real feather in their collective caps if Eisenhower's first veto of the session could be upset. Conservative leader Howard W. Smith of Virginia claimed he had thirty Democrats, primarily southerners, who would depart from the party stand. Democratic strategists estimated fifteen Republican defections to their side. Most observers expected a close vote; the result was a narrow victory for the President. With 406 members casting their votes, the tally was 249 in favor of overriding to 157 against. With this total voting, it would have taken 271 votes to provide the necessary two-thirds majority. The party division was sharp: 234 Democrats voted to override and 27 voted to sustain; the expected 15 Republicans voted to override while 130 voted to sustain.

The veto did not disrupt the program established by the 1956 law. Since H.R. 3610 was a series of amendments to this law, the original act still stood intact, including the grants provisions. In many respects Blatnik had accomplished what he set out to do when he introduced his bill in 1959. He had attracted considerable attention to his cause throughout the nation. His bill was now indelibly stamped as a Democratic measure, providing ammunition for the fall campaign. The fight had been a successful holding operation: although Eisenhower had submitted proposals in 1958 and 1959 designed to eliminate the pollution control grants, his 1960 budget proposal only called for their reduction to a level of $20 million. Clearly the proposal to end the grants would not be resurrected and it was also likely that the proposed reduction would fail. With these factors in mind Blatnik could conclude that the unsuccessful attempt to force the Eisenhower administration's hand had not actually been a defeat for proponents of an expanded program. There would be another day and more favorable circumstances; until then, the program would remain intact.

*The 1960 Presidential Campaign.* In the fall presidential campaign the Democratic team of John F. Kennedy and Lyndon B. Johnson charged that Eisenhower's veto of the pollution bill was a "national tragedy."

The Natural Resources Advisory Committee (headed by Congressman Frank Smith of Mississippi, a member of the Public Works Committee and consistent supporter of the antipollution legislation) publicized the veto while extolling Kennedy's position on water pollution control. Kennedy declared:

> The problem of water pollution is not a local problem. Our great natural rivers flow past hundreds of cities and towns, carrying with them the refuse and filth of all they touch. The need for clean, healthy water goes beyond political boundaries—it is a national need—and our nation's welfare and health are gravely affected by the stubborn insistence of the Republicans that pollution "is a uniquely local problem." We must step up the fight against water pollution. We must stimulate construction of needed sewage and waste treatment plants and prevent further spread of water pollution. Our goal must be abundant clean water for all Americans, with full utilization of every drop of water in every river system in the nation.

*The National Conference on Water Pollution.* The conference proposed in Eisenhower's veto message became the next focal point of the battle between the Republican administration and the Democratic Congress. Inspiration for the conference stemmed from a suggestion by Vivian Whitfield, chairman of the North Carolina State Stream Sanitation Committee, in testifying on H.R. 3610 in 1959.

As perceived by the White House, the strategic purpose of a national conference was to demonstrate that Republicans and the outgoing administration were committed to and vitally interested in controlling the nation's pollution. The conference would serve to mitigate somewhat the antagonisms aroused by the veto among many groups interested in pollution control. At the same time it might give a succeeding Republican administration a benchmark from which to proceed. Finally, bringing together various parties to pollution control efforts could yield salutary results in terms of pushing toward solutions.

After the election in November the conference became something of an embarrassment for the outgoing administration. Plans had been made for months, however, and the program was set; cancellation would make the administration appear to be poor losers; and there was no assurance that something of value might not emerge after all. For these reasons the conference had to be held, lame duck or not.

The conference, organized efficiently by the Public Health Service, was held in Washington from December 12 to 15. Major topics included the effect of pollution on the nation's health, welfare, and economy; the importance of water pollution control on the management of water resources; the responsibilities of government, industry, agriculture, and the public in combating pollution; and the need for research and professional training. Few surprises emerged: everybody was against pollution and the respective roles of localities, states, and the federal government did not become a burning issue.

Blatnik and his allies felt that the conference did not hurt their cause and possibly aided it. Certainly it focused further attention on the problem of pollution, although how much of this publicity reached people not already aware of the problem is a matter of conjecture. At least it generated a substantial amount of information that was disseminated by the mass media. The conference also put a number of people, including Congressman Cramer of Florida, on record as favoring stronger federal action. (Cramer's statements were to be thrown back at him when he battled against some of the provisions in the legislation advanced in 1961.) As a meeting organized in part to atone for a presidential veto of increased grants, the session produced much praise and little criticism of the grants program.

## The 1961 Legislation—Progress under a New Guard

In the first session of the Eighty-seventh Congress the context for water pollution control legislation was radically different from the previous eight years. Blatnik looked forward to working with the Kennedy administration, which was likely to favor a vigorous program of enforcement and aid. With a Congress still heavily Democratic (262 of 437 in the House and 65 of 100 in the Senate) some of his proposals now stood a good chance of being enacted. Nonetheless, he decided that the pollution control bill would have its best chance of success if it was not an administration proposal, but was initiated and pushed from Capitol Hill. The administration was still feeling its way, and it was by no means certain that the new regime would want as much as he wanted. After being partially checkmated by the Republicans for several years, Blatnik and his associates were in no mood to settle for anything less than some striking changes in P.L. 660. The administration was likely to be more cautious.

A number of other factors led Blatnik to favor going it alone. The Kennedy administration had assigned top priority to five legislative proposals, and water pollution control was, understandably, not among them. Blatnik also desired to keep his name on pollution control legislation. If the new bill became known as "the Blatnik bill" it would immediately be identified with his experience and past performance in this area. A final consideration confirmed his decision. Some administration personnel were considering including the water pollution control program in the proposed Urban Affairs Department. (As it turned out, the Urban Affairs Department did not emerge until four years later, but early in 1961 its prospects appeared bright.) Blatnik opposed this because he feared that other programs, such as housing, hospitals, and airports, would receive higher priority, and felt that pollution control was not strictly an urban problem. Interestingly enough, at one stage Blatnik was considered by the incoming administration as a possible secretary of the interior, and Sonosky had prepared a memo showing how all water activities, including pollution control, could be included in the Interior Department.

In his message on natural resources, submitted to Congress on February 23, President Kennedy indicated his approval of H.R. 4036, the new Blatnik bill. This endorsement did not make it an administration bill in the strict sense, however; H.R. 4036 had been in the making for nearly two years. Some of its provisions were carryovers from previous bills such as H.R. 3610 of 1959. Even as that doomed bill wound its way through the Eighty-sixth Congress to an eventual veto, the 1961 bill was being drafted. Again primary initiative for the legislation lay with Sonosky and Stein. By July 1960 a draft was circulated to many of the same people who had been involved in earlier bills, including Milton Adams. In the fall of 1960, Adams had solicited the views of members of the State and Interstate Water Pollution Control Administrators. These and other soundings, not all of which were favorable, helped to prepare the way for the introduction of bold legislation in 1961.

As originally submitted H.R. 4036 was an ambitious bill. It increased the annual authorization from $50 million to $125 million and total grants authorization from $0.5 billion to $1.25 billion; it increased maximum grants to 30 percent of project cost or $600,000, whichever was lower (the old figure was $250,000); it allowed municipalities to cooperate on projects with no penalty in grant allowances to the participants; it authorized reallocation of unused grants money. Although the figures for annual grants and total authorization were higher than previously advocated, these proposals caused little debate. Indeed the $125 million figure was purposely inflated because it was known that Senator Kerr in his S. 120 was proposing a $75 million figure. Blatnik was willing to settle for $100 million and considered the $125 million as a starting point for later bargaining.

*The Politics of Administrative Arrangements.* More controversial was the proposal to establish a Federal Water Pollution Control Administration as a separate independent operating agency within HEW—the provision deleted from the 1959 bill in committee. The conservationists, most of whom had been in Blatnik's camp since 1956, endorsed this proposal strongly. Blatnik himself felt the need for more autonomy and higher status for the program, but perhaps would not have pressed for this change without their pressure.

Many of the conservationists did not like the orientation of Public Health Service personnel on water pollution control. They felt that the PHS professionals tended to treat the subject primarily as the health matter of making water potable. By conservationist standards the "medical men," as they called the PHS personnel, treated the symptoms but not the source, and were not sufficiently interested in control and enforcement at the roots. In the process, the conservationists believed, the PHS overlooked the recreational, aesthetic, natural, and wildlife aspects of pollution problems.

Accountability for program decisions was also difficult to determine in the existing administrative structure. Some conservationists protested that except for the grants-in-aid money no one could tell how the PHS was spending the money appropriated for the program. Critics of the program's hierarchical location found another source of irritation in a proposed reorganization that would place it in a Bureau of Environmental Health. This was suggested in the final report of a study group on the mission and organization of the Public Health Service, released June 7, 1960. Conservationists, and others as well, were incensed by the study group's proposal, because it would emphasize even more the "health" approach taken by the PHS to the pollution problem. More significantly, it left the program at a division level within a bureau, thus making no upward adjustment in its status. Finally, and this was perhaps the most annoying factor, as a division in the Bureau of Environmental Health the water pollution control program would probably be carrying various other minor operating programs on its back. Other divisions proposed for the new bureau would have such titles as "office of toxicology intelligence," "division of occupational health," "division of environmental economics and organization," "division of air pollution," and about a half dozen others—all with programs significantly smaller than that of the existing Division of Water Supply and Pollution Control.

While strong support for reorganization existed, there was also vigorous opposition. The PHS was not likely to abandon a large-scale program, although some sentiment within the Water Supply and Pollution Control Division itself favored administrative alterations to elevate the status of its program. Those members of Congress, and in particular of the Public Works Committees, who were especially good friends and admirers of the PHS could be expected to defend the retention of the program in the "able" hands of the service. Various associations of state health officers, sanitary engineers, and legal officials had opposed the establishment of a separate commission in 1959, and they behaved similarly in 1961. As one of the key state people explained, "The 'medical' men might not be the best people to run the program, but they are at least a known quantity. The state people know what to expect from them; there are patterns of cooperation and work which have developed over the years. If the function were moved to another department or agency these patterns would be broken down." State officials also feared that a reorganization might be linked to tighter federal enforcement, especially in regard to pollution of intrastate waters. Those states that were derelict would not welcome being prodded by the federal government; those doing commendable jobs of enforcement might justifiably feel that federal intervention would hurt rather than help them.

Newly appointed HEW Secretary Abraham A. Ribicoff represented the most important source of opposition to a separate agency. After viewing the reorganization plans as embodied in H.R. 4036, Ribicoff told Blatnik that he would not like to be faced with a substantial change immediately. The projected reshuffling was certain to create a controversy and he was not eager for such a fight. Meanwhile, Senator Kerr and his staff let it be known that on the Senate side such a proposal would not be viewed favorably. Since Blatnik would probably have to bargain on some other points, it seemed inadvisable to press forward on this front.

After consulting with the proponents for change, particularly the conservationists, Blatnik agreed to Ribicoff's entreaty upon two conditions: first that Ribicoff explain his position in the formal hearings; and second that Ribicoff publicly declare his intention to initiate a departmental survey to consider possible administrative changes. Ribicoff met these provisos in his statement before the committee on March 29.

In this fashion, then, the decision was made to delete the proposals for administrative change. Blatnik retreated because of Ribicoff's intervention and because he did not want to jeopardize any of the other innovations he sought for the program. The conservationists expressed disappointment but they took solace in a subsequent development.

After it became clear that drastic alteration was out of the picture, a modified organizational change was proposed by the Water Supply and Control Division. Under the existing law the surgeon general was charged with administering the program. The division proposed that the secretary of HEW be charged with overall responsibility for the act. This would give central direction to the program and make it possible to circumvent the surgeon general's office when and if necessary.

At first Blatnik rejected this suggestion, partly because he could see no legitimate rationale. Then the idea came back from the division with an honorable justification, namely, recommendation fourteen from the first report of the Hoover Commission on Organization of the Executive Branch of the Government. The commission injunction read: "Under the President, the heads of departments must hold full responsibility for the conduct of their departments. There must be a clear line of authority reaching down through every step of the organization and no subordinate should have authority independent from that of his superior." Blatnik, now satisfied that he had legitimized the suggestion, incorporated the proposal into the clean bill reported out of committee (H.R. 6441). In a sense the committee had tossed the organizational problem back to Ribicoff, but it gave him such ambiguous instruction that he could avoid an immediate reorganizational crisis.

*Expanding Federal Enforcement.* H.R. 6441 also contained significant innovation in the field of enforcement. Under the existing act federal enforcement operations applied only to interstate waters, defined in the 1956 legislation as "all rivers, lakes, and other waters that flow across, or form a part of, boundaries between two or more states." Of the 26,000 bodies of water in the United States, only an estimated 4,000 were interstate. Those beyond the reach of the 1956 statute included, for example, the greater part of the Great Lakes and their tributaries, many coastal streams, international boundaries such as the St. Lawrence, Niagara, lower Colorado, and Rio Grande, all bodies of water in Florida, Alaska,

Hawaii, the Virgin Islands, and Puerto Rico, the greater part of the Hudson River and important reaches of the Tennessee, Columbia, Colorado, and Merrimack Rivers. Furthermore, federal enforcement was legitimate only in cases involving pollution of interstate waters that "endangers the health or welfare of persons in a state other than that in which the discharge originates."

To correct these presumed deficiencies Blatnik's original draft (H.R. 4036) set out a bold extension of the federal domain: "The pollution of *navigable* [emphasis added] waters in or adjacent to any State or States which endangers the  health or welfare of any persons, shall be subject to abatement as provided in this Act." Here was a clear directive for the federal government to move from purely interstate pollution to intrastate as well. Federal jurisdiction in intrastate cases was to be exercised only upon request from a state or from a municipality with the concurrence of the governor or the state water pollution control agency. Nevertheless, it was inevitable that strong reactions would be forthcoming.

Another major change had to do with the toughness of enforcement proceedings. P.L. 660 gave the secretary of HEW authority to call a conference of offending and affected parties in cases where pollution was charged, and to issue an abatement notice if he felt it justified. He could then initiate court action if necessary, but only with the consent of the offending state. H.R. 4036 allowed him to issue an *order* directing the abatement, subject to challenge in a U.S. Court of Appeals. Such orders would be enforced by U.S. District Courts in actions brought by the attorney general at the request of the secretary.

Finally, an enforcement construction grants fund of $25 million was proposed to help financially pressed communities that had been required as a result of federal enforcement proceedings to construct treatment facilities. In some respects this fund was a "sweetener" to offset reaction against the further extension of federal authority.

The far-reaching changes excited considerable interest and debate. The conservationists and the American Municipal Association favored them, and the AFL-CIO provided active support. The state associations of health officers, sanitary engineers, and their legal aides were inclined to oppose the changes, or at least not to endorse them vigorously.

On the issue of administrative reorganization Secretary Ribicoff's plea that it be cut from the bill had been decisive for Blatnik. In the case of extending enforcement powers to all navigable waters the secretary proved cooperative. The recent appointment of Jerry Sonosky to HEW's legislative liaison section undoubtedly served to strengthen the voices within the department speaking for broader enforcement powers, since part of his assignment was water pollution control legislation. His presence in HEW proved to be an asset for Blatnik as developments unfolded, particularly in working out a compromise with the Senate bill.

In addition to supporting the navigable waters definition of the scope of federal authority, HEW and the PHS supported the provision authorizing the secretary to issue orders rather than requests for abatement. They opposed the $25 million fund for enforcement construction grants.

The bill reported out of committee (H.R. 6441) contained both major provisions of the enforcement section. The enforcement construction grant provision was deleted by the committee after advice from many quarters that it would encourage municipalities to delay undertaking construction projects until federal enforcement proceedings were initiated. Blatnik never considered this a priority item anyway.

The committee report on H.R. 6441, filed April 25, 1961, contained a strong minority report by ten Republicans. They recommended an annual authorization of $75 million for construction grants, with a requirement that funds exceeding $50 million be matched by the states; they also rejected extension of federal enforcement powers. There was little doubt that there would be a floor fight when the House took up H.R. 6441 for debate. There was also little doubt that the Republicans would be defeated.

On the floor Cramer first moved to amend the bill to reduce the authorizations to $75 million, place an overall limit of $750 million on the program after June 30, 1964, and require the states to match all grants over $50 million. This was defeated on a standing vote, 138 to 69. Subsequently Cramer incorporated the same provisions in a recommittal motion, which was defeated by a roll call vote of 256 to 165 (Democrats 232 to 21 against, Republicans 144 to 24 for recommittal). He then moved to strike out the extension of federal power to all navigable waters, and this was rejected by a standing vote of 151 to 70. Final passage came on a vote of 308 to 110 (Democrats 229 to 22 in favor and Republicans 88 to 79 against).

While Blatnik's objectives had for the most part been achieved in the House, problems were developing in the Senate. Senator Kerr's S. 120, reported out June 7, differed in three major respects from H.R. 6441: it contained no administrative changes, it provided for no further federal enforcement powers, and it authorized federal agencies constructing reservoirs to include facilities for stream flow augmentation and other water quality control features. There were other less serious discrepancies. S.

120 was a bit more frugal on the construction grants and provided for a sliding scale; but it also contained more elaborate demonstration and research provisions.

The low flow augmentation provision in S. 120 was a creation of Senator Kerr to permit the inclusion of reservoirs of water that would be used in improving seasonal low flow conditions. Adding good water to low flow streams and rivers is one way of reducing pollution. Although there was a difference of expert opinion on its effectiveness, there was general agreement that the idea was basically a good one and should be part of the 1961 legislation. Kerr had previously tried to put a similar provision in the Omnibus Rivers and Harbors Bill, without success. Blatnik's staff had discussed the proposal with the Division of Water Supply and Pollution Control and received a generally favorable reaction, but he and his aides felt that it would be wise to leave it out of H.R. 6441 because this would give them something to bargain with at the conference table. As it turned out, their expectations proved sound.

The main difference between S. 120 and the bill passed by the House lay in the enforcement section. Whereas S. 120 offered nothing new in this respect, Blatnik's measure contained the navigable waters concept and more authority for the HEW secretary. Since 1955–56 Senator Kerr had become a staunch defender of the Water Pollution Control Act, but it was doubtful that he would encourage extending federal power to intrastate waters. Moreover this extension of federal enforcement power represented a fundamental change, and if the Kerr bill were reported out without it, the chances of obtaining it in the conference committee would be slim. Therefore Blatnik and his strategists decided to attempt to get it incorporated into the Senate bill before the Senate Public Works Committee reported the bill out.

Senator Frank E. Moss, Democrat from Utah, was chosen to introduce the amendment. Senior enough not to be afraid of Kerr, Moss was a westerner, a liberal, and a fighter. In addition he had cosponsored S. 861, companion bill to Blatnik's original H.R. 4036. Thus if he pressed in committee for the navigable streams concept it would appear that he merely wanted something put in that he had been backing all along. Moss was agreeable to the strategy, and the amendment was adopted in committee by a close vote. The language of the amendment differed slightly from the Blatnik bill, specifying interstate and navigable waters rather than just navigable, but this was a question of semantics and did not affect the substantive implications.

S. 120 had no trouble on the Senate floor. With one minor amendment the language of S. 120 replaced that of H.R. 6441 and passed by voice vote on June 22.

In the conference committee sessions that followed, the conferees accepted the Senate's idea of a sliding scale on grants-in-aid but provided for reaching the $100 million level earlier (1964) than the Senate version (1966). The Senate bill repealed the restriction that at least 50 percent of the funds appropriated go to cities of 125,000 or less; the House conferees insisted on retaining this provision. The House conferees acceded to the section calling for a total of $25 million for the development of new methods of sewage treatment, but rejected the proposed $10 million for field demonstration facilities. On the subject of enforcement the Senate version of "interstate or navigable" rather than merely "navigable" waters was agreed upon. The Senate conferees rejected the House provision giving the secretary of HEW the power to issue orders for abatement. The conference substitute provided that if pollution is not abated within the specified time in the *notice* following the public hearing, the secretary may ask the attorney general to bring suit to secure abatement in cases of interstate pollution. In the case of intrastate pollution he may ask for such a suit only with the written consent of the state involved. The low flow augmentation provisions of the Senate bill were adopted, as was the House language making the secretary rather than the surgeon general directly responsible for the program.

On the face of it Blatnik appeared to secure most of what he wanted. It was true that he agreed to the low flow augmentation provision and the new methods of treatment section, but these were certainly not provisions to which he was opposed. On the key section regarding enforcement he had scored a major victory and on reorganization he had at least placed "the camel's nose under the tent." The conference report of July 6 was adopted by the House on July 13 and by the Senate on July 14, both by voice votes. President Kennedy signed the bill on July 20, culminating a long effort by advocates of federal action.

## Analysis of the Legislative Events, 1956–61

*The Predominant Effect of Party.* Analysis of the House roll call votes that occurred in the 1956–61 period indicates three features: (1) the degree to which votes were predicated on an urban interest; (2) the differ-

Table 1: *Percentage of Votes in Support of Water Pollution Control on Related Roll Calls in the House of Representatives, by Type of District*[a]

| Roll calls | Rural | Suburban | Urban |
|---|---|---|---|
| 1959 recommittal | 58 | 59 | 66 |
| 1959 final passage | 61 | 70 | 67 |
| 1960 veto override | 58 | 56 | 70 |
| 1961 recommittal | 56 | 58 | 72 |
| 1962 final passage | 70 | 76 | 80 |

[a] All percentages reflect the pro votes on water pollution control regardless of the specific direction of the original vote. Thus on the 1959 recommittal vote a nay vote was actually a vote in support of the measure, so in this table the percentage of nay votes has been listed because that shows the support for the bill. The specific numbers upon which the percentages are based vary from vote to vote. The distribution of districts by the threefold categorization used here is 57 percent rural, 14 percent suburban, and 29 percent urban. This is the classification scheme developed in the *Congressional Quarterly Weekly Report*, week ending February 2, 1962, pp. 153–56. Experimentation with other indexes of urbanism did not produce marked differences from those found in Tables 1–3.

ences between the voting records of Republicans and Democrats; and (3) the characteristics of those congressmen who deviated from the voting patterns of their colleagues of the same party.

If the water pollution control measure was one to which urban congressmen and their constituents were particularly sensitive, then it would follow that urban representatives might show a more favorable voting record than nonurban congressmen. As Table 1 demonstrates, however, classification of the distribution of votes according to rural, suburban, or urban character of the district represented shows meager support for this hypothesis. Only on the 1960 veto vote and the 1961 recommittal vote is there more than a 10 percent difference between the pro water pollution

Table 2: *Percentage of Votes in Support of Water Pollution Control on Related Roll Calls in the House of Representatives, by Party of Representative*[a]

| Roll calls | Democrats | Republicans |
|---|---|---|
| 1956 recommittal | 88 | 21 |
| 1956 final passage | 97 | 85 |
| 1957 appropriation deletion | 84 | 23 |
| 1959 recommittal | 89 | 9 |
| 1959 final passage | 89 | 19 |
| 1960 veto override | 90 | 10 |
| 1961 recommittal | 92 | 14 |
| 1961 final passage | 91 | 47 |

[a] All percentages reflect the pro votes on water pollution control regardless of the specific direction of the original vote.

control votes of the urban members and of the suburban and rural members. Even those differences are so slight as to be of questionable practical significance.

Obviously this analysis neglects many aspects of the congressmen's situation that might override any rural or urban constituency differences. The prime factor, of course, is the member's party. Table 2 illustrates that Democrats consistently tended to support the pollution control legislation and Republicans tended to oppose it, with two exceptions. In the final passage vote of 1956 a majority of Republicans voted affirmatively, and in the final passage vote of 1961 nearly half of them voted for the bill. Such behavior is not uncommon; the revealing vote, the best indicator of individual and party preferences, comes on the motion to recom-

Table 3: *Percentage of Votes in Support of Water Pollution Control on Related Roll Calls in the House of Representatives, by Party and Type of District*

| Roll calls | Democrats | | | Republicans | | |
|---|---|---|---|---|---|---|
| | Rural | Suburban | Urban | Rural | Suburban | Urban |
| 1959 recommittal | 85 | 100 | 93 | 9 | 21 | 0 |
| 1959 final passage | 86 | 100 | 91 | 16 | 43 | 6 |
| 1960 veto override | 85 | 93 | 96 | 11 | 15 | 6 |
| 1961 recommittal | 87 | 100 | 97 | 16 | 17 | 6 |
| 1961 final passage | 86 | 100 | 97 | 50 | 53 | 33 |

mit. The 1959 final passage vote did not fit the 1956 and 1961 final vote pattern because of the special situation that then existed: the issue had become decidedly partisan, the administration had gone out of its way to label the grants provisions of the program as objectionable, and there was a strong probability that Eisenhower would veto the legislation; thus Republican congressmen did not feel the same sense of freedom they felt in 1956 when a majority of them voted for final approval.

There is little question, then, that partisanship directly or indirectly was decisive in establishing the configuration of voting in the House, in contrast to the rather undifferentiated pattern by type of district.

Nevertheless, it might be that within each party the congressmen from the more urbanized districts showed more support than their nonurban colleagues. This possibility is examined in Table 3, where Democrats and Republicans are each grouped according to the nature of their constituencies. While support generally ran high among the Democrats, it is apparent that those from rural constituencies were less enthusiastic than those from urban and suburban districts. On the other hand, the least support among Republicans came from those with the most urbanized constituencies, and those from suburban districts were slightly more favorable than their rural colleagues. Unquestionably, party was more important than the nature of the district. The legislative majority pushing liberal pollution control legislation through the House was primarily a partisan one.

The identity of those who defected from the party line is important, especially since some of the votes were close. Among the Democrats, de-

Table 4: *Defection by Democratic Congressmen on Water Pollution Control Roll Call Votes*

| Roll calls | Total number of defectors | Number who were southerners |
|---|---|---|
| 1956 recommittal | 25 | 23 |
| 1956 final passage | 5 | 5 |
| 1957 appropriation deletion | 35 | 32 |
| 1959 recommittal | 29 | 26 |
| 1959 final passage | 28 | 24 |
| 1960 veto override | 27 | 26 |
| 1961 recommittal | 21 | 20 |
| 1961 final passage | 22 | 21 |

fections occurred proportionally more often among rural-based congressmen. Table 4 shows that they were a particular type of rural congressman: southerners.

The majority of the southern defectors were from predominantly rural and small-town districts, although there was a sprinkling of big-city southerners among their ranks. Democratic opposition to the water pollution control legislation was concentrated in states and localities where, in most cases, the financial needs were among the greatest in the country. Considering the disproportionately low contribution of these states to the national revenue and the federal aid they were to receive from the legislation, the southerners were voting against a financially rewarding proposition. Clearly ideology and/or perceptions of constituency preferences were influencing them.

Democrats in opposition to the legislation proved to be consistently opposed. Thus among the twenty-one Democratic deviants on the 1961 recommittal vote seventeen had also voted in opposition in 1957 and sixteen were opposed on one of the 1959 votes.

While Republicans in general voted against the legislation as submitted to the House, there were always a few who broke ranks. The number ranged from a high of forty-five on the 1957 appropriation deletion vote to lows of thirteen and fifteen respectively on the 1959 recommittal motion and the 1960 attempt to override President Eisenhower's veto. The pattern among Republican deviants is much less clear than that prevailing among Democrats. Nonconformers came from both urban and rural constituencies and from all sections of the country. Both in absolute numbers and proportionally, however, they were found most often in the

Table 5: *Defection by Republican Congressmen on Water Pollution Control Roll Call Votes*

| Roll calls | Total number of defectors | Number who were from Pennsylvania |
|---|---|---|
| 1956 recommittal | 37 | 8 |
| 1957 appropriation deletion | 45 | 11 |
| 1959 recommittal | 13 | 5 |
| 1959 final passage | 27 | 6 |
| 1960 veto override | 15 | 5 |
| 1961 recommittal | 24 | 9 |

middle Atlantic and northeastern states. Members of the Pennsylvania delegation were particularly likely to break with their party, as Table 5 shows.

Pennsylvanians are particularly sensitive to water pollution problems. Natural resources form a vital part of the state's economic base, but mining and other industries using these resources have contributed to the pollution of the state's streams. Some members of the delegation apparently perceived the water pollution control legislation as a way of combating a difficult problem in an economically productive fashion.

Like the Democrats, the Republican deviants were rather consistent in their behavior. Out of the twenty-seven who defected to vote for final passage in 1959, seventeen also deviated on the 1957 appropriation deletion vote, thirteen on the 1956 recommittal motion, and eleven on the 1960 attempt to override Eisenhower's veto. Just as Blatnik could anticipate a core of Democratic defections, he could also count on some Republican support. The support varied, of course, with the political context: it was considerably greater in 1956 and 1957 than in 1959 and 1960 when the administration laid its prestige on the line.

*The Minor Impact of Urban Interests.* The pollution of water has ramifications for both urban and nonurban areas; but the urban dimensions of pollution and pollution control have received special attention partly because the disposal and treatment of sewage and the purification of polluted waters are traditionally conceived as the responsibility of urban governments. Also, most of the polluting industries are in urban areas.

In the sense that virtually all pollution control has some impact on urban localities and their inhabitants, the legislative process described here may be viewed as having served the needs and interests of urban areas. By 1962 the urban areas had more resources for fighting pollution than existed in 1955 largely because congressional leadership, abetted by the bureaucracy and the interest groups, had forged weapons designed to benefit municipalities. Nevertheless it remains true that several constraints worked against an all-out focus on urban areas and their needs.

One such constraint may be adduced from the fact that the *most* highly urbanized areas—the large metropolitan areas—received disproportionately small shares of the construction grants, even though their needs loomed exceedingly large in dollar amounts. To establish the grants program it was essential to attract the support of congressmen and state officials representing the smaller to medium size municipalities, and therefore the program was shaped to give relatively more aid to the smaller urban locales. Another constraint was dictated by federalism and state police powers. Satisfying the interests and sometimes jealously held privileges of state officials produced legislation that placed nonfederal responsibility and initiative in the state house rather than in the courthouse or city hall where there was likely to be more zeal. A third constraint lay in the web of relationships between the Public Health Service and its allies in Washington and particularly in the states. These established ties did little to advance the special needs and desires of urban governments. Finally, even though industrial interests apparently had little direct effect on the legislation, the desire to foster industrial development and to refrain from punitive action undoubtedly restrained the Congress from permitting even more direct federal intervention to abate industrial pollution in urban areas.

The legislative history of the pollution control bills makes it hard to contend that urban interests were particularly instrumental in enacting the legislation. Neither were nonurban interests particularly significant in attempting to block or modify the legislation. To a great extent the water pollution control program as it stands today was congressionally inspired and constructed. The principal architect came from an essentially nonurban congressional district, and his motives were not so much directed toward helping urban areas as toward conserving a natural resource for the benefit of all sorts of people and interests. The second most active figure in the development of the legislation, Senator Kerr, came from a state with a small proportion of its population living in urban areas. He, too, was more concerned with natural resources than with helping urban areas.

The most influential interest groups were the state officials and the conservationists. In terms of helping to shape the bills, supplying information and group support, and exerting constituency pressure on Congress, these groups and their spokesmen helped make legislation possible. But they could hardly be called urban interest groups, though they believed that their objectives would benefit both urban and nonurban dwellers. What the naturalists and conservationists wanted to protect were often areas quite removed from the metropolis, although important to urban dwellers seeking recreation.

The American Municipal Association and the AFL-CIO, both of which came to play important roles only toward the end of the period, were more representative of the urban localities. But in the case of the Municipal Association at least, its activities in support of broader pollution control legislation were probably no more effective than those of individual municipal officials.

The help that came from the Eisenhower administration was not the result of any great desire to aid the municipalities, and urbanism was hardly the leitmotif of the Kennedy administration, although Kennedy was more inclined to place the welfare of the urban areas at the top of the agenda as far as water pollution control was concerned. During both administrations the Public Health Service was more concerned with maximizing good working relationships with the states than with focusing on urban localities as such. In the final analysis, one must conclude that urbanism per se was not an issue in this series of legislative events. Urban interests both aided and hurt the legislative program, and the same could be said of nonurban interests.

It must be concluded, too, that the chain of events from 1956 to 1961 was extraordinarily influenced by the actions of one man—Congressman John Blatnik. While some water pollution control legislation would probably have passed without his exertions, it probably would have been more modest. Not only did he perform the major legislative roles of sponsorship, marshalling of support, negotiating and bargaining with others, and planning of overall strategy, he also played an innovative and initiatory role.

## Epilogue

The most significant water pollution control legislation since 1956 was enacted in the Water Quality Act of 1965. In addition to increasing the annual construction grants to $150 million, facilitating multicommunity and large construction programs, the act also incorporated two signal departures.

The first was the long-sought administrative reorganization. A federal Water Pollution Control Agency was established within the Department of Health, Education, and Welfare, and a new assistant secretary post created to supervise the agency. The line of command flowing directly to the secretary at last wrested control of the program from the PHS and its "medical men" in the "seventh sub-basement of HEW." The consequences of this reorganization and gain in status for the day-to-day operations of the program remain to be seen.

The second major innovation lay in the establishment of water quality standards. No clear standards of violation existed previously. Prevention of pollution is now the keynote, and violation of the quality standards constitutes grounds for abatement procedures. The states are required to establish standards and adopt a plan for their implementation and enforcement. If the plans are not satisfactory to HEW the secretary may authorize a collaborative federal-state procedure for the development of suitable criteria.

Blatnik's role in the 1965 proceedings had a somewhat different character from previous sessions. True to past behavior he pressed for and gained more funds for construction grants. He also ensured that *all* water pollution control activities would rest with the new agency. But Democratic Senator Edmund S. Muskie of Maine, with strong Johnson administration backing, seized the legislative initiative and rammed through a bill giving HEW stronger authority in setting water quality standards than the House version.

Thus for the first time the Senate provided for a stronger federal regulatory role than did the House. For this reason some of Blatnik's long-time supporters accused him of selling out to "the interests." Blatnik argued that HEW did not have the technical personnel and the knowledge required to develop and implement immediately the kind of program contained in the Senate bill. Furthermore, there was intense lobbying from states and industries on the issue, and he believed that a floor fight might jeopardize the entire bill.

From the conference committee, which did not file its report until four months after both houses had acted, a compromise emerged whereby the states were first given the opportunity to show good faith. Most observers, including Blatnik, felt the compromise was reasonable. Nevertheless, it seemed clear that the federal government held the high cards. Proponents of a strong control program expected the new legislation to curb much previously tolerated pollution.

JOHN E. MOORE

# Controlling Delinquency: Executive, Congressional, and Juvenile, 1961–64

THIS IS THE STORY of a modest proposal for federal action to help cope with a major problem—juvenile delinquency. From the layman's viewpoint juvenile delinquency appears to be a predominantly urban problem. Although this superficial impression is belied by statistics comparing the rate of increase of juvenile crime in urban and rural areas, it is shared by many members of Congress and by interest groups active in mobilizing support for legislative or administrative action. Organizations that at various times supported juvenile delinquency legislation include the National Urban League, the American Municipal Association, and the United States Conference of Mayors. The roster does not include the 4-H Clubs, the American Farm Bureau Federation, the Farmers Union, or the National Grange.

This case is particularly concerned with the way in which Congress handled a piece of legislation of major concern to urban areas; in broadest outlines it is an explanation of how a bill became law, and how differing interpretations of legislative intent led to controversy between Congress and the executive branch.

## Initial Attempts To Legislate, 1955–57

Prior to 1952 federal concern with juvenile delinquency was limited to the often disputed statistics compiled by the Federal Bureau of Investiga-

110

tion (FBI), activities incidental to the child welfare work of the Children's Bureau in the Department of Health, Education, and Welfare (HEW), and—beginning in 1948—a series of research projects sponsored by the National Institute of Mental Health (NIMH). In 1952 a more active interest in juvenile delinquency emerged simultaneously in both the legislative and executive branches.

In testimony that year before the Senate's Special Committee to Investigate Organized Crime in Interstate Commerce, FBI Director J. Edgar Hoover had offered evidence supporting his contention that "during the past decade, youth has led the criminal army in the United States." Already alerted to the problem by his work on organized crime, the committee's chairman, Democrat Estes Kefauver of Tennessee, proposed the creation of a Senate Judiciary Committee subcommittee to investigate juvenile delinquency. Authorized by voice vote in the spring of 1953, its objectives were outlined in a joint statement by Senator Kefauver and Republican Senator Robert C. Hendrickson of New Jersey: "To root the problem out at its core; to alert local authorities to the methods of combating this evil, and where those methods might be falling short; to establish the menace firmly in the public mind for the problem it is." There appeared to be no contemplation of direct federal aid, or the creation of an administrative counterpart to the subcommittee.

Meanwhile Dr. Martha M. Eliot, chief of the Children's Bureau, had appealed successfully to private foundations for funds to support a special delinquency project to be housed in the bureau but privately administered. The project sponsored a set of background studies and reports, demonstrated the interest of private organizations in action at the federal level, and—most importantly—attracted the attention of HEW Secretary Oveta Culp Hobby.

The combined activities of the Children's Bureau and the Senate Judiciary subcommittee culminated in Secretary Hobby's call for a national conference on juvenile delinquency in June 1954. According to one participant, "this was the gimmick to provide the desired recommendations. Eliot got Ike interested by working up through the administrative hierarchy, then using the Senate Judiciary Subcommittee proposals and National Conference recommendations as leverage."

The national conference proved to be an effective precipitant: in his 1955 State of the Union message President Dwight D. Eisenhower proposed federal legislation to assist the states in dealing with juvenile delinquency, and in his subsequent special health message he recommended "new grants to the States to enable them to strengthen and improve their programs and services for the prevention, diagnosis, and treatment of delinquency in youth. There should be assistance for State planning, for coordination of all State and local agencies concerned with juvenile delinquency, for training of personnel, and for special research and demonstration projects." An administration bill to achieve these objectives was drafted by the Children's Bureau, and sponsored in the Senate by Republican Alexander Wiley of Wisconsin.

Although primarily concerned in its first two years with investigating sources of juvenile crime in selected metropolitan areas, the Judiciary subcommittee had turned up some requests for the creation of a permanent federal agency to deal with juvenile delinquency. The interest of the Children's Bureau in becoming that agency was safeguarded on the subcommittee staff by two members who were recent HEW alumni. Shortly after the Eighty-fourth Congress convened in January 1955, three of the four members of the subcommittee—Democrats Kefauver and Thomas C. Hennings, Jr., of Missouri and Republican William Langer of North Dakota—cosponsored a separate bill establishing a federal grants-in-aid program to be administered by an upgraded Children's Bureau. Title 1 of the bill elevated the bureau to an Office of Children's Affairs, reporting to the secretary directly rather than through the Social Security Administration.

In July 1955 a Special Subcommittee on Juvenile Delinquency of the Senate Labor and Public Welfare Committee, chaired by New York Democrat Herbert H. Lehman, held hearings on the administration and Kefauver bills. Referring to Title 1 Senator Kefauver commented that "much of what is proposed in this bill can be done by Departmental order," and he observed that "it is a shame that the press had to report recently that within a year, the Secretary of the Department of Health, Education, and Welfare has not even spoken to the Chief of the Children's Bureau." The senator and Dr. Eliot may well have hoped that appropriate administrative action would be prompted by Title 1, and that it could then be stricken from the legislation. Just the opposite occurred: HEW refused to have its hand forced by Kefauver (or by Eliot, who was eased into a professorship at Harvard within the year), and Title 1 stirred up a controversy that served to obscure the legislation's principal objective of providing federal grants-in-aid for strengthening and improving state programs to combat juvenile delinquency.

The other major difference between the administration and Kefauver bills related to the composition and responsibilities of the federal and state advisory councils contemplated in both proposals. Where the administration bill was vague about the composition of the advisory councils, the Kefauver bill named specific agencies, including a liberal salting of private organizations; where the administration bill limited their role to advice and consultation, the Kefauver bill called upon the advisory councils to supervise administration of state plans.

In their testimony private welfare agency representatives generally preferred the Kefauver bill because it specified the inclusion of their agencies on federal and state advisory councils, and because it would improve the status of the Children's Bureau—the federal agency with which they worked most closely. State agencies, on the other hand, resented the inclusion of volunteer organizations in a supervisory capacity, and were opposed to the isolation of Children's Bureau activities from the other social welfare programs for which the Social Security Administration provided a single point of contact.

In his budget message of January 16, 1956 President Eisenhower noted that "during the last 8 years there has been a 60% increase in the number of children appearing before our courts" and renewed his request for legislation. Senator Lehman's subcommittee split the Kefauver bill into two separate measures, and approved both. The troublesome proposal to elevate the Children's Bureau was isolated in a bill devoted exclusively to establishing an Office of Children's Affairs in the Department of Health, Education, and Welfare. A revision of the program of grants to states that had been included in both the Kefauver and administration bills was introduced as a new bill (S. 4267).

The issue relating to the composition of the advisory councils was compromised in S. 4267. Specific groups were not identified, but it was made clear that the membership was to be widely representative of the many professions and agencies concerned with the prevention and treatment of juvenile delinquency. Administration of state programs would be entrusted to designated state agencies, but each state would have an advisory council, and state proposals for grants-in-aid would be required to show that there had been consultation among state and local public and voluntary agencies.

The new bill contemplated a seven- to eight-year program instead of the five-year program proposed in the administration bill, and authorized $11 million for the initial year instead of the administration bill's $3 million. It followed the administration bill in authorizing grants-in-aid to the states for strengthening existing programs, for training of personnel, and for support of special projects. The committee recommendation was unanimous, and S. 4267 passed the Senate by voice vote on the final day of the session. With no time remaining for consideration in the House of Representatives, the bill died when Congress adjourned.

Following approval of S. 4267 in 1956, the Senate consistently supported juvenile delinquency legislation. Its fortunes thereafter hinged on action in the House.

As in the Senate the preceding year, two sets of bills were introduced in the House in 1957. Democratic Congresswoman Edith Green of Oregon introduced a measure corresponding to Lehman's S. 4267 of the preceding Congress, except that she specified the private agencies to be represented on the federal advisory council. Republican Peter Frelinghuysen, Jr., of New Jersey and Democrat Carl Elliott of Alabama introduced the administration's proposal.

Hearings were held between May 19 and May 24 by the Special Education Subcommittee of the Committee on Education and Labor. The chairman of the subcommittee was Carl Elliott, a moderate southern Democrat who chose the administration program because it seemed politically more feasible than the costlier approach supported by Mrs. Green. But the chairman of the full committee was Democrat Graham A. Barden of North Carolina, an exceptionally skillful legislative tactician who measured his success in terms of the number of proposals he managed to block in committee. One committee member observed that "during my first years on the Committee, Chairman Barden did his best to avoid committee meetings—he preferred to go fishing." He declined to institute formal committee rules, set regular meeting days, or establish standing subcommittees with specific jurisdiction. In a terse recollection Mrs. Green summed up the prospects of both juvenile delinquency bills under Barden's chairmanship: "*No* legislation got support from Barden, including juvenile delinquency. Hearings were held in the hope of establishing a record that might, by some miracle, lead to committee action."

Like the Kefauver bill in the earlier Senate hearings, the Green bill was generally preferred by spokesmen for private welfare organizations —and opposed by administration officials and officers of public welfare agencies—because of its provisions relating to the composition and role of the advisory councils. Apart from this question a majority of witnesses favored Mrs. Green's bill because it contemplated a longer program (eight as opposed to five years), and authorized larger appropriations ($11 million as opposed to $3 million during the initial year). Some of them expressed a willingness to compromise, however, in light of the administration's emphasis on budget trimming.

The 1957 hearings served to establish a record, but the miracle Mrs. Green felt would be necessary to get committee action was not forthcoming, and no effort was made to produce a bill reconciling the administration and Green proposals. Although both bills thus died in committee, their resurrection was supposed to be assured, as Mrs. Green had occasion to point out in 1959: "The Chairman of the Committee, at that time [1957], said that if we dropped the juvenile delinquency bill then and spent all of our time and energy on the National Defense Education Act, we would make juvenile delinquency the next order of business."

## Failure of Renewed Efforts, 1959–60

The revival of juvenile delinquency legislation in 1959 after a two-year interval may be attributed in part to the persistence of Elliott and Mrs. Green and in part to a revolution that took place within the committee following the Democratic landslide in the congressional elections of 1958. The enlarged majority entitled the party to additional seats on committees generally, and with the help of Speaker of the House Sam Rayburn of Texas the party ratio on Education and Labor was revised to favor the Democrats by twenty to ten instead of seventeen to thirteen. All of the six new Democrats appointed in 1959 were supported by organized labor; none of the southern Democrats who applied was accepted. As one committee member recounted it, the liberal majority that was thereby secured "simply took the Committee away from Barden, establishing [its] own rules, scheduling Committee meetings for every 2nd Monday, and clarifying the jurisdiction of the subcommittees." Barden was still a force to be reckoned with, but for the first time appropriate weapons were available.

While changes in the composition and control of the Education and Labor Committee improved prospects for a juvenile delinquency bill, changes in the Eisenhower administration's attitude diminished them. In his 1957 budget message President Eisenhower had renewed his request for the prompt enactment of legislation, but in 1958, for the first time in three years, this request was omitted. The Bureau of the Budget (BOB) listed grants for juvenile delinquency among programs that had been "deferred." As an HEW official commented, "When Sputnik went up [in October 1957], domestic spending went down."

*Controversy over Political Expediency.* Mrs. Green's new bill was considerably briefer than its predecessor, emphasizing training, special projects, and improved coordination. The most significant change was the deletion of grants to states to strengthen and improve existing programs, which was the primary objective of President Eisenhower's original proposal. This deletion reduced the cost of the program from $11 million to $6 million during the first year. It also eliminated the need to obtain agreement on another controversial question: whether all grants were to be made to a single agency specified by each state. The American Public Welfare Association and individual state agencies wanted such a requirement written into the bill, but Mrs. Green sought greater flexibility and opposed it.

Representative Elliott's new bill was even more limited, providing $5 million a year for "projects which will demonstrate or develop techniques and practices leading to a solution of the Nation's juvenile delinquency control problems."

This introduced a new point of controversy because the Elliott bill made no reference to training of personnel, and in a program that Mrs. Green said had been very dear to her heart for some time, training was perhaps most dear. At the hearings on the two bills held by the Special Education Subcommittee in March 1959 the omission of training provisions became the focus of some heated exchanges between the congresswoman and interest group spokesmen supporting the Elliott bill. Mrs. Green came to the conclusion that she had been betrayed by a political sellout, and any prospect of agreement within the subcommittee on compromise legislation in 1959 was virtually eliminated.

The problem was clearly revealed in the following exchange between subcommittee members and George J. Hecht, publisher of *Parents Magazine* and president of the American Parents Committee. His position was particularly important to Mrs. Green because, as she later recollected, "the only really active group in the early days was George Hecht's parents group."

ELLIOTT: It is apparent to me from what you [George Hecht] have said that while you urge the passage of a bill which provides for research and demonstrations, you would not oppose grants to the States to carry out some of the work that they are already doing and grants to provide education and training. If you thought we could get such a bill through the Congress would you not be happy to support a bill like that?

HECHT: Yes, we have supported such a bill right along. I would not want the bill too big. I want to get something through and passed. We supported a bill in the two sessions of the last Congress and it did not get passed. I think this bill you introduced, Mr. Elliott, for $5 million a year for 5 years is a good beginning. Let us get it passed and get the money appropriated. . . .

GREEN: Well, I have noticed you have repeated several times that this is the bill you think will pass, this is the bill that Congress will support.

HECHT: This is the bill I hope will pass.

GREEN: I understood your passing of a political judgment. I would be much more interested if you would discuss the needs of juvenile delinquency control rather than the political merits of a specific bill.

The principal actor for the Parents Committee had not been Hecht himself, but one of his associates. Working with Children's Bureau officials and members of Congressman Elliott's staff, she served as midwife for a bill that no one really liked, but that appeared to offer the greatest promise of being enacted. Although Hecht himself was an innocent party to administration strategy, Mrs. Green believed—as she later said— that he had "worked something out with Elliott or his staff to get a bill limited to demonstration projects. This was an emasculation motivated by political expediency."

Among the few witnesses expressing a strong preference for the Green bill was Walter Reuther's administrative assistant, Richard Leonard. He mirrored Mrs. Green's appraisal of the administration's attitude toward juvenile delinquency legislation:

> Last year's administration proposal was wholly inadequate and paid little more than lip service to this growing problem. Under the terms of that bill, 35 states would have received only $30,000 during the first year for strengthening and improving juvenile delinquency programs. This year, the administration is apparently unwilling to provide any Federal funds. Like the delinquency itself, the administration has taken a step backward.
>
> While we do not know all the causes of juvenile delinquency, we do know that it will not disappear with the coming of a balanced budget. We are concerned that a juvenile delinquency bill may again be sacrificed in the holy name of "economy."

A slightly revised version of the Elliott bill was reported to the full committee, but the disagreement that had developed within the subcommittee persisted, depriving the liberal members of the unanimity required to force action from Graham Barden.

On April 27, 1959 the Senate Labor and Public Welfare Subcommittee began five days of hearings on a variety of bills that covered nearly all the alternatives that had been presented to Congress since 1955. In the Senate, as in the House, there was a preoccupation with the political feasibility of alternative proposals. Since the Senate had earlier approved the most comprehensive of the bills under consideration, a majority of the subcommittee members and witnesses simply assumed that they were looking for a measure that would pass the House, and the Senate companion bill to the Elliott bill appeared to be the most promising candidate. This was S. 694, cosponsored by Democrat Lister Hill of Alabama, chairman of the full committee, and Democrat Joseph S. Clark of Pennsylvania, chairman of the subcommittee.

New York's Republican Senator Jacob K. Javits was troubled by the limited scope of S. 694 and Democratic Senator Wayne Morse shared the concern of his colleague from Oregon, Edith Green, over the omission of any reference to training. Morse summarized the dilemma confronting both himself and the committee:

> Now we have before us a choice of bills, one a broader bill that would deal with training and research, . . . and the other a much more limited bill, . . . a bill not nearly as broad as the Lehman bill formerly passed by the Senate.
>
> Now, this choice is one of the difficult problems that confronts each Senator in the legislative process.
>
> Do you vote for something that you know is inadequate? Do you do so, knowing that even its authors are perfectly honest and frank to say it is not as good as they would like to have it, but which they think there is some political chance of getting passed, and which, to the extent of its provisions, will do some good? Or do you hold fast to what you consider to be at least the minimum program that ought to be adopted? . . .
>
> I will finally vote for anything that will do some good, but I will hope that those of us that believe we ought to be voting for more than is contained in the Hill-Clark bill . . . can at least persuade the Senate to go as far as we went in the Lehman bill, because time has passed and the Lehman bill is none too adequate for today.

Where Mrs. Green had seen a "sellout" for purposes of political expediency, Senator Morse perceived a misguided effort by men of good will. The attitude of Senators Javits and Morse permitted compromise; Mrs. Green's attitude did not. In any case, Senator Morse succeeded only in obtaining a minor concession—the inclusion of improved methods of training among the purposes of demonstration projects—before the bill was reported out of committee on August 25.

Once again the Senate was debating a juvenile delinquency bill at the end of the session—it was in fact the last piece of legislation to be considered, in the evening of a characteristically prolonged final day. Supporters of S. 694 on both sides of the aisle—including its cosponsor, Senator Clark—agreed that the bill was just an entering wedge. Clark observed: "It is quite true that we should have in this juvenile delinquency study bill a provision for training. The unfortunate thing is that the administration has opposed it; and in the committee . . . we have thought that if we could get half a loaf, if we could get a foot in the door, if we could get the Federal government committed, by making a small start in the way of studies of juvenile delinquency, that would be the wise thing to do. . . ."

But the Senate was not permitted to pass even the most limited of bills. Supporters were frustrated when Democrat Strom Thurmond of South Carolina threatened a filibuster that would have prevented adjournment. A single sentence was all that Thurmond required to state the automatic response of conservatives to juvenile delinquency legislation: "First, that the Federal Government has no jurisdiction in the field, under the Constitution; and second, even if it did . . . it would be more advisable to leave this field in the places where it more rightly belongs —in the home, the school, the community, and, if necessary, action by the State."

*Obstacles to Action.* Juvenile delinquency legislation got off to a hopeful start during the second session of the Eighty-sixth Congress. The Senate debate that was suspended on adjournment day the year before was resumed on January 26, 1960. Senator Clark reopened the debate on S. 694 by reversing his tactical position on the training question. Referring to 1959 he said: "At that time we were hopeful that we could get the bill through the Senate and the House before the end of the last session of Congress, [and] we had advice from our friends in the other body that it would be easier to achieve that result if we did not add a training provision. . . ." Noting that subcommittee members Morse and Javits had objected to the original bill because it made no provision for training, Clark observed that "we are confronted with a different situation now" and offered an amendment to add a new section entitled "Training of Personnel." The amendment involved no increase in authorizations—it simply divided the original $5 million equally between demonstration projects and training programs, the latter to include development of courses, fellowships, and traineeships.

Senator Clark's amendment was enthusiastically supported by advocates of juvenile delinquency legislation, including former dissenters Morse and Javits. The only significant opposition to the bill in floor debate came from Thurmond, who again raised the conventional states' rights banner ("there is no authority whatever under the Constitution for the Federal Government to enter into the field of juvenile delinquency"), and from Minority Leader Everett McKinley Dirksen of Illinois, who offered amendments limiting the program to two years and appropriations to $1 million a year. Senator Clark made effective use of the ambiguous statements tendered by the Budget Bureau and HEW to counter Dirksen's amendments. Quoting the BOB's lack of opposition and HEW's preference for S. 694, Clark concluded that "The influential agencies of the Eisenhower administration support the amount of money in the bill." The Dirksen amendments were rejected and the Clark amendment and the revised bill were passed, all by voice vote.

S. 694, as passed in the Senate, held promise of resolving the controversy that had stymied the House Education and Labor Committee the previous year. It contained an express provision for support of the training programs that Representative Green and others had considered to be essential, yet required no increase in funds. Although Mrs. Green would have preferred a larger allocation for training, she accepted the compromise and introduced a bill similar to the amended version of S. 694 on May 6. It was reported out by the full committee on May 18—with surprising ease.

Chairman Barden's first line of resistance having failed, he looked for aid to the conservative balance of power in the House Rules Committee, and the sympathetic viewpoint of its chairman, Judge Howard W. Smith of Virginia. The problem confronting liberal Democrats in the Rules Committee was analogous to that faced in the Education and Labor Committee prior to 1959: an exceptionally knowledgeable, conservatively inclined chairman possessing power to determine when the committee would meet, what it would consider, and who would testify; and a party ratio that on paper gave the Democrats an 8 to 4 margin but, with the defection of Chairman Smith and ranking Democrat William M. Colmer of Mississippi, often produced a 6 to 6 tie vote pigeonholing social welfare measures. To get a rule for legislation such as the juvenile delinquency bill, it was essential—though by no means sufficient—to have the support of the chairman of the committee from which the bill was reported. As Mrs. Green recalled, "When we finally managed to report a bill in 1960 [and] it got stuck in the Rules Committee, . . . Graham Barden wasn't about to get it out." Even if Barden gave his support, however, it would still have been necessary either to get the indulgence of Judge Smith or to use vigorous presidential leadership to persuade Republican members on the Rules Committee to join liberal Democrats in an attempt to wrest control from the chairman. Given the conservative persuasion of the Republican members, President Eisenhower's preoccupation with budgetary limitations, and a traditional disinclination to bypass the committee chairman, the latter solution offered little promise. Since Judge Smith believed that the answer to juvenile delinquency problems was to be found in more frequent trips to the woodshed, his indulgence was not forthcoming. Thus, after finally overcoming many of the afflictions that had plagued juvenile delinquency legislation since it was first introduced in 1955, Mrs. Green's latest bill languished and died in the House Rules Committee.

Among the more significant factors contributing to the difficulties encountered by juvenile delinquency legislation was the kind of leadership President Eisenhower provided. As noted earlier, the first proposals for federal action in this field followed his call for federal assistance in the 1955 State of the Union message. The administration bill at that time, while less generous than the Kefauver and Lehman bills, authorized a comprehensive program of grants. A similar program was requested in 1956 and 1957, but thereafter President Eisenhower's concern for juvenile delinquency legislation—and for domestic welfare legislation generally—was eclipsed by military priorities and an intensified interest in fiscal responsibility. No further requests for congressional action on the subject issued from the White House during his term.

Even during the period of formal presidential support, however, the degree and nature of that support had disappointed the bill's backers. An interest group spokesman commented that "Eisenhower talked some, but he provided no help whatever—he didn't do anything." A Democratic member of the House Education and Labor Committee called Eisenhower's support "lip service," adding: "neither he nor members of his administration pushed the legislation, or provided any direction. His attitude here, as elsewhere in the field of social welfare, seemed to be, 'I said I supported it, and that should be enough.' " The highest ranking administration official to testify in support of the Eisenhower program was Assistant Secretary of HEW Elliot L. Richardson; and by 1958 Richardson found himself in the awkward position of endorsing in principle a measure that the Budget Bureau had listed among items deferred. In short, Eisenhower's lukewarm interest in juvenile delinquency legislation deprived members of the House Education and Labor Committee of Republican support that might have helped them to report a bill as early as 1957; it diminished prospects of getting some assistance from Republican members of the House Rules Committee; and it decreased the likelihood of House approval if a rule could be obtained.

One more obstacle should be mentioned: the opposition normally encountered, especially in the House, by legislation that appears primarily beneficial to urban areas. Advocates of juvenile delinquency legislation were sensitive to the potentially crippling impact of its association with urban problems, and took pains to point up the rural aspects of juvenile delinquency. During Senate hearings in 1959 Senator Clark asked Norman Lourie, the deputy secretary of the Pennsylvania Department of Public Welfare, about juvenile delinquency in rural areas:

> LOURIE: Our impression is that, relative to the size of the population, relative to the economic distribution of the groups of population, there is no difference between the urban and the rural incidence of delinquency.
>
> CLARK: This is despite the fact that, as far as publicity is concerned, it is largely pictured as an urban problem?
>
> LOURIE: I think because it is less protected in the urban communities from the spotlight of the public. When you get the concentration you do in the urban communities, you can't help but get the publicity.

In the same exchange Lourie made one of the few explicit references to another association that was likely to reinforce the opposition of the conservative coalition of northern Republicans and southern Democrats: "I cannot help but comment on [the] race question because I think that we sometimes are misled by concentration of populations and people sometimes tend to feel that we are involved in a race problem. If we, in any city, imposed on any group, racial, ethnical, cultural, or religious, the same conditions we impose on some of our racial groups in our large northern cities, we would get the same degree of angry expression from the children." The juvenile delinquency program was viewed, especially by southern congressmen, as being both urban-oriented and Negro-oriented.

## The New Frontier and Passage of the Act, 1961

With the election of President John F. Kennedy the political context for juvenile delinquency legislation changed decisively. A Democratic administration could be expected to look more favorably upon an expanded federal concern with domestic welfare problems, and the 1960 Democratic platform had specifically called for federal leadership to control and prevent juvenile delinquency. Even more important, the Kennedy family took a lively personal interest in the problem.

There was also a significant change in the House Education and Labor Committee. Chairman Graham Barden retired and was succeeded by Democrat Adam Clayton Powell, Jr., of New York. This key position thus passed into the hands of a liberal congressman from an urban constituency in Harlem.

A third change involved President Kennedy's narrowly successful effort to enlarge the House Rules Committee. On January 31, 1961 the House of Representatives voted 217 to 212 in favor of expanding the membership of its Rules Committee from 12 to 15. While the 2 to 1 party ratio continued, it was hoped that the addition of two moderate Democrats and one Republican would provide the House leadership with an 8 to 7 majority to overcome the conservative coalition of Republicans and southern Democrats that had previously dominated the committee. Given the power of Judge Smith this was not a comfortable margin, but prior to the end-of-session logjam that served to enhance the chairman's influence, it might prove sufficient. Supporters of juvenile delinquency legislation received an additional boost from this action when Carl Elliott was appointed to the enlarged Rules Committee. Since he was succeeded as chairman of the Special Education Subcommittee by Representative Edith Green, the move did not entail any loss of interest in juvenile delinquency within the subcommittee.

*The Administration Mounts an Attack.* "We have talked a lot about preventing delinquency, but have not acted with equal vigor. Action, rather than debate, is what we need now." Attorney General Robert F. Kennedy's charge to the House Special Education Subcommittee in July 1961 captures the spirit of the New Frontier, and provides a forceful contrast with the attitude of the Eisenhower administration. Within a week of the 1960 elections the President-elect and his attorney general-designate had asked a member of their campaign organization to head an administration effort to launch a national attack on juvenile delinquency. The man called on was David Hackett, a former prepschool roommate of Robert Kennedy, and one of the family's favorite amateur athletes (an Olympic hockey player). Hackett's intimate relationship with the Kennedy family, which continued during the presidency, was indicative of the Kennedys' close personal interest in the juvenile delinquency project. Hackett was immediately interested, but as he later noted, he "had no background or experience—just a list of names."

At the top of Hackett's list was the name of Democrat John E. Fogarty of Rhode Island, chairman of the House Appropriations Subcommittee on Labor and Health, Education, and Welfare. Throughout his career in Congress Fogarty had shown a special interest in mental health problems. He steered Hackett to Mike Gorman, the executive director of the National Committee Against Mental Illness, who became a key actor in the 1961 campaign to obtain juvenile delinquency legislation.

In 1959 Fogarty had requested a report on juvenile delinquency from the Children's Bureau and the National Institute of Mental Health. A joint report was submitted in February of 1960. Predictably, it recommended legislation along the lines of the bill that had been pending since 1955. It identified research studies, demonstration projects, and training of personnel as the major areas requiring increased action. Following a special subcommittee hearing, the House Appropriations Committee directed the NIMH to earmark $1 million of the increased funds provided for fiscal 1961 for new programs and activities aimed at solving the problem of juvenile delinquency.

Among the NIMH programs in which Congressman Fogarty developed a particular interest—with the good offices of Mike Gorman—was a project on New York's lower east side known as Mobilization for Youth. The ubiquitous Gorman had been instrumental in securing a planning grant from NIMH for this project, jointly sponsored by the research center of Columbia University's School of Social Work and a number of neighborhood civic groups, and initially financed with the help of the Ford Foundation.

Mobilization for Youth was distinguished by the emphasis it placed on a comprehensive approach to juvenile delinquency within a given community. Rather than attempting to develop particular techniques directed at controlling certain kinds of delinquent acts irrespective of the community in which they occurred, this project concentrated on improving the opportunities open to potential delinquents in their immediate neighborhood through a revitalization of the physical and social environment. The text for this approach is the book *Delinquency and Opportunity,* coauthored by Richard A. Cloward and Lloyd E. Ohlin, both of whom were then members of the faculty of Columbia's School of Social Work. As Cloward later explained, "When we became involved in Mobilization for Youth, the importance of these ideas was generally credited by the sponsors of this program, [and the book] became the basis for much of our thinking in the planning phase about the development of our program."

The central hypothesis of the Cloward-Ohlin study was based upon "differential opportunity structures":

> This approach permits us to ask, for example, how the relative availability of illegitimate opportunities affects the resolution of adjustment problems leading to deviant behavior. We believe that the way in which these problems are resolved may depend upon the kind of support for one or another type of illegitimate activity that is given at different points in the social structure. If, in a given social location, illegal or criminal means are not readily available, then we should not expect a criminal subculture to develop among adolescents. By the same logic, we should expect the manipulation of violence to become a primary avenue to higher status only in areas where the means of violence are not denied to the young. . . . In short, there are marked differences from one part of the social structure to another in the types of illegitimate adaptation that are available to persons in search of solutions to problems of adjustment arising from the restricted availability of legitimate means. In this sense, then, we can think of individuals as being located in two opportunity structures—one legitimate, the other illegitimate. Given limited access to success-goals by legitimate means, the nature of the delinquent response that may result will vary according to the availability of various illegitimate means.
>
> When we say that the form of delinquency that is adopted is conditioned by the presence or absence of appropriate illegitimate means, we are actually referring to crucial differences in the social organization of various slum areas, for our hypothesis implies that the local milieu affects the delinquent's choice of a solution to his problems of adjustment.[1]

On March 16, 1961 David Hackett, by this time formally designated assistant attorney general, held the first of a series of conferences designed to develop some consensus on approach and criteria. In preparing the invitation list Hackett relied primarily on the advice of Phillip Green, director of the Juvenile Delinquency Division in the Children's Bureau. In addition to representatives of public and private agencies who had frequently appeared before congressional subcommittees in support of juvenile delinquency legislation, Green included David Hunter of the Ford Foundation, and Lloyd Ohlin. In 1961 Ohlin was serving as part-time adviser to both NIMH and the Children's Bureau. He was also

[1] Richard A. Cloward and Lloyd E. Ohlin, *Delinquency and Opportunity* (The Free Press, 1960), pp. 151–53.

among the professional personnel to whom Hackett had been guided by the Ford Foundation. It was becoming increasingly apparent that Ohlin was peculiarly well placed in the constellation of public and private agencies that from Hackett's viewpoint had made the most promising assault on juvenile delinquency.

The main working paper at the conference had been prepared by Hunter. It incorporated many of Ohlin's ideas about the importance of opportunity and the necessity of a comprehensive approach, and might fairly be called a trial balloon. Hackett was familiar with the paper's content, and had encouraged Hunter to distribute it to conference participants. The professional viewpoint that Hackett found most appealing was summarized by Lloyd Ohlin: "I think that the community ought to be the central arena of action. . . . My own view is that the answer lies in enlarging the opportunity structures for youths in the areas of large cities. . . . I would think that the Hunter report represents the closest statement that I have found yet to the kind of view which I would seek to propose."

Although the conference was primarily concerned with establishing technical criteria, neither administration spokesmen nor professional participants were oblivious to political considerations. When pressed by the chairman of the conference, Judge Thomas Waxter, Hackett indicated that the administration anticipated a five-year program involving sums of approximately $10 to $20 million a year, including NIMH funds allocated to juvenile delinquency. He said an executive order was being drafted to create a committee representing HEW, Labor, and Justice to coordinate the activities of the three departments. Wilbur J. Cohen, assistant secretary of HEW, observed that "If we do come up with a piece of legislation . . . we would like to see it enacted this session. We would not like to see a piece of legislation that is so involved that it will take another three or four years to get through Congress. There have been interminable hearings already, and a lot of differences of opinion. . . ."

As attention began to focus on the Ohlin-Hunter proposal, David Hunter placed a prescient finger on one of its chief political shortcomings: "There may be problems in getting a program of this kind through Congress because this does not have something in it for everybody. It would be concentrated in certain large urban areas . . . in relatively limited spheres so that some kind of visible impact is made. . . ." An urban focus would do nothing to attract essential support from representatives of rural constituencies, and a concentrated attack would severely limit even the number of urban communities involved. Moreover, a comprehensive approach would leave little room for the discrete research and demonstration projects that were uppermost in the minds of congressional advocates of juvenile delinquency legislation. The immediate concern with obtaining congressional approval might be satisfied through the common device of employing ambiguous statutory language, but a foundation would also be laid for disagreement over congressional intent.

There would be still another problem: bridging the gap between professional and lay viewpoints. This first became apparent during the March 16 conference when HEW Secretary Abraham A. Ribicoff, after listening briefly to a part of the discussion, offered a peremptory criticism: "It seems to me as if you are going pretty far afield . . . scattering a lot of your energies. You are dealing with a problem that is like quicksilver. It is a very difficult problem to grasp. There is a lot of talk pro and con on this in America, but nobody gets down to brass tacks from my standpoint." Having thus offended all the participants Ribicoff promptly departed. He was later persuaded by Assistant Secretary Cohen to return and make amends, but in the meantime Judge Waxter had pointed out that "these are the same kinds of questions you are going to get when you get to Congress, that you have got to nail down something to the mast that is understandable, but the lay person who has no technical knowledge in this field does not understand it."

David Hackett, though more sympathetic than Ribicoff, had also been struggling to grasp what the participants were talking about. As he later remarked, "I quickly learned from the March meeting that you can't get consensus among professionals, so I had to pick one of the best and rely on his judgment." He chose Lloyd Ohlin.

*The Senate Acts.* Meanwhile Congress was beginning to move. At an Appropriations subcommittee hearing on March 14, Chairman Fogarty, whom David Hackett considered the administration's congressional anchor man, sought to reinforce the record in support of federal action on juvenile delinquency. Witnesses called for this purpose included Mike Gorman; James McCarthy, project administrator of Mobilization for Youth; Richard Cloward; and Dean LeMasters of the University of Wisconsin School of Social Work, who attempted to underline the rural impact of juvenile delinquency.

The Senate required no prodding. On January 9 Senators Hill and Clark had introduced S. 279, almost identical to the bill passed by the

Senate in the previous session. It was reported by the Labor and Public Welfare Committee on April 6, and passed on April 12.

Noting the omission of a grants-in-aid program, the Senate used the debate preceding passage as the occasion to read a lengthy lesson to the House. Senator Thomas J. Dodd, Democrat from Connecticut, said that under the circumstances that had prevailed in the past he would have been happy with the bill, "for we were then operating in a rather hostile atmosphere. The public was not as concerned with the problem; the Congress was not as informed; and the administration was not as sympathetic. . . . The circumstances which in the past made a skeleton bill necessary have all changed, yet the skeleton bill is still before us." Senator Clark pointed out that "We are legislating within the art of the possible. I hope that when the bill gets to the House, it will be possible to have the Administration persuade the House that a larger program is necessary."

Senator Javits made the point perfectly explicit:

> . . . the purpose of my statement today is to have the public understand why we are taking this action. When the bill gets to the House, we do not want the House to say "Oh, well, this is another one of those spendthrift programs which the Senate liberals are sending to us." The House will realize that we have exercised a great sense of restraint and a great sense of discipline in a common effort to get something done. . . .
>
> There is no problem about having the bill passed by the Senate. Certainly if it is left as it is . . . there should not be a great problem in having it passed by the other body. . . .

*The Administration's Draft.* When David Hackett endorsed the comprehensive, community-oriented attack on juvenile delinquency advanced in the Hunter paper, and when he later selected Lloyd Ohlin as his professional adviser, it became apparent that the administration had in mind a different approach from that reflected in legislative proposals calling for demonstration and evaluation projects. The administration was primarily concerned with developing integrated programs in a few communities, while Congress in its earlier efforts to legislate on juvenile delinquency had contemplated a number of discrete projects involving such things as the early identification of potential delinquents, the impact of school dropouts on delinquency, and the effect of state laws regarding the employment of minors. Although the two approaches were not mutually exclusive, there was a significant difference in emphasis. But Hackett was familiar with the tortured progress of juvenile delinquency legislation, and reluctant to create new problems by making the difference explicit. He therefore chose to work within the framework of existing proposals: "We looked at the legislation which had just been passed by the Senate, took it and added an improved preamble, and made provision for the President's Committee that was to be established by Executive Order."

The "improvement" in the preamble (technically, the declaration of "Findings and Policies") consisted mainly of an increased emphasis on coordination—a deceptively innocent term that sheltered the administration's interest in a comprehensive approach. The administration was not attempting to mislead Congress about its intentions; the ambiguous terms reflected as accurately as possible the general direction of its thinking. In his letter to the President transmitting the draft bill on May 5, Secretary Ribicoff stated that with respect to demonstration and evaluation projects, "major emphasis would be given . . . to the selection of a limited number of communities or states that show promise of having programs for the prevention or control of juvenile delinquency or youth offenses that might be useful or applicable in other parts of the country." Ribicoff reiterated this emphasis during his testimony before the House Special Education Subcommittee. In a letter to Speaker of the House Sam Rayburn on May 11 transmitting the administration bill, President Kennedy stressed that "We must undertake a program integrating specific remedies into a total attack upon the prevention and control of youth offenses." In retrospect, terms like "coordination," "integration," and "total attack" were seen to have far-reaching implications, but at the time they provoked little reaction in Congress.

On the day he sent his legislation to Congress President Kennedy issued an executive order establishing a President's Committee on Juvenile Delinquency and Youth Crime. The committee was composed of the attorney general, the secretary of labor, and the secretary of HEW. Although HEW would be responsible for administering the program, the executive order designated the attorney general as chairman. David Hackett attributes this curious division of responsibility to three primary considerations: Attorney General Kennedy's personal interest in juvenile delinquency; the fact that Hackett, who was to become executive director of the President's Committee, was an assistant attorney general; and the apparently more limited involvement of the Department of Justice, which would enable it to play the role of arbiter.

The executive order also established a citizen's advisory council to the

President's Committee, consisting of between twelve and twenty-one members drawn from both public and voluntary organizations and designated by the chairman. By this action the President forestalled further debate in Congress over the composition of a national advisory council, and the method of appointment ensured the council's sympathy with the viewpoint of Attorney General Kennedy.

In addition to modifying the preamble, the administration's bill doubled the $5 million annual appropriations authorized in the Senate bill and extended the program from four to five years. It also indicated in purposely vague terms the relationship contemplated between the secretary of HEW and the President's Committee: "The Secretary shall consult with the President's Committee on Juvenile Delinquency and Youth Crime on matters of general policy and procedure arising in the administration of this Act, and shall consider the recommendations, if any, of such Committee on program applications submitted under [the Act]."

The biggest problem at the time the bill was drafted concerned the role of the President's Committee. According to Hackett, "We had a big fight with HEW, and especially with its Budget Officer, over the authority to be vested in the President's Committee." Hackett wanted an explicit acknowledgment of the committee's primary role. "We finally compromised on 'consultation,' but there was a clear informal understanding among members of the President's Committee that I would administer the program—they didn't want to fight the Attorney General."

*The Bill in the House.* The administration bill was introduced in the House by Edith Green on May 18. Hearings before her Special Education Subcommittee were scheduled to begin July 10, and on that day subcommittee member John Brademas, Democrat from Indiana, introduced an identical bill (H.R. 8028) that was later substituted for the Green bill. Sensitive to the political fortunes of her fellow Democrats, Mrs. Green followed a policy of sharing the subcommittee's wealth among its majority members. Brademas had expressed an interest in juvenile delinquency and volunteered to do the homework necessary to become an effective advocate. In effect Brademas became a cosponsor of the bill introduced by Mrs. Green, but under the rules of the House this required the introduction of a separate, identical bill.

Apart from a consistent emphasis on coordination and community planning, the principal contrast with previous hearings was to be found not so much in the testimony as in the lineup of witnesses. The highest-ranking member of the Eisenhower administration ever to appear in behalf of juvenile delinquency legislation had been an assistant secretary of HEW. When the Kennedy administration bill came before the House subcommittee it was supported by the combined forces of the secretary of HEW, the secretary of labor, and the attorney general. Mrs. Green remarked to Attorney General Kennedy, "In the 7 years I have been here, this is the first time I have seen any active interest on the part of the Department of Justice in this particular area." Cabinet members were available for preliminary conferences with members of the subcommittee, and members of the executive branch helped to draft the committee report. According to the subcommittee clerk, this evidence of active support had a profound impact on the bill's prospects in the House.

Hearings before the subcommittee were completed on July 18. On the following weekend members of the subcommittee traveled to New York City to take a firsthand look at some of its high crime neighborhoods. Mrs. Green said she was "concerned" and "shocked" by what seemed to be "almost a hopelessness on the part of the hundreds of young people to whom we talked." Congressman Brademas told the House, "My awareness of the seriousness of juvenile delinquency and my concern that we undertake effective countermeasures were both sharpened by the experience of the trip." The trip to New York City also increased the sense of urgency of Republican members who had not been inclined to support juvenile delinquency legislation actively. H.R. 8028 was unanimously approved by the Special Education Subcommittee.

With the accession of Adam Clayton Powell to the chairmanship of the Committee on Education and Labor, no difficulty was anticipated in reporting the bill out of the full committee. Mrs. Green later observed that the change in committee chairman was the single most important factor contributing to the enactment of juvenile delinquency legislation in 1961. But while Powell—unlike his predecessor—was not actively opposed to this legislation, he was not actively interested in it either. His attitude was perhaps most accurately characterized, by a member of the President's Committee staff, as "sympathetically indifferent." The bill came up near the end of the session and according to David Hackett, "Powell either wasn't going to schedule the bill for Committee consideration, or else he wasn't going to be around to hold a committee meeting." At this point the attorney general made one of several critically important contributions to enactment of H.R. 8028: "He called Powell and persuaded him to schedule a meeting to report the bill."

H.R. 8028 was reported on August 17. The committee had made two changes designed to reduce opposition in the Rules Committee and on the floor: it reduced the federal commitment by cutting the term of the program from five to three years, and it eliminated the controversial provision of fellowships for the training of personnel. The amended bill also instructed the secretary of HEW to give special consideration to a major demonstration project in the District of Columbia.

As of August 17 the bill had reached the previous highwater mark for juvenile delinquency legislation: it was in the Rules Committee, where Mrs. Green's bill of the preceding session had become stuck. The Rules Committee had been enlarged to provide an 8 to 7 liberal majority, but Congress was once again approaching adjournment, and Chairman Howard Smith's power to control the agenda was reaching its peak. The administration would either have to obtain Judge Smith's cooperation, or to persuade its agents on the committee—Democrats Richard Bolling of Missouri and Ray J. Madden of Indiana—to fight for the one-vote majority they could usually command when a bill was sufficiently important to warrant the struggle.

The administration first got an important assist from Congressman Fogarty. He reportedly got in touch with two members of the committee who had opposed a rule in 1960 and persuaded them to reverse their position. This strengthened the administration's hand but did not in itself assure that a rule would be forthcoming. To the surprise of virtually everyone but Robert Kennedy, that assurance finally came from the chairman himself.

Shortly after the inauguration of President Kennedy an improbable friendship began to develop between Judge Smith and the President's brother. Realizing that the Rules Committee could prove to be one of the New Frontier's principal stumbling blocks, Robert Kennedy endeavored to establish cordial relations with its conservative chairman. They did not find much common ground so far as policy was concerned, but they did discover a personal affinity for one another. The attorney general invited the judge over to his estate in McLean, they found mutual pleasure in gentleman farming in Virginia, and a kind of father-son relationship began to evolve.

When Robert Kennedy called Judge Smith in August he was assured that the chairman would make no effort to block a rule. Congressman Fogarty's ability to shift two votes may have given the attorney general the backing he needed to make his call effective. The administration might have had the votes in any event. But rather than fighting for an 8 to 7 liberal majority the administration obtained Judge Smith's indulgence; although he was not sympathetic to the purposes of the juvenile delinquency bill, it did not involve much money, and, as a member of the President's Committee staff put it, "the Judge liked Bobby." A rule was granted on August 24.

David Hackett and his aides, following the advice of Congressman Fogarty, Mike Gorman, and the House Democratic leadership, had, in Gorman's estimate, "talked to just about every Democrat in the House." According to Hackett, "We expected little trouble on the floor of the House—the proposal wasn't that difficult or major. The main problem was getting a rule."

Going to the floor on August 30, the juvenile delinquency bill had basic bipartisan support. As Congressman Brademas stated during the debate, H.R. 8028 "was adopted unanimously by our subcommittee and given almost unanimous support by the full committee." Even a little bipartisanship was hard to come by on the Education and Labor Committee, so the confidence of the administration did not appear to be misplaced. It was known that Robert P. Griffin of Michigan, a Republican member of the Education and Labor Committee, intended to offer a crippling amendment limiting demonstration projects to the District of Columbia, but both Hackett and Gorman believed they had a comfortable margin: "We figured on a maximum of 150 votes for the Griffin amendment." What they had failed to anticipate was that the juvenile delinquency bill would come up immediately following an attempt to obtain Calendar Wednesday consideration of the emergency aid to education bill of 1961. The vote against consideration of the education bill was surprisingly lopsided (242 to 170), and still flushed with this victory over the administration, Minority Leader Charles A. Halleck of Indiana decided to use the Griffin amendment for another partisan test vote. Hackett and Gorman had not taken for granted the votes needed to defeat the Griffin amendment—"there must have been about 15 of Bobby's lawyers working in the cloakroom while the bill was being debated"—but they did not expect a test vote. As Hackett was to comment later, "We had the votes, but many of them had left the floor after the aid-to-education vote."

When the question was taken on the Griffin amendment, it carried on a teller vote, 106 to 98. But the rules of the House permitted a later roll call vote, giving the administration additional time in which to muster its forces. When the roll was called the Griffin amendment was defeated, 217 to 187. Then the bill was passed by voice vote.

*Debate and Voting Patterns.* After six years of hearings, revision, and hesitation the House of Representatives had at last passed a juvenile delinquency bill. Prior to 1959 discussion in both Houses had focused on the relative merits of alternative proposals; thereafter, the primary concern had been political feasibility, with special emphasis on the difficulty of securing House approval. The major obstacles on the way to the House floor were personified by the chairmen of the Education and Labor and the Rules Committees, but even when these had been overcome, disproportionate representation of rural constituencies in the House still left the outcome in doubt.

The principal arguments advanced on the floor against the juvenile delinquency bill fell into two related categories—skepticism regarding the value of governmental assistance generally, and particular opposition to the intrusion of the federal government in this field. In discussing congressional action on this and earlier proposals, the director of the Division of Juvenile Delinquency Service of the Children's Bureau once remarked that "There is a funny emotional involvement in juvenile delinquency problems." Among the outgrowths of this emotional involvement is a strong preference for old-fashioned remedies, and a tendency to blame government, especially the federal government, for their failure. Many examples of this viewpoint are to be found in the debate over H.R. 8028, but none can match the folksy eloquence of Michigan's Republican Clare E. Hoffman:

> The bill is a little late in coming here. This bill should have been here when the Members of the House, apparently God-fearing, intelligent men and women, were children. . . . How much better in every respect each of us might have been if the Government—instead of the loving mother, the stern father—had guided us. . . .
>
> ***
>
> Most of our trouble grows out of our own doing. We do one thing this week and then the next week we have to fix it up—try to lessen the harm we have caused. That has been the course here for many years—interference by the Federal Government in personal and local affairs, then a bill and an appropriation to make good, but only in part, the loss.
>
> ***

There was a time—every time I get to thinking about this subject, I feel so sorry for my poor old grandfather and grandmother . . . they did not have any of the advantages we had; the Government did not tell them how to regulate their daily lives. They worked; they read the Scriptures; said a prayer each morning and each night; attended to their own business; helped the neighbors when help was needed; lived in peace; saw to it that the children —and in mother's family there were 13—traveled the straight and narrow road. All that without Government direction or advice.

\*\*\*

I cannot see how as parents, as most of us are, we are going to help by turning control of our families, our children, over to some Federal official and let him direct what the boys and girls should do. Much of the trouble grows out of crowding, nothing to do. But the recreation, the work, must be furnished and directed by local authorities after the parents have done all they can.

\*\*\*

It is possible the parents as well as the girls and boys need instruction, or, at least that they do a little thinking on their own—then try by example as well as by precept—old home remedies. And, I might add, a little enforcement of present laws. Pass this bill—then sit back and watch the agency grow.

As Clare Hoffman's last remark indicated, a preference for solutions reached in the individual family or community was intertwined with suspicion that this bill marked the first step along a path leading to massive federal intervention. The pervasiveness of this suspicion was reflected in Ohio Republican John M. Ashbrook's withdrawl of the support he had promised as a member of the Special Education Subcommittee:

I must say to my distinguished friend from Rhode Island [John Fogarty] that I was very much concerned at his statement that . . . he looked forward to a grant-in-aid program or a direct Federal-aid program to combat juvenile delinquency.

\*\*\*

It was my impression up to this time that the seed money would be of the type which would be designed to produce reports and know-how with the idea in mind of helping other levels of government. . . . Now it seems that almost certainly the seed money will bring forth a crop, a harvest, of Federal intervention, a harvest of Federal bureaucracy. . . . I will oppose this bill for that reason.

Congressman Griffin's amendment, which stemmed from a similar suspicion of spiraling federal involvement, provided a rallying point for opponents of a larger federal role:

. . . there are two provisions in this bill, one providing for Federal grants to establish projects and another to provide for the training of personnel, which are the "camel's nose under the tent," and which inevitably, in my opinion, will lead in the direction of a gigantic Federal program to take over State and local responsibilities to control the problems of juvenile delinquency. There is only $10 million a year in this bill, a ridiculously small sum, to try to do anything in this field on a nationwide scale.

If we sprinkle this small sum of money around the country for a few projects here and there, what will be the result? Next year or the year after the administration in power will be back to say, "We have not made much progress in dealing with this problem because we didn't have enough money. We need a great deal more money."

Almost without exception those who spoke in opposition to H.R. 8028—or in favor of the Griffin amendment—represented rural constituencies. Alert to the connection, Congressman Fogarty attempted to underline the rural impact of juvenile delinquency in answering Clare Hoffman's tribute to the virtues of country life: "The gentleman from Michigan left the impression that this is a city problem. The gentleman from Michigan is not right when he says it is a city problem. It has been going on for a good long time; I venture to say it was going on when he was born about 80 some years ago, or whenever it was. But, it was going on in the small towns in Michigan as it is going on in the small towns today. Maybe it should not happen, but it does happen in small towns."

If Hoffman's testy reply was indicative, then Fogarty's argument had fallen on deaf ears:

HOFFMAN: Does the gentleman concede much of the trouble grows out of the fact we have crowded so many people in small areas with nothing to do, and I refer to the young folks?

FOGARTY: I think that has a bearing, but in your State, sir, you have this problem. It exists in the smaller towns.

HOFFMAN: We do not have much of it.

FOGARTY: You have a lot of it, the gentleman would be surprised.

HOFFMAN: I know what is going on in my district.

In analyzing the roll call vote it will be helpful to make some comparisons with the earlier vote of the same day on consideration of the emergency aid to education bill. Both were partisan test votes, that is, the minority leadership had made clear the position of the Republican party and the expectation that its members would adhere to the party's position. Because of this, and on the basis of many studies of roll call voting in Congress, it might be expected in examining the two votes that party cohesion would be the most reliable predictor of the positions taken by individual congressmen.

The aid to education vote provides an excellent example of minority party cohesion supported by a conservative coalition with southern Democrats: 160 of 166 Republicans were joined by 82 Democrats, including 69 of 90 southerners, to reject consideration of the bill. While partisan lineups were also the most prominent feature of the Griffin amendment roll call, a comparison of the two votes reveals significant departures from Republican party unity,[2] and equally important inroads on the conservative coalition with southern Democrats: 29 Republicans joined with 188 Democrats, including 40 of 92 southerners, to defeat the Griffin amendment.

In view of the critical issues identified in floor debate on the juvenile delinquency bill, it might be expected that these deviations would correspond with: (1) a pattern of support for a larger federal role;[3] or (2) predominantly urban or suburban constituencies.[4] The defenders of the juvenile delinquency bill tallied 217 votes against the Griffin amendment (203 were required to defeat it). A total of 188 Democrats voted against the Griffin amendment; of these, 158 also voted in favor of the aid to education bill, and 30 switched from opposing aid to education to supporting juvenile delinquency on the Griffin amendment roll call. Of the 30 who switched, 25 had supported a larger federal role on 6 or more of 10 roll call votes that session (including both aid to education and the Griffin amendment). Twenty of the switching Democrats were from southern states, including the 5 who had not supported a larger federal role in 6 or more of 10 roll call votes. Of the 55 Democrats who voted in favor of the Griffin amendment (and thus against the juvenile delinquency legislation) 52 were from southern states, 51 represented rural constituencies, and 38 supported a larger federal role on 5 or less of 10 roll call votes.

These two sets of data indicate that: (1) among those Democrats who switched from opposition to the aid to education bill to support of the juvenile delinquency legislation on the Griffin amendment vote there

[2] It should be noted that the slapdash nature of the aid to education bill to some extent reinforced Republican party unity by reducing the level of support from customarily friendly Republicans. See Richard F. Fenno, Jr., "The House of Representatives and Federal Aid to Education," Robert L. Peabody and Nelson W. Polsby (eds.), *New Perspectives on the House of Representatives* (Rand McNally, 1963), p. 234.

[3] As shown in *Congressional Quarterly*'s analysis of 10 roll call votes in the first session of the Eighty-seventh Congress, including both the aid to education and Griffin amendment votes. *Congressional Quarterly Almanac, 1961,* p. 633.

[4] As estimated in *Congressional Quarterly*'s breakdown of all congressional districts on the basis of the 1960 census figures. *Congressional Quarterly Almanac, 1963,* p. 1170.

was a general pattern of support for a larger federal role; and (2) among those Democrats who voted in favor of the Griffin amendment there was an equally clear correspondence between the rural composition of their constituencies and opposition to the juvenile delinquency legislation.

Support from 30 Democrats who had defected on the aid to education vote still left the administration 15 votes short of the 203 necessary to defeat the Griffin amendment. Nearly double this margin was supplied by 29 Republicans, only 3 of whom had voted in favor of the aid to education bill. Of the 26 who switched, *none* had supported a larger federal role on 6 or more of 10 roll calls, and only 8 had supported a larger federal role on 4 or more roll call votes.

In the absence of a direct relationship to patterns of support for a larger federal role, how can the switch of the 26 Republicans be accounted for? One answer seems to be provided by urban-suburban constituency factors, which for the Democrats were also generally reflected in support for a larger federal role. In the exceptional instances when these Republicans did support a larger federal role, it might be argued that constituency factors had a special bearing on gaining their support in the particular case. The argument is in fact substantiated by an examination of the constituencies represented by the 26 Republicans opposing the rurally sponsored Griffin amendment: 4 represented urban districts; 9 represented suburban districts, largely in the New York metropolitan area (where delinquency in well-to-do suburban settings was getting frequent notice in the press); and 7 represented "mixed" districts in which the rural population ranged from 44 percent to 56 percent. Altogether, only 6 of the 29 Republicans voting against the Griffin amendment represented predominantly rural districts.

This brief analysis of the debate and roll call vote indicates that efforts to underline the rural implications of juvenile delinquency, and to discount the length and depth of the federal government's involvement, correctly anticipated the bill's greatest obstacles. The national scope of the juvenile delinquency bill was finally preserved by a narrow margin of votes supplied by Republicans and southern Democrats more likely to oppose than support a larger federal role.

*Enactment.* At Senator Hill's request the House amendments to the Hill-Clark bill were accepted by the Senate without debate on September 11. In signing the bill into law on September 22, President Kennedy observed that "With this legislation the Federal Government becomes an active partner with state and local communities to prevent and control the spread of juvenile delinquency. Though initiative and primary responsibility for coping with delinquency reside with families and local communities, the Federal Government can provide leadership, guidance, and assistance."

After six years of what Carl Elliott called "an enormous amount of talk about juvenile delinquency," why was action finally forthcoming in 1961?

(1) All that "talk" led to the deletion or compromise of some of the more controversial features in the original bills. (2) The unflagging interest of several members of Congress—including Representatives Green, Elliott, and Fogarty, and Senators Hill, Clark, and Javits—sustained the legislative effort during the lean last years of the Eisenhower administration. (3) The changes in the chairmanship of the House Education and Labor Committee, in the party ratio within that committee, and in the size and composition of the House Rules Committee made it possible to overcome the blocking power of the conservative coalition of Republicans and southern Democrats. (4) The Kennedy administration expressed strong support and interest by designating a member of the presidential campaign force to work full time on enactment of the legislation; creating by executive order the President's Committee on Juvenile Delinquency and Youth Crime; publicly marshalling three cabinet members to testify at committee hearings; privately expending much time and effort to win over individual congressmen; and making effective use of the influence of Robert Kennedy, who in the dual role of attorney general and brother of the President provided an uncommonly forceful symbol of presidential concern. As Mike Gorman pointed out: "In many ways, it's easier to get a big bill than a little one. With big bills, the issue is posed, the objective is clearly important, and there is very likely going to be a decision one way or the other. With little bills like this óne you go around and talk to people, they say they're all for it, but they haven't got the time to do anything. They have to worry about aid to education, or medicare." The interest of the Kennedy administration "put this legislation in the big leagues."

## Executive-Legislative Conflict over Program

Three years after the Juvenile Delinquency and Youth Offenses Control Act of 1961 was signed into law, the House of Representatives voted to extend the program for an additional two years. As reported by the *Washington Post* on June 17, 1964, "No attempt was made to defeat the bill, but friends and critics alike complained that the 3-year program which expires in two weeks has been too long on planning and too short on action." In fact, House approval of a limited extension climaxed two years of bitter argument over congressional intent. The struggle affords a revealing illustration of congressional involvement in administration.

*Executive Refinements as the Program Takes Shape.* When the administration bill was drafted in the spring of 1961, responsibility for administering the act was lodged with the secretary of HEW, but he was directed to "consult with the President's Committee on matters of general policy and procedure. . . ." It was informally understood that the policy judgments of the President's Committee would be controlling. The danger that conflict might develop between HEW and the President's Committee was minimized by locating the Office of Juvenile Delinquency and Youth Development (OJD) in the office of the secretary of HEW, and by placing at its head the man David Hackett had turned to for professional guidance, Lloyd Ohlin. The development of a top-heavy staff in the secretary's office was avoided by distributing juvenile delinquency personnel among HEW line agencies, including the Office of Education and the Children's Bureau. A few people in the Department of Labor were also detailed to juvenile delinquency work. The major staff, however, was attached to the President's Committee. There could be little doubt that David Hackett was in charge of the juvenile delinquency program; and, as one participant later remarked, "Because of the Attorney General's virtual identification with the President, and Hackett's association with the Attorney General, this program was administered with a freer hand than 99 out of 100 other Kennedy programs."[5]

The seeds of controversy with Congress were sown when David Hackett first subscribed to the "opportunity theory" formulated by Lloyd

[5] Even after a major reorganization of HEW's welfare activities in 1963 moved the Office of Juvenile Delinquency from the secretary's office to a newly created Welfare Administration headed by Dr. Ellen Winston, Hackett retained control. As commissioner of welfare for North Carolina Dr. Winston had been troubled by the fragmentation of responsibility for administering welfare programs at the federal level; neither her background nor her new assignment promised much sympathy for the free-wheeling approach of the President's Committee. But she was in no position to challenge the attorney general by a proposal to alter the committee's structure or its style of operation.

Ohlin. The early legislative proposals had contemplated federal aid for research and demonstration projects designed to develop and test a number of specific approaches to juvenile delinquency control. Subjects for investigation frequently cited by Chairman Edith Green of the House Special Education Subcommittee included the early identification of potential delinquents, the use of former delinquents to reach the unrepentant, the impact of school dropouts, and the laws affecting the employment of minors. What Mrs. Green and several of her subcommittee colleagues sought primarily was the rapid implementation of such specific and discrete experimental approaches. The President's Committee, on the other hand, was most interested in integrating isolated programs in a few communities; short-term benefits stemming from individual projects would be incidental.

The "discrete," "limited," or "special" projects may be contrasted with the "total attack" advocated by President Kennedy in his letter accompanying the administration's draft bill of 1961 and presumably incorporated in the preamble through language calling for "intensive and coordinated efforts on the part of private and governmental interests." In retrospect, David Hackett might justifiably view the preamble's reference to coordination as a significant amplification of the congressional mandate. But coordination had been a consistent and prominent objective of juvenile delinquency legislation ever since 1955. There is no reason why this reference should have particularly impressed members of Congress, or—even if it had—why it should have been seen as conflicting with the discrete projects they had in mind.

As the President's Committee began to implement the program, however, it became increasingly apparent that its concern with effective coordination and comprehensive planning would overshadow the individual projects that were of principal interest to the House Special Education Subcommittee. In his statement in September 1961 to the Senate subcommittee for HEW appropriations, Assistant Secretary Wilbur Cohen made clear the administration's emphasis:

> The most urgent need in the field of delinquency prevention is to show what a fully mobilized community can do to control its delinquency problem. We need several communities where we can demonstrate what effective coordination of service means and what a truly effective prevention program should have. There are very promising projects in many communities throughout the country which deal with some part of the total delinquency problem. . . . We can find no single community where all of these desirable programs have been brought together to demonstrate what a complete program can do.

The Federal Government can provide leadership, "seed money," and technical assistance in creating a number of such model community programs. . . .

Each community undertaking a major demonstration effort will be encouraged to create a comprehensive "community development plan for delinquency prevention." Technical assistance services will be made available to these communities in developing their plans and bringing about the necessary coordination. . . .

The underlying reasoning was expressed this way by an HEW official in 1964:

> The President's Committee . . . proceeded on the assumption that past efforts directed at changing the delinquent—instilling him with middle class values and aspirations, then telling him to go out and do good—have proved ineffective. What is the use of trying to change the values of the delinquent if the environment that made him a delinquent remains the same—if he continues to live in a slum area, if payments made to him so that he can participate in juvenile delinquency projects are offset by deductions from his parents' welfare allotments, if the schools fail to take into account his lack of preparation and motivation from the kindergarten grade on up, if they train him for jobs that will have been automated away by the time he is ready to enter the job market, etc.?
>
> While the juvenile delinquency program cannot itself wholly finance projects in all these areas, it can use the money available to finance community planning efforts aimed at bringing together the public and private agencies that are concerned with each of them, and then make a substantial contribution to an action program that coordinates the activities of these formerly independent groups. It is in this sense that the administration conceives its programs as involving a "seed money" approach—not simply in the sense of developing some new techniques which, upon being proved successful, will be widely adopted.

These views resulted in an almost exclusive emphasis by the committee on coordination and comprehensive planning. As outlined in its first report to the President in May 1962, the criteria for award of demonstration project grants called for a "comprehensive attack on the sources of delinquency. [This] means coordinating a broad combination of social services and related resources. The idea is not only to combat the pressures which urge youth toward delinquent behavior, but to create the opportunities that are essential, if these young people are to realize creative and productive lives." Since careful planning was viewed as "an essential prerequisite" to a comprehensive program, initial emphasis was to be placed on "planning demonstrations," which were expected to outnumber action grants by a ratio of about three to one.

As a corollary to its encouragement of integrated programs capable of covering the multiple causes of delinquent behavior, the committee stressed the importance of "mobilizing sufficient authority for organizational change behind the planning process." Its report stated:

> Planning an effective prevention program may require pervasive changes—changes which reorganize existing youth services and create new ones. Inevitably many organizational or personal investments in the community will be affected. These interests need to be represented and to participate for the planning process to succeed. They must lend authority and support to the changes contemplated by the planning operation. No planning organization can hope for success if it lacks sufficient authority or excludes sources of community influence whose support is mandatory if the necessary social changes are to be achieved.

Two years after the above report was submitted, a member of the OJD staff described what the administration's concern with mobilizing authority for organizational change entailed:

> [It] goes well beyond the formal involvement of related groups and services. Efforts are made to identify the power structure of a given community—who wields political influence, who controls the purse strings, who determines educational policy—and then to achieve a cooperative approach that integrates the activities of the power wielders and the professional social workers. Not only must the plan recognize the need for such integration—the people who will implement it must have a good idea of what they will do if trouble develops. The screening panels, for example, may ask proponents of a plan what they would do if such and such a community influential refused to cooperate.

This ambitious attempt to rearrange the community power structure bearing upon the administration of social welfare programs forced the President's Committee to concentrate its energies on community liaison. As Attorney General Kennedy's spokesman, David Hackett provided the symbol of political power necessary to gain access to political notables in the community; Don Ellinger, a former regional director of the AFL-CIO's committee on political education who joined the staff in the spring of 1962, tempered Hackett's raw power with political finesse; and Lloyd Ohlin supplied the credentials of professional competence. Reflecting on the committee's apparent (and surprising) success in mobilizing community support for juvenile delinquency demonstration projects, Hackett commented that

> one of the main problems in administering this program was to marry the academician and the practitioner, the professional and the politician. The need for an experienced politician to perform a kind of brokerage function

among these different groups is why Don Ellinger was brought in. The reason we were successful was our access to and judicious use of power, in combination with the advice of bright professionals. Ohlin was the brain, I was the agent of power, and Ellinger was the politician.

*Congressional Opposition Aroused.* During his first few months with the President's Committee, Don Ellinger did not devote any of his mediating talents to congressional liaison. Since the subcommittee members who would have a continuing interest in the program were assumed to be sympathetic with its objectives, no one was specifically designated to handle congressional relations. A tenuous link to Congresswoman Green's office was maintained through periodic communications with her administrative assistant, but no effort was made to familiarize her with the controversial approach that was being taken. There is unanimous agreement among the participants that they made a basic mistake in failing to keep Mrs. Green fully informed.

Differing explanations are advanced for this lapse. One staff member of the President's Committee contends that "we just didn't do our homework. . . . We assumed that [Mrs. Green] was pleased with the bill, and that she liked the people who were administering it. We viewed her as a friend rather than a potential enemy. We knew that HEW would be unhappy with our approach, but we didn't anticipate any trouble with Mrs. Green." Oversight may have been a significant factor, but in retrospect Hackett offered a less ingenuous explanation: "This was partly a calculated risk that didn't pay off. The danger of not too deeply involving members of Congress was whether we could get away with it. We had run into lots of trouble in the communities, and had nothing really to show in support of our approach. But it was a mistake—if I had it to do over, I would try to explain to Mrs. Green what we were doing."

By the spring of 1962 Representative Green had begun to receive a few complaints from disappointed applicants for project grants. She also learned—from a newspaper article, rather than from the President's Committee—that sixteen planning grants were about to be awarded. Since administration witnesses before her subcommittee had contemplated demonstration grants to no more than five or six communities, Mrs. Green was disturbed by the larger figure mentioned in the newspaper article. She asked David Hackett to come up and explain the discrepancy, and during their conversation he said several things that converted her mild concern into genuine apprehension.

As Mrs. Green recalled, the meeting got off to a bad start when Hackett justified the award of sixteen planning grants by arguing that if the money had not been committed during the fiscal year, it would have reverted back to the Treasury. Failing to perceive Mrs. Green's unhappiness with this explanation, Hackett proceeded to compound his error with the assertion that the President's Committee contemplated a total of twenty-six planning grants, in anticipation of a campaign for extension of the program: grants to twenty-six communities would presumably increase the administration's leverage with Congress. Since the program still had two years to run under the original legislation, Mrs. Green saw in this statement the first indication "that politics was a predominant concern in administering the juvenile delinquency project."

Hackett had clearly misjudged this woman. As one observer remarked, "He could have said the same things to Adam Clayton Powell and got nothing more than an understanding nod, but Mrs. Green hit the ceiling." Mrs. Green's growing suspicion that grants were being made exclusively for political purposes was confirmed during the same conversation by Hackett's specific reference to a project proposal sponsored by the city of Portland in her own district. An accurate understanding of this crowning error requires some background on the policy for reviewing project applications.

The juvenile delinquency staff acknowledged that some members of the President's Committee had made political commitments during the campaign, and that these and other political considerations were taken into account in awarding demonstration grants. Technical review panels were established to keep these considerations from subverting the objectives of the program, and particular care was taken in reviewing "political" grants in order to guard against the possibility that the professional panel members might themselves become so entranced with the opportunity to use political muscle in implementing the program that they would slacken their standards. According to Hackett, a total of three political grants were awarded; the communities involved had to meet the same criteria as other applicants, but they enjoyed preferred access. Hackett recalled that two of these were promised in return for congressional support of other HEW proposals. The third grant—to the city of Providence, in Congressman John Fogarty's district—had both political and professional support.

Political considerations were made to conform to professional objectives, but they were clearly present. Among them was a desire not to offend key members of Congress by rejecting, out-of-hand, poor proposals submitted by communities located within their constituencies. One such proposal had been submitted by the city of Portland, Oregon, and rather than flatly rejecting it, the Office of Juvenile Delinquency was providing technical assistance, trying to "bring it along" to the point where it would qualify for a grant. As David Hackett prepared to leave the meeting with Mrs. Green, which he later called "a disaster," he mentioned the Portland project, leaving the impression that it could be funded if Mrs. Green so desired. This gesture simply reinforced her belief that the administrators of the program were more concerned with politics than with juvenile delinquency.

Following her conversation with Hackett, Mrs. Green met with the majority members of the Special Education Subcommittee, still hoping to iron things out privately. They decided to ask for a meeting with the President's Committee, presumably to determine if Hackett's attitude was representative. The meeting was held in July 1962. In addition to the majority members of the subcommittee (Mrs. Green, Neal Smith of Iowa, Robert N. Giaimo of Connecticut, and John Brademas of Indiana) the participants included Anthony J. Celebrezze, the newly appointed secretary of Health, Education, and Welfare; David Hackett, in his dual capacity as executive director of the President's Committee and spokesman for Attorney General Kennedy; Bernard Russell, director of the Office of Juvenile Delinquency; and several staff members of the President's Committee. It was an unhappy occasion for all concerned: program personnel were stunned by the force of Mrs. Green's criticism; subcommittee members, with the exception of John Brademas, were dismayed by the program's commitment to an approach that they viewed as a departure from congressional intent; and Secretary Celebrezze, who had barely begun to acquaint himself with the program, was thoroughly confused.

According to one of the HEW officials present, the President's Committee agreed at this time to award no more planning grants. Mrs. Green, however, could recall no immediate response to her criticism: "The attitude of the President's Committee was one of impatience with our criticism. Rather than listening to what we had to say, they spent their time defending what had been done." Mrs. Green left this meeting deeply impressed by the arrogance of the President's Committee: "They evidently felt it was Congress' job to pass the bill, and theirs to administer it."

Mrs. Green's impression that no immediate action was taken to curtail planning grants may have stemmed from the subsequent award of one or two grants that had been conditionally approved at the time the moratorium was imposed. This apparent discrepancy may also have contributed to the harsh criticism Neal Smith later directed at the program. Prior to the moratorium, the Office of Juvenile Delinquency had had some contact with Smith in connection with what it considered to be a poor project proposal submitted by the city of Des Moines. Smith was told that the proposal would require a lot of work before it could qualify, and he seemed to understand and agree. Then came the meeting described above, and the agreement not to make any more planning grants. Des Moines was among the projects washed out, but no one explained the reason for this to Smith, nor why the Providence project, which had been conditionally accepted, was approved several months after the moratorium.[6]

Two of the four majority members of the Special Education Subcommittee thus shifted from support of the juvenile delinquency program to either vigorous criticism or outright opposition. The defection of a third member, Robert Giaimo, apparently stemmed in part from local political considerations and in part from an unforeseen lapse in protocol. According to an administration official Giaimo had hoped to use the New Haven project, Community Progress, Inc., to strengthen the position of his partisans in the continuing struggle between the Irish and Italian factions that characterizes Democratic politics in New Haven. Mitchell Sviridoff, executive director of Community Progress, had submitted a sophisticated project proposal that was among the first to be funded under the Juvenile Delinquency Act. Approval of the grant happened to coincide with HEW Secretary Ribicoff's announcement of his candidacy for

[6] This incident does not fully explain the vehement attack Smith eventually directed at the entire program. At the April 1963 hearings on extending the program Smith had more general grounds for indicting the President's Committee:

"The intent of Congress was that you find some projects and you haul off and try them, you determine which ones will work, and there is actual value in finding out which ones will not work. That was the intent of Congress.

"It seems to me that the criteria you have set up and the way you have administered it, go exactly contrary to that. . . . Although I supported the bill before, if there is not a great improvement in administration, I just think I am going to have to oppose an extension rather than support it.

"The testimony here this morning seems to indicate that you not only do not intend to try to comply with the intent of Congress, you do not believe the intent of Congress is right and you are going to go ahead just like you have."

the Senate. The day he was to declare his candidacy he indicated to the Office of Juvenile Delinquency his intention of including an announcement of the grant to be awarded New Haven. When the OJD protested that the order had not yet been signed by the secretary, Ribicoff simply signed it. As a result of this last minute approval, Giaimo was neither informed of nor included in the announcement. (The OJD profited from this experience, and subsequently made certain that announcements were coordinated with the congressmen in whose districts the grants were awarded.) This episode certainly did not help strengthen ties between the juvenile delinquency program and Giaimo, but OJD officials felt that the real break came later, when Sviridoff and New Haven Mayor Richard C. Lee resisted Giaimo's efforts to place some of his supporters on the Community Progress staff. According to one possibly apocryphal story, Giaimo was told that "the only place we could put the people you've been sending us is in the illiteracy project—and it wouldn't be on the staff." The final blow was struck when the Office of Juvenile Delinquency refused to appoint to its staff a man sent down by Giaimo who failed to meet civil service requirements.

From the administration's standpoint some friends of the program remained friends throughout the two-year struggle for extension—Brademas and Fogarty, for example. Others, however, were severely shaken by Mrs. Green's criticism, which was difficult to refute in the abstract. Results, in the form of a startling new approach or a reduced rate of juvenile delinquency, are much easier to sell than planning and coordination. Because of her deep interest and reputed expertise in the area Mrs. Green could be very difficult to argue with. Moreover, her ability to cite personal knowledge of particular projects made her an effective "switch hitter." During House debate on the extension, when Republicans H. R. Gross of Iowa and Peter Frelinghuysen of New Jersey were making political hay out of Adam Clayton Powell's involvement in a controversy over patronage control of two Harlem projects, Mrs. Green could respond, "I went up and visited the program in central Harlem. I think even then, about a year and a half ago, there were 200 young people who were actually working in these slum areas. . . . In regard to this particular matter, I think it has been carried out by professional people." Her knowledge of the strengths and weaknesses of specific projects could be used with equal facility against subcommittee members who attempted to defend the program.

In addition, the administration felt that she marshalled support for her position by "enormously skillful" manipulation of her subcommittee members. The trouble with Giaimo was cited as an illustration. In this case she presumably capitalized on the dissatisfaction of someone not nearly as interested in the program itself as she was, and gave him shelter for critical public statements under the umbrella of departure from congressional intent. The administration saw her wielding the seniority power of a subcommittee chairman over freshman Democratic members like Sam M. Gibbons of Florida and Carlton R. Sickles of Maryland, or distributing favors to gain the support of other members. Democrat James Roosevelt of California was supposedly neutralized by a legislative trade-out. Republican Charles E. Goodell of New York, whose attitude toward the program had previously been "very positive," was anxious to have a vocational training center established in his district, so Mrs. Green included the provision of such centers in an early amendment to the proposed extension that was subsequently dropped. Albert H. Quie of Minnesota and Robert P. Griffin of Michigan, the other two minority members of the subcommittee, were especially interested in laws affecting the employment of minors, so another amendment directed the secretary of HEW to "make a special study of the compulsory school attendance laws and of the laws and regulations affecting the employment of minors. . . ."

It should be emphasized that the preceding account describes what the administration *believed* it was facing. The hazards of accepting these perceptions at face value are indicated, for example, by a quite different explanation of the origin of the amendment relating to the employment of minors. As early as 1961 Mrs. Green had suggested that employment regulations might have an important bearing on juvenile delinquency. According to her administrative assistant, A. Wesley Barthelmes, Jr., this interest was reawakened in the summer of 1963 in a way that is illustrative of the casual manner in which legislative proposals may arise. Jack Goldberg, director of Washington Action for Youth, had come to discuss the juvenile delinquency project in the District of Columbia. In describing efforts to improve employment opportunities he mentioned that sixteen- and seventeen-year-old girls were having trouble getting jobs in local department stores because they were prohibited by law from working after 6 p.m. This started Representatives Green and Goodell thinking more generally about possibly antiquated legal obstacles to juvenile employment, and led to the amendment quoted above. During House debate of the extension Goodell specifically referred to the amendment as "my proposal."

*Mrs. Green's Substantive Objections.* Many factors contributed to
Mrs. Green's opposition to the way the administration was handling the
juvenile delinquency program. Her impression that the President's Committee was acting from political considerations in its emphasis on and
distribution of planning grants initially aroused her concern, but she
also became greatly distressed at the committee's focus on a comprehensive approach: "What I had in mind, and what I believe is in the
record, is a number of experimental projects, such as the controlled
group experiment sponsored by the 'Back Yards' program in Chicago,
using professionals in one group and rehabilitated delinquents in another; the early identification of potential delinquents; the increased
study of biochemical factors that may influence behavior in the adoles-
cent stage; the anchoring of a ship near slum areas for recreation purposes, and so forth. I surely wasn't thinking of what they refer to in the
profession today as 'the thirty million dollar test of Ohlin's opportunity
theory.' " From Mrs. Green's perspective the legislation was barely adequate to train some new personnel and develop some new approaches:
"We didn't intend to try to achieve any social reform, and we certainly
didn't expect to do it with a $10 million a year appropriation."[7]

The local political cooperation that a comprehensive approach seemed
to require disturbed her too, as can be seen in the following exchange
with OJD Director Bernard Russell during the April 1963 hearings:

GREEN: Does the law require that you deal with the governmental head,
or did you have authority to deal with any group or public or private agency?

RUSSELL: [The latter], but the law explicitly refers to extensive and coordinated efforts on the part of private and governmental interests. To
achieve the coordination of governmental interests, it is almost essential to
get the active cooperation of the governmental head in a particular community. . . .

GREEN: Do you really believe that you could not make progress on any
demonstration project unless you had the cooperation of the political head
of the city? Do you really believe that?

RUSSELL: Yes, Madam Chairman, I do.

Mrs. Green was also disturbed by delays in the District of Columbia

[7] Regarding the feasibility of accomplishing community reform with modest appropriations, a member of the President's Committee staff argues that "you can do more in the
way of genuine social reform in a small program. Too many concessions are necessary to
get Congressional approval of a big program. A big bill would have attracted more objections based on federalism prior to passage, and more pressure for money afterwards. If
some communities won't cooperate, you don't want them in, and if you have more money
to dispense, you can't keep them out. Moreover, there is little possibility of getting sufficient qualified personnel to administer a large program."

project, particularly in view of the clear indications of special congressional interest in such a project. But departures from congressional intent were not the only aspects of the program that troubled her. When the administration did approve relatively modest experimental projects of the kind Congress had in mind, it sometimes appeared that she was as much concerned with the nature of the innovation as with the scope of the project.

For example, Mrs. Green had specifically cited a proposal to anchor ships near slum areas for recreational uses as illustrative of the sort of projects she contemplated. Mobilization for Youth came up with what would seem to be an imaginative adaptation of this device to the environment of New York City's lower east side. They bought and refurbished a former night club, attempting to preserve the original atmosphere so that it would be attractive to the delinquent youth they were trying to rehabilitate. Mrs. Green approved, until she discovered that admission to the club was restricted to members of a certain gang who had succeeded in kicking the narcotics habit. She later explained that "It seemed to us that this was a method of rewarding the gang members, making gang membership more attractive and in effect penalizing the youngsters who, out of choice, sought other friendships than within the gangs. It also seemed a paradox that they were trying to cut down on gang memberships and yet by requiring membership in the gang they were, in fact, recruiting members. . . ." According to a member of her staff, however, "That night club business was a little wild for Mrs. Green and some other members of the subcommittee. They were really looking for innovation within a conventional framework."

This observation is especially noteworthy because it corresponds with an assessment of the substantive basis of the conflict between Mrs. Green and the administration advanced by a member of the President's Committee staff. His view, slightly paraphrased, was that

Mrs. Green really wanted a regular grant-in-aid program [this had been the principal objective of early legislative proposals submitted by both Mrs. Green and President Eisenhower], but she found too much objection in the House to this kind of extension of the Federal government's role, and so tried to sell the program under the labels of "leadership" and "innovation." The influential social scientists like Lloyd Ohlin, on the other hand, became interested in the program because of the opportunity it afforded for *real* innovation—comprehensive planning and coordination or, if you will, social reform. These divergent objectives were temporarily brought together in the ambiguous wording of the law, which—because the ideas of reform and leadership had to be included by Mrs. Green in order to sell her traditional approach—actually comes closer to reflecting the goals of the social scientists.

***

We had to be cautious about our description of these goals [however] because most Congressmen find it somewhat frightening to be told that the school system, the physical environment, job opportunities, etc., all have something to do with juvenile delinquency. So Mrs. Green's conception of the problem and of Congressional intent in dealing with it was quite different from that of the administration.

Mrs. Green had made clear her displeasure with the program's emphasis on planning and a comprehensive approach as early as 1962. With two years remaining in which to recapture her support before the law expired, why did the President's Committee fail to meet her objections?

One obstacle was the difficulty of achieving any effective communication. The technical jargon employed by the professional staff members who attempted to explain the program simply did not register with Mrs. Green. After observing a meeting of the committee's technical review panel, she reportedly commented to a member of her staff that "I just couldn't make sense of what they were saying."[8] Mrs. Green's attempt to communicate subcommittee expectations in layman's terms was no more successful. Following the April 1963 hearings on the proposed extension of the program, the director of the Office of Juvenile Delinquency had several conversations with Mrs. Green. He hoped to allay her suspicion that political concerns governed administration of the program, to explain the administration's conception of program objectives, and—perhaps most importantly—to understand what kinds of alternative projects Mrs. Green had in mind. The result was mutually frustrating: "She wasn't won over to the administration's viewpoint, but neither did she clearly articulate her own viewpoint. Many of the projects she used for illustrative purposes—early identification, roving leaders, half-way houses—were already being supported by the National Institute of Mental Health."

If Mrs. Green was indeed looking for *new* techniques, this would by definition exclude existing projects, and make difficult any very precise description of alternatives. So long as the professional enjoys the layman's confidence, the communications gap between laymen in Congress

[8] Mrs. Green, after reviewing the manuscript of this case in draft, challenged this interpretation: "This is in error. My criticism was based on the fact that the review panels came to Washington for one or two days, went over voluminous amounts of material that had been screened by the staff prior to their coming to Washington and that because of the limited time no really independent valid judgments could be made. As a matter of fact, members of the review panels came to my office and voiced the same self-criticism."

and experts in the executive branch is not especially important. Once that confidence has been lost, however, the layman is unwilling to let the expert proceed independently, and is frequently unable to specify alternative approaches.

With respect to planning grants, the administrators contend that they responded promptly to Mrs. Green's criticism by declaring a moratorium covering all but a few proposals that had already been conditionally approved. The subsequent award of these pending grants may account for Mrs. Green's impression of a "totally negative response" following the July 1962 meeting with the President's Committee. So far as planning grants were concerned Mrs. Green's criticism apparently achieved the desired result, but the administration failed to make this clear to her.[9]

Revision of the administration's comprehensive approach posed more difficult problems. There was a natural reluctance to abandon the professional commitment around which the juvenile delinquency program had been built, but the most inflexible commitment was financial. According to Hackett, "after 1962 we didn't really have any money for discrete projects. We set aside $500,000 in our minds, but we had obligations and commitments to 16 communities which had received planning grants. We gambled in awarding 16 grants with so little money available." The gamble hinged upon the expectation of obtaining an extension of the program that would enable the administration to make good the commitment for demonstration grants implied in the award of planning grants. As Hackett learned during his "disastrous" first conversation with Mrs. Green in the spring of 1962, there was a real possibility that the gamble might not pay off. The original authorization would then have to be stretched to cover qualified project proposals resulting from an inflated number of planning grants, "and the review panel found between 6 and 8 demonstration projects—rather than the projected 5—which seemed promising." This left little money for the development of the discrete projects that, paradoxically, appeared to be a prerequisite for Mrs. Green's support of the program's extension.

[9] From HEW's standpoint the objection to the number of planning grants awarded or anticipated may have had greater merit than could be officially acknowledged. The 1962 moratorium came at a time when the program was in some danger of overextending itself by commissioning more projects than it could possibly hope to fund if a satisfactory action proposal resulted from the planning grant. The agreement with Mrs. Green provided a convenient excuse for refusing applications that would have been rejected in any event, or if accepted for political reasons, would have committed more resources than were available. With the moratorium some of the burden of responsibility for these rejections could be shifted from the President's Committee to the House subcommittee.

Moreover, according to the director of the OJD:

> While we did set aside $500,000 during that first year to fund discrete projects, we were concentrating so intensively on the comprehensive projects that we failed to shake a man loose to handle them. And then we hoped that some components of comprehensive projects, together with a few planning projects that weren't comprehensive, would satisfy her requirements. I don't know how we could have kidded ourselves into believing that this would be enough. There was no conscious abrogation of the agreement, but there was a failure to concentrate on the kinds of projects Mrs. Green had in mind.

The political vulnerability of a comprehensive approach was underlined at the outset of subcommittee hearings on the proposed extension. Reading a prepared statement, Director Russell of the OJD noted that "if annual funding were continued in 1964 and no extension granted, it would mean that only one demonstration project can be carried to completion." Mrs. Green picked up this remark, determined that the project was Mobilization for Youth, pointed out that it had been initiated in 1957, and observed: "then the only one, according to your testimony, that could be carried to completion would be the one that was started approximately 4 years before this bill was passed and made a law." Near the end of the day she added: "I am concerned to find that a year and a half later we have spent millions on plans and programs, and that apparently not one dime has gone for the people who really are working with juvenile delinquents."

In summary, Mrs. Green's criticism focused on three substantive features of the juvenile delinquency program: its concentration on a comprehensive approach, which she equated with social reform; its emphasis on planning at the expense of action projects; and the administrative requirement of local political cooperation. Among the program's major errors of omission, from Mrs. Green's viewpoint, were its failure to initiate a project in the District of Columbia, despite clear indications of Congress' special interest in a D.C. project, and its inability to demonstrate any discernible impact on the incidence of juvenile delinquency. Wesley Barthelmes, Mrs. Green's administrative assistant, summed up the divergent premises of the administration and Congress in these words:

> Congress expected more tangible results—as in urban renewal, where you can point to the number of slums torn down and new buildings raised, it was hoped that there might be a reduction in the rate of juvenile crime. While this might have been recognized as wishful thinking, the expectation was still there. On the other hand, there was a feeling downtown that this

wouldn't *really* be a temporary program—that like the temporary buildings scattered all over Washington, it would be continued, and that it would therefore be wise to require careful planning, and a comprehensive approach which in the long run could be expected to yield the best results.

*Personal and Political Aspects of Mrs. Green's Opposition.* In addition to the basic disagreement over the substantive features of the juvenile delinquency program, there were other reasons for Mrs. Green's opposition. The juvenile delinquency program was closely identified with the Kennedy administration and, through Attorney General Kennedy's active role in its enactment and administration, with the President himself. Mrs. Green had been among the first prominent members of the Democratic party to publicly support John F. Kennedy's bid for the presidential nomination, and she had looked forward to a close relationship with the President following his election. Her confrontation with members of the President's Committee in July 1962 happened to coincide with what administration officials later construed to be one of several disappointments in this regard—the appointment of Anthony Celebrezze to succeed Abraham Ribicoff as secretary of Health, Education, and Welfare. Throughout her career in Congress Mrs. Green had concentrated on policy issues falling within the purview of HEW. While she may not have expected to be offered the appointment herself—as many in Washington believed—she might reasonably have expected to be consulted about it. She was not consulted and, in the view of staff members of the President's Committee reconstructing events relating to the July meeting, she considered the choice of Celebrezze a transparent bid for the Italian vote, reinforcing her growing concern about the partisan political orientation of the Kennedy administration. From their viewpoint her criticism of the juvenile delinquency program was magnified by Celebrezze's involvement, and by what his appointment represented in terms of her relationship with the President.

The discrepancy between the perceptions of Mrs. Green and administration officials is exemplified by the fact that Mrs. Green thoroughly discounts these expectations and responses attributed to her. Since the preceding appraisal rests to some extent upon a presumed coincidence, it should also be noted that she had known for some weeks prior to the July meeting that she would not receive the HEW appointment, having been so informed at a White House meeting with the President.

Whether or not the program's fortunes were affected by any falling-out between Mrs. Green and the Kennedy administration, David Hackett's initial approach did not improve the atmosphere. According to one observer (a friend), "Hackett was inexperienced in legislative-executive relationships, he had no professional background, his political experience was pretty much limited to presidential campaigning, and he was still riding the cloud of the New Frontier, along with many others—the world was theirs, and they were quick to let people know it." Hackett subsequently tempered his reactions and approach and developed a cordial relationship with Mrs. Green, but at a critical juncture in the campaign for extension of the juvenile delinquency program, both friends and critics used the same word to describe his attitude toward her —"arrogant."[10]

For Mrs. Green, David Hackett's behavior was symptomatic of the administration's patronizing attitude toward Congress, and the juvenile delinquency program illustrative of the administration's preoccupation with political objectives. When Hackett appeared before her subcommittee in April 1963, she concluded the hearing by remarking: "I was much disturbed when I read in the paper last week there was a mutuality of contempt between the Legislative and Executive Branches. I assure you that as far as the Legislative Branch is concerned, this is not true. . . . Maybe I do not speak for everyone, but let me say I know I speak for the majority, and the majority of us are deeply concerned about the way this program has been administered."

Mrs. Green was first alerted to the juvenile delinquency program's political orientation by David Hackett's justification of additional planning grants on the ground that they would broaden the base of support for extension. She was disturbed by this apparent confusion of means and ends, but not nearly as disturbed as she was to become over what impressed her as the calculated manipulation of the program to strengthen the political underpinnings of the Kennedy administration. From Mrs. Green's viewpoint planning and demonstration grants were awarded to large urban communities not because they were the principal sources of juvenile crime, but because "that is where the votes are." She also saw a

[10] By 1964 Hackett's relationship with Mrs. Green had improved to the point that both were able to joke about the "arrogance" that had earlier contributed to her disaffection. When a young lawyer working on the poverty bill met with Hackett and OJD Director Bernard Russell, his intolerance of criticism visibly pained Hackett, who finally leaned over to Russell and whispered, "Now I know what you had to put up with." This same young man, when later informed of an amendment that the Education and Labor Committee intended to offer, replied, "We won't accept that," Mrs. Green burst into laughter and exclaimed, "Shades of Dave Hackett!"

political explanation for the administration's delay in making a grant to the District of Columbia: "There aren't any votes in the District."

The final count in Mrs. Green's indictment was directed at the "political pressure" exerted by the administration on herself, members of her committee, and witnesses appearing before her subcommittee during the spring 1963 hearings. She remarked at one point in the hearings that "I do not recall in the nine years in which I have been in Congress that I have received as much political pressure because I have raised questions about a program as I have on this one." Her impression is corroborated by a staff member of the President's Committee—who would of course take exception to the word "pressure": "This program was probably more congressionally active than any Kennedy administration program, with the possible exception of the domestic peace corps proposal. There was certainly more activity over the juvenile delinquency extension than over the poverty program. . . . We talked to every member of the committee, and to every potentially influential member of the House."

Because Mrs. Green personified congressional interest in juvenile delinquency and was in a position to determine whether or not congressional support of the 1961 program would continue, the preceding analysis focused on factors contributing to her alienation. It should be emphasized, however, that her views were shared by a number of her fellow congressmen. And, as the analysis indicated, the sources of congressional displeasure were both varied and complex.

## A Successful Campaign for the 1964 Extension

*Defense of the 1964 Appropriations.* In the spring of 1963 an effort was made to reduce juvenile delinquency program appropriations for fiscal 1964. The attack was spearheaded by former Special Education Subcommittee members Neal Smith and Robert Giaimo, both of whom had moved to the Appropriations Committee. When Mrs. Green scheduled the Special Education Subcommittee for April hearings on extension of the program she invited Giaimo and Smith to participate. The hearings provided a convenient forum for developing criticism aimed at the appropriations request. Nonetheless, when the House took up the appropriations bill on April 30 the anticipated move to cut the juvenile delinquency program did not materialize. Before the House clerk reached that provision of the bill Democratic Congressman Charles A. Vanik of

Ohio found an opportunity to commend Subcommittee Chairman John Fogarty "for making necessary allocations for programs under the authority of the Juvenile Delinquency Control Act," and Democrat Roman C. Pucinski of Illinois remarked that he was "very pleased to see that apparently no effort will be made to reduce the appropriations to carry on the work outlined in the Juvenile Delinquency Control Act of 1961. We had heard reports that an effort would be made to reduce this year's appropriations of $6.7 million by 2¼ million."[11]

Smith and Giaimo used the debate on the appropriations bill to warn "that a close look should be taken at the authorizing legislation when [it comes] up for an extension next year with a view to either changing it or not extending it." But they did not press for the cut in 1964 funds. Giaimo's explanation was graceful, but not altogether persuasive:

> As a member of the Appropriations Committee, it was my thought that the people dealing with juvenile delinquency could get along with somewhat less than the money which was given to them by the committee. However, having a great deal of respect for and confidence in the chairman and the subcommittee, I shall abide by the wishes of the full committee and I shall not offer an amendment at this time to reduce the amount of money for the juvenile delinquency program.

Mrs. Green had a different explanation: "There was terrific pressure from the administration on Giaimo and Smith." If the administration did in fact exert direct pressure on Giaimo and Smith, it was insufficient to dissuade them from seeking a 30 percent reduction in juvenile delinquency funds when the HEW bill came before the full Appropriations Committee. There the motion was opposed by Congressman Fogarty, and defeated by a five to one margin. A handful of critics on the committee were no match for Fogarty's personal prestige and the deference customarily accorded to the subcommittee chairman. Mrs. Green later indicated that if an amendment had been offered on the floor she probably would have voted for curtailment of the appropriations. But Smith and Giaimo did not offer an amendment because, according to Congressman Fogarty, "they didn't have the votes."

The burden of defending the juvenile delinquency program at the Special Education Subcommittee hearings was borne by Congressman Brademas. At Robert Kennedy's request Brademas cancelled a visit to his district in anticipation of testimony that the administration believed

---

[11] Vanik and Pucinski represented portions of Cleveland and Chicago respectively. Both cities were recipients of planning or action grants under the juvenile delinquency program.

would be aimed directly at the program's pending appropriations. The vehicle for this attack was George Von Hilsheimer, a board member of Mobilization for Youth known to be critical of that particular project and the juvenile delinquency program generally. Von Hilsheimer had dealt with the President's Committee before, in connection with an unsuccessful project proposal submitted by the Fund for Migrant Children in Fort Pierce, Florida. His description of that experience directly supported some of Mrs. Green's earlier criticisms:

> We were told by the Committee that our proposal failed to meet its criteria for several reasons. First of all, it was a small town, and grants were not being given in small towns, despite the fact that the greatest increase in juvenile delinquency in the past 10 years has been in the small town setting. We were told, as well, that our program could not be considered unless it had the full involvement of all social agencies in cooperation in this area.

Congressman Brademas was sympathetic with the administration's comprehensive approach, and might have been critical of Von Hilsheimer's testimony simply on substantive grounds, but his conviction that Von Hilsheimer had been planted for the express purpose of sabotaging the program's appropriations request moved him to attack the witness rather than his testimony. Brademas later remarked that "this left a bad taste in my mouth, but if they wanted to play dirty, that's the only way to fight it." From Mrs. Green's perspective this "character assassination" was symptomatic of the raw political approach employed by the President's Committee. Mrs. Green says she chose Von Hilsheimer because he was associated with Mobilization for Youth and was therefore in a position to offer informed criticism. "Apparently he had some time ago written a book endorsing homosexuality or something of the sort, and during the hearing Hackett was feeding the lurid details about this fellow's past to Brademas, to be used to discredit his testimony." The Von Hilsheimer episode, in which Representatives Brademas and Green played equally uncomfortable roles, is indicative of the extent to which relations between the President's Committee and Mrs. Green had deteriorated by the spring of 1963.

Although sparks flew in the hearing rooms, the most significant defense of the juvenile delinquency program was conducted quietly, in the offices and through the mailboxes of individual congressmen. In January 1963 Don Ellinger and an assistant from the staff of the President's Committee had begun a concerted drive to muster congressional support for extending the program. During the early months of this effort they devoted equal attention to protecting the 1964 appropriations request, and among the congressmen whose votes Smith and Giaimo "didn't have" were those who had previously been reached and persuaded by Ellinger.

*Aid from the Conference of Mayors.* Throughout the campaign for extension and the related defense of the 1964 appropriations request, the administration received vital support from the United States Conference of Mayors. In enactment of the legislation in 1961 interest group activity had not been a critical factor. But early in 1963 the Conference of Mayors began to hear expressions of concern from several members whose cities had received planning grants that the program would expire before demonstration projects could be funded. Among those concerned was Mayor Richard Lee of New Haven, president of the organization. At Lee's request officials from the project cities met in Washington for "emergency sessions" on April 15, followed by an evening meeting with Attorney General Kennedy.

Thereafter the Conference of Mayors gave extension of the juvenile delinquency program top priority: a "coordinating center" was established in the Washington office and a special counsel was hired to devote full time to the juvenile delinquency project. At this point the mayors anticipated a brief but intensive campaign, designed to dislodge the extension bill from the Special Education Subcommittee. Money had been budgeted to pay special counsel Richard Cramer for a maximum of six weeks. As John Gunther, the executive director of the Conference of Mayors, later observed, "We lost our shirts on this one." The special counsel was retained through December, and Gunther allocated much of his own time to the juvenile delinquency project through March of 1964.

The first indication that the extension bill was going to require a greater effort than they had anticipated came during the mayors' evening meeting with the attorney general. Sharing the mayors' early optimism, Kennedy called Mrs. Green to ask if she would come down to his office to discuss the program with them. The answer was a blunt "no." He then asked if they could come up to her office, and got the same response, though Mrs. Green left open the possibility of meeting with some of the mayors the following day.

On the evening of April 15 Mrs. Green had reason to be unhappy with the Conference of Mayors: on the periphery of the formal meeting held earlier in the day she had been the subject of some extremely uncomplimentary remarks. The substance of these comments had been relayed to her prior to Robert Kennedy's call, and had added an emotional charge to her response.[12] Executive Director John Gunther had known Mrs. Green for several years, but when he tried to arrange a meeting with her a few days after the mayors' "emergency session," she flatly refused to discuss the juvenile delinquency program, referring him on this matter to her administrative assistant.

At this point Mrs. Green was on the verge of walking away from the juvenile delinquency program: "The program had taken more time and drained me of more energy than it appeared to be worth. The political pressure exerted was completely out of proportion to the importance of the program."

Mrs. Green's evident irritation with the Conference of Mayors argued for a cooling-off period, and the impact of the group would in any event depend as much on its ability to muster constituent support for the extension as on its success in achieving a rapprochement with Mrs. Green. Working closely with David Hackett and his legislative liaison, Don Ellinger, the Conference of Mayors concentrated on the cities that had received planning grants. John Gunther wrote the mayors of these cities on April 26 informing them that a coordinating center had been established, and asking them to provide local impetus for congressional support of the program:

> As a first assignment on your part, it is suggested that the Mayors of cities with grants contact every member of the United States Congress from their communities—both House members and Senators. Members of the House should specifically be urged to talk with members of the Special Education Subcommittee of the House Committee on Education and Labor. It is hoped that your home town Congressmen can persuade the Subcommittee members of the absolute necessity of continuing the program for three years. In order to do this your Congressmen must be informed in some detail as to what has been going on under the program in your city and what the future plans are. As I am certain you recognize this is the most effective means of convincing the Congress that legislation is needed.
>
> May we respectfully suggest that your efforts in this direction begin im-

[12] Mrs. Green gave the following, comparatively dispassionate account during the next meeting of the Special Education Subcommittee: "I was especially disappointed when the Mayors had their Conference in Washington, D.C., about two weeks ago, and no member of the subcommittee was invited to attend the Conference. It was entirely on the question of the juvenile delinquency program. It was a quarter to 6:00 that night, after they had been extremely critical all afternoon, and after friends had already reported to me various things that were said by various individuals—it was a quarter to 6:00 that I was invited to meet with some of them to discuss the problem."

mediately. The bill is now stuck in the House Subcommittee and cannot be pried loose until considerable support from back home has been shown to House members. Please keep us informed of reports from your Congressmen....

At the same time a more urgent appeal was made—by wire—to marshall support for the 1964 appropriations request. The combined efforts of the President's Committee, Congressman Fogarty, and the Conference of Mayors dissuaded House critics from seeking an appropriations cut, and the following week Attorney General Kennedy sent a note to John Gunther "to express my appreciation to you and the Conference of Mayors for the magnificent job you did in mobilizing support for the juvenile delinquency appropriation. . . ."

In the Senate Chairman Joseph Clark of the Subcommittee on Employment and Manpower had agreed to introduce a straight three-year extension bill, though he expressed a certain amount of sympathy with Representative Green's argument that after nearly two years the program should have been able to get more action projects under way. Since little if any opposition was anticipated in the Senate, Clark allowed the President's Committee to take the initiative in determining who would testify during six days of hearings scheduled in August 1963. When city officials came to appear before the subcommittee the Conference of Mayors arranged meetings with appropriate congressional delegations. Thus, Mayor Arthur Naftalin of Minneapolis met four Minnesota congressmen, including Republican Albert H. Quie of Mrs. Green's subcommittee, and also taped a television show on juvenile delinquency with Senator Eugene J. McCarthy.

Concurrently the Conference of Mayors worked with the President's Committee on concessions that might lead to a reconciliation with Mrs. Green. The approach throughout was based upon the premise that, as sponsor of the enabling legislation, Mrs. Green should be considered a friend rather than an enemy, and every effort should be made to work through her. By July the group had concluded that she was genuinely apprehensive that an extension bill might not carry in the House, but of more immediate importance, as Richard Cramer pointed out to them, "she isn't going to worry about it until she settles the problem of what the extension bill is going to call for." The Conference of Mayors suggested that the administration award no more planning grants, undertake some action phases of the program as soon as possible, and draft special legislation to deal with juvenile delinquency in the District of Columbia. According to the President's Committee the first recommendation had already been implemented. The second had not produced results that were convincing to House skeptics. This forced the Conference of Mayors to place greater weight on the District of Columbia project and other amendments proposed by Mrs. Green in order to demonstrate their willingness to compromise. John Gunther later recounted: "We kept talking with Wes Barthelmes about amendments, and although some were terribly objectionable, we didn't oppose tacking things on so long as the comprehensive programs weren't curtailed. We tried not to fight Mrs. Green." In the long run these tactics proved to be successful, and most of the "objectionable" amendments were deleted before the bill was reported out of subcommittee. There was one crucial exception, however; despite a last-minute appeal, mustering all the forces available to the Conference of Mayors, the bill approved by the subcommittee in the fall of 1963 provided for a two- rather than a three-year extension.

While the Conference of Mayors was mobilizing selected urban constituencies, the National Committee Against Mental Illness was working through its executive director, Mike Gorman, to develop congressional support based upon sympathy with the general objectives of the program. Both groups, as Gorman pointed out, assumed that "unless Mrs. Green's propaganda could be countered, most Members would take it at face value," and both concentrated on providing information responsive to Mrs. Green's criticism, but the Mental Illness Committee's appeal was not limited to delegations from project cities. Gorman himself recognized, however, that where the Conference of Mayors' campaign was effective it had an extra bite—in addition to supplying information to the mayors and their congressional delegations, it "established the point that a lot of important people in the communities themselves were behind the program."

*The Administration's Tactics of Persuasion.* The administration focused on Mrs. Green and the members of her subcommittee, attempting to meet criticism of the program's emphasis on planning with the argument that—in the words of one mayor—"planning *is* action." Having once made a major tactical mistake in failing to keep Mrs. Green fully informed, Don Ellinger sought to compensate for this lapse by encouraging her to take a first-hand look at the project communities. Here, occasionally paraphrased, is his account:

> This was a difficult job, because a little knowledge of what was happening in the communities was more damaging to the program than complete ignorance—the malcontents usually spoke with the loudest voice. The Cleve-

land experience is illustrative: this hadn't been one of the more successful projects, in terms of bringing together competing factions within the community, and the people who were most unhappy with the project complained to their Congressman, Charles Vanik. Vanik asked Mrs. Green to hold hearings in Cleveland, relating loosely to Federal impact legislation, but aimed largely at administration of the juvenile delinquency program. The witnesses were loaded with critics, and Vanik found out too late that he had been fed a bill of goods. Vanik subsequently spoke in favor of the extension on the House floor, but Mrs. Green tended to remember the criticism she heard at these hearings, rather than the evidence of widespread support that subsequently came to Vanik's attention.

The point is that to rebut criticism of the program, it is necessary to get the critics to the communities, then persuade them to spend enough time there to get an accurate picture of what has been accomplished. Mrs. Green personally visited the projects in Boston, New York's lower east side (Mobilization for Youth), Harlem, the District of Columbia, and Cleveland, and though she may have been looking for negative evidence, these visits at least provided a basis for explaining to her what some of the problems were and how they were being overcome. Perhaps more useful to the President's Committee were the trips made by her administrative assistant, Wes Barthelmes, to Charleston and New Haven. His viewpoint tended to be more objective, and his opinion was valued by Mrs. Green.

In responding to the charge that the program had failed to produce tangible results, the administration attempted to salvage what had earlier appeared to be a total loss. The enabling legislation had provided for "full funding" of demonstration projects—that is, grants for the duration of the project were to be reserved from the appropriations for the fiscal year in which the original grant was made. This provision was especially important to the communities because of the difficulty of attracting qualified personnel if funds were not assured beyond the initial year. In its second year, however, full funding was lost when one of the program's staunchest supporters, Chairman John Fogarty of the Appropriations subcommittee, objected to the procedure as a matter of general subcommittee policy.

Although an extension of the act would have been sought in any event, the loss of full funding provided an extremely useful rationale. Here was something beyond the control of the President's Committee that enabled it to plead that the program *could* have been substantially completed had full funding been continued. As Attorney General Kennedy pointed out in a letter to Senator Clark, "In large part, this extension is required because of the loss of full funding authority in the second year of the program." The Conference of Mayors developed this theme at considerable length, arguing that "this loss of funds has retarded and crippled the program. . . ."

The administration still had to convince Mrs. Green. The Conference of Mayors was making headway with other members of the committee and the House, but while Mrs. Green paid attention to this lobbying effort, she viewed it as further verification of her suspicion that planning grants had been awarded primarily for political reasons. And her administrative assistant characterized the work of the mayors' group as "a conventional lobbying effort" requesting members and friends to send letters and telegrams to Mrs. Green in support of a straight three-year extension—communications that he dismissed as "waste-basket material."

In its effort to combine persuasion with pressure the administration sought help both in and out of Congress. The President's assistant for District of Columbia affairs, Charles A. Horsky, was helpful in replying to Mrs. Green's criticism of the program for failing to get a project under way in the District. In response to Robert Kennedy's call and because of his own interest in continuing support for the Harlem project, Education and Labor Committee Chairman Adam Clayton Powell let Mrs. Green know that he actively favored an extension. John Fogarty asked Speaker of the House John W. McCormack of Massachusetts and House Majority Leader Carl Albert to talk with Mrs. Green. Meanwhile, a simple three-year extension passed the Senate without objection on September 25. This did not improve prospects in the House subcommittee, however. It appeared to Mrs. Green that program officials were using the Senate bill to persuade members of her subcommittee to override their chairman and insist on a counterpart to the Senate measure. Whether or not this impression was accurate, it impeded negotiations at a time when agreement appeared to be within reach.

On several occasions during the months following the April hearings, the attorney general, Hackett, and OJD Director Russell met separately with Mrs. Green to try to work out an understanding on the juvenile delinquency program. At the last of these meetings Mrs. Green made a general commitment not to oppose a limited extension. On October 10 identical bills calling for a two-year extension were introduced by Congressmen Sickles and Goodell and shortly thereafter reported out by the Special Education Subcommittee.[13]

[13] Regarding sponsorship of the extension bill, the administration felt that Mrs. Green simply did not want to have her name associated with it. However, it was her policy to distribute bills among interested subcommittee members, especially freshmen. Sickles'

Mrs. Green had been prepared to wash her hands of the extension bill. What caused her to change her mind? "I finally concluded that a few of the projects held out some promise, and it didn't seem fair to abandon some of the communities that had been counting on help." David Hackett, focusing on methods of persuasion rather than substantive concessions, attributed the recovery of Mrs. Green's support to: (1) the series of meetings between Mrs. Green, himself, Attorney General Kennedy, and Russell; (2) Chairman Powell's active involvement; (3) Congressman Fogarty's influence with the majority leaders, who conveyed their concern to Mrs. Green; (4) the Conference of Mayors' effective mobilization of community support, which in addition to demonstrating significant political backing outside the administration itself, "reflected our success in winning the support of local political leadership"; and (5) the day-in, day-out efforts of Don Ellinger, who—in Hackett's words—"didn't get nervous."

Commenting on the difficult role he was required to play as buffer between Congress and the more impatient members of the Kennedy administration, Ellinger observed that "we tried to avoid a bloody battle that would put Mrs. Green on the spot. . . . We tried to keep the temperature down, kept talking, kept explaining, and generally kept Hackett from taking off. Mrs. Green kept the door open, and I tried to see to it that she wasn't forced to close it."

Hackett's summary omits the concessions required to achieve agreement. Among the *quids pro quo* for Mrs. Green's support were the following: (1) The extension was limited to two years rather than three. (2) Funds were authorized for only one year, requiring an annual justification of the agency's request before her subcommittee as well as before the Appropriations subcommittees. (3) There was an express agreement that new projects initiated under the extension would be limited, rather than comprehensive. To avoid any possibility of misunderstanding on this point Mrs. Green requested a written commitment from the director of the Office of Juvenile Delinquency, which she read into the record *twice* during the floor debate: "We plan in fiscal 1965 to maintain not more than eight and possibly less, of the comprehensive projects that we have started. In addition, we plan to spend $1,800,000 for a number of limited demonstration projects focusing directly on delinquency in communities other than the present project cities." (4) An

---

suburban Maryland constituents would have a particular interest in the District of Columbia amendment, and Goodell's support made the measure bipartisan.

amendment was added calling for a special project in the Washington metropolitan area, with a supplementary authorization of $5 million. The amendment was not objectionable in itself, but congressional specification of features to be included in the District of Columbia project displayed little confidence in administrative discretion. (5) There was a clear understanding that, so far as Mrs. Green was concerned, the two-year extension would be terminal.

*Passage of the Extension.* The bill was reported by the Committee on Education and Labor on February 13, 1964. Robert Kennedy had been assured by Chairman Howard Smith that there would be no problem in securing Rules Committee approval, but for a variety of reasons Mrs. Green did not request a rule until early June. While she may have been certain of her intentions, the administration was not. Mike Gorman recalled: "One week she would be all for it, say she was going to get a rule; but then she'd go up to Boston and be unhappy again. Another week it would be New York, and another Cleveland. Then the Education and Labor Committee got tied up with the poverty bill, parts of which were patterned after the juvenile delinquency program. We were up and down, never sure whether she would try to get a rule or not." Once the request was made, Rules Committee consideration was perfunctory, as Judge Smith had promised.[14]

House consideration was scheduled for June 16, and the administration correctly anticipated no trouble on the floor. When the enabling legislation was being considered in 1961 an effort had been made to underline the rural aspects of delinquency, to draw some of the teeth from rural opponents of the program. In working for the extension the administration pointed with pride to its one rural project in Lane County, Oregon, but no conscious effort was made to emphasize rural problems in order to broaden the base of support in Congress. In 1961 marginal rural votes had been needed to overcome resistance to federal entry into this field, but by 1964 the legitimacy of federal action had been accepted. Criticism focused on departures from legislative intent, and while the administration's failure to concern itself with rural delinquency was occasionally included among the alleged departures, it was not a significant factor. The two-year extension, with authorization of appropriations lim-

[14] Although Mrs. Green appeared before the Rules Committee in its support, formal responsibility for requesting a rule is vested in the chairman of the full committee. Chairman Powell may thus have contributed to the delay for which the administration believed Mrs. Green was solely responsible.

ited to one year, was approved by voice vote. This final condition assured Mrs. Green an opportunity to enforce the others. It also permitted the graceful capitulation of the program's bitterest critic, Congressman Neal Smith of Iowa.

> I believe this is one of the worst administered commissions in the U.S. Government, and I measure my words carefully when I say that. I believe it is one of the worst administered commissions we have ever had in the U.S. Government, and I speak from the standpoint of carrying out the intent of the Congress and accomplishing the objectives set forth in the authorizing legislation.
>
> ***
>
> I do not have much hope that they are going to want to change much in the future, so the only hope we have is to limit this authorization to 1 year so that they have to come back to the committee soon, so their actions will be scrutinized soon and thus cause them to be more apt to follow the intent of Congress.

House debate closed with a ringing defense of the program by Congressman Fogarty, who was livid with anger when he rose in response to Smith's attack: "Mr. Chairman, I should like to disagree wholeheartedly with my friend from Iowa on the administration of this program. I do not agree with anything he said when he was in the well. . . ."

There had been little liaison between the Senate and House subcommittees, but once the House had approved a limited extension Mrs. Green called Senator Clark to find out if it would be possible to avoid conference. After polling the members of his committee Clark reported that the House version would be acceptable to them, despite their unhappiness with House protocol. When the House bill was laid before the Senate on June 29 Senator Clark observed, "The House of Representatives, ignoring the Senate bill entirely—which I may state in passing is somewhat less than the courtesy usually extended to this body by the other body—passed a different bill." Having thus expressed its rebuke, the Senate proceeded to approve the House version by voice vote, and the extension bill was signed into law by President Johnson on July 9, 1964.

The Juvenile Delinquency Act originally authorized expenditures of $30 million over a three-year period; of that amount, only $19 million was actually appropriated and spent. This was less than the cost of ten failures in operational training missions involving Atlas missiles, Mrs. Green calculated. What accounts, then, for the high degree of controversy surrounding the proposed extension of this modest program? Why was this program, in the words of a President's Committee staff member, "more congressionally active than any other Kennedy administration program?" Why was the Conference of Mayors willing to employ a special counsel to work exclusively on this project for eight months? And why did Mrs. Green spend what she has called a "disproportionate" amount of time and energy on juvenile delinquency, second only to her investment in aid to education programs?

At first the administration had been concerned with obtaining the money necessary to fulfill its general commitment to a comprehensive approach and its specific commitments to individual cities. As proposals for a large poverty program began to take shape, however, the administration sought to defend the comprehensive projects because they would be used as a pattern for Title II of the poverty bill. The interrelationship of these two programs raised the stakes of the game. According to Don Ellinger, who with an assistant devoted nearly two years to rescuing and extending the juvenile delinquency program, "Such an investment was not justifiable unless a major innovation resulted, and could be fed into Title II of the poverty bill." Failure to mount an effective defense of the $10 million-a-year juvenile delinquency program would have weakened the administration's case for its proposed $1 billion-a-year poverty program, for which the prospects of obtaining House approval remained uncertain until the roll was called on Judge Smith's motion to strike the enacting clause. Less than two months intervened between House consideration of the juvenile delinquency and poverty bills.[15]

The Conference of Mayors committed its resources primarily because it was interested in protecting the investment of members' cities in project plans that could not be implemented unless the program was extended. However, in 1963 and 1964 the group also vigorously supported the administration's comprehensive approach.

Mrs. Green became so involved not only because of her genuine interest in juvenile delinquency control and because personal clashes increased the intensity of her relationship with the administration, but because she was looking beyond this particular program to the principle of administrative adherence to legislative intent, to the effectiveness of

---

[15] While the successful defense of the juvenile delinquency program helped to secure passage of the poverty bill, the administration felt that its efforts to gain the program's extension had been complicated by the overlapping consideration of the two bills. OJD Director Russell noted: "[New Jersey Republican] Peter Frelinghuysen, Jr., for instance, admired the juvenile delinquency program, yet he had to get up on the floor of the House and criticize it in order to lay a base for his attack on the poverty program."

congressional oversight of administration, and to the preoccupation of the administration with political concerns to the exclusion of substantive goals. As a result of her experience with the juvenile delinquency program Mrs. Green suggested to Chairman Powell that the Education and Labor Committee explore the possibility of establishing a permanent subcommittee on legislative oversight.

Summarizing the program's achievements David Hackett said, "We have achieved our goals remarkably well; we have shown that coordination is essential, and though the process may have been painful, we have developed a public concern with juvenile delinquency. Perhaps our greatest contribution was in setting a framework for poverty legislation, and demonstrating the value of a comprehensive attack." Hackett's summary suggests the absence of any genuine agreement with Mrs. Green. What he saw as achievements, she saw as flaws: planning, coordination, and a comprehensive approach. Mrs. Green had succeeded in pointing the juvenile delinquency program in a direction that she and many of her colleagues felt was more consistent with legislative intent, but she did not believe that the administration had made any real concessions to congressional preference: "We can get more limited projects now because the poverty program will pick up the comprehensive projects."


Epilogue

Controversy over the 1964 extension had some unanticipated consequences. Jurisdiction over juvenile delinquency legislation was transferred from Mrs. Green's Special Education Subcommittee to the General Education Subcommittee chaired by Democrat Carl D. Perkins of Kentucky. The one-year authorization of appropriations, conceived as a sanction to assure compliance with legislative intent, afforded an ideal opportunity to press for a further extension of the program, and the critics' emphasis on limited projects provided the perfect rationale. One year after the 1964 extension had been approved the House was considering an administration request for an additional two-year extension, and advocates of the extension like Democrat William Ryan of New York were using the substance of Mrs. Green's criticism for justification:

> In the next 2 fiscal years, these [comprehensive] demonstration projects will be phased out—not because they have been unsuccessful but because their work is being carried on through other media: local community or-

ganizations that have been inspired to create similar programs of their own and community action programs funded and organized through the programs of the Economic Opportunity [Poverty] Act.

\*\*\*

In turning away from the comprehensive demonstration projects that aimed at affecting the general environment surrounding youth in low-income, trouble-prone areas, the legislation is devoting new attention to developing special anti-delinquency programs for specific types of youth problems. . . . This represents a departure from general community action and reaffirms the legislation's stated purpose of blazing new frontiers in the battle against youth crime and problems.

Characteristically, the Senate approved the full request, the House approved a committee amendment limiting this second extension to one additional year, and the Senate then acceded to the House version. But there was a marked difference in the atmosphere of House debate. The bill's sponsor, Congressman Brademas, observed with some confidence that "I know of no serious criticism of the program at this time," and as if on cue received support from Neal Smith: "Since I have been one of the strongest critics of the way this program has been administered in previous years, I am very happy to note that finally, after 4 years, they are getting some special demonstration projects. . . ." Although illness prevented Mrs. Green from participating in the debate, her position of the previous year was upheld by Congressman Pucinski, who served notice that he would "very strongly oppose any further continuation of this program beyond the period we are now agreeing to." But the odds were now in favor of the administration, and the door was left open for further extension. Chairman Perkins pointed out that his General Education Subcommittee had undertaken an extensive study of the program being conducted under the Juvenile Delinquency Act, and that he "was convinced from the testimony that there was justification for a longer extension than that approved."

Compliance with congressional instructions to concentrate on limited projects had aided the administration's cause, as had the transfer of jurisdiction over juvenile delinquency legislation from the Special Education to the General Education Subcommittee. Perhaps the most significant assist, however, was provided by the poverty program, which moved the more controversial aspects of the juvenile delinquency program to a new battleground. Congressional artillery was accordingly realigned, as is apparent in this contrived exchange between Congressmen Pucinski and Quie:

PUCINSKI: . . . I was wondering if the gentleman from Minnesota cared to comment on whether or not there was any significance in the fact that most of the people who have been associated with this program have now moved over to the Office of Economic Opportunity and are working in the poverty program, having abandoned the juvenile delinquency agency.

QUIE: I will surely agree with the gentleman from Illinois, because the mistakes we saw were occurring in the juvenile delinquency program have all been shifted over to the poverty program. . . .

JUDITH HEIMLICH PARRIS

# Congress Rejects the President's Urban Department, 1961–62

JOSEPH S. CLARK, Democratic Senator of Pennsylvania, and Dante B. Fascell, Democratic Representative of Florida, introduced on April 18, 1961, identical bills known to be sponsored by President John F. Kennedy. These measures (S. 1633 and H.R. 6433) proposed abolition of the Housing and Home Finance Agency (HHFA) and its constituent parts: the Public Housing Administration (PHA), the Urban Renewal Administration, the Federal Housing Administration (FHA), the Federal National Mortgage Association (FNMA), and the Community Facilities Administration. In their place the bills proposed to establish a cabinet-level Department of Urban Affairs and Housing headed by a presidentially appointed secretary. On February 21, 1962, by a vote of 264 to 150, the House of Representatives rejected this reorganization. The following case study is a history of the legislative struggle underlying that vote.

## The Growth of Federal Attention to Urban Needs

The Kennedy administration took office at a time when opinion leaders were giving increasing attention to the implications of the new urban way of life. When the first generation of government officials took the initial census in 1790, a mere 5 percent of the total population lived in 24 "urban areas" of 2,500 people or more. By 1960 some 69.9 percent of Americans were city dwellers, living in over 5,000 cities across the country. The clustering of the population in metropolitan areas—defined

173

for census purposes as core cities of at least 50,000 people, plus the adjacent communities with which they form an integrated economic system —presented an equally dramatic indication of the twentieth-century growth pattern. In 1900 31.7 percent of the total population lived in these metropolitan areas; by 1960 the figure had climbed to 62.9 percent. The urban population during this period was growing at a rate nearly double that of the country as a whole.

As population densities increased in the twentieth century, so did city problems. More housing and community facilities were needed. Environmental pollution became more evident. Transportation systems became inadequate. Many immigrants to the city, particularly Negroes, remained locked in downtown ghettoes, rather than moving up after a time to more prosperous neighborhoods as previous immigrants had. Many of those trapped in such pockets of poverty resented their alienation from the affluent America their fellow countrymen knew. This resentment often took the form of antisocial behavior—street crime, drug addiction, juvenile delinquency of all kinds, and so on. The middle class became concerned and even frightened. Meanwhile, the new affluence meant that society as a whole demanded higher standards of urban living. In 1900 residents of Washington, D.C., boiled their brackish water as a matter of course; by the middle of the twentieth century such a daily ritual was unthinkable.

Throughout the twentieth century concern for "urban affairs" grew among the attentive public. A consensus slowly emerged that the federal government had a general responsibility in this area. A variety of federal programs aimed at cities were created, and support increased for proposals to establish a federal organization at a high level to deal with the broad sweep of urban problems. The gradually developing consensus helped bring an urban department closer to reality. The divergent interests of its proponents, however, made for a shaky coalition of supporters.

Early advocates were kinsmen of the muckrakers; their interest was ideological. Some believed that a federal department would minimize the traditional corruption in city government, others that it would provide a more efficient and logical means of coordinating urban programs. The first man to propose such an agency in writing was Philip Kates, who in a 1912 article for *American City* called for a federal Department of Municipalities. "Municipal government," he said flatly, "has been our national failure." He urged that Congress create a department that would study municipal conditions in the United States and abroad.

*Concentration on Housing.* The issue lay dormant for a number of years thereafter. The pattern of federal activities that emerged in metropolitan areas had housing as its core. The Reconstruction Finance Corporation, created in 1932, was authorized, among other more important purposes, to make loans to state and municipally regulated housing corporations for low-income dwellings and slum clearance. The Federal Home Loan Bank Board, established the same year, was the first federal agency designed to provide credit for home finance. In 1933 passage of the Home Owners Loan Act established a program of relief for home owners and financial institutions in difficulty as a result of mortgage defaults, and authorized chartering of federal savings and loan associations. The National Industrial Recovery Act of 1933 authorized the use of federal funds to finance low-cost and slum clearance housing and subsistence homesteads. The initial Housing Act, passed in 1934, set up the Federal Housing Administration to insure mortgage and improvement loans made by commercial financial institutions. The act also established the Federal Savings and Loan Insurance Corporation under the Home Loan Bank Board. The Housing Act of 1937 created the U.S. Housing Authority. It authorized local housing authorities established under state laws to receive federal loans and grants for the provision of low-income housing and slum clearance. Regulation of mortgage banking began in February 1938 when the Federal National Mortgage Association was chartered at President Franklin Delano Roosevelt's request by the federal housing administrator. Its original name, "National Mortgage Association of Washington," was changed in April of the same year. Its function was to provide a secondary market where lending institutions could sell their eligible FHA-insured residential mortgages, much as commercial banks can rediscount their short-term paper and replenish their reserves at the Federal Reserve Banks. The FHA program, backed by the FNMA, made it financially feasible for middle-class families to move from cities to the suburbs and become homeowners, as they did in swelling numbers. In 1942 the Federal Housing Administration, the Home Loan Bank Board, and the Public Housing Administration—which had been created to administer the 1937 Housing Act programs—were incorporated into the National Housing Agency, whose administrator was designated to head the new agency and report directly to the President. After World War II, however, housing programs burst through the machinery of coordination again when the Veterans Administration was authorized to guarantee GI loans outside the purview of the Housing Agency. In 1947 President Harry S. Truman by an executive reorganization plan created the Housing and Home Finance Agency with the FHA, PHA, and the Home Loan Bank Board as constituent units.

Housing officials who took the long view soon began to foresee the time when their rapidly expanding agency, which increasingly extended its activities into the broad field of community development, would grow to cabinet stature. However, they realized that such a radical change was unlikely during the conservative administration of Dwight D. Eisenhower. Yet the Eisenhower years did see an increase in federal housing machinery. In 1954 an order of the HHFA administrator created the Community Facilities Administration to deal with programs tangential to housing, and the Urban Renewal Administration to handle rehabilitation, redevelopment, and slum clearance. The same year the FNMA was rechartered as a part of the Housing and Home Finance Agency. Democratic Congresses, despite White House opposition, secured gradual increases in housing authorizations and appropriations during the five ensuing years.

Despite the numerous attempts to consolidate and coordinate federal housing activities the incoming Kennedy administration found housing programs administered by four departments outside the HHFA: Agriculture, Commerce, Defense, and Health, Education, and Welfare. Other community development programs requiring coordination with existing HHFA undertakings were being carried on by the Commerce Department, the Labor Department, the Tennessee Valley Authority, the Veterans Administration, and the Atomic Energy Commission. The Home Loan Bank Board had been removed from HHFA jurisdiction in 1955 and established as an independent executive agency. There were also internal problems: the FHA, the PHA, and the FNMA held unique statutory status as so-called "constituent units" and were not subject to the direct line authority of the HHFA administrator. Thus it was something more than mere pique that prompted Robert C. Weaver, when he became the administrator in 1961, to term his agency "a bureaucratic monstrosity."

*The Idea of a Cabinet Unit.* Transforming the HHFA into a cabinet-level agency seemed an appropriate and desirable step to take: it could help to coordinate the numerous housing-related programs, to remedy internal administrative problems, and to meet the rising demand for increased community development activities. Yet little enthusiasm was roused before 1950 for the idea. During the 1930's and 40's the interest in urban programs was still manifested almost exclusively by intellectuals. Like Philip Kates they sought not personal benefit but rather what they thought would promote the civic welfare. Thus, the President's Committee on Administrative Management of 1937, a landmark in official recognition of public administration problems, recommended that the Bureau of the Budget assume responsibility for coordinating urban affairs programs. The same year the National Resources Committee called for an urban policy coordinator. Charles E. Merriam, the distinguished political scientist who sat on both committees, in 1942 urged the creation of a federal bureau or department to deal with urban affairs.

After World War II concern for such administrative matters was spurred by the report of the first Hoover Commission in 1949. The report propounded a principle that was an article of faith among most advocates of reorganization: "There must be a clear line of authority reaching down through every step of the organization." In its specific reference to housing the commission recommended unification of all programs under a single administrator.

The idea of a separate department moved from the intellectual realm into the political arena by way of housing and planning circles. The National Housing Conference in 1952 became the first interest group to propose a department measure along the lines ultimately considered by Congress. Founded by early proponents of public housing, the National Housing Conference over the years became one of the foremost groups supporting community development in its broader aspects. For it the department meant an institutional mechanism for coordinating such programs. Others backed the proposal for different reasons. In 1953 Thomas P. Coogan, former president of the National Association of Home Builders, publicly called for the HHFA's elevation to cabinet status. Such a move, Coogan said, would help assure adequate housing for all Americans and make home ownership possible for more people.

About this time opinion leaders among city officials caught onto the idea as a means to help alleviate their problems. In 1955 Mayor Richardson Dilworth of Philadelphia urged the national congress of the American Municipal Association to endorse the idea of a Department of Urban Affairs. Dilworth was a reform mayor, the sort of politician for whom the traditional intellectual view of the department as a mechanism for civic welfare was most meaningful. For his rather less idealistic colleagues a more convincing case was necessary. Not until 1958 did the

Municipal Association adopt the proposal as part of its official policy recommendations.

But before that time the idea had struck the fancy of some members of Congress. The initial bill came in 1955. Its sponsor was a man with prior experience in municipal programs, Representative J. Arthur Younger, a Republican from California. His proposal called for a Department of Urbiculture with the existing housing agencies as the basis. Younger had served as chairman of the San Francisco Municipal Conference, a civic group composed of the city's largest taxpaying organizations. Having seen at first hand the problems of coordinating municipal programs, Younger became convinced that urban dwellers needed representation at the cabinet level at least equal to the representation enjoyed by their rural brethren through the Department of Agriculture. In the Eighty-third Congress three other bills were introduced to create a similar department. They differed primarily in administrative detail. Their sponsors were all northern liberals, most of them with urban-oriented constituencies. All the bills died in committee.

In 1957 a new Congress brought three new bills on the subject, two of them updated versions of earlier measures by their previous sponsors. The third bill was introduced by Democratic Representative Albert Rains of Alabama, chairman of the Subcommittee on Housing of the House Banking and Currency Committee. Rains's support was the first to come from a congressman primarily concerned with housing rather than with urban problems. His endorsement lent to the measure the weight of a housing expert highly regarded within Congress.

Support continued to rise outside the legislative halls. Both housing and urban leaders endorsed the idea. In 1957 Nathaniel S. Keith, a former federal housing official, circulated a comprehensive memorandum on community development that called for a federal department to promote overall planning. The same year the President's Advisory Committee on Government Organization, headed by Nelson A. Rockefeller, reported that a Department of Urban Affairs was greatly needed and suggested that the HHFA be reconstituted to form the basis for it. Rockefeller, long a civil defense advocate, was anxious that this function be included in the new cabinet unit.

The Eisenhower administration was also concerned. White House staff members gave sporadic consideration to the department idea and also to the possibility of a White House urban affairs coordinator. The Eisenhower HHFA administrators themselves supported cabinet status for the agency through a reorganization plan. However, the President was the final maker of administration policy, and neither the department idea nor the alternative of a coordinator ever received official White House backing. The administration did not endorse any of the pending legislation. It had little political motivation to do so: the big-city vote was heavily Democratic. The administration opposed broadening existing housing programs; hence, federal housing officials did not support an institutionalized framework for such expansion.

The national Democratic party supported the proposed department on a semi-official basis. The Democratic Advisory Council, formed by National Chairman Paul Butler as a forum for developing the policy positions of the "out" party, had a committee on urban and suburban problems. Headed by Mayor Richard C. Lee of New Haven, the committee formed a close link between Democratic mayors and the national party. Its members warmly endorsed the department idea.

The impetus provided by such recommendations generated considerable congressional activity. The Eighty-sixth Congress saw some thirteen bills introduced on the subject. Sponsorship was bipartisan and came mostly, although not exclusively, from members with urban constituencies. In 1959 for the first time hearings were held by both houses, and the Senate on September 10 passed S. 1431. Sponsored by Senator Clark, this measure would have established a Federal Advisory Commission on Metropolitan Problems. The commission would have studied existing needs, capabilities, and federal programs, and reported its findings—presumably including the need for a department—to the President and Congress by February 1, 1961. A companion bill, H.R. 7456, was sponsored in the House by Representative Fascell. Although reported by the Government Operations Committee, it died in the Rules Committee. Three of the other bills also dealt with a commission to study urban problems. Eight additional bills called for establishment of an urban department. None received a hearing except S. 3292, also introduced by Clark, which the Banking and Currency Committee amended and reported out during the summer of 1960. It was then passed over in the press of legislative business near the end of an election-year session.

*Democratic Party Endorsement.* Yet this very election-year atmosphere also helped the proposal. During the summer of 1960 the measure was thrust into the arena of presidential politics. Department advocates, headed by the powerful Mayor Richard J. Daley of Chicago, testified before the Democratic platform committee. Fortuitous circumstances at the convention aided their cause. The platform committee's secretary was James L. Sundquist, administrative assistant to Senator Clark and a long-time proponent of a department. Edward Logue, New Haven development coordinator and a leading department supporter, was an associate of Chester Bowles, chairman of the platform committee. Moreover, staff of the United States Conference of Mayors were billeted across the hall from the committee and hence enjoyed continuing access to its people and their deliberations. The Democratic platform endorsed the department idea.

In September Professor Robert C. Wood of the Massachusetts Institute of Technology promoted the issue in the intellectual community. Wood, also a member of the Democratic Advisory Council's committee on urban and suburban problems, took the occasion of a speech before the annual convention of the American Political Science Association to discuss the proposed department. Between the time he had been asked to deliver a paper to the gathering and the appointed hour, the idea of a department had become perhaps the most well-known new proposal in the urban affairs community. Wood conceded that such a reorganization would not mean any immediate succor for urban needs. Nonetheless, he argued, it would put HHFA officials on an equal footing with their opposite numbers in cabinet agencies. If they got no new programs at least their status aspirations would be realized. Such a bureaucratic boon, Wood said, was probably the most that could be done for urban affairs proponents at the federal level at that time.

In the meanwhile John F. Kennedy was seeking to build a grass roots constituency for his platform. When Mayor Richard Lee urged an urban affairs conference—an idea developed by Logue and Wood at a meeting at Logue's house at Martha's Vineyard that summer—the Democratic nominee was receptive to the idea. At the conference in Pittsburgh on October 10 Mr. Kennedy called for a broad-scale program of community development under a cabinet department, and he pledged his own efforts to that end if elected to the presidency. He thus became the first presidential nominee ever to support the measure.

The content of the Pittsburgh speech was by no means a foregone conclusion. As a senator Mr. Kennedy had never cosponsored legislation to set up such a department. He did not sit on the Banking and Currency Committee and had shown no particular interest in housing. Though a former big-city congressman, he was not closely linked with local officials. In 1956, as chairman of the Senate Government Operations Subcommittee on Executive Reorganization, he had requested and received an HHFA memorandum on a department bill. Still he had not espoused the cause. In July of 1960, however, he changed roles. In becoming his party's presidential nominee he took on different political needs and obligations. He gained the allies of a liberal presidential candidate, many of whom were either manifest or latent department supporters. Moreover, since the New Deal, Democratic presidents have been elected because of large pluralities among big-city voters; offering them a department was a handy way to woo their votes.

The Kennedy victory had considerable bearing on the department issue. Most fundamentally, it kept the measure alive. The Democratic platform had called for a department; the Republican document had not, despite the urging of GOP mayors at platform committee hearings. In addition, since the man elected to the highest office in American politics had committed himself to the department, its fate was now squarely in his hands. This elevation of the issue helped its original proponents by bringing their case before a vast public and attaching to it some of the prestige of the presidential office. At the same time, however, it caused them to suffer a loss of personal influence. They could no longer finally determine the strategy toward creation of the department, for they had been eclipsed by the power of the presidency. Now they could seek their objectives only through an alliance headed by the President—or through one opposed to him. Everything depended upon the way the man in the White House construed the situation.

## Devising the Kennedy Administration's Proposal

Having successfully shifted from congressional politics to the politics of a presidential campaign, the new President now had to shift again to the politics of an incumbent dealing with a lukewarm Congress. His legislative majority would be as precarious as his popular-vote majority had been at the polls. The membership of the new Senate included 65 Democrats and 35 Republicans; the membership of the new House, where there were some vacancies, included 260 Democrats and 172 Republicans. But this paper majority was certain to be reduced in practice by the refusal of some conservative southern Democrats to support many liberal programs. Only with the votes of moderate southerners and liberal Republicans could he get his measures passed.

The President's reaction to his position in congressional politics affected all his campaign pledges, including his endorsement of the department. He chose—the choice of necessity—to work with his less-than-liberal Congress, rather than to dramatize the differences between its orientation and that of his platform. This course required him to woo the moderate southern Democrats and liberal Republicans. Indeed, in order to get bills to the floor he would have to woo some committee chairmen who were more conservative than moderate. He had little influence to waste, and so needed to establish priorities among the proposals in his 1960 platform. Although the message of Governor David L. Lawrence of Pennsylvania, former mayor of Pittsburgh, fell on sympathetic ears when he urged the President-elect to give the new cabinet agency a high priority in his program, the department was only one of an overwhelming number of items. Indeed, it ranked below such other measures as aid to depressed areas like West Virginia, whose primary had given him a key victory in his fight for the nomination; medical care for the aged through social security; tax reform; civil rights; and aid to education.

*Advisers.* With his working strategy established, the President parcelled out proposals to his advisers. A variety of advisers worked on the department measure during this transition period between the election and the end of January 1961. Their concerns and their views diverged at a number of points. A presidential task force on long-range problems of housing and urban affairs included the department within its purview for recommendations. Career bureaucrats from the Bureau of the Budget (BOB) approached the proposal with a view to its organizational implications: whether the HHFA was sufficiently large to justify cabinet status and what functions might appropriately be included. Attorneys from the HHFA were primarily concerned with promoting the agency and with operating as a liaison with housing groups. Spokesmen for the nation's mayors were less interested in the technicalities of the legislation than that the word "urban" should have a prominent place in the department's title and should be of corresponding importance in its subsequent operations. Richardson Dilworth and Mayor Don Hummel of Tucson, presidents respectively of the Conference of Mayors and the American

Municipal Association, had met with Mr. Kennedy in December 1960 and spoke with White House staff members in January to press these points. Staff assistants from Capitol Hill were generally conspicuous by their absence from early discussions, although James Sundquist did give the White House a detailed memorandum on the subject during this period. Central to the deliberations were White House staff advisers Lee C. White and Richard E. Neustadt. General-purpose assistants, they evaluated the recommendations of the experts and advised the President on what they considered to be in his best interest. Neustadt, a Columbia University professor who officially was adviser to the President on the presidency, handled the department matter between the election and the inauguration. White, deputy assistant counsel to the President, took it over thereafter. Both worked closely with White House Special Counsel Theodore C. Sorensen and his deputy, Myer Feldman. Mr. Kennedy himself consulted continuously with his own aides and spoke in January with legislative leaders including Democratic Senator John L. McClellan of Arkansas, chairman of the Government Operations Committee to which the proposal was slated to go.

The first recommendation from this diverse lot of advisers came on December 30, 1960 in the report of the presidential task force on long-range problems of housing and urban affairs. The group was chaired by Joseph P. MacMurray, at the time considered a front runner for the post of HHFA administrator and subsequently named chairman of the Home Loan Bank Board. Its other members included Professor Robert Wood; John E. Barriere, staff director of the House Subcommittee on Housing; Harry Held, senior vice president of the Bowery Savings Bank of New York; and Charles Wellman, executive vice president of the Glendale, California, Federal Savings and Loan Association. The task force strongly endorsed the proposed cabinet agency, and favored including in it along with the HHFA the water pollution control program of the Public Health Service.

About the same time James Sundquist's memorandum, submitted on behalf of Senator Clark, was given to the White House. Sundquist pointed out the two main issues to be resolved: the scope of the department, and whether the measure should be presented to Congress as a reorganization plan or as a conventional bill. He argued that no functions outside the present scope of the HHFA should be assigned to the new department. To propose any transfers, he said, would stir up opposition both within and outside the government; transfers could be better considered after the department had been created. He held that the reorganization should be presented as a simple change of name. Sundquist also noted the key importance of Senator McClellan. In the Eighty-sixth Congress the Senate bill on the department, unlike previous bills, had gone to the Banking and Currency Committee under a voluntary relinquishment of jurisdiction by McClellan. By rule, however, reorganization plans must go to Government Operations; so, too, must the legislation that was required in 1961 to renew the President's authority under the expiring Reorganization Act. McClellan would probably oppose the department in any event, but it was most desirable that he not be alienated by the White House.

Before these matters could be considered another event took place that had considerable impact on the fate of the proposal. A completely different set of presidential advisers, including Ralph A. Dungan and Adam Yarmolinsky, had been working on another problem. These were the men charged with the task of finding candidates qualified for high executive appointments. While housing and organizational advisers were embroiled in the technicalities of legislation, the talent seekers were concerned with the politics of appointments. The recruitment group finished its work first. On the first day of 1961 President-elect Kennedy, accompanied by Robert Weaver, met the press in an impromptu session at Palm Beach, Florida. The new chief executive announced his intention to appoint Weaver as his HHFA administrator. Weaver, holder of a Harvard Ph.D. degree in economics, had attained considerable distinction in the field of housing. A former deputy state housing commissioner in New York, he was at this time vice president of New York City's Housing and Redevelopment Board. An active champion of Negro rights, Weaver was also serving as board chairman of the National Association for the Advancement of Colored People (NAACP). If the HHFA became a department he was clearly in line to become the first Negro to sit in the cabinet. Henceforth that prospect remained just below the surface in the minds of department planners.

*Decisions on Policy, Strategy, and Tactics.* In theory, the President and his staff could choose to name a White House urban affairs coordinator rather than seek a department. In fact, Mr. Kennedy as a general principle favored giving his White House staff flexible, frequently ad hoc assignments, rather than permanent special-area ones. This approach allowed more room for alternative sources of information and recommendation. He was also willing to use his department heads—who were responsible for broad functional areas—as staff members of his own. Hence, in the new President's mind "urban affairs" was more a realm for a cabinet department than for a White House staff office.

Decisions about the key issues the Sundquist memorandum had noted involved more detailed scrutiny. Shortly after the election the task of evolving an answer to the question of scope for the department was assigned to the Bureau of the Budget's Harold Seidman, acting director of the Office of Organization and Management. As an institution the Budget Bureau had dealt with similar problems, notably the elevation in 1953 of the Federal Security Administration to cabinet status as the Department of Health, Education, and Welfare. The bureau's approach was to group together units with like purposes and, when an agency's role had broadened sufficiently, to recommend its promotion to cabinet level. During the Eisenhower administration the Budget Bureau did not publicly state a position on the HHFA's eligibility for cabinet status. Nonetheless, while leaving the matter to President Eisenhower's discretion, it did clear letters supporting the idea from HHFA Administrator Albert M. Cole to congressional subcommittees. There was a consensus among the BOB staff that a department for community development with housing as its core was justifiable, though not a matter of highest priority.

There was, however, some disagreement about the agencies to be included. The Rockefeller committee had recommended inclusion of civil defense. The MacMurray committee had called for inclusion of the water pollution and sewage programs then being administered by the Public Health Service. At least one BOB adviser, who had served previously with the Public Health Service, favored this idea. Another thorny point concerned whether the Home Loan Bank Board and the Veterans Administration housing and loan guarantee sections, not parts of the HHFA but closely related by function, should be brought into the proposed department. After a good deal of staff discussion at the BOB, it was tentatively decided to include them. However, White House staff members and HHFA General Counsel Milton P. Semer encountered distaste for the idea among relevant interest groups. The clientele of the Home Loan Bank Board strongly opposed any change in its existing status. Spokesmen for veterans' organizations were against moving the veterans' housing programs from the one-stop service of the Veterans Administration. That left water pollution control as the only outside function being considered for admission to the department. Therefore the HHFA and the White House advisers recommended that the President offer an unchanged package of existing agency units and postpone the question of including water pollution until later.

At the same time that staff from the Budget Bureau, the White House, and the HHFA were working out these policy decisions, the measure itself was being drafted. For this task the BOB turned outside the government to B. T. Fitzpatrick, a Washington housing attorney who had served as HHFA general counsel during the Truman administration. At about the time of the inauguration he wrote two draft bills at the request of Elmer B. Staats, the Budget Bureau's deputy director. One draft provided for the maintenance of the FHA and the PHA as semi-autonomous "constituent units," and the other vested all powers in the department's secretary. Neither draft called for an undersecretary for housing, which had been requested by the National Association of Home Builders in its official 1960 policy statement. The Budget Bureau felt such a move would unnecessarily rigidify the structure of the new agency. Instead, it proposed a general deputy and three assistant secretaries. Only the HHFA and its constituent units were included in the Fitzpatrick drafts. The completed drafts were referred to the HHFA legal staff for comments and modifications. Ultimately, Budget Director David E. Bell recommended to the President the bill that gave all authority to the secretary. This followed the precedent of existing departments. If pressure were exerted for maintaining the special status of the FHA and the PHA, the legislation could be amended. Mr. Kennedy accepted this recommendation.

The White House had a choice of methods for presenting the proposal to Congress. A conventional bill to create the new cabinet unit could be sent to Capitol Hill. Alternatively, the President could exercise his authority to make desirable administrative reforms by an executive reorganization plan. Such a measure becomes operative unless expressly disapproved by either house of Congress within sixty days after the time it is proposed. Ultimately, the decision was made on political grounds. Senator McClellan was known to be hostile to reorganization plans as devices for diminishing congressional prerogatives. If this method was used, he might retaliate by opposing the bill to renew the President's reorganization authority. Thus the White House decided to introduce an ordinary bill to establish the new department.

McClellan's position settled the matter, but conventional legislation had other advantages. The Bureau of the Budget cited technical problems of reorganization plans. Such plans must be administrative rather than legislative in content, and thus no statement of national urban policy could be incorporated. Similarly, BOB advisers doubted that a reorganization plan could give new appointment power to the department head. The chiefs of the FHA and the PHA would therefore continue to be chosen by the President, limiting the secretary's control over his own household. Further, the Budget Bureau spokesmen noted that a reorganization plan cannot be amended. This fact could provide an avenue of escape for legislators opposed to the department who did not want to appear unconcerned with urban problems. They could justify a negative vote on the procedural ground that amendments were needed.

Conventional legislation might also prevent the loss of a few votes on Capitol Hill. It was the traditional approach for this matter since bills to create the department had been introduced previously. Other lawmakers besides McClellan had little liking for reorganization plans. A bill would surely be more acceptable to traditionalists than a reorganization plan with "executive" in its title.

With policy and strategy decided the next problem was tactics. The principal question involved the personnel to handle the bill—the congressional sponsors and the administration spokesman. Ideally, the two committee chairmen would serve as sponsors. But McClellan opposed the measure on its face. Democrat William L. Dawson of Illinois, chairman of the House Government Operations Committee, generally preferred not to sponsor major legislation; in addition, as a Negro he would underscore the Weaver issue. Clark and Fascell, the past sponsors, ultimately were chosen. Clark was widely regarded as a loner in the Senate; moreover, he could not manage the bill on the floor because he was not a member of the Government Operations Committee. Fascell was a relative unknown in the House.

For the administration spokesman Budget Director Bell, rather than Weaver, was chosen. The administration felt Bell's presence would dramatize the proposal as a White House, and not simply an agency, request. Reorganization, of course, touched upon the total structure of the executive branch, and by protocol alone Bell was the appropriate lead witness for the administration. The White House stamp of approval would also add political impetus to the measure. This approach further served to keep Weaver in the background. Weaver had by now become controversial. His nomination to the post of HHFA administrator had been uncharitably received by some members of the Senate Banking and Currency Committee, though it was eventually approved by a wide margin.

Thus many precedents and many decisions, seemingly unrelated, slowly began to shape the course of a legislative battle on the proposed Department of Urban Affairs and Housing. The political climate for the measure at the beginning of the Kennedy administration left room for negotiation. Considerable political and interest group pressure was being generated in Washington for establishment of the proposed new cabinet unit. However, different groups were supporting the measure for different reasons. What would serve the mayors and their allies might not please housing spokesmen, nor were housing groups themselves in complete accord. Levels of concern also varied considerably. Departmental status was of some urgency to some interest groups, but in fact had rather low priority at the White House. The Kennedy administration as it assumed command was preoccupied with conciliating Congress. Within the Washington community jealousy was quietly coming to life in existing departments, where many tended to view an additional cabinet unit as another competitor for the President's ear. Yet these officials were Kennedy appointees who could raise little public objection to the proposal. On Capitol Hill a quick rundown of the Government Operations Committees that were expected to handle the legislation revealed a membership apparently divided but probably favorable. Presidential advisers concerned with the department assayed the House chairman as an ally but the Senate chairman as an opponent, though not so adamantly opposed as to become an obstructionist. No one really knew, and only a few speculated about, how much the latent racial issue injected by Weaver's appointment might affect the chances of the proposal.

Thus Clark and Fascell introduced the White House bills amid considerable apathy, some quiet jockeying for political advantage, and in general a sense of optimism among the proponents. The arena shifted from executive offices to congressional committee rooms.

## Congressional Response to the Administration Bill

*Hearings.* Once the administration bills had been introduced they quickly began moving through the legislative mills. By agreement with the White House Senator McClellan and Representative Dawson scheduled hearings at once. The House Subcommittee on Executive and Legislative Reorganization held hearings May 14, June 6–7, and June 12. Elmer Henderson, the subcommittee counsel, organized the witnesses. In some cases they approached him with a request to be heard; in others, he sought their views. On the Senate side McClellan, when announcing the hearings on the floor, called for prospective witnesses to contact committee staff members. Senate hearings were held by the Subcommittee on Reorganization and International Organization June 21–22. The White House played no central part in setting up the hearings. Like other interested parties outside the Capitol Hill world, at this point it mostly watched, fully occupied with a host of other problems, but prepared to exercise its influence wherever possible.

The first opportunity to exercise that influence came in the presentation of the administration statement on the department. Budget Director Bell received cordial treatment by both subcommittees. The upshot of his testimony was that the scope of existing HHFA programs and of urban problems justified the agency's elevation to cabinet status. Senators Edmund S. Muskie of Maine and Hubert H. Humphrey of Minnesota, both loyal administration Democrats, were entirely favorable to Bell's remarks. Republican Senator Karl E. Mundt of South Dakota expressed concern with the word "urban" in the department's title. He said that the term was unclear and added that it would seem to discriminate against small communities. Bell replied that no such discrimination was intended and pointed out that he himself had been born in a small town in North Dakota. On the House side Chairman Dawson praised Bell for "a very fine statement." Fascell, sponsor of the bill, handled all the cross-examination. No problems were raised. Five senators and nine representatives —a bipartisan contingent—offered endorsements of the department for inclusion in the printed hearings. Only Republican Representative Richard H. Poff of Virginia submitted a statement in opposition to the measure.

Interest group patterns of support and opposition had emerged swiftly during the hearings. The nation's mayors were perhaps the foremost allies of the administration. They predated President Kennedy as proponents of the measure, and stood to gain most directly from it. As they said time and again, at stake was a seat for the cities at the cabinet table. The mayors symbolized the urban vote to which the administration owed a sizable debt, and the administration was counting on the reciprocity of their interests. The title of the proposed cabinet body, "Urban Affairs and Housing," was coined at the mayors' behest. To no one's surprise both the American Municipal Association, representing small and middle-sized cities, and the United States Conference of Mayors, speaking for larger urban areas, expressed a wholehearted endorsement of the proposal at the hearings. Various leagues of municipalities and individual mayors followed suit.

The mayors' theme was sounded with a number of variations. Mayor Ben West of Nashville contended that equity demanded an urban department because there had been a rural department—Agriculture—for about a hundred years. Ed E. Reid, executive director of the Alabama League of Municipalities, noted that big cities already had large and well-equipped staffs to deal with their problems. Thus small and middle-sized communities lacking such assistance stood to gain most from the services of a department. The mayors also termed ongoing urban programs inadequate. James M. Felt, New York City planning commissioner, pointed out that some metropolitan problems overlap not only city but also state jurisdictions. Tucson's Mayor Hummel added that local governments lack the tax base available to the federal government for the financing of local programs. Several mayors argued that increased federal activity would challenge the states and localities to step up their flagging efforts in the urban field.

A second source of aid for the administration came from the liberal-labor lobby. Longtime allies of the Democratic party, they were heir to two traditions. One was support for urban planning for reasons of good government and optimum administrative efficiency. The other and far more important tradition was the conception of an urban department as a needed institutional mechanism for social welfare measures. Among the groups articulating these two views in support of the administration bills were the Americans for Democratic Action, the American Federation of Labor-Congress of Industrial Organizations, the Cooperative League of the U.S.A., the American Veterans Committee, the American Jewish Committee, and the Urban League.

Liberal groups specializing in community development each added a plea in the interest of its own constituency. Nathaniel Keith, speaking for the National Housing Conference, made a special point of stating that "housing in my opinion will continue to be perhaps the most important single legislative aspect" of the measure. Throughout the period Congress was in session the National Housing Conference held continuing strategy meetings on urban affairs legislation including the department. The American Institute of Architects and the American Institute of Planners voiced the hope that a department would increase coordination of urban programs. The National Association of Housing and Redevelopment Officials added that establishment of the department would considerably simplify dealings with Washington by the local officials for whom the association speaks.

Yet for all this support the hearings also brought opposition to the administration's proposal. Notable protests came from the private housing industry. Conservative in their attitude toward the role of the federal government, the spokesmen for real estate, lending, and home building interests were suspicious of any move implying extension of the federal involvement in housing. They were generally expected to speak against the bill, and they did. The National Association of Real Estate Boards, for instance, contended that a widened public sector inevitably infringes upon the private sector, to whose maintenance the organization considers itself dedicated. Certain spokesmen were concerned over the role to be played within the new department by the already existing agencies with which they dealt. On such issues, relatively minor to its own purpose, the administration was conciliatory. It was willing to make small changes in return for support. Knowing this, the groups made their apprehensions clear. The mortgage bankers and others expressed the fear that the Federal Housing Administration might be submerged within a large cabinet unit. Similarly, the United States Savings and Loan League denied its support to any measure that would alter the existing independent status of the Home Loan Bank Board and its constituent unit, the Federal Savings and Loan Insurance Corporation.

The key group in the housing industry, the National Association of Home Builders, was internally divided and vacillated in its position. Elevation of the HHFA to cabinet status had been favored by large builders, who were accustomed to dealings on high levels. Within the association, however, they were at a disadvantage numerically. Small builders, comprising about 95 percent of the membership, tended to dislike what they suspected would be an increase in comprehensive planning and government control under a cabinet agency. Nonetheless, the organization's leaders felt that mortgage interest rates were being dictated by the Treasury, the Council of Economic Advisers, and the Federal Reserve Board rather than by the FHA, which was more responsive to the Home Builders, and that upgrading the housing agency might give more authority in this field to the FHA. Therefore, in 1960 a Home Builders' policy statement declared that existing needs "make essential a voice for home-building at the highest governmental policy level." But the 1961 policy statement hedged: "We favor a Cabinet Department but only one in which housing is given primary importance." Then came the administration bill, with the clear imprint of the mayors' stamp. The association was piqued by the secondary position for housing in the proposed department's title, which suggested a deemphasis on residential construction. It also wanted promotion of the home building industry included in the bill's statement of national policy, and it wanted an undersecretary for housing in the department. Only on these conditions would the Home Builders support the measure.

Nor were the spokesmen for geographic units other than cities enthusiastic about the bill. At the request of Chairman McClellan, the views of the executive committee of the 1961 Governors' Conference and the Council of State Governments were set forth in writing by Brevard Crihfield, executive director of the latter body. Crihfield contended that a direct link between cities and the federal government would tend to weaken the states. Two governors wrote to McClellan in support of this view. However, seventeen Democratic governors attending the Governors' Conference wired their endorsement of the department as a means to coordinated urban development. County officials were clearly suspicious of the bill. The federal government was threatening to enter their political jurisdictions. Moreover, the national Democratic party—and its President—had little direct influence on local officials. Stanley B. Frosh, a member of the Montgomery County, Maryland, County Council in suburban Washington, D.C., suggested in his testimony that the vague scope granted the proposed cabinet agency threatened the integrity of state and county governments. He noted also that the suburban counties encounter developmental problems different from those of the core cities, which he contended would be the principal beneficiaries from the pending legislation. Bernard F. Hillenbrand, executive director of the National Association of County Officials, testified that the proposal would not bring about better coordination in urban development. Rather, he said, it would create additional problems as the new secretary dealt with other federal agencies having their own ongoing urban programs.

Spokesmen for the nation's rural interests stood diametrically opposed to the proposed department. Their generally conservative orientation to politics was strongly reinforced by opposition to the advancement of big-city interests. Presumably such advancement could take place only at the disadvantage of rural areas. The American Farm Bureau Federation foresaw dangerous centralization of power in the federal government. Republican Representative Glenn C. Cunningham of Nebraska expressed alarm at a trend toward urban domination of the country and consequently introduced a bill to create a Department of Small Town and Rural Affairs. "Are you a leader of the back-to-the-farm movement?" Fascell asked him. "Frankly, I would sometimes rather go back to the farm myself," Cunningham replied. Democratic Representative Wright Patman of Texas took a more moderate approach. He urged the subcommittee to amend the bill so as to include a Division of Smaller Community Development within the department. Even more modestly, Republican Senator Kenneth B. Keating of New York, sponsor of legislation closely paralleling the administration bill, suggested that the cabinet agency be called the Department of Community Affairs.

Far more fundamental opposition was voiced by the two foremost business interest groups in the country, the National Association of Manufacturers (NAM) and the United States Chamber of Commerce. As spokesmen for the business community they opposed extension of the federal role in the economy and, by inference, of federal authority in general. The NAM was primarily concerned with the alleged threat to local power from Washington. The Chamber of Commerce echoed this fear, contending that creation of a department would be the first dangerous step down "the 'primrose path' of centralism," and that it would help concentrate power in the federal government, particularly the executive branch. The group also protested the "socialistic" tendencies of the welfare measures presumed to be in the offing under a newly created department. A degree of opposition from the business community is expected by liberal Democrats on many proposals. But the heat of the opposition to this measure, particularly from the Chamber of Commerce, came as something of a surprise to presidential advisers.

With the completion of the hearings political positions were apparent. The Bureau of the Budget had finished its work. HHFA lawyers prepared to cooperate with the committee staffs. White House aides had given some attention to the cause amid their other problems, but they had not made any special effort to build an interest group constituency for the proposal before or during the hearings; other matters were more pressing. The President himself was concentrating primarily on a Vienna summit conference with Soviet Premier Nikita S. Khrushchev. Congressional consideration of the urban affairs department was taking place well off the center of the Washington stage.

*The Committee Bills.* After the hearings were over two HHFA lawyers were dispatched to Capitol Hill to help Senator Muskie work over drafts of the bill. Spokesman for a rural state, former governor, and sponsor of the bill to create the Advisory Commission on Intergovernmental Relations, Muskie's interest in the department was more intellectual than political. Though a loyal administration Democrat, he had originally been lukewarm to the idea and refused to cosponsor the measure. Testimony at the hearings, however, converted him to the White House view. Senator Humphrey, a former Mayor of Minneapolis, brought in a special assistant from that city to work on the bill and in December of 1961 published an article advocating the department. Senator Clark and his aides also worked closely with this group on the measure.

On the House side Representative Fascell and Elmer Henderson, counsel of the Reorganization Subcommittee, worked on their draft. On August 1 Fascell introduced H.R. 8429, a version of the administration bill incorporating the changes made in committee. On August 28 the House Government Operations Committee reported the measure favorably.

After some delay in getting the minority views and printing the report, the Senate Government Operations Committee on September 6 favorably reported an amended S. 1633. The House and Senate measures were exactly the same.

The amended bills would have abolished the Housing and Home Finance Agency, the Urban Renewal Administration, the Public Housing Administration, and the Community Facilities Administration and replaced them with a cabinet-level agency. The Federal Housing Administration and the Federal National Mortgage Association would have been transferred intact into the new department. The secretary's duties were to:

> conduct continuing comprehensive studies, and make available findings, with respect to the problems of housing and urban development; advise the President with respect to Federal programs and activities relating to such problems; develop and recommend to the President policies for fostering the orderly growth and development of the Nation's urban communities; exercise leadership at the direction of the President in coordinating Federal activities affecting urban areas; provide technical assistance and information including a clearinghouse service to State, county, town, village or other local

governments in developing solutions to urban problems; and encourage comprehensive planning by the State and local governments with a view to coordinating Federal, State, and community development activities at the local level.

Four major modifications of the original White House bill, all acceptable to the administration, had been made in committee. First, the FHA and the FNMA were maintained as separate constituent agencies rather than vesting authority for these functions in the secretary subject to delegation by him. Distrust was rather widespread in the housing industry that the FHA's unique functions might become buried in a large department. Similarly, there was justification for the FNMA's status as a specialized agency; it predated the Housing and Home Finance Agency, it was considered a distinct entity within the housing complex, and only through preservation of its corporate status could the rights of its common stockholders be maintained adequately. Preservation of the semiautonomous status of the FHA had already been proposed in B. T. Fitzpatrick's alternative draft bill for the White House in January. The administration had considered it preferable to vest all power in the secretary, however, and the bill sent to Congress was so written. But political advantages the following summer outweighed the bureaucratic disadvantages of maintaining the two constituent units. The administration had only minor qualms about this change. It did not, however, accept the exact language requested by the National Association of Home Builders, preferring instead to provide that the FHA commissioner should conduct his agency under the direction of the secretary of the proposed department.

Secondly, specific references to the housing objectives of the proposed agency were incorporated into the bill. This addition was made in an attempt to reassure the Home Builders that their industry would receive major attention from the new department. Both Government Operations Committees stressed this point in presenting their reports. Here again the administration was happy to go along in order to gain additional political support, particularly since the proposed alterations were fully consistent with its views. The Home Builders had many friends in Congress, and the White House was willing to smooth their ruffled feathers if minor changes would mean more votes.

Third, a statement of national policy contained in the original bill was deleted from the amended version. The phrases of this statement were rather sweeping:

National policy . . . shall be to encourage and facilitate the efforts of our urban communities to develop and carry out local programs to meet effectively the needs resulting from urban, suburban, and metropolitan growth and change, including the preparation of comprehensive plans for necessary community development and redevelopment; the elimination of slums and blight; the provision of decent homes in a suitable living environment for all American families; the provision of adequate locations for industrial and commercial facilities to create new employment opportunities and to assist in the establishment of an increased and more stable tax base; the promotion of effective mass transportation within urban areas and the coordination of transportation plans with the needs of urban communities as part of the overall planning for such communities; the provision of additional public facilities and improvements commensurate with current and future needs; the provision of open areas, parks and other facilities for recreation, and the fostering of the provision or expansion of facilities for educational and cultural pursuits, thus contributing to the improvement of conditions under which people live and work and under which business enterprise may expand and prosper, to an economy of maximum production, employment, and purchasing power, and to the growth and security of the Nation.

The policy statement had originally been included as a preface to the bill in order to articulate officially the administration's concern for urban problems. Very early it had been decided that although the secretary would be granted no new responsibilities under the measure he would be given a broader mandate by way of this introductory statement. However, feeling was expressed at the hearings that such a declaration implied federal programs and outlays that went far beyond the simple administrative overhaul involved in upgrading the HHFA. In an attempt to allay such fears the statement was removed. The White House was less concerned with legal rhetoric than with passing legislation.

Finally, amendments added specific references to the problems of small communities. The stigma of a "big-city" bill dogged the proposal throughout its days, but direct reference to smaller localities was intended to combat this argument of opponents. So long as the department was called "Urban Affairs and Housing" the big-city clientele of the White House would be satisfied. If modification of small print in the bill could gain support from the small-town constituency in Congress, the administration had no objections.

*Doubtful Prospects.* The committee votes brought reason for some cheer to the White House. Of the House committee's thirty members, only five—all Republicans—signed the minority report. None of the seven southern members raised formal objections; it appeared that perhaps the Weaver issue might not be raised in public or at any rate might not alienate the southern delegations.

On the Senate side the battle was more closely fought. The two southern members of the Senate Government Operations Committee did vote against the bill. The measure passed the committee by a slim 5 to 4 margin. The White House had a change in the Republican membership on the committee to thank for the victory. At the beginning of the Eighty-seventh Congress Senator Homer E. Capehart of Indiana had left Government Operations for another committee; Senator Jacob K. Javits of New York replaced him. Capehart had little enthusiasm for the department; Javits' backing had been a foregone conclusion.

Despite the narrow margin of the Senate committee vote, recent experience made the White House legislative staff, headed by Lawrence F. O'Brien, expect that it would have working majorities on the floor of both houses. On June 28 the conference report on the innovative Housing Act of 1961 had passed both houses with comfortable majorities. The administration got 53 votes in the Senate and 229 in the House. That kind of support for the HHFA, administration strategists reasoned, might well carry over to the department measure.

Actual head counts belied this reasoning. On the House side the bill had to be approved by the Rules Committee. The expansion of that unit at the beginning of the session had given the Kennedy administration an 8 to 7 majority on most measures. But this majority was shaky. The group of eight included two southerners who were liberal on many issues but not on civil rights. If the Weaver issue became visible they could not be counted on to vote for the department. Further, Capitol Hill allies of the administration reported that in the House votes for the bill were at least twenty shy of a majority. Duly warned, the White House made no attempt to get the bill out of the Rules Committee and onto the floor before the end of the session. In the Senate the count was closer; victory seemed possible. Yet why risk defeat in the Senate when House passage before adjournment appeared impossible?

This situation was discussed on September 7 at a strategy conference of legislative leaders called by Senate Majority Leader Mike Mansfield of Montana. S. 1633 had been scheduled to go to the Senate floor on September 10; however, Mansfield changed his plan. Speaking to the press after the meeting he argued that the House should act first on the department since it had been less productive of legislation than the Senate during that session. This statement was a thinly veiled admission that he lacked the votes to pass the bill. Meanwhile, the House Rules Committee took no action on H.R. 8429 during the first session, which ended in September.

For the White House the failure to pass the department bill during the first session was a minor disappointment. The administration was more concerned with the urgency of such proposals as medical care for the aged through social security and federal aid to education, neither of which passed Congress in 1961. It had not pushed Mansfield or the Rules Committee to act on the proposed department. With its influence in Congress in limited supply, only the most important measures could be given all-out backing. The extension of the President's reorganization authority and the omnibus housing bill were considered more important by the White House and the bureaucratic sponsors, the Bureau of the Budget and the HHFA. Thus the department bill was shelved temporarily while administration forces concentrated on getting through these two bills; their passage more than compensated for postponement of the department measure.

Yet at the same time it was known in the White House that dealings with Congress would probably not become any easier during the second session. The honeymoon was over. The aura of political glamour in which the youthful New Frontiersmen had swept into Washington was shadowed by the Bay of Pigs debacle in April 1961. The promise of bold departures in Kennedy rhetoric had not been matched by performance in this first major test. The Washington community lost its optimism. The administration's self-assurance was thoroughly shaken. Although confidence about and within the new administration was gradually restored, the mood was never again quite the same. Even the brilliant Kennedy circle had made a human mistake—and a serious one; Washington old-timers could relax again. This change in mood was felt in the White House, but there was not much that could be done about it.

The administration had little time between sessions to brood about its relations with Congress. The three major executive statements—the State of the Union, budget, and economic messages—had to be prepared. To be sure, the department was included in the first two of these. But it was only one item on the presidential list. The matter, as far as the administration was concerned, would have to wait until Congress came back.

If the administration gave scant attention to the urban affairs department between sessions, one closely concerned interest group was discussing the matter with considerable heat. The National Association of Home Builders, gathering in annual convention in December, officially went on record against the administration bill: "Since S. 1633 does *not* accomplish the objectives of NAHB policy with respect to a Cabinet Department for housing, we oppose the bill as reported." The association was disturbed by its failure to secure a post within the proposed new department for an undersecretary for housing. Originally the group had supported the department as a means of promoting its industry; but this objective was not mentioned in the policy statement of the bills coming out of committee. Opposition to the proposal had been growing within the membership during the late spring and summer of 1961. In December a president who supported the department, E. J. Burke, Jr., was replaced by one who opposed it, Leonard L. Frank. The same convention that witnessed this change in leadership produced the policy statement in opposition to the department. The position of the Home Builders was received as a blow by the housing experts at the HHFA; to the generalists at the White House who ultimately determined administration policy, it was only a minor setback to a bill of no more than middle-level priority.

White House concern for the department was renewed when the President met with congressional leaders in early January 1962. The measure, along with others in the legislative program, was on the agenda for discussion, and the consensus was that it was in serious trouble.

To pass any bill the White House needed to add some combination of Republican and southern Democratic votes to its core strength, which came chiefly from northern Democrats. In 1961 White House legislative tacticians had set about building such a coalition for housing legislation. Then Weaver increasingly became an issue. The President, hoping to avoid the controversy as much as possible, still had made no commitment to name the HHFA administrator as the secretary-designate. Yet Mr. Kennedy had also refused to assure Democratic Senator John J. Sparkman of Alabama, chairman of the Senate Banking and Currency Subcommittee on Housing and ordinarily an administration ally, that he would not appoint Weaver. By now most of those close to the scene thought that Weaver was slated for the job, and few southern legislators could face with equanimity the prospect of helping a Negro into the cabinet. Sparkman, liberal on every issue except civil rights, champion of the HHFA, and one-time advocate of the department, refused to support the bill. If Sparkman did not support the measure, it was clear to the White House that few southern senators would.

In the House, where the administration's working majority was still narrower, the outlook for votes from the southern bloc was even more bleak. Alabama's House delegation was in a particularly painful plight. The state had lost a House seat as a result of its relative decline in population in proportion to other states between 1950 and 1960. Yet none of the nine incumbents was willing to step aside, and the state legislature was unable to work out a satisfactory redistricting plan. Thus all nine Alabama Democrats were scheduled to run at large in the spring 1962 primary. Two were key men in the department battle. Carl Elliott, normally an administration man, sat on the Rules Committee, which was soon to take up the bill. Albert Rains, chairman of the House Banking and Currency Subcommittee on Housing, supported the department in principle—although not publicly—and had considerable influence within the southern bloc. In January it seemed to the White House and the HHFA legislative staff that with Elliott's support they could probably get the bill through Rules, and with Rains's backing they might get it through the House. But Elliott and Rains would be hard men to persuade. On Capitol Hill it is an axiom that in order to be a statesman one must first be elected.

In this situation Republican votes assumed new importance. But by the time Congress convened in January the President's head-counters on Capitol Hill knew the Republicans were not disposed to give them any help on the bill. Most congressional Republicans tend to be conservative; they had little taste for appearing to expand the federal government by creating a new cabinet agency. Few congressional Republicans have predominantly urban constituencies; there was little potential for grass-roots pressure for the department. Above all, the legislators were beginning a campaign year. When a Democratic President elected by the big-city vote requested a Department of Urban Affairs, seasoned GOP politicians thought they sensed the beginnings of a political maneuver. They wanted no part of it.

With Republicans banding together in opposition and virtually all southerners slipping over to the other side, the White House was under considerable pressure to minimize the racial issue. Yet considerable pressure was thrusting the administration in the opposite direction as well.

As the Democratic nominee Mr. Kennedy had pledged solid backing to civil rights measures. During the campaign he had remarked that a President could "with a stroke of the pen" issue an executive order banning racial discrimination in federally aided housing. As the Eighty-seventh Congress reconvened no administration civil rights bill was being actively pursued, and no executive order had been signed. The President was being openly chided for his inaction. Rumors circulated through Washington that the executive order lay on his desk. Civil rights groups stepped up their demands. Thus, Mr. Kennedy could not afford to abandon Weaver even though whatever southern support the department might once have had was collapsing. The political support of the urban North, including the Negroes, was of greater importance to him than the voting support of the South in Congress. Indeed, if the matter came to a simple choice, a public posture as champion of the big cities and a Negro cabinet member was far more valuable than the housekeeping advantages of promoting the HHFA to cabinet status.

A push for the department, whatever its outcome, would publicize the President's stance and redound to his political advantage. Therefore the White House told Speaker of the House John W. McCormack of Massachusetts to press for the Rules Committee vote. Meanwhile, the administration's legal staff at the HHFA began work on a reorganization plan as an alternative device if, as expected, the bill was pigeonholed in the Rules Committee.

Action came swiftly. On January 22 the House Republican Policy Committee officially went on record against the bill, bearing out the pessimistic counsel of Democratic legislative tacticians. On January 24 the five GOP members of the Rules Committee followed the lead of their Policy Committee. Joining with four southern Democrats, they formed a 9 to 6 majority against clearance of the department bill for floor action. Two of the southern Democrats were consistent conservatives: Chairman Howard W. Smith of Virginia and William C. Colmer of Mississippi. The other two negative southern votes were cast by Alabamian Elliott and James W. Trimble of Arkansas. Earlier Trimble had privately expressed his willingness to go along with the measure, but he joined his fellow southerners when his affirmative vote would not have saved the bill.

Thus the bill for a department met with a decisive defeat. But in the administration's view the real battle had not yet been lost.

Confrontation over a Reorganization Plan

A presidential press conference had been scheduled for the afternoon the Rules Committee voted on the department bill. Mr. Kennedy announced he would submit the proposal to Congress again as an executive reorganization plan, which would become law unless vetoed by either the House or the Senate within sixty days of its submission. In response to a question he said that he intended to appoint HHFA Administrator Weaver to head the new agency.

President Kennedy's remarks reflected his strategic choices. With a high sense of drama he publicly abandoned cultivation of the southern Democrats and Republicans. He pointed out that all Republicans on the Rules Committee had voted against the department. At that moment the issue became overtly partisan. Previously a number of GOP spokesmen had voiced opposition to the bill, but it was the President who officially served notice that a partisan battle had been joined.

The chief executive also took a strong stand on the Weaver issue. He added that certainly the appointment had been expected as a logical move for some time in Washington circles, and he expressed admiration for Weaver's performance as HHFA administrator. The President was formally casting his lot with the civil rights advocates. In backing their cause he was asking that they back his. He was giving them an ongoing legislative issue in Washington for their restless energy, which was then being worked off primarily at the grass roots in sit-in demonstrations. The administration was uneasy with sit-ins; it considered Weaver's appointment a more meaningful approach to the elimination of racial discrimination—not to mention its greater political value to the administration. At the same time Mr. Kennedy was turning the lack of southern support into a justification for northern support. He was daring any congressman vulnerable to a liberal constituency to cast an opposing vote that would be interpreted as a vote against civil rights.

In sum, the President had the perfect moment and the perfect forum in which to chastise his political opposition, and he took full advantage of it. He was faced with a lack of enthusiasm about the department and, indeed, the Kennedy program in general. But with the eyes of the television viewers on him, the President attempted to put the reluctant legislators on the defensive by terming them opponents of civil rights and of large cities, tangible symbols of modern progressive society. He was simultaneously transmitting this interpretation to the voters and telling the Washington community that a major legislative battle was in the offing.

In addition, Mr. Kennedy at his press conference made public a fundamental decision regarding timing. Once he had made up his mind to resort to the reorganization plan he still could have picked any one of a variety of moments to initiate it. He could, for example, have said merely that such a plan was being drafted for presentation to Congress later in the session. Instead, he took the option of immediate action. In so doing he failed to pick up votes like that of Albert Rains, which he might have gleaned after the spring primaries. Yet a push for action on the heels of the Rules Committee vote seemed to have several advantages. First, it would serve notice that the President would not abandon a measure simply because it was opposed by some influential House members. In addition, it would provide a chance to make the issue clear to the public. And the publicity would have its effect on Congress. Drama surrounded the department proposal in January; it was at the center of the legislative stage and feelings were running high. By mid-May it might be forgotten; there would be other bills and other priorities to impede its progress. The President stood to gain only a few votes in waiting for the Alabama delegation—and most of these were doubtful anyway because of the racial issue. In the interim he might lose any number of other votes he had assembled on the measure. To wait four months with such risks simply was not feasible. The moment after the Rules Committee veto seemed the psychological moment to seize the initiative and force the issue.

The executive reorganization plan with which the administration confronted Congress was in substance identical with the bills that had been reported from committee. One minor change had been made by the White House. Certain sections were deleted that, according to the Bureau of the Budget, "constituted legislation outside the purview of a reorganization plan." The measure was officially received on Capitol Hill January 30. The presidential message accompanying the plan repeated the familiar arguments.

Congress responded at once. The same day Republican Representative George Meader of Michigan and Democratic Senator Gale W. McGee of Wyoming introduced resolutions disapproving the plan.[1] The resolutions

---

[1] Senator McGee explained carefully that he was acting to secure prompt congressional consideration of the President's request. In the voting he supported the proposed department.

were referred to the Government Operations Committee of each house.

*Opposition at the Hearings.* The hearings, held in the House February 6–7 and in the Senate February 14–16, were by no means only a rerun of earlier testimony. Most earlier witnesses did appear again, but in addition a number of new witnesses came to support the administration. A group of Democratic state and local officials championed the reorganization plan. Other liberal allies, including labor unions and religious groups, spoke for the department. The National Association for the Advancement of Colored People sent a terse telegram to Chairman Dawson expressing the organization's interest. Elsewhere the NAACP charge that votes against the department would be interpreted as racially motivated was widely publicized. The telegram to the House committee, however, merely reported a one-sentence endorsement of the department made by the organization's national convention the previous July, and requested that this position be included in the formal record of the hearings.

Advocates of the department attempted to present the support for it as broadly based. But their statements rang hollow, and both the administration and Congress knew it. Few who testified for the measure were not across-the-board liberals from northern constituencies. Only two Republicans expressed public support: Representative John V. Lindsay, spokesman for a midtown Manhattan district, and David M. Walker, an Eisenhower administration urban renewal commissioner. The only southern backing the administration and its allies mustered came from the Tennessee League of Municipalities and P. R. Olgiati, mayor of Chattanooga.

If the White House could find little cause for optimism in the showing of its own side at the hearings, it had good cause for gloom in the showing of its opponents. Support from the organized mayors was undercut by testimony in opposition from the Southwide Association of Municipal Officials. Working with the National Association of Home Builders and other antidepartment forces, the Southwide Association charged that the favorable resolutions of the American Municipal Association and the Conference of Mayors had been pushed through the organizations by big-city mayors who allegedly controlled their conventions. The association took the position that a federal department would stifle local initiative and impinge upon legitimate local authority. A majority of the nation's mayors, it contended, shared this view. Taking an-

other tack the League of California Cities wrote to McClellan informing him that they had unanimously voted disapproval of the department.
They said the new secretary would not be able to coordinate all federal
urban programs and thus was not worthy of the title of secretary of
urban affairs. The league explained that it did not object to a promotion
of the Housing and Home Finance Agency to cabinet status; its opposition lay in giving the agency a title beyond its capabilities.

Meanwhile, pressure from housing interests against the department
was mounting. The National Association of Home Builders, unable to
get its original demands, contended that the proposal would downgrade
the role of the housing industry and its governmental ally, the FHA. The
department, the Home Builders said, had become merely a device to aid
large cities. These positions were reflected in the mail received by Chairman McClellan. Inserting into the record a raft of telegrams and letters
from realtors, home builders, and city officials against the department,
McClellan said his mail was running 50 to 1 in opposition. Even the
mail of Senator Clark, sponsor of the original administration bill, was
arriving in about the same lopsided proportions. The administration and
its allies had apparently failed to develop a sustained grass-roots following.

Support by members of Congress was also on the decline. No senators
and only four representatives testified for the department. Senators A.
Willis Robertson, Democrat from Virginia, and J. Caleb Boggs, Republican from Delaware, argued that the department was an unwarranted
intrusion into state and local affairs. Four congressmen spoke against the
measure. Republican Robert R. Barry represented New York City's West-
chester suburbs; he argued that the federal cabinet agency would
weaken the states. J. Arthur Younger, who had started the whole idea in
Congress with his Department of Urbiculture, contended at this point
that the proposed reorganization plan did not go far enough in attempting to coordinate federal urban affairs programs. Representative Thomas
M. Pelly, Republican from Washington, argued that experience in Seat-
tle with the federal highway program had demonstrated that decisions
about urban programs were best handled at the local level. Democrat
Walter S. Baring of Nevada, who was outraged with the HHFA for an
allegedly mismanaged urban renewal program in his district, testified
that the department would mean federal usurpation in the state and local
domain. His governor, Grant Sawyer, originally wired his support for
the department; at Baring's request he wired again in opposition. Baring

also had sent a letter on January 15 to every member of Congress in which he argued that the proposed cabinet agency would lead to the destruction of states' rights through big government, centralization of power, and, ultimately, socialism.

The administration was not only outnumbered by its opponents on Capitol Hill; it was also subjected to a much stiffer attack than during the previous hearings. Budget Director Bell, testifying on February 6 before the House committee, found himself under serious fire from the Republicans and southern Democrats whom the President had semi-officially acknowledged as antagonists on this measure. Representatives Meader and John B. Anderson, Republican from Illinois, questioned him closely on the implications that the creation of a department would have for the overall expansion of federal power. Republican Representatives Odin Langen of Minnesota and R. Walter Riehlman of New York pressed the point that a new department probably meant increased outlays of public money.

Massachusetts Republican F. Bradford Morse questioned Bell sharply. If no new powers would be created by the reorganization plan, the congressman contended, then the whole battle was a sham. He said: "The one-stop service statements and this sort of thing, I think, have given rise to the attitude that something more was being created." Morse then asked Bell for a definition of "urban affairs." Bell termed such a definition beyond the scope of a reorganization plan and declined to give his own view as a tacit understanding for the future. Picking up another point, Morse questioned whether the administration considered housing more important than space or veterans' activities. Was this not a reasonable conclusion, since the HHFA and not the National Aeronautics and Space Administration or the Veterans Administration—of which Morse was a former deputy administrator—was being considered for cabinet status? Bell said he did not consider that a reasonable conclusion. Morse pursued one final line of inquiry. Could not the administrative improvements being sought be achieved without cabinet status, by statute or by a less drastic reorganization plan? "It seemed much more sensible at the present stage to create this proposed Department," said Bell, citing the added prestige of a cabinet post. Morse countered: "Your emphasis on prestige tempts me to inquire into this business of government by status symbol, but I will not do it."

Ordinarily, prolonged questioning by the junior Republican member of a committee would be no cause for alarm to a Democratic administration. But the obvious hostility of Morse to the Kennedy reorganization plan boded ill. Morse was the kind of liberal GOP congressman who served as a weathervane for White House legislative tacticians. His district, an ethnic hodgepodge, was composed largely of Boston suburbs and exurbs. He had been one of a handful of GOP representatives to back the administration on enlarging the Rules Committee. If Morse was against the White House on the department, it was unlikely that there was much Republican support. It appeared that even Republicans with constituencies disposed to support an urban department would have nothing to do with what they construed as a partisan venture.

The White House also received scant encouragement in the Senate hearings. John McClellan, chairman of the full committee, conducted the meetings. He did not damn the reorganization plan outright, but he made his opposition clear when questioning David Bell:

MCCLELLAN: [The plan] does present, I think you will agree, to the Congress, a rather difficult decision, does it not?

BELL: In what way, sir?

MCCLELLAN: In that the regular constitutional processes of legislation being available, of having been attempted and not having succeeded through those channels, Congress now is confronted with a decision as to whether, having turned from the regular legislative procedure, those having failed, to proceed by this process and do what couldn't be done by the regular legislative process. That presents a difficult decision, and, as I said earlier, Congress has to take its share of responsibility because it provided this means.

The Arkansas Democrat reiterated this point as he cross-examined Bell for most of the nearly five hours the Budget Bureau director spent before the committee on February 14. Senator Ernest S. Gruening, Democrat from Alaska, pointed out that because the House Rules Committee had refused to send the conventional bill to the floor the House had been unable to work its will on the administration proposal. McClellan then sparred with Bell about the meaning of "urban area." Bell noted, as he had previously in responding to Representative Morse, that a definition would constitute legislation outside the scope of a reorganization plan. McClellan then asked in an offhand manner whether Robert Weaver would testify in favor of the plan. Bell cited the precedent of the reorganization plan to create the Department of Health, Education, and Welfare; he said that Oveta Culp Hobby, the secretary-designate, had not testified at that time. McClellan demurred; the record was consulted; Mrs. Hobby had testified. The following colloquy ensued:

BELL: The only comment I need to make, sir, was that I was obviously misinformed and Mrs. Hobby certainly did appear on Reorganization Plan No. 1 in 1953, and, as I said, I am sure Dr. Weaver would be delighted to appear.

MCCLELLAN: As I said, I do not think that is of any major importance except to mention it so that the record would be cleared up.

Next McClellan questioned Bell regarding the extent of the administrator's authority within the housing agency. He suggested that the administrator already had sufficient authority under a provision in the Independent Offices Appropriation Act of 1955 to coordinate programs and reorganize the agency to meet his needs. Bell disagreed without further comment. McClellan then took up the issue of the scope of HHFA activity. The Veterans Administration, he pointed out, expended more funds than the housing agency; why then was departmental status justified for the HHFA and not for it? Bell replied that the status of the Veterans Administration was not at issue; moreover, there were other considerations involved in judging an agency ready for cabinet status. McClellan also questioned whether Weaver would in fact be better able to coordinate programs as a secretary than as an administrator, and whether creation of the department would necessitate new programs of federal spending. Bell once again replied that the prestige of cabinet status was an important consideration but that such status did not necessarily imply additional outlays of money.

Republican Senator Carl T. Curtis of Nebraska picked up the spending issue. Conceding that the reorganization plan itself involved no new programs, he contended that the mayors were backing the measure in anticipation of additional programs after the creation of the department. Certainly they were, but it was hardly politic to concede the fact publicly. Instead, Bell suggested that Curtis ask the mayors about their motives. His own impression, he said, was that a department would give them a central place to visit when calling on Washington for assistance and greater prestige for their advocates in the federal government.

The administration's spokesman was hard pressed, although he did get some reinforcement as he was cross-examined by Senator Humphrey. However, in his enthusiasm to help the administration by demonstrating the neglect of cities, Humphrey requested comparative figures from Bell on the amount of federal money spent on research about the environment of urban dwellers and research about the environment of farm livestock. The question was so broad that assembling an answer posed real problems for Budget Bureau statisticians.

*Failure.* By the time the Senate hearings on the reorganization plan ended, the White House no longer expected to win the battle to create the new cabinet agency. Nearly all the urban Republicans whose support the administration had hoped to gain, particularly because of the civil rights issue, were refusing to rise to the bait. The South appeared to be lost. Head counts by HHFA legislative experts and their Capitol Hill allies —using past votes on civil rights as well as on housing issues—suggested that with enough support from the ranks of rural western Democrats the reorganization plan might escape a resolution of disapproval from the Senate. Senators like Alan Bible and Howard W. Cannon of Nevada, Clinton P. Anderson and Dennis Chavez of New Mexico, Carl Hayden of Arizona, and Robert S. Kerr of Oklahoma would cast the swing votes. But in any event chances in the House were almost nil. On February 18 Speaker McCormack stated on a nationwide television program that he lacked the votes in the House to defeat the resolution disapproving the reorganization plan. A resolution of disapproval passed in either chamber would kill the plan.

Nonetheless, the President wanted every member to stand up and be counted in response to an official roll call. If he won Republican votes after all, he might possibly get the department. If he lost them, he had a ready-made campaign issue to take to the urban and Negro voters who were the core of his electoral strength. He therefore instructed the Democratic congressional leaders to maneuver a vote first in the Senate, where chances of approval were greater, and then in the House.

Somewhere between the White House and Capitol Hill the administration plan went astray: the White House failed to get either a department or clear-cut votes on the merits, which the President needed if he was to use the issue as a campaign weapon. The immediate cause of this failure lay in the realm of legislative tactics. The administration's men on Capitol Hill did not coordinate their efforts to optimum advantage. The Senate had fallen behind the House in its hearing schedule. While the Senate panel was still hearing testimony, the House committee on February 15 unfavorably reported the resolution of disapproval, thus in effect supporting the reorganization plan. Meanwhile, Senate committee Chairman McClellan, always a deliberate legislator, was in no hurry to push this particular measure. Moreover, the Budget Bureau could not quickly assemble the statistics requested by Senator Humphrey, and the Senate report was delayed. Knowing White House strategy well, a group of House Republicans—including Minority Leader Charles A. Halleck of

Indiana, Whip Leslie C. Arends of Illinois, senior Government Operations Committee member Clarence J. Brown of Ohio, the ubiquitous H. R. Gross of Iowa, and George Meader, author of the resolution of disapproval—seized the opportunity at hand. On February 19 Representative Meader announced his intention to call up his resolution in two days.

This eventuality had been anticipated by neither the administration nor its congressional leaders. Although under House rules Meader's resolution could be called up as a highly privileged motion by anyone at any time ten days after the House committee had reported it out, McCormack did not expect the Republican action. He felt assured that the GOP would not call it up until somewhat later. Dante Fascell, scheduled to champion the department on the floor, so little anticipated a quick House vote that he was home in Miami campaigning in a closely fought primary race. He rushed back to Washington, going directly from the airport to the Capitol, where he spoke for fifty minutes on the floor without the notes he would otherwise have had time to prepare.

However, the President was determined to get a record vote in both houses. Accordingly, although Majority Leader Mansfield had previously told Chairman McClellan that no attempt would be made to discharge his committee from further deliberation, the day after Meader's announcement Mansfield tried to secure a vote in the Senate. He called for a resolution discharging the Government Operations Committee, which would have cleared the way for a floor vote. This resolution was defeated by a vote of 58 to 42. The following day, after a full-scale debate, the House defeated the plan, 264 to 150. A Department of Urban Affairs and Housing was dead for the Eighty-seventh Congress.

## The Grounds for Defeat

What killed the proposed department? Certainly the tactics employed for the measure by no means worked to its advantage. But tactics alone do not fully explain the yeas and nays. The battle surrounding the cabinet post was fought on several grounds—and it was lost on several grounds.

*Problems of Procedure.* One was procedural. Congress is jealous of its prerogatives; the administration's reorganization plan had touched upon some of them. This issue reached its zenith in the Senate, as the key vote was taken on whether the Government Operations Committee should be discharged. Mansfield's remarks were patently defensive. He specifically singled out Senator McClellan to praise the way in which his committee had been handling the proposal to date; but in an exchange with Democratic Senator Spessard L. Holland of Florida he urged the Senate to approve the discharge proposal, arguing that this would be the only chance the Senate would have to vote directly on the merits of the department. Holland asked why the Senate could not take up the conventional bill, S. 1633, instead. Mansfield termed such action futile in light of the House Rules Committee position. He noted that "the President's hand was forced" by the Rules Committee veto and that the reorganization plan had been the only recourse of the White House. If the House was going to kill the reorganization plan, Holland continued, was not a Senate vote futile? No, Mansfield declared; each senator could make his views known, and in addition Senate passage might influence the House. Democratic Senator John O. Pastore of Rhode Island backed up Mansfield. He pointed out: "After all, the proposal is within the procedural structure of the Senate. We have a perfect right to discharge the Committee." What neither Mansfield nor Pastore could concede publicly was that the upset timetable had thrown the administration's tactics into disarray. Without sufficient time to gather the votes to win, the only truly compelling reason for the Senate floor vote was the President's decison to use the department issue for partisan ends—to put himself and his supporters on the side of the angels and his opponents on the other side.

Administration spokesmen were evasive and defensive to no avail. Several of their colleagues from both parties denounced the legislative methods they sought to employ. Republican Leverett Saltonstall of Massachusetts said: "At the present time the question is one of procedure," for the Government Operations Committee "has been expeditiously conducting its hearings and is almost ready to report." Republican Prescott Bush of Connecticut objected that the discharge petition would unduly rush a committee that had been making its inquiry with exemplary diligence. By far the most significant rhetorical volley against the discharge petition, however, was hurled by the Government Operations Committee chairman himself. McClellan said:

> Although in recent years there has been a very ominous trend toward the surrender of the legislative functions of the Congress to the executive, Members of this body should not now take this most serious step to further undermine and eventually destroy the normal and legitimate legislative procedure. . . . The brightness of the legislative skies is clouded, the brilliance of statesmanship is dimmed, and the light of fairness and justice in this Chamber is

darkened today by this proposed deplorable action and the irrevocable injury that it would inflict upon the historic dignity and integrity of the legislative processes of the Senate.

The influence of such sentiments as these was reflected in the vote of thirteen of the sixteen standing committee chairmen against the discharge resolution—and hence against the department.

Another, although probably less important, procedural issue arose over the reorganization plan itself: some members of both houses argued that it was an ill-advised executive excursion into legislative territory. Several such comments were made during the course of the floor debates. Senator Saltonstall noted that this was the first time a President had submitted a reorganization plan while there was a live bill to the same effect before Congress. Representative Lindsay used the occasion to jeer at the administration's inability to get high-priority legislation through the Rules Committee; still, he was willing to vote for the measure despite its deviation from the normal legislative process. Representative Younger argued that a cabinet agency whose structure had been hammered out through conventional legislative operations was more likely to be managerially sound than one created by executive fiat. Representative Barry made the most blunt criticism of White House intervention: "This January H.R. 8429 was considered and rejected by the Rules Committee. Normally this would be the end to a bill. Those who propose and support it are naturally disappointed at its failure, but they bow to our legislative process. Not so the present administration." Despite the fact that the reorganization plan technique generated such comments as these, objection to it probably was not one of the prime motivations of voting behavior. Nonetheless, it did provide a two-edged sword with which department opponents could at once confuse the issue and attack the administration.

*Partisanship.* Sharp partisan infighting also marked the struggle over the proposed department. Like the procedural issues, partisanship became a factor because of Mr. Kennedy's own decision. Although GOP congressional leaders, including the House Republican Policy Committee, House Minority Leader Halleck, and Senate Minority Leader Everett McKinley Dirksen of Illinois, had gone on record against the Kennedy proposal, and *Battle Line,* the publication of the Republican National Committee, attacked the reorganization plan, it was the President's public support of the measure and criticism of the Republicans on the Rules Committee who voted against it that sharply etched the party issue.

Accordingly, remarks during the floor debates pointed up the partisan battle. A Republican member of the House Government Operations Committee declared: "Reorganization Plan #1 of 1962 is a politically inspired document which a Member of the other body and a former chairman of the Democratic National Committee has excitedly labeled the first big political issue of the 1962 and 1964 elections." A number of the congressman's fellow Republicans echoed his sentiments. On the other side of the aisle, Representative William Fitts Ryan of New York recalled the Democratic platform endorsement of the department and said: "It is now 1962. Let us redeem this pledge of 1960." Most appeals to party, however, were oblique. Neither Speaker McCormack nor Minority Leader Halleck participated in the House floor debate. House Majority Leader Carl Albert of Oklahoma spoke for the department measure, but his remarks dealt primarily with the procedural issue of how the matter had been brought to the floor. His one flatly partisan comment was without elaboration: "I should hate to see the vote on President Kennedy's plan confirm what some people say about my Republican colleagues: That is that they have not voted in accordance with what they know is best for the country but rather have voted to secure some momentary political gain."

Debate in the Senate was concerned almost exclusively with the discharge petition. Mansfield and Dirksen both spoke to this point. There were no overt appeals for or against the President's position. Senator Humphrey rose to his feet to speak; an aide from the Government Operations Committee told him that his request for statistics had held up the report and thus in a sense forced the discharge confusion; Humphrey reseated himself. The administration's men on the Hill could only make a faint, wistful partisan statement like Albert or remain silent like Humphrey.

The partisan antagonism affected the voting, as a numerical summary indicates. Only 4 GOP senators voted for the department by voting for the discharge resolution, while 32 opposed it. In the House only 13 Republicans voted for, while 153 were against. Party did not hold the Democrats together, though. In the Senate 38 Democrats supported the department, but 26 opposed it. Similarly, 137 Democratic representatives voted for, but 111 voted against.

*The Racial Issue.* The White House had gambled and lost a chunk of Democratic votes on the racial issue. The position of the southern Democrats was clear. However loyal they were to President Kennedy, or to government housing, or even to help for big cities, most Dixie members just could not afford to cast a vote that might be construed as favoring a place for a Negro in the cabinet. Overtly they ignored the civil rights issue. None made any comment on the floor about Weaver's race, and indeed few of them even participated at all during the floor debate. But the votes of the southern delegations spoke louder than their words. Albert Gore and Estes Kefauver of Tennessee and Ralph W. Yarborough of Texas were the only senators from Old Confederacy states recorded in favor of the department. Each was a liberal, none was from the Deep South, and all three were distinctly men apart from the southern bloc of the Senate. In the House all southern Democrats except four voted against the department. The four—Representatives Fascell, Henry Gonzalez of Texas, Albert Thomas of Texas, and J. Carlton Loser of Tennessee—all represented urban or suburban constituencies outside Deep South areas.

Members of Congress were well aware of the racial aspect of the controversy. Robert Weaver had warned in a television broadcast a few days before the vote that Negroes would view votes against the department as anti-Negro. The NAACP had said a vote against the proposed cabinet agency would be interpreted as "racially motivated" and had urged GOP National Chairman William E. Miller "to prevent the Republican Party acquiring this stigma." Virtually everyone casting a vote against the department who did not have a predominantly white southern constituency made some complimentary remarks about the ability of Weaver. Senator Bush's words were typical of the many Republican lawmakers who deplored the existence of the Weaver problem: "The President's injection of racism into this issue was ill-considered and unworthy of his high office." The GOP attempted to attach the Weaver matter to its general criticism of crass political maneuvering by the Democratic White House.

The President had defied the South and the Republicans and now they in turn had defied him. Of course, as White House legislative hands knew, the pressures on most Republicans and southern Democrats were likely to work against the department measure even if the President had been conciliatory. Most came from constituencies outside big cities where few Negroes vote. Southern Democrats are not strongly compelled to vote with their national party on most issues; sustained by local opinion, they can more readily afford to differ from the position of a northern Democrat in the White House than from the position of their constituents. Dixie legislators and Republicans are also especially concerned with the fine points of legislative procedure, both because such an attitude dovetails with their general conservatism and because they would like to keep liberal measures from possible passage on the floor. More southerners and Republicans than northern Democrats come from safe districts, which gives them a vested interest in supporting the will of committee chairmen since they themselves stand a good chance of becoming chairmen one day. The opposition of many southern senators was reinforced by their view as committee chairmen—or prospective chairmen—that the discharge resolution was an infringement upon the prerogatives of the committee chaired by McClellan, also a southerner. Moreover, the South is the least urbanized area of the country.

*The Urban-Rural Conflict.* The most obvious basis for the votes on the department issue lay in the urban-rural split. Of the nonsouthern House Democrats voting against the department, not one represented an area within the twenty-five largest cities of the United States. The White House got the big-city vote on which it had been counting, but as this statistic implies, the other side of the coin was less fortunate. Although the original administration bill had been amended to extend it specifically to smaller communities, it was still conceived of—and in opposition circles criticized—as a "big-city" measure. The attempt to create an urban bloc had instead solidified an anti-urban bloc. In 1956 Senate sponsors of the department bill included western Democrats with sparse constituencies; after the tactical maneuverings of Kennedy lieutenants, the proposal was constantly attacked as a measure to benefit city slickers. Congressmen who did not represent big-city districts had no reason to support such a department. Indeed, with farmers' and ranchers' organizations as prominent as they were in many districts, a congressman stood to lose a great deal by supporting a proposed cabinet agency of this sort. The personal activities of many nonsouthern Democrats who opposed the department underscored the rural influence. Representatives J. Floyd Breeding of Kansas and W. R. Hull, Jr., of Missouri were farmers. Representative Thomas G. Morris of New Mexico was a rancher and farmer. Representatives Tom Steed and Victor Wickersham of Oklahoma were born on farms. Representative Thomas F. Johnson owned a farm on Maryland's eastern shore. Representative Walter H. Moeller of Ohio was born on a farm and owned one. Representative M. Blaine Peterson of Utah, an attorney, had specialized in mining law.

The same situation in reverse appeared among Republicans supporting the department. Nearly all were from the East Coast megalopolis and most from its large cities. Paul A. Fino, Seymour Halpern, and John V. Lindsay represented New York City districts. New Jersey areas in the New York metropolitan complex also gave Republican votes: those of Representatives Florence C. Dwyer and George M. Wallhauser. Similarly, the district of Californian William S. Maillard included a part of the San Francisco area. Some suburbanites also backed the measure. John F. Baldwin's district was located on the edge of the San Francisco-Oakland region. William T. Cahill's New Jersey district included sections of the Camden-Philadelphia metropolitan area. The New Jersey district of Milton W. Glenn was also close enough to this urban complex to be strongly suburban. Moreover, Glenn had been born in a large metropolitan area, Atlantic City, and had served as a municipal magistrate in Margate City before going to Washington. The Maryland district of Representative Charles MacC. Mathias, Jr., included some rural counties bordering on West Virginia, but the bulk of his constituents lived in the Montgomery County suburbs of Washington. Although James E. Van Zandt represented a predominantly rural district in Pennsylvania, it was very much to his advantage to support a big-city department: he was running for the Senate against Joseph Clark in the fall of 1962 and needed the votes of Philadelphia and Pittsburgh. Chester E. Merrow of New Hampshire and Stanley R. Tupper of Maine both spoke for rural constituencies and nevertheless voted for the department. However, Merrow was an ideological liberal; and Tupper, moderately liberal, supported the measure as a means toward providing greater administrative coordination and simplified procedure for localities seeking federal aid.

All four Republican senators who backed the department—Clifford P. Case of New Jersey, Javits and Keating of New York, and Hugh Scott of Pennsylvania—came from states where rural interests are strong but where the urban population is a prime concern. Each is a swing state politically. Each has many Negro votes. Republicans can count on most of the rural votes since these are traditionally GOP, but to win election they must also pick up a large number in the cities, where a majority of voters live.

Considerations such as these, which the White House tried to exploit, did not always prevail with the individual legislator weighing the ramifications of his own vote. Republican Senator Thomas H. Kuchel of California, for instance, voted against the department although his situation was similar to that of the Republican senators who supported the measure. He, too, came from a state with sizable urban concentrations and meaningful rural influences; he supported civil rights legislation; his senatorial colleague voted for the department. Yet his vote ultimately hinged on the procedural issue. Prepared to deliver a lengthy speech endorsing creation of the department, he was outraged by what he considered to be cavalier tactics on the part of Mansfield in announcing a discharge petition attempt after assuring McClellan that the committee could proceed at its own pace. Thus the White House tacticians attempting to win votes had first to recognize the presence of a variety of influences and then to contend with their intensity.

*Lack of Grass Roots Support.* The administration lost votes for reasons of procedure, partisanship, racial antagonism, and rural and small-town opposition; but it would not have lost all these votes had there been any strong commitment to the department in the constituencies of the legislators. The White House did not, either unilaterally or in conjunction with its allies, develop significant grass roots support for the proposed cabinet unit. The President did not appeal directly to the people about it. The issue was mentioned at regional White House conferences on housing and urban affairs held during the winter of 1961, but it was only one issue among many. With the exception of the formal State of the Union and budget messages, from the time of the Pittsburgh urban affairs conference in 1960 until his press conference after the Rules Committee veto in 1962 the President did not actively promote the measure to an audience broader than the Washington community.

His omission probably had several reasons. In the first place, Mr. Kennedy did not as a matter of course take legislative issues to the people; he engaged in nothing truly corresponding to Franklin D. Roosevelt's fireside chats. Moreover, the urban department was relatively low on his agenda of priorities; when he did speak to the people directly through the media of mass communication he concentrated on issues such as the state of the economy or foreign affairs. Also, the issue was abstract to the man in the street, translatable only with the greatest difficulty or risk into a measure offering potential personal gain. On domestic issues public appeals nearly always must be to programs. In this case if this had been done—if, for example, the administration had promoted the department as a means by which urban blight could be combated by specific kinds of federal activities—opponents of the measure would have been fully aroused to attack federal spending, government control, socialism, and so on.

Yet the strategy of avoiding this kind of attack by keeping the issue purely administrative on its face did not wholly succeed. Conservative interest groups, particularly the United States Chamber of Commerce and the Council of State Chambers of Commerce, knew that the clientele of the proposed department were more interested in money than in administration. It was well known in Washington that the mayors and others had sought to include within the cabinet unit government functions in addition to those then in the HHFA. No one doubted that they wanted more funds for their undertakings; some even continued to say so publicly. Accordingly, the Chamber of Commerce concentrated its lobbying efforts on the department measure, sending out large mailings containing copies of an article from *The Nation's Business* entitled "Washington Reaches for Your City Hall." They urged their local members to write their congressmen. The local businessmen, frequently prominent citizens and civic leaders known to their congressmen, responded to the appeal. And many congressmen, not strongly predisposed to vote for the measure to begin with, backed away from the proposal. Support for the department dropped sharply between the hearings in the spring of 1961 and the second round in February 1962. The loss was particularly marked among western Democrats, who would ordinarily have gone along with the President even though few of them were particularly concerned with the role of the HHFA; very few ultimately cast their vote for the measure on the floor.

The White House—basically caring little about the department, but controlling strategy in a way that neither the mayors nor the HHFA and its clientele could much affect—aimed its approach at the Washington community. It assumed the support of urban-oriented liberals and sought to attract the moderate and the indifferent by terming the proposal a matter of administrative housekeeping. Only when positions had hardened and the administration appeared to be losing did the White House turn its attention to the grass roots, charging its opponents with partisanship and racism and obstruction to progress. But to its own misfortune the White House found that it had no real support or even interest mobilized at the local level; what concern there was had been organized by the opposition. Faced with the enormous task of conciliating a balky Congress, the President and his lieutenants had in this battle all but forgotten the folks back home. Their friends there were correspondingly indifferent; only their enemies came out in full force.

President Kennedy himself explained the matter in terms of the Washington community. Speaking to Tom Wicker, then White House correspondent for *The New York Times,* he said: "I played it too cute. It was so obvious it made them mad." Even after the struggle the President did not conceive of the department issue as one based primarily on citizen petition to legislative representatives.

Political victories are won in Congress when a policy maker, using strategy and tactics he deems appropriate, persuades enough of his colleagues that what he wants is in their interest. This the Kennedy administration failed to do in the case of its legislative proposals to create a Department of Urban Affairs and Housing.

## Epilogue: Passage in 1965

"We'll be back," one department supporter told the House as the measure went down to defeat in 1961–62. Back they came, and not long after. In 1963 President Kennedy in his budget message called for creation of a Department of Housing and Urban Affairs. President Johnson the following year requested creation of the cabinet unit—this time named the Department of Housing and Community Development. Congress did not vote on the proposals.

The 1964 elections brought fresh hope to department proponents. President Johnson won a landslide 61 percent of the presidential vote. The Democratic sweep was also reflected in a net gain of three Senate and thirty-four House seats over the Congress faced by Mr. Kennedy in 1961. Most of the freshmen in the Eighty-ninth Congress were northern liberals and many felt that they owed their election at least in part to the presidential coattails. It seemed likely that they would support the department proposal.

President Johnson advocated a Department of Housing and Urban Development in his 1965 State of the Union and budget messages, and the Budget Bureau on March 23 sent identical draft bills to the speaker of the House and the president of the Senate. The measures were in substance the same as the Kennedy era proposals. Essentially they elevated the HHFA to cabinet status and vested in the secretary full authority over the affairs of the new agency and over coordination of related programs. There were, however, a few important changes. First, the 1965 bill called for a Department of Housing and Urban Development, responding to prior opposition from the home builders and others by restoring housing to a primary place in the department's title and in its prospective operations. Second, the 1965 bill authorized an additional assistant secretary to be appointed by the President and confirmed by the Senate, and another assistant secretary for administration to be appointed by the secretary with the President's approval. Prospects of considerable internal reorganization made the two additional posts desirable. Finally, under the 1965 bill the FHA's functions were transferred to the secretary, but the FNMA was maintained as a constituent unit of the new department. The Kennedy measures had called for both the FHA and the FNMA to remain intact within the new cabinet body. The Johnson administration believed that the secretary should have firm control within his own household; it was felt that sufficient assurance had been given to alleviate interest group fears that the FHA might suffer a loss in importance as a result of the shift.

The Johnson administration bill was introduced on March 23 by Representative Henry S. Reuss, Democrat from Wisconsin, and on March 25 by Senator Abraham A. Ribicoff, Democrat from Connecticut. Representative Dante Fascell, Kennedy administration floor manager of the bill in the House, introduced an identical bill on March 30.

The House Subcommittee on Executive and Legislative Reorganization held hearings on the measure on April 5 and 6. The Senate Subcommittee on Executive Reorganization heard testimony on March 31, April 1 and 2, and May 19. The Budget Bureau presented the administration case that the department would represent recognition of urban problems and the need for their solution, and would better serve to coordinate the HHFA's internal programs and its relations with other agencies undertaking relevant activities. Spokesmen for the nation's mayors and the liberal-labor lobby who had supported the measure in the past endorsed it again. The National Association of Real Estate Boards, the United States Chamber of Commerce, and the National Association of Manufacturers opposed it once more as unnecessary, undesirable, and inadequate because it did not coordinate all housing and all urban programs. The Mortgage Bankers Association again voiced concern that the FHA, a credit institution, would be submerged within an urban affairs department.

Significantly, three groups switched their position from their 1961–62 stance. Most important was the National Association of Home Builders. The Home Builders believed that elevation of the HHFA to cabinet status would promote the housing industry, provided housing was not eclipsed by concern for urban development. Accordingly, the organization proposed an amendment to the administration bill designating an assistant secretary with specific responsibility for the private mortgage market. The National Association of Counties, formerly the National Association of County Officials, also moved from opposition to support of the department as part of an overall program of community development for urban, suburban, and rural areas. The U.S. Savings and Loan League said that it would back the department so long as the Home Loan Bank Board—the agency with which the league had most of its dealings—was kept independent, as the administration bill provided.

The House committee on May 11 approved the bill with the Home Builders' amendment by a 20 to 8 vote. In addition to the minority report, four Republicans submitted separate views calling for an Office of Community Development in the Executive Office of the President as a substitute for the department. On June 15 the bill was called up in the House. After debate focusing primarily on the administrative merits of the department, the House on June 16 rejected a GOP move to recommit the bill with instructions to report the Republican substitute. The House then adopted the committee amendment, rejected various other amendments, and by a 217 to 184 vote approved the bill.

The Senate committee voted 9 to 4 on August 2 to report the bill favorably. No minority report was filed. The committee had added the Home Builders' amendment. The senators also added amendments underscoring the future role of the private housing industry, directing the President to study possible transfers from other agencies to the new cabinet unit (but requiring express congressional approval for transfer of the Interior Department's outdoor recreation program), and providing machinery to coordinate federal-state community development programs and relevant federal programs outside the new department. Senate floor debate began August 10. Once again discussion centered on the advantages of the measure as a matter of administrative housekeeping. The committee amendments were agreed to en bloc. An amendment was approved preserving the FHA as a component unit within the department headed by a commissioner appointed by the President with senatorial confirmation. Another amendment was added substituting the word "community" for "urban" in various sections of the bill. The secretary was directed in still another amendment to hold hearings at the request of any governor in whose state programs of the department were being proposed or administered. On August 11 the Senate approved the amended bill, 57 to 33.

In conference the FHA matter was worked out in a compromise designating an assistant secretary as commissioner of the FHA also; the FHA was to be a constituent unit with prime responsibility under the secretary's supervision for private mortgage market programs. In the matter of coordinating machinery the secretary was required to consult state and local officials and hold hearings at his own discretion, and an urban program coordination director was provided for in compromise language. The Senate amendment regarding further transfers of functions was accepted, as was the substitution of "community" for "urban" at several points in the bill. Finally, the conferees agreed to the Senate provision directing the secretary to encourage a maximum role for, and cooperation with, the private sector and added similar wording to the statement of purpose. Both houses adopted the conference report by voice vote without debate, the Senate on August 30 and the House on August 31.

*Grounds for Success.* How was it that a department proposal resoundingly rejected in 1962 could win approval rather handily in 1965? Certainly the obvious answer is the group of administration supporters, particularly in the House, added as a result of the 1964 elections. These additional backers made 1965 a spectacularly successful legislative year for President Johnson. Some 68.9 percent of all his 1965 legislative proposals were enacted, the greatest legislative success for a President in over a decade.

Yet passage of the department bill was facilitated for other reasons as well. Legislative tactics did not provide the stumbling block they had in 1962. The urban bloc in Congress, backed effectively by the White House, functioned more cohesively and adequately. Moreover, partisan division over the measure had become more complex. Liberal and moderate Republicans, whose party in 1965 had not been subject to public presidential chastisement over the issue, chose not simply to oppose the measure but to offer a substitute. In the end, after defeat of their bill, only nine House Republicans voted for the department, four fewer than in 1962; but ten GOP senators—an increase of six—supported it. The administration gained more clearly among southern Democrats. A total of six Dixie senators and twenty-seven congressmen voted for the successful measure; in 1962 the figures had been three senators and four congressmen. In 1965 it was not at all clear that Robert Weaver would be named secretary of the new department; and even if he were, his appointment seemed a less important race relations matter after passage of the 1964 Civil Rights Act. In addition, the urban-rural cleavage was less severe in 1965. The title and language of the bill and general climate of debate served to alleviate its prior big-city stigma. Finally, the bill had more support outside Congress and the administration. Three relevant interest groups, one perhaps the key group, reversed their positions and endorsed the measure. State and local officials were giving more attention to community development efforts. The growing consensus supporting federal responsibility for alleviation of urban problems provided a better climate for such a measure than in 1962. The new poverty program had aroused citizen interest in their communities' undertakings. And the majority of the country as a whole seemed to be backing the President and his programs. All these factors caused a bandwagon mentality and added votes for the department. Urban affairs had become a more relevant concern for policy makers.

Within this favorable context Mr. Johnson signed the department bill on September 9. Although the new cabinet agency was scheduled to come into existence sixty days later, its early days were clouded with uncertainty. There was legal confusion because the President appointed no one to exercise the powers of the secretary. He delayed his decision while waiting for a task force report on the transfer of various functions to the new department. Several names were mentioned; Robert Weaver publicly acknowledged his interest; civil rights groups publicly endorsed him; and nothing happened. Finally, on January 13, 1966 Weaver's appointment was announced, along with that of Robert C. Wood, chairman of the task force, as undersecretary. But despite a strong statement from Mr. Johnson endorsing Weaver and Wood and the need to build great urban areas in the Great Society, substantial presidential enthusiasm for the new department was not clearly evident. The President made no public comment on the various transfers recommended by his task force. The Department of Housing and Urban Development had become a reality, but the ultimate significance of the change was still an open question.

RANDALL B. RIPLEY

# Congress and Clean Air:
# The Issue of Enforcement, 1963

ON DECEMBER 17, 1963 President Lyndon B. Johnson signed H.R. 6518 into law. This bill, sponsored by Democratic Representative Kenneth A. Roberts of Alabama, was designated the Clean Air Act (P.L. 88–206). It was designed to promote a substantial federally led attack on air pollution in the urban areas of the United States. It included provisions for research, for a new grants-in-aid program aimed at helping state and local air pollution agencies, and for limited federal enforcement powers in both interstate and intrastate instances of harmful pollution. The act had been produced largely through congressional initiative over a number of years. Roberts had been the chief initiator in Congress since 1959.

By 1963 air pollution in the United States had become a serious problem, although there was some dispute over the exact extent and nature of this problem. Air pollutants are any foreign objects—solids, liquids, and gases—that change the normal or "pure" composition of air. In the words of a 1963 staff report from the Senate Public Works Committee, these pollutants

> mirror virtually all of our activities which utilize materials for domestic, commercial, agricultural, industrial, or other purposes. The burning of fuels to heat our homes, and to propel our automobiles, trains, planes, and missiles; the conversion of raw materials into finished goods; the application of pesticides and fertilizers to increase our crops; the exploration into the capabilities of nuclear energy; the burning of trash and garbage; the clearing of land; the construction of roads and buildings—each of these puts foreign substances into the air.

224

Once in the air the pollutants, through processes not fully understood, can cause further chemical reactions that can be harmful to people and to objects. Weather—in the form of winds, vertical air currents, and temperature—plays an important part in dispersing and also in concentrating pollutants. Particularly important in creating serious pollution problems are "thermal inversions." These exist where a layer of warm air develops over cooler air, thus preventing pollutants from being dispersed.

Urban areas develop the most serious air pollution problems because of the large numbers of pollutants emitted locally. Where large-scale pollution is combined with a geographical setting particularly susceptible to thermal inversions—as in Los Angeles—monumental problems can result. By 1963 over 58 percent of the American people lived in urban areas with some kind of air pollution problem. Forty-one percent of the population lived in areas with either moderate or major problems. Almost a quarter of the population lived in urban areas with major air pollution problems.

There was some dispute even by the early 1960's about what the harmful results of air pollution were. The Public Health Service (PHS) felt there was "strong evidence" that air pollution contributed to a number of respiratory ailments, including the common cold, bronchitis, pulmonary emphysema, bronchial asthma, and lung cancer. "Classic" smogs in London had killed 4,000 people in 1952 and 340 in 1962. A similar smog in Donora, Pennsylvania, in 1948 had made one-third of the population ill and killed about 20. Statistical evidence brought to light some years later revealed that a bad smog concentration in New York City in 1953 had killed about 200.

Damage to property resulting from air pollution is harder to evaluate, although there is no doubt of its existence. Agricultural damage caused by ozone, fluorides, and other pollutants costs hundreds of millions of dollars each year. Property damage in urban areas—resulting principally from deterioration of all kinds of materials but also from soiling—has been estimated to cost as much as $11 billion annually. Further effects of air pollution on visibility (and thus on air and auto safety), weather patterns, and aesthetic sensibilities cannot be measured precisely but also exist.

Even though some facts were in dispute, and even though there was some damage to crops in rural areas, everyone who was concerned about air pollution, both in Congress and in the executive, made it clear that the problem was centrally urban in character. Draft legislation, speeches, and reports from the late 1940's through 1963 all pictured the need for cleaner air as primarily an urban need.

California in 1947 and Oregon in 1951 had led the states with the first laws relating to air pollution. By 1963 thirty-three of the American states and territories had some kind of air pollution law. Only fifteen had a control authority, however, while twelve others allowed local control authorities to be set up by local option. Only California and Oregon had extensive standards for air quality, although four other states had emission standards for one or more specific pollutants. In 1961 only seventeen states were spending $5,000 or more on fighting air pollution. California spent 57 percent of the total of $2 million. At the local level only 43 percent of the urban areas with a major or moderate air pollution problem had a control agency spending more than $5,000 yearly. The eighty-five local agencies serving these communities spent about $8 million in 1961. Fifty-five percent of these funds were spent in California—almost four-fifths of that in Los Angeles alone. This limited state and local activity had resulted in some recognized successes—as in Pittsburgh—and in some recognized advances—as in Los Angeles. But by 1963 most areas had not even begun to make a dent in their problem.

Industries and some universities also attacked the problem of air pollution. University research projects in 1962 accounted for over half a million dollars. Research sponsored by industrial organizations in 1962 amounted to almost $2 million. Industrial groups also pointed out that they had spent tens and even hundreds of millions of dollars installing pollution control devices through the years.

One factor hampering state and local governments and industries in their attack on air pollution was an incomplete technology of identification and control. Various air sampling programs, most of them federal, had helped to develop the technology throughout the 1950's and early 1960's. New developments in the science of meteorology had also been helpful. On the basis of this knowledge various control devices had been developed for some of the worst industrial pollutants and for a minor part of automobile exhaust. But many problems still remained unsolved in 1963, two of the most important being automobile exhaust as a whole and the discharge of sulfur dioxide in the burning of fossil fuels. This situation of course gave those opposed to enforcement in the field of air pollution the argument that it was wrong to penalize polluters if the technology was not complete, and that the first priority should be technological development.

Another problem, which was related to the incomplete state of the technology, was the high cost of some of the effective devices developed to control pollution. A few examples taken from the Senate staff report mentioned above illustrate this. The control equipment used in fiberboard production cost 50 percent more than the production equipment itself. The control equipment for a bulk gasoline loading rack cost almost 60 percent as much as the production equipment. The control equipment for a yellow brass crucible furnace cost almost seven times what the furnace itself cost. An open hearth furnace used in the steel industry cost $200,000. The electric precipitator used to control pollution cost $150,000.

Other industries, however, were more fortunate. A crude oil distillation unit costing over $3 million required a control device costing only $10,000. Machinery for the manufacture of liquid hydrogen cost $8.4 million. Satisfactory pollution control equipment for it cost only $17,700. The pollution control unit for a rotogravure press costing $340,000 was only $40,000. Clearly, though, a major technological effort would be required to make pollution control less costly in many industrial processes.

By September 1962 those favoring a larger federal role in the attack on urban air pollution had generally agreed that the Public Health Service should have more research funds and should administer a grant-in-aid program that would encourage effective state and local antipollution activity. Before this time few persons knowledgeable about air pollution had seriously considered proposing that the federal government be given enforcement power in the drive to abate pollution. But during the fall of 1962 this idea was put forth and began to draw support. Those favoring federal enforcement power were, in the minds of many of those involved in the legislative process, "liberal" and supporters of "strong" legislation. Those opposed to federal enforcement during late 1962 and early 1963, whether motivated by principled opposition to federal involvement in this field or by a political or technical judgment that 1963 was too soon to ask for these powers, were labeled as "conservative." It is in this sense that the actors in the story that follows will be called "liberal" or "conservative."

Looked at in one way the story of the passage of the Clean Air Act is a story of cooperation and common purpose. The parts of the legislation dealing with research and grants-in-aid were widely recognized as necessary and occasioned great support from the executive, the Congress, and many of the private groups involved. Looked at in another way, however, the story is one of conflict and misunderstanding. There was no agreement among the concerned parties about the necessity or value of that part of the legislation dealing with federal enforcement powers. This case will attempt to tell both stories—that of cooperation and that of conflict—at once. Necessarily, the issue that provoked conflict—federal enforcement powers—will receive more attention, although it should not be forgotten that large portions of this act were the object of widespread support and the occasion of little conflict.

## Federal Recognition of the Problem

In 1907, five years before Kenneth Roberts was born in Piedmont, Alabama, the Smoke Prevention Association was formed. At that time smoke was thought to be the only serious pollutant of the atmosphere. The federal government became interested in the problem a few years later and in 1912 the Bureau of Mines in the Department of the Interior published three bulletins on the causes and means of preventing excessive emission of smoke from coal-burning equipment. As the Bureau of Mines developed its interest in smoke prevention it became the principal location within the national government for the study of air pollution. The bureau had an Office of Air Pollution. But most efforts to identify and control sources of smoke were made on the local level.

After World War II persons acquainted with the fight to prevent smoke became aware that air pollution was a complex phenomenon that encompassed exhausts other than smoke. In December 1949 President Harry S. Truman wrote to his secretary of the interior requesting him to organize an interdepartmental committee that would call the first United States technical conference on air pollution. In early May 1950 this conference was held in Washington. Over 750 persons from all levels of government and industry attended and urged that the federal government help identify air pollution problems and develop the technology to combat them.

In 1950 the American Municipal Association adopted its first resolutions on the subject of air pollution. Thus part of the so-called "urban lobby" began to interest itself in this problem.

The first stirrings of congressional activity in the field of air pollution also occurred in 1950. Two resolutions were introduced in the House to provide for research into the health hazards of air pollution. They were referred to the House Committee on Interstate and Foreign Commerce, where no further action was taken.

In November 1950, after serving as city attorney in Piedmont, Alabama, Ken Roberts was elected to Congress from Alabama's Fourth District. Upon his arrival in January 1951 he was given membership on the Interstate and Foreign Commerce Committee. This committee would consider all of the major air pollution legislation in the House in subsequent years.

In 1952, the year in which a smog in London was blamed for the deaths of several thousand persons, congressional interest in the problem was again in evidence. The House Committee on Interstate and Foreign Commerce reported a resolution "providing for intensified research into the causes, hazards, and effects of air pollution, into methods for its prevention and control and for recovery of critical materials from atmospheric contaminants." This resolution directed the surgeon general, the secretary of the interior, and the secretary of agriculture "to intensify their respective activities within the scope of their existing authority" to conduct research and publish and disseminate the resulting information. The Public Health Service had general research authority, provided in Section 301 of the Public Health Service Act of 1944, that would cover some aspects of air pollution.

The House passed this resolution on July 2, 1952. Its manager estimated it would cost $75,000 to $100,000 annually for five years, although the resolution itself contained no specific figures. The Senate Committee on Labor and Public Welfare reported it the following day. The Senate was conducting its floor business by unanimous consent at this point in the session in an effort to adjourn before the beginning of the national nominating conventions. Thus a single objection on the floor of the Senate on July 4 killed the legislation. The objection, from a highly conservative Republican senator, was on the grounds that no money figures were available for what the resolution would cost and yet it empowered three agencies of the government to increase their spending. Congress adjourned three days later. Similar resolutions were introduced in the House in both sessions of the Republican Eighty-third Congress, but received no attention in committee.

*The First Legislation, 1955.* In 1954 Republican Senators Thomas H. Kuchel of California and Homer E. Capehart of Indiana made an unsuccessful attempt to add air pollution sections to the housing bill. After it became clear that no air pollution legislation would be passed that year, Kuchel and Capehart wrote President Dwight D. Eisenhower on August 5, 1954 that "it might be constructive to have an interdepartmental committee set up comprising representatives of various federal agencies responsible for framing and carrying out policies regarding health, housing, industrial, and agricultural matters, transportation, the national economy, and scientific research, which could make a canvass of the resources of the Government which might be employed in furtherance of efforts to control 'smog.' " The White House replied promptly, saying that the suggestion of an interagency committee had been discussed with the secretary of health, education, and welfare "and the Secretary agrees that the proposal is an excellent one."

Thus, in the fall of 1954 the secretary of HEW appointed an ad hoc Interdepartmental Committee on Community Air Pollution. The surgeon general was the chairman and the members were representatives of the Departments of Defense, Agriculture, Commerce, Interior, and HEW, the Atomic Energy Commission, and the National Science Foundation. The committee reported later in the fall of 1954 and urged legislation authorizing a broad federal program of research and technical assistance in air pollution problems. This report helped to shape subsequent PHS positions favoring research and grants-in-aid programs and opposing federal enforcement powers.

In accord with the recommendations of the committee President Eisenhower in his January 6, 1955 State of the Union message said he would propose "strengthened programs to combat the increasingly serious pollution of our rivers and streams and the growing problem of air pollution." Eisenhower followed this on January 31 with a special message recommending a health program. The President saw a need to "step up research on air pollution. As a result of industrial growth and urban development, the atmosphere over some population centers may be approaching the limit of its ability to absorb air pollutants with safety to health. I am recommending an increased appropriation to the Public Health Service for studies seeking necessary scientific data and more effective methods of control."

The Senate Public Works Subcommittee on Flood Control—Rivers and Harbors held hearings on water and air pollution in late April 1955. Only a small part of one day was devoted to the administration's bill on air pollution. The chairman of the subcommittee was Democrat Robert S. Kerr of Oklahoma. Kuchel, although a Republican, chaired most of the section on air pollution. At one point, however, Kerr made it clear that he had no sympathy for any proposal to give enforcement power to the federal government. The Senate committee reported the bill, which provided for $3 million annually for five years, on May 31. The report stressed the committee's determination that "it is the primary responsibility of State and local governments to prevent air pollution." The bill, which had come from the committee by unanimous vote, now passed the Senate by voice vote without dissent.

The House Interstate and Foreign Commerce Committee reported the bill in late June. It increased the money authorized to $5 million annually for five years. On July 5 the House passed the bill by voice vote under suspension of the rules. Democrat J. Percy Priest of Tennessee, chairman of the House committee, summed up the purpose of the legislation by saying that although the committee recognized the problem to be primarily the responsibility of state and local governments, it "feels also that the Federal Government has a stake in this question, that it may well conduct research, provide technical services and some financial aid to agencies and individuals concerned with the problem of air pollution."

The following day the Senate agreed to the House amendments by voice vote, without debate. On July 14 Eisenhower signed the bill into law (P.L. 84–159). This law, which was the basic federal air pollution statute until the passage of the 1963 Clean Air Act, declared that it is "the policy of Congress to preserve and protect the primary responsibilities and rights of the States and local governments in controlling air pollution, to support and aid technical research to devise and develop methods of abating such pollution, and to provide Federal technical services and financial aid to State and local government air pollution control agencies and other public or private agencies and institutions in the formulation and execution of their air pollution abatement research programs." The law further provided for federal surveys of specific local problems upon request and for the publication of reports by the surgeon general. It authorized $5 million annually for five years (through fiscal 1960), which could be spent in part for contracts for research, training, and demonstration projects and for grants-in-aid to state and local government agencies and other public and private air pollution agencies, as well as for research within the Public Health Service.

*Growing Attention but Little Action, 1956–62.* In 1955, at the beginning of the Eighty-fourth Congress, Ken Roberts had become third-ranking Democrat on the Health and Science Subcommittee. In 1956 Chairman Priest appointed him chairman of the newly created Special Subcommittee on Traffic Safety. In that year Roberts held extensive hearings focusing on highway traffic accidents. One witness, however, dealt briefly with automobile exhaust as a form of air pollution.

In 1957 the National Advisory Committee on Community Air Pollution was created by the surgeon general. It had members from industry, local control agencies, and medical and public health research centers. Also in 1957, at the urging of the California House delegation, Democratic Representative L. H. Fountain of North Carolina took his Government Operations Subcommittee on Intergovernmental Relations to Los Angeles for a one-day hearing on the progress of the federal air pollution efforts.

The problem of automobile exhaust received more attention from the Roberts subcommittee in 1958. Republican Paul F. Schenck of Ohio, a member of the subcommittee, introduced a bill prohibiting the use in interstate commerce of any motor vehicle discharging unburned hydrocarbons in an amount determined by the surgeon general "to be dangerous to human health." Roberts held a day of hearings on this proposal. HEW recommended against passage because the technology for defining "dangerous" was not developed. The subcommittee killed the bill.

Also in the spring of 1958 the Fountain subcommittee again touched on air pollution in its survey hearings involving federal-state-local relations. At these hearings Surgeon General Leroy E. Burney opposed federal enforcement powers because of the incomplete state of the technology for controlling pollution.

In June 1958 the National Advisory Health Council of the Public Health Service stressed the need for greater research and education in environmental health. As part of the program stimulating more activity in the air pollution field the surgeon general called a National Conference on Air Pollution, which was held in Washington November 18–20, 1958.

The official in the executive who took the need for increased federal activity most seriously was the recently appointed secretary of HEW, Arthur S. Flemming. At a press conference on December 1, 1958 he recommended that the federal government be allowed to hold public hearings on specific problems of pollution and make findings and recommendations based on those hearings. The Public Health Service, although a part of HEW, was quick to oppose the secretary's position. At a meeting in early April 1959, prior to the introduction of HEW-sponsored legislation on air pollution, Flemming was opposed by seven PHS representatives. His views, however, remained unchanged. Draft legislation was prepared in accord with his wishes.

There was a general reason for the Public Health Service opposition. The institution construed the power to hold public hearings as a kind of enforcement power and it was "conservative" in terms of seeking enforcement powers for itself. Traditionally, its only major enforcement authority was in the quarantine field, though some limited water pollution enforcement powers had been added in 1948, 1956, and 1961. It neither sought nor wanted such powers in the air pollution field. It saw itself as an apolitical, highly professional, research-oriented organization that developed health standards to be used and enforced by state and local officials. It prided itself on the good relations it enjoyed with these officials and it thought that enforcement powers, by taking away some of their initiative and authority, would disrupt the close cooperation it had developed with them in promoting the health of the nation.

The specific reason for the Public Health Service opposition to Flemming's suggestion at this time, however, was the fear that a negative reaction to it in Congress would jeopardize any chance of passing other aspects of the legislative proposals concerning air pollution. In 1959 the five-year program enacted in 1955 had yet another year to run. But the PHS was anxious to get the program extended for an indefinite period and to have the limitation on funds removed. Actual appropriations were authorized both by the 1955 law and by general research provisions of the Public Health Service Act. Two hundred thousand dollars had been expended in fiscal year 1955, $1.7 million in fiscal 1956, $2.7 million in fiscal 1957, $4 million in fiscal 1958, and $4 million in fiscal 1959. The budget for fiscal 1960 called for $4.2 million.

The Senate Committee on Public Works considered a bill removing time and authorization limits. It reimposed both limits and reported a bill calling for a four-year extension at $7.5 million annually. Secretary Flemming sent a letter to the committee suggesting his idea of permitting the Public Health Service to hold hearings, but no such provision was added to the legislation. The Senate passed the bill as reported.

At the beginning of the Eighty-sixth Congress in 1959 Ken Roberts had become chairman of the Subcommittee on Health and Safety. His subcommittee held two days of hearings in May and June 1959 on the proposal to extend the Air Pollution Control Act. The subcommittee was pleased with the new activity at all levels of government, as well as in private industry and research institutions, which it felt the 1955 law had stimulated. It felt, however, that it should extend the law for only two years so as to be able to review the program in the Eighty-seventh Congress. The bill reported to the House simply continued the existing authorization level of $5 million for two years. The House passed it under suspension of the rules with little debate. Only Republican H. R. Gross of Iowa indicated skepticism: "This is getting to be a pretty expensive program, is it not?"

The subsequent conference kept the $5 million figure but extended the program for four years, as in the Senate bill. On September 22, 1959 Eisenhower signed this extension into law.

The problem of automobile exhaust also concerned the Roberts subcommittee in 1959. Paul Schenck introduced more legislation prohibiting the use in interstate commerce of any car discharging substances in amounts that are "dangerous to human health." Again HEW opposed the enactment of this bill. It cited the lack of technical know-how and also the philosophy of local responsibility for enforcing solutions to pollution problems. The subcommittee weakened the bill and reported it in a form that merely directed the surgeon general to undertake a study of automobile exhaust. The House passed this bill on August 17, 1959 and it was referred to the Senate Committee on Labor and Public Welfare.

The Senate committee reported the bill the following May and it passed the Senate with no difficulty. The President signed it on June 8, 1960. The law, known as the Schenck Act, simply required that the surgeon general conduct a "thorough study" of motor vehicle exhaust and report to Congress within two years. This report, over 450 pages long, was filed in June 1962.

In 1960 the Roberts subcommittee again held hearings that concentrated on automobile exhaust. No further legislation was reported on the subject, however. The hearings were designed merely to review the progress being made in the control of the harmful portions of auto exhaust.

In June 1960 the Senate Committee on Public Works reported a bill to give the surgeon general the power to hold hearings on air pollution problems "which are interstate in nature and are of broad significance." This power, although desired by Secretary Flemming, was still not generally desired in the Public Health Service—even though Senator Kuchel, sponsor of the bill, emphasized that it was not an enforcement power.

The bill also extended the air pollution program for two more years, through fiscal 1966. The Senate passed this bill in late June and sent it to the Roberts subcommittee. Roberts had introduced a similar bill in February 1960, but his subcommittee took no further action on this legislation that year.

In 1961, at the beginning of the Eighty-seventh Congress, Senator Kuchel, who had been the sponsor of virtually all air pollution bills in the Senate since the initial law, reintroduced the bill that had passed in the Senate the previous year. In presenting the bill on the floor he again stressed that the hearing boards it provided for would not be construed as federal enforcement. Late in September the Senate again passed this bill, and again the Roberts subcommittee took no action.

In February 1961, President John F. Kennedy indicated that he was going to support efforts to get a more substantial federal air pollution program. President Eisenhower, after his initial 1955 effort, had been little interested in the problems of air pollution and an expanded federal role in the effort to control it. But now the new President, in a special message on natural resources, proposed a new unit in the Public Health Service to work on the water pollution problem. And:

> this same unit should provide new leadership, research, and financial and technical assistance for the control of air pollution, a serious hazard to the health of our people that causes an estimated $7.5 billion annually in damage to vegetation, livestock, metals and other materials. We need an effective Federal air pollution control program now. For although the total supply of air is vast, the atmosphere over our growing metropolitan areas—where more than half the people live—has only limited capacity to dilute and disperse the contaminants now being increasingly discharged from homes, factories, vehicles, and many other sources.[1]

[1] It should be noted that the history of the attempts to give the federal government a role in controlling air pollution follows somewhat the same pattern as the attempts in the field of water pollution. The major difference is that the water pollution chronology started a few years before the air pollution chronology and therefore was usually at a more "advanced" stage. Thus, for example, the federal government was given substantial though limited enforcement powers in the water pollution field seven years before receiving air pollution enforcement powers. It should also be noted that those working in the air pollution field—in the executive, in Congress, and in some of the private groups—viewed the relations between control of water pollution and control of air pollution in widely varying ways. Some viewed them as absolutely analogous. Others viewed them as completely separate—especially since water pollution can sometimes be alleviated by removing the pollutants from the water whereas pollutants cannot be removed from the air but must be prevented from entering it. The differences in how the relationship between the two fields was viewed had some importance in the way in which the 1963 air pollution legislation took shape.

In November 1961, after the adjournment of Congress, Roberts held a single day of hearings on the subject of air pollution in Birmingham, Alabama. This city was adjacent to his own district. At these hearings Dr. Richard Prindle, deputy chief of the Division of Air Pollution of the Public Health Service, summed up the PHS philosophy of the federal role in air pollution control. "I believe the role of the Federal Government is just as our law has outlined, provision of technical assistance, research knowledge, and the information on which a State and local government might act."

Early in 1962, on February 27, President John F. Kennedy sent to Congress his special message on health care. In this message he asked that the House pass the Senate bill from the previous year. Two days later, to implement the President's requests, Roberts introduced an administration bill into the House.

Roberts held a day of hearings on the administration bill and other air pollution bills in June 1962. The administration bill provided for elimination of time and money limits and authorized programs of research and grants-in-aid to state and local air pollution control authorities. It also provided for federally initiated conferences on specific air pollution problems—either interstate or intrastate—that could make recommendations to state and local officials. Roberts introduced the bill at the request of the administration but by the middle of the summer felt that his subcommittee needed more time to study these proposals before approving them. The subcommittee therefore reported favorably a simple two-year extension of the 1955 law. This would carry it through fiscal 1966.

In September the House passed this extension by voice vote under suspension of the rules. Roberts stated his desire to go into the broader proposals more thoroughly in the next session of Congress. The Senate concurred in the House amendment to the bill it had passed the year before. On October 9, 1962 President Kennedy signed the two-year extension of the $5 million program into law. The only other provision of the law directed the surgeon general to continue his studies of motor vehicle exhaust.

The administration was disappointed with this outcome. In April 1962 Secretary of Health, Education, and Welfare Abraham A. Ribicoff had announced that the second National Conference on Air Pollution would meet in Washington in December. It had been thought that this conference would celebrate and publicize the new law and help get its implementation started rapidly. Now, however, the conference would take place before any substantial new legislation could be enacted.

During the years from 1955 through 1962 the pattern of private group activity both for and against stronger federal action had been emerging. The chief groups urging more federal action were part of the urban lobby—the United States Conference of Mayors, the American Municipal Association, and the National Association of Counties. The Conference of Mayors and the Municipal Association both began to work for broader legislation. The individual behind the activities of both groups in this field was Hugh Mields, Jr., who was assistant director for federal activities for the Municipal Association from 1956 to 1961, and associate director of the Conference of Mayors after July 1962.

Few groups after 1955 totally opposed federal work in the field of air pollution. The National Association of Manufacturers opposed any increase in or extension of the program. Most of the industrial groups that were directly involved—such as the chemical manufacturers, the iron and steel industry, and the coal industry—felt that they had a voice in making policy through their participation in the National Advisory Committee on Community Air Pollution. The automobile industry directed its major effort to fighting the passage of any strong laws, such as those urged by Schenck, against cars that emitted unburned hydrocarbons and other pollutants. It was successful.

The American Medical Association approved of limited federal expenditure for research on air pollution as long as primary responsibility in taking action was preserved for the states and localities. The Association of State and Territorial Health Officers held much the same position, although going further in hoping for increased federal expenditure.

By September of 1962 virtually all parties had conceded that the federal government had at least a research role to play in combating the problem. Many parties had become aware that an expanded federal program of monetary aid to state and local authorities would be useful However, no one in a prominent position, at least publicly, had suggested that the federal government had a role to play in enforcing abatement proceedings aimed at specific situations involving dangerous pollution.

By mid-1962 the House subcommittee chaired by Roberts had held numerous hearings and had built up substantial expert knowledge about air pollution problems and technology. All of its recommendations had been enacted by voice vote under suspension of the rules on the House floor.

In the executive branch the Public Health Service certainly possessed many of the most knowledgeable people in the field of pollution control. It remained an open question, however, whether either the PHS or the Department of Health, Education, and Welfare would commit itself to a battle for legislation that included enforcement powers.

Among the private groups the Conference of Mayors had developed some knowledge of the problems of air pollution and had worked at the local level to create substantial interest in solving the problems of pollution.

In the Senate there were knowledgeable and interested senators, like Kuchel, who probably would support expanded federal activity in the pollution field. But with Kerr as chairman of the subcommittee empowered to handle any such legislation, it was doubtful how far the Senate would go with new proposals.

Thus, for those interested in a vigorous new federal effort against air pollution the problem was twofold. First, someone must be found to initiate the legislation providing for a new effort. Second, support must be mobilized for it.


Conflict in the Executive, 1962–63

In 1960 the Public Health Service combined two existing units and created a Division of Air Pollution within its Bureau of State Services, thus bringing together the men actually working on the problem. The division was headed by Vernon G. MacKenzie, a sanitary engineer educated at the Massachusetts Institute of Technology. After graduation he had worked for the cities of Chicago and Detroit and had joined the PHS in 1939 in Cincinnati. He came to Washington in 1954 and worked in the air pollution field, becoming chief of the new division. One of MacKenzie's chief assistants in the division was Samuel Rogers, who had been with the PHS since 1949 and had been working in air pollution since 1956. The principal legal adviser for the division was Sidney Edelman. Edelman was the assistant chief of the Public Health Division in the general counsel's office of HEW. He had been with the Public Health Division since 1952 and had been working in the field of air pollution for about four years prior to 1963.

Shortly after its creation the division worked out its legislative proposals for 1961. The division favored having amendments added to the Public Health Service Act, rather than to the air pollution law itself. The proposals, as reported in early October 1960, included a recommendation for public hearings on specific problems, the elimination of time and money limits, and a grant-in-aid program. In sending these proposals to the deputy chief of the Bureau of State Services in January 1961, Mac-Kenzie noted that "A number of air pollution bills have already been introduced into the current session of the Congress; a number of these bills outline various approaches to the problem. We have been approached informally by members of Congress for our thoughts on Federal air pollution legislation. It is important, therefore, that review of these specifications receive high priority so that there is internal Public Health Service agreement on the concepts proposed."

In February 1961, Hugh Mields, then of the American Municipal Association, wrote to Ivan A. Nestingen, the undersecretary of health, education, and welfare. He included draft legislation on air pollution, stating that "No other bill currently before the Congress is . . . as comprehensive or as appropriate in view of the growing seriousness of the problem." This draft legislation provided for federal fostering of interstate cooperation, increased authority for research, training, and informational activities, and a grant-in-aid program to state and local pollution agencies. In replying to this letter Wilbur J. Cohen, the assistant secretary of HEW for legislation, indicated general agreement with the principles stated by Mields.

In mid-March Nestingen gave a speech in which he expressed both the desire of the new administration to do something more in the air pollution field and the desire of the PHS and of HEW as a whole not to go too far. "In general, the current Federal policy would appear to be sound; we believe the time has now come, however, for the Federal Government to take a more active role. The research and technical assistance efforts of the Federal Government should be supplemented by vigorous leadership to stimulate greater air pollution control effort on the part of industry, States, and local governments."

But the more conservative views of the Public Health Service were also expressed in this first year of the Kennedy administration, in a memo from the deputy chief of the Bureau of State Services to the surgeon general. The deputy chief equated the proposed hearings with a step toward federal enforcement. "The initiation of any Federal enforcement activity or action which would lead thereto has considerable opposition from some public agencies and particularly from industry. In our opinion, it is much more desirable at this time to take effective action to stimulate State and local control programs than to initiate any activity leading toward Federal enforcement action." He added that ultimately federal authority might be needed on some problems.

In July 1961 MacKenzie met with Cohen, representatives from the general counsel's office, and Jerome N. Sonosky, Cohen's special assistant. At this meeting it was agreed that the department would consider sponsoring legislation in the 1962 session of Congress.

In early 1962, when the administration began to shape its legislative proposals for the year, it was agreed that authority for expanded research, grants-in-aid, and federally initiated public conferences should be requested. The main difference of opinion in the executive was between the Public Health Service and the Bureau of the Budget (BOB). The BOB objected to general federal grants to support the operation of state and local air pollution control programs, although it was willing to support grants that would aid in the evaluation of specific air pollution problems. It based its objections on two grounds: the art of controlling air pollution was not far enough advanced to warrant the granting of money to local agencies; and such efforts should be financed locally. The President's message, in late February, indicated support for grants for specific projects.

In discussing the draft legislation with other agencies the Public Health Service was confronted with particularly strong and often repeated objections from the Bureau of Mines in the Interior Department and from the Bureau of Standards in the Commerce Department. Both insisted that the Interdepartmental Committee, which in theory was to coordinate air pollution efforts throughout the federal government, had been used insufficiently. They also argued that the PHS should finance the activities of the other departments in the air pollution field. The PHS prevailed in the wording of the draft legislation but the losing agencies were unhappy through the remainder of 1962. By 1963, however, they apparently realized that the major federal air pollution effort was irrevocably under the control of the Public Health Service.

Conditions within the executive thus did not seem auspicious for a large new legislative effort in 1963. Nevertheless, the activity of Hugh Mields, now with the Conference of Mayors, bolstered by the technical assistance of a few persons in the Public Health Service, generated activity within the executive that by mid-February 1963 had the President of the United States publicly committed to federal enforcement of air pollution abatement.

After Mields became associate director of the Conference of Mayors in July 1962 he immediately began drafting legislation in the air pollution field. He took the bulk of the 1962 administration bill and made a few changes and persuaded Democrat George M. Rhodes of Pennsylvania to introduce it in the House in early October 1962. The most important change from the administration bill was in the policy section, where Mields's draft declared it to be the purpose of the act "to authorize and direct the Secretary of Health, Education, and Welfare to mount a concentrated national effort to achieve the prevention and control of air pollution *within the next ten years . . .*" [italics added]. The policy section also omitted the customary reference to "the primary responsibilities and rights of the States and local government." Instead it stated that "The Congress recognizes that the Federal Government has an obligation to provide the leadership in the initiation of national programs of research and development necessary to the ultimate prevention and control of air pollution."

The office of Senator Clair Engle, Democrat from California, asked Mields if Engle could introduce the same bill in the Senate at the same time. Mields of course agreed. He realized that it was much too late in the 1962 session to expect any action but wanted this draft before Congress to stimulate discussion. He also felt it would be a basis for discussion at the National Conference on Air Pollution that was scheduled for December.

Throughout the rest of the fall of 1962 Mields worked with Samuel Rogers and Sidney Edelman in considering and wording drafts of even stronger legislation. Rogers and Edelman formally cleared their participation as technical advisers with their superiors.

*The National Conference on Air Pollution.* The National Conference on Air Pollution, which had been in the planning stage for almost a year, finally took place December 10–12, 1962 in Washington. Almost 1500 people participated in it. Another killing smog in London occurred before and during the conference and gave an added urgency to the deliberations.

Congressman Roberts spoke on December 11 to a conference panel on "Applying Present Know-How to Air Pollution Control." Roberts stated that "I do not think the Federal Government has any business telling the people of, say, Birmingham or Los Angeles how to proceed to meet their air pollution problems. That was made clear in the 1955 act." He listed the areas in which the federal contribution could be substantial: research, encouraging state and local cooperation, collecting and disseminating information, and conducting investigations and surveys on request. The panel discussion that followed endorsed Roberts' position. An air pollution official from Chicago was the only one who made specific and favorable mention of the broader policy suggested by the Rhodes-Engle bill. The others who spoke, all representatives of industry, stressed the need for state and local control of abatement proceedings. The report from this panel session to a plenary session stressed the consensus on "the desirability of local control programs."

Two statements made at the conference favored federal enforcement of abatement, at least in interstate pollution problems. These statements made a stronger bill, including enforcement procedures, seem more feasible to Mields and to proponents in the executive. The first came in a banquet speech by Arthur Flemming, president of the University of Oregon and formerly President Eisenhower's secretary of health, education, and welfare. Those planning the conference had chosen Flemming to speak both because he knew the problem and had been particularly interested in it as secretary and because he was a Republican and thus would help give the conference a bipartisan flavor. In his speech Flemming proposed four ways in which the federal government should increase its activity. First, it should have an environmental health unit in the Public Health Service. Second, its research and training programs should be expanded. Third, it should develop a grants-in-aid program. Fourth, "the Federal Government should be given enforcement authority in air pollution comparable to the authority it now has in water pollution." He expanded on the need for this authority:

> Now I know there are many who would say that this authority is not needed, and they would point to the substantial progress that has been made without such authority. I respect those who are responsible for this progress. But I submit to you that there is still too much evidence pointing to the fact that there are those who put selfish economic interests ahead of the health of our Nation and resent and resist the efforts of others who put the health of the Nation ahead of all other considerations.

The second statement came from the American Medical Association, in the form of a telegram on December 12 from Dr. F. J. L. Blasingame, executive vice president, to Dr. Luther L. Terry, the surgeon general. The full text of the telegram read:

> Congratulations on your extremely productive conference on air pollution. One of our most serious environmental health problems is air pollution. It can and should be controlled. The American Medical Association endorses the concept of local, state, and federal joint enterprise. Local, state, and industrial groups should participate to the utmost of their capacity. The federal government should engage in:
>
> (1) Responsible leadership through the Public Health Service;
> (2) Research and discovery; and,
> (3) Enforcement in interstate or interjurisdictional difficulties in the manner of the successfully implemented Water Pollution Act.
>
> Enough has been said. Let's clear the air.

This telegram was drafted by two Medical Association staff representatives attending the conference in Washington. They felt that such a telegram was needed. After consulting with others at the conference, including representatives of the PHS, they sent it to Dr. Blasingame's assistant in the Chicago headquarters of the association for his approval. This assistant felt the telegram to be in accord with American Medical Association policy and sent it back to the conference over Dr. Blasingame's signature. Interestingly enough, the Medical Association went beyond the preferences of Dr. Terry, who in closing the conference quoted the telegram but muted the point about enforcement.

Representatives of industries and local and state government, as well as elements of the medical profession, were quick to point out to the association that its position in favor of enforcement in air pollution was distasteful to them. Consequently Dr. Blasingame wrote a clarifying letter to Dr. Terry on January 9, 1963. This was printed in the proceedings of the conference. In the letter Dr. Blasingame said that his telegram had only summarized a long-standing attitude on the part of the Medical Association. He spoke about enforcement in more guarded language than in the telegram: "Where local efforts fail, where proper agreements cannot be reached between the States involved, where the air pollution is interstate in nature—the Federal Government should exercise leadership to see that air pollution is controlled."

The day after the conference ended the National Advisory Committee on Community Air Pollution held its annual meeting. This meeting, attended by representatives of industry, private research institutes, state and local government, and the Public Health Service, was in part devoted to a discussion of possible legislation on air pollution. The committee endorsed the removal of limits on time and appropriations and also endorsed the grants-in-aid section of the Rhodes-Engle bill. Federal enforcement powers were not discussed.

*The Question of Federal Enforcement.* In mid-December 1962 Mields, Edelman, and Rogers produced a draft of a bill calling for federal enforcement procedures. This draft began to circulate in the Public Health Service and was also shown by Mields to possible sponsors in Congress.

A more conservative alternative, based on the recommendations of the National Advisory Committee, was also drafted and circulated by PHS staff members. Surgeon General Terry reported to Secretary of HEW Anthony Celebrezze on December 13 on the nature of these recommendations. He felt that the recommendations, which left no room for federal enforcement, "represent a middle ground which was acceptable not only to the industry, state, local, and public members of the advisory committee but also the Public Health Service. I recommend that they form the basis for an administration air pollution bill to be offered the next session of Congress."

A draft bill was ready by December 20 reflecting this position. The bill included provisions encouraging cooperation among various levels of government, stimulating research, providing grants-in-aid, and making the cooperation of officials at federal installations mandatory. On the question of public hearings the bill provided only for investigations into specific intrastate problems at the request of the governor or local air pollution control agency and into interstate problems only at the request of one governor or air pollution control agency.

At this time Dean Coston, the special assistant to Wilbur Cohen, became the chief moving force in the Department of Health, Education, and Welfare behind a strong bill with enforcement provisions. Coston had taught radio-television at the University of Michigan until coming to HEW in 1961. He had also been active in Democratic politics in Michigan. In July 1963 he was to be promoted to deputy assistant secretary of HEW for legislation. Coston felt that the most decisive way to defeat the conservatives in the Public Health Service and get administration endorsement of a strong bill was to get the President himself committed to a strong position. Consequently, on December 26, the day before Cohen was to go to Palm Beach to discuss the HEW legislative program with

President Kennedy, Coston advised him of how the battle for enforcement provisions in the bill stood:

> A burning desire for Federal enforcement has not yet emerged from the States and municipalities. Until many more local jurisdictions get disturbed and excited about the problem, widespread support may be difficult to obtain.
> Strong enforcement proposals may well jeopardize the enactment of any other legislation on air pollution. Congressman Roberts, in his speech to the National Conference, made it clear that his interest was in strengthening State and local programs, and not in Federal enforcement.
> A position statement on air pollution should be made in either the State of the Union or the Health messages. In this statement, some recognition of the need for more adequate enforcement could be given without specifically endorsing a full Federal enforcement program. This would give some freedom in choosing what course the administration would take.

Cohen spent the next two days in Palm Beach and was successful in getting the President interested in supporting federal enforcement. Following Coston's suggestions Cohen argued that the administration could not afford to find itself to the political right of Republican Arthur Flemming and the American Medical Associaton.

As the new year opened disagreement within the executive continued. Few were aware of the President's probable support for enforcement powers. Many were hoping to get Secretary Anthony Celebrezze to take a definite position on the issue. This the former mayor of Cleveland never did, even though he was a former president of both the American Municipal Association and the United States Conference of Mayors.

On January 3, 1963 MacKenzie and Coston met with representatives from the general counsel's office and from the surgeon general's office. Those present felt that it might be pointless to include air pollution recommendations in the President's health message, since they thought the message would not get to Congress before March 1. They were also undecided about introducing just one administration bill. The White House had made it clear that it desired a "stronger" air pollution bill to be prepared. The meeting included a discussion of whether this bill should contain provisions for federal enforcement. The consensus of the meeting was that it should not. MacKenzie and the associate general counsel of HEW, Harold W. Horowitz, were appointed to draft legislation in accord with the White House's unspecific wishes.

Coston, however, in a memo to Cohen on January 7 indicated that he did not agree with the consensus of the January 3 meeting and was proceeding to draft his own bill "with some kind of *limited* enforcement provisions, although there is a sharp disagreement on this question."

The MacKenzie-Horowitz draft was ready by January 14. In general it was the same as the Rhodes-Engle bill of the previous year, except that the conference provisions had been deleted.

On January 17 the President's budget requests were no more specific than to request an "increase" in funds for air pollution activities.

On January 25, Coston, Edelman, and MacKenzie met with Mields, Donald Slater of the Municipal Association, and C. D. Ward of the National Association of Counties. The discussion focused on the provisions of two bills that had just been introduced into the Senate. The first was S. 432, which provided for federal enforcement both in interstate and intrastate problems. This had been introduced by Democrat Abraham Ribicoff of Connecticut, who until July 31, 1962 had been Kennedy's secretary of health, education, and welfare. The second was S. 444, essentially the old Rhodes-Engle bill, again introduced by Senator Engle.

Mields, Slater, and Ward all said their organizations would support the enforcement section of either bill if the administration supported either. They also favored the other provisions of the bills. All at the meeting agreed that the important thing was for the administration to come to a decision and make a public statement on air pollution legislation.

The Public Health Service continued to fight against an administration endorsement of enforcement powers. On January 29 it produced a staff analysis on "Federal Enforcement Authority in Air Pollution Control." This had been requested by the Budget Bureau, and a copy was sent to the White House for its reactions. After rehearsing arguments on both sides, the analysis summarized the PHS position: "For the present at least, no Federal regulatory authority beyond that proposed by the Administration in 1962 is desirable." The analysis concluded with these comments: "The inclusion of Federal regulatory authority in . . . legislation at this time is subject to fundamental differences of opinion. The basic questions to be considered are: First, is such regulatory authority necessary to obtain effective progress in dealing with the air pollution problems nationally; and Second, will the inclusion of the Federal regulatory authority in the Administration-sponsored legislation proposal jeopardize the enactment of any legislation in this field at this time."

In the few days following the release of the staff analysis the debate within the executive reached its highest pitch. The assistant surgeon general for plans sent a copy of the analysis to the chief of the public health branch in the Bureau of the Budget with his endorsement of its contents. Simultaneously the general counsel's office began to raise questions about the constitutionality of federal enforcement in the air pollution field. On January 30 Edelman wrote a nineteen-page memo upholding the constitutionality of federal enforcement. Coston and the assistant general counsel for legislation clashed over the constitutional question in memos on January 31 and February 1.

The Cohen and Coston position, developed without the active support of the secretary, came to be that the administration should endorse the Ribicoff bill or a bill along those lines, that is, one containing some kind of federal enforcement provisions. Coston drafted language to that effect for inclusion in the President's special message on health, which was slated to be released on February 7. Cohen took this draft to the White House.

The most powerful PHS ally against federal enforcement in those closing minutes of the debate was the Bureau of the Budget. The BOB knew of the tentative decision at Palm Beach to support interstate enforcement, and it knew that the draft of the health message contained support for this position. But Budget Bureau discussions with HEW had revealed many unanswered questions, prompting its request for the analysis of the pros and cons that had then been prepared by the Public Health Service. On January 31 the bureau recommended against endorsement in talking with the White House. It cited the split within HEW and the Public Health Service as evidence of the wisdom of this position. It felt that state and local enforcement should be given a longer trial period in which to prove itself. If this produced no results then federal enforcement might be considered as an alternative.

In raising these points the Bureau of the Budget felt that it was simply performing its normal staff function for the President of pointing out difficult issues in looking at proposed legislation. It disclaimed any interest in making, or power to make, policy. Those favoring presidential support for enforcement powers, however, took a strikingly different view of the BOB's role. In their eyes the bureau possessed the power to make policy decisions and in this instance used that power on the "conservative" side in the controversy over federal enforcement. Whatever the motivation of the BOB, its questions and objections were apparently answered to the satisfaction of the White House. The Cohen-Coston position on enforcement was included in the President's message.

*The President's Decision.* The President's message on health recommended legislation:

authorizing the Public Health Service of the Department of Health, Education, and Welfare:

(a) To engage in a more intensive research program permitting full investigation of the causes, effects and control of air pollution;

(b) To provide financial stimulation to States and local air pollution control agencies through project grants which will help them to initiate or improve their control programs;

(c) To conduct studies on air pollution problems of interstate or nation-wide significance; and

(d) To take action to abate interstate air pollution, along the general lines of the existing water pollution control enforcement measures.

Despite some reservations about the presidential decision, the Public Health Service immediately ceased its protests against enforcement provisions. The general counsel's office retained some of its constitutional doubts, however, and worked throughout the rest of the year to build the strongest possible constitutional case where it could. Wilbur Cohen in a letter on February 21 summarized the state of the executive branch two weeks after the President's message: "The whole question of air pollution legislation is moving to some kind of resolution. There has been great interest in the Ribicoff approach, with the general feeling that the Federal Government at last means business in this area. The President's Health Message gave us all stronger marching orders than we have had in the past, and now that the blow has fallen, even the most conservative USPHS'ers are beginning to like it."

Coston summarized the prospects for the strong bill on the day of the President's message. He felt that it would attract liberals because "it *does* something, and indicates forward movement" but would also attract conservatives because it "does it at relatively small cost." He recognized that industrial groups would be likely to oppose strong legislation but emphasized the value of the support that the municipal groups would give. In assessing the congressional situation Coston indicated that the Senate prospects looked good. "The House presents more of a problem. . . . Mr. Roberts has not been willing to take a position for enforcement, and Mr. Harris' [Oren Harris, Arkansas Democrat and chairman of the Interstate and Foreign Commerce Committee] position is at best unknown."

The major decision left for the executive, once the President had spoken on enforcement, was whether to draft an administration bill or merely testify on bills introduced by senators and representatives. Virtually all the supporters of the legislation favored not introducing an administration bill. Those who wanted a strong bill did not want to become involved in the formal legislative clearance process with the Public Health Service and the Bureau of the Budget. There would surely be disagreements over the specific wording of a bill. These disagreements could produce delay that would prevent congressional action in 1963. The urban groups favoring strong legislation agreed with this reasoning. The White House had a particular interest in not offending Senator Ribicoff by introducing what would be thought of as an alternative to his bill. Those opposing a strong bill did not object to the lack of an administration bill. Perhaps they reasoned that without administration support for a specific proposal the chances of natural political processes producing a weak bill would be better. They might have felt that they were now free to support the weakest alternatives before the Congress.

What legislation would emerge, if any, was now up to the Congress. The executive at this point was speaking timidly and with reservations. Its formal support of a strong bill was important but did not represent a clear and united executive position. Thus, after February 7 the eyes of all interested parties turned to the Hill, where the newly elected Eighty-eighth Congress had organized and was beginning to get to the legislative tasks at hand.

## The Work of Roberts in the House, 1963

*Senator Ribicoff's Initiative.* At the time that Engle had introduced his bill in early October 1962 he released a statement for the press saying that he hoped "to give all interested persons and agencies concerned ample opportunity to study the proposal before hearings get under way in Congress early next year." He also indicated that his bill "implements the proposals of the U.S. Conference of Mayors." On December 10, 1962, in a statement prepared for the mayors, Engle said, "I intend to reintroduce the bill with such modifications that may be appropriate in January 1963."

There was growing misunderstanding between Mields and the member of Engle's staff responsible for air pollution during this October to January period. Engle's staff member got the impression that Mields and the others supporting the legislation in effect wanted the 1962 bill reintroduced without change. Actually Mields felt that no progress could be made merely by reintroducing the Rhodes-Engle bill, but he thought that Engle's man was consciously rejecting a bill containing enforcement powers. Engle made his plans along the lines suggested by his staff member and began to recruit cosponsors in the Senate on that basis.

At the same time the new senator from Connecticut, Abraham Ribicoff, became interested in sponsoring air pollution legislation. In addition to being secretary of health, education, and welfare from 1961 until July 1962, Ribicoff had been the governor of Connecticut and knew the problems of air pollution firsthand. As his legislative assistant he picked Cohen's former special assistant, Jerry Sonosky. Sonosky had also worked a short time for Democrat John A. Blatnik of Minnesota, a water conservation leader in the House. Ribicoff looked on air pollution as a logical first bill for him to sponsor and told this to Sonosky.

Sonosky, consulting with both Mields and Edelman and doing some of his own drafting, put together a far-reaching bill. The language was a combination of new material and material borrowed from other air pollution bills and water pollution bills of previous years. He got the title "Clean Air Act" from Mields, who had taken it from the British law. Ribicoff circulated the completed draft to all members of the Senate. He introduced the bill on January 23. Nineteen senators subsequently joined as cosponsors. These included Democratic Majority Leader Mike Mansfield of Montana, Majority Whip Hubert H. Humphrey of Minnesota, and Minority Whip Thomas Kuchel.

Engle and Democrat Maurine B. Neuberger of Oregon, another longtime advocate of greater federal programs in air pollution, were angered by what they considered to be the excessive aggressiveness of a freshman senator. Engle introduced his own milder bill, S. 444, on the same day Ribicoff introduced his. He had nine cosponsors, including three who had also cosponsored the Ribicoff bill.

At the time he introduced his bill, S. 432, Ribicoff wanted and expected to be named to the Public Works Committee, which had jurisdiction over air pollution legislation. His preferences for committee assignments were (1) Finance, (2) Public Works, and (3) Government Operations. He was given his first choice and, because he was one of only a few senators with a real interest in Government Operations, his third choice. Thus, although he could keep abreast of developments, Ribicoff was effectively removed from a position where he could help determine the outcome. He had played a crucial role, however, by introducing early in the session strong legislation that was then a major focus of debate throughout the year.

*Roberts' Support of Enforcement.* By February 1963 Representative Roberts and the members of his subcommittee had developed unquestioned expertise in the field of air pollution. The problem, from the viewpoint of those who wanted strong legislation including enforcement provisions, was to get Roberts to support enforcement and then act on the bill.

In December 1962 Roberts had appeared to oppose enforcement. As late as February 7 Dean Coston had indicated he was unsure of Roberts' position. But on February 21 he supplied Roberts with a draft bill including enforcement procedures in cases of interstate pollution, and on February 28 the congressman introduced this bill as H.R. 4415. What made him change his mind?

The chief factor was that he simply began to see the problem of air pollution in broader terms than he had before. He had become increasingly aware of the serious problem in Birmingham, near his home. In discussions with Dr. Prindle of the Division of Air Pollution he learned more about the killing smog in London in December 1962, which Prindle had observed firsthand. He became convinced both that the problem was a truly national one and that it offered an immediate threat to the health of millions of Americans.

During the February 7 to 21 period Roberts and Coston had a number of conversations that led Roberts to believe federal enforcement of a limited variety was both needed and feasible. Mields also saw Roberts as much as he thought prudent. The Municipal Association was instrumental in getting Ed E. Reid, the executive director of the Alabama League of Municipalities and a power in Alabama Democratic politics, to urge the necessity of a strong bill on Roberts.

On February 21, when Coston sent the draft bill to Roberts, he indicated it had been modified in line with the congressman's wishes. Roberts had been insistent that the grant-in-aid section of the bill name a specific figure and length of program and so the bill called for a five-year program of $30 million. Roberts had also asked for some modifications in abatement proceedings involving intrastate problems. Coston also indicated that the bill had not been cleared within HEW or anywhere else in the executive branch and that the administration position would be "presented in the form of reports and testimony on this and other legislation introduced in the 88th Congress."

Roberts introduced the bill a week later. In a speech on the floor during the week following the introduction he said that "The need for such an effort has become increasingly apparent to me after careful study of the problem in my capacity as chairman of the Subcommittee on Health and Safety of the Committee on Interstate and Foreign Commerce." He gave special praise to Congressman Schenck for his work on automobile exhaust. He summarized by saying that:

> The purpose of the bill I have introduced is to develop a comprehensive national program for the prevention and control of air pollution, providing for Federal leadership while recognizing fundamental responsibilities of State and local governments.
> The bill provides for—
> First. Establishment of a national research and development program . . . .
> Second. A 5-year, $30 million matching grant program to State and local agencies . . . .
> Third. Enforcement measures against air pollution, with Federal enforcement of interstate pollution, and State enforcement of intrastate pollution. Federal, State and local governments would become partners in effective action to abate pollution.

*The Subcommittee Hearings.* Roberts held two days of hearings on March 18 and 19. His subcommittee members were Democrats George Rhodes, Leo W. O'Brien of New York, and Paul G. Rogers of Florida, and Republicans Paul Schenck, Ancher Nelsen of Minnesota, and Donald G. Brotzman of Colorado. Only O'Brien showed no interest in the proceedings. Schenck was unavoidably absent much of the time because his wife was ill.

The subcommittee considered two pairs of identical bills. Republican Seymour Halpern of New York had introduced a bill identical to the Roberts bill. Democrat Peter W. Rodino, Jr., of New Jersey and Republican James G. Fulton of Pennsylvania had introduced identical bills that contained the same language as the Ribicoff bill in the Senate. These bills, as with all others that were considered in 1963, had three areas in which major controversy could arise: (1) the grants-in-aid program to assist state and local agencies with their pollution control programs; (2) the provisions for federal involvement in abatement proceedings; and (3) the power given to the secretary of HEW to require reports from persons whose activities result in emission of pollutants into the air.

The Roberts bill provided for a gradually increasing grants-in-aid program of $30 million over five years. The Ribicoff bill (Rodino-Fulton in the House) provided for a gradually increasing program of $74 million over ten years. The figures in the two bills were the same for the first five years, however. The two bills were also identical in calling for the secretary to contrive a formula for allotting the money to the various states for use on specific projects. These funds were to be allotted on the basis of "the population, the extent of the air pollution problem, and the financial need of the respective states." Both bills provided that the federal grant to a state or local air pollution program could cover up to two-thirds of the cost of "establishing and maintaining programs for the prevention and control of air pollution." The Ribicoff bill provided for "special financial incentives" for regional control programs (defined as programs sponsored by two or more cities, counties, or states). The Roberts bill specifically limited this support to three-fourths of the total cost.

In the matter of enforcement both bills provided the secretary with power to call conferences of involved parties in both intrastate and interstate pollution problems. He could call these conferences when requested to do so by local officials and could also call them on his own initiative in interstate cases. Following the conference the secretary would make recommendations. If after at least six months the secretary felt that progress was unsatisfactory he could call a public hearing for the purpose of making findings. If after another six months progress was still unsatisfactory the secretary then could proceed to "request the Attorney General to bring a suit on behalf of the United States to secure abatement of the pollution." Here the two bills differed. The Ribicoff bill allowed this action both in interstate and intrastate situations. In intrastate cases, however, the written permission of the governor would have to be given. The Roberts bill made no provison for a federal suit in intrastate cases. Instead it provided that the secretary should send all of the papers to the governor or state attorney general so that they could institute judicial proceedings, if they so desired. The secretary could also give technical assistance in any legal proceedings that ensued, if so requested by the state officials.

Both bills had an identical section on "Requirement of Reports":

The Secretary is authorized to require any person whose activities result in the emission of air pollutants causing or contributing to air pollution which has been the subject of a conference . . . to file with him, in such form as he may prescribe, a report, furnishing to the Secretary such information as may reasonably be required as to the character, kind, and quantity of pollutants discharged and the use of devices or other means to prevent or reduce the emission of pollutants by the person filing such reports.

The executive departments involved were requested to report their views on both the Roberts bill and the Ribicoff bill. The two most important reports, from Secretary Celebrezze and from the Bureau of the Budget, took the same position. They preferred the Roberts bill to the Ribicoff bill, feeling that a five-year grants-in-aid program would be "more appropriate for a new grants program" and preferring the intrastate enforcement procedure in the Roberts bill.

The one major executive complaint about the Roberts bill involved the grant program. HEW objected to the provision for "maintaining" existing and new programs. The department wanted the secretary to have more flexibility to assist in "the initiation, expansion, or improvement of air pollution control programs, rather than the cost of 'maintaining' such programs." Celebrezze also requested that the allotment provisions be eliminated in favor of more flexibility for the secretary. He wanted the grants to be for specific projects only. The Bureau of the Budget supported these requests but also stressed economy by asking for an amendment that would require "that Federal grant support be provided on a declining basis over the duration of the projects in order to facilitate the gradual assumption of financial support for the control programs by the States and localities."

At the House hearings twenty-eight persons appeared to testify. The major executive witnesses were Undersecretary Nestingen and Dr. Prindle of the Division of Air Pollution. Division Chief MacKenzie and Surgeon General Terry accompanied Nestingen.

Among the urban groups the Conference of Mayors was represented by a statement from Mayor Richard J. Daley of Chicago, read by one of his aides. The Municipal Association sponsored the appearance of the Mayor of Pittsburgh. The National Association of Counties was represented by the chairman of its air pollution committee.

State and local officials working directly with the problem of air pollution were represented by the National Association of Attorneys General, the Association of State and Territorial Health Officers, and the Conference of State Sanitary Engineers. Individual air pollution officials from Florida, Los Angeles, and the New York-New Jersey-Connecticut Interstate Sanitation Commission also testified.

Only five representatives of private industry testified. These witnesses came from the National Association of Manufacturers, the Manufacturing Chemists Association, the Incinerator Institute of America, the Weyerhaeuser Lumber Company, and the Idaho Mining Association.

In his testimony Nestingen of course followed the line taken by Secretary Celebrezze in the department's report on the legislation. He also introduced material making clear the need for a federal effort of sizable proportions in this field. He attempted to play down the enforcement aspects of the legislation, emphasizing that the Roberts bill was aiming at a total program of "control" of air pollution, and that "enforcement" was only one aspect of "control." He also stated his feeling, based on experience with similar powers in the water pollution legislation, that only rarely would the attorney general of the United States be asked to bring an abatement suit. Prindle, MacKenzie, and Terry limited their testimony to technical matters.

The urban lobby witnesses made it clear that they supported either the Roberts or the Ribicoff bill and that they felt that both bills respected the rights of state and local officials.

The spokesman for the National Association of Manufacturers, Daniel Cannon, devoted most of his testimony to emphasizing that local effort was enough and that the federal government was not really needed in either the grant or enforcement fields. He urged deletion of the grants program and the enforcement authority provisions of the bill. He cited the enormous sums spent by industries to control their own pollutants and felt that a sizable federal effort on top of this would be both wasteful and wrong. In what he thought to be a convincing conclusion to his argument he quoted from the speech Roberts had given at the National Conference on Air Pollution to the effect that abatement and enforcement must remain at the local level.

Roberts responded immediately with the proverbs, "Consistency is a hobgoblin of little minds" and "The wise man changes his mind and the fool never does." He elaborated on the reasons for changing his mind: "I do feel . . . that there have been some things that happened, particularly the recent London smog, which make me feel that the Federal Government does have a responsibility in this field particularly when it involves the death and health of our people. Now I think there are some of these situations that we cannot reach other than by legislation of this type. It seems to me that we have here in H.R. 4415 what is a very modest approach to the problem."

The only other major industrial group to testify was the Manufacturing Chemists Association. This group took a much more affirmative position than Cannon had taken. It endorsed and urged "a continuation and expansion of the activity of the Secretary and his staff in the areas of research, development, and training of personnel." It had no objection to a grants program, although asking for more control over the secretary's discretion in distributing the funds. In the enforcement field it favored the provisions of the administration bill in 1962 that conferences could be held on specific problems of pollution—either interstate or intrastate—and the conferences could make recommendations to the state and local officials.

The only local official fully endorsing the enforcement provisions of the Roberts bill was the representative from Los Angeles. The others, with one exception, resented any federal action without specific state invitation. Most vocal on this point was the representative of the National Association of Attorneys General. The Association of State and Territorial Health Officers and the Conference of State Sanitary Engineers were particularly insistent that the federal government should not be allowed to make grants directly to localities but that they should get state approval first.

Throughout the course of the hearings Chairman Roberts interjected comments designed to stress the moderate nature of his bill. He wanted to recognize the primary place of states and localities in controlling air pollution but he felt that his bill authorized indispensable federal services. The only member of the subcommittee to show skepticism about the bill was Nelsen. Rogers was a little hesitant about the enforcement provisions. The other members took no clear positions.

*The Roberts Bill.* Following the hearings Roberts undertook to discuss the bill further with groups that had opposed substantial parts of it. He felt that it was necessary to neutralize hostility to the bill before it reached the House floor. Thus he initiated meetings with industrial representatives—principally from the coal, chemical, and steel industries. He found out their exact complaints and sought to make changes that he thought reasonable to meet their objections.

After talking with the objecting groups and developing some ideas on what changes would be acceptable, he talked with Mields and MacKenzie to make sure that the changes would not affect their view of the bill as a good one. Roberts thought of himself as a broker between these various points of view and he felt that by doing his job well he could prevent any meaningful opposition. He thought it important that, if possible, no major group should oppose the bill actively.

The subcommittee held one executive session on the proposals, using the Roberts bill as the basic text for amendment. Following this session Roberts introduced a clean bill, H.R. 6518, which was then the subject of an executive session of the full Interstate and Foreign Commerce Committee in late June.

At these two meetings three important changes were made. First, in the enforcement section the procedure for bringing an abatement suit in federal court in interstate cases of pollution was modified. The modification provided that the secretary of HEW could not request the attorney general to bring a suit until the governor of the injured state certified that he "has made a good faith effort to enter into an agreement or compact with the State" where the pollution originated "in order to secure abatement of such pollution and has not been able to secure such an agreement or such a compact." Roberts felt this amendment was necessary in order to gain House approval for the bill. In effect, it made the prospect of any federal suit for abatement quite unlikely, and thus further protected state and local autonomy. The remaining sections pertaining to enforcement that provided for conferences followed by public hearings in both interstate and intrastate instances of pollution were left unchanged.

Second, in the grants program the figures, which had been progressively larger in the original Roberts bill, were now limited to $5 million per year.

Finally, in line with its general campaign to recover control of certain programs from the Appropriations Committee, the Interstate and Foreign Commerce Committee added specific amounts of money that were authorized to be appropriated. The bill as reported called for $5 million additional for fiscal 1964 (to cover the first year of the grants program), $20 million for fiscal 1965, $30 million for fiscal 1966, and $35 million for fiscal 1967. It also provided that no appropriations were authorized by the general research provisions of the Public Health Service Act "for any purposes for which appropriations may be made under authority of this Act."

*House Approval.* On June 27 the bill was ordered reported favorably to the House by unanimous vote of the thirty-three members of the committee. The report itself was made on July 9. It stated that "the blight of air pollution . . . has become a real menace to all urban areas." In justifying the enforcement procedures the report said, with reference to intrastate problems, "The bill provides specifically for cooperation with the States, and the conference and hearing procedures authorized are intended to encourage and assist State and local communities in their efforts to control air pollution, not to usurp or preempt their rights, powers, or responsibilities in this field." With respect to interstate problems, "The committee believes that the procedures provided constitute a reasonable balance between the primary rights of the States to control air pollution within their boundaries and the rights of States seriously affected by pollution from another State to have available to them a practical remedy."

On July 16 the Rules Committee granted an open rule with one hour of debate and on July 24 the House debated H.R. 6518. Roberts was the floor manager of the bill. Nine members spoke in favor of it, including four Republicans. Roberts again stressed that the bill was designed to aid states and localities and still protect their rights. Nelsen indicated that he had resolved any doubts he had about the legislation in committee because H.R. 6518 was a more moderate bill than the original Roberts bill. He felt the committee had done "a very thorough job in modifying the bill in all respects." Roberts congratulated him for having helped to write the legislation.

Only four members, all Republicans, spoke in opposition. Thomas B. Curtis of Missouri resented the short time allotted for debate and thought it did not allow a sufficient probing of the provisions of the bill. Robert McClory of Illinois, a freshman, wanted the bill rejected because of the bad experiences he felt had come from the same enforcement procedures in the water pollution field. H. R. Gross taunted Roberts with having changed his mind about enforcement. Roberts again replied that only fools do not change their minds. He added that "States' rights are protected in this bill. . . . I think this is both a State and a Federal problem. I do not think air stays in one State all the time. . . . It moves across State lines."

Republican Ralph Harvey of Indiana moved to recommit the bill. This was defeated 41 to 29 by a division vote. The House then passed H.R. 6518 by a roll call vote of 272 to 102. Ninety-five percent of the voting Democrats voted for the bill and 42 percent of the voting Republicans favored it.

Thus, with remarkably little opposition the House passed its version of the Clean Air Act. In addition to little formal opposition in the hearings there had been only a small amount of lobbying against the bill. Most industries were more interested in the fate of the water pollution bill, which was also going through Congress during 1963. Some of the industrial representatives had expected that an air pollution bill would not pass before the water bill. They had thought that because Roberts had not supported enforcement in the past there was no particular need to concentrate their energies on him or his subcommittee. In effect, most of the industrial groups who opposed all or part of the Roberts bill had not taken the hearings and committee action on it seriously.

After the industrial groups realized that the Roberts bill was going to be stronger than they had anticipated and partially unsatisfactory to them, they looked for access points on the House side to see what could be done. Representative McClory was particularly unhappy with the legislation and let it be known, through a friend of his employed by the United States Chamber of Commerce, that he would welcome industrial support. When the representatives from a few industries went to see McClory, however, all he offered them was strong criticism for not having paid attention to the legislation at an earlier stage.

There was little lobbying in favor of the bill once Roberts decided to support it. Both Mields and Coston felt that success would come in the House without much further effort on their part.

## The Senate Prepares a Stronger Bill, 1963

The deaths of two Democratic senators played an important part in clearing the way for Senate action on a strong air pollution bill in 1963. Dennis Chavez of New Mexico, chairman of the Public Works Committee, died on November 18, 1962. Robert Kerr, second-ranking on the full committee, chairman of the Rivers and Harbors Subcommittee, and a foe of federal control in this field, died on January 1, 1963. This made Pat McNamara of Michigan, an urban-oriented liberal, the new chairman.

The committee had three standing subcommittees. McNamara himself took Rivers and Harbors and gave the other two to the next senior Democrats. The fourth-ranking Democrat on the committee of seventeen was Edmund S. Muskie of Maine. Muskie had expressed his great interest in water pollution legislation and he had already introduced the principal new bill in that field. Chairman McNamara faced the question of how to handle this legislation. He decided that a special subcommittee would be the logical solution, with Muskie as chairman. McNamara also knew that air pollution legislation had been introduced and he gave the Muskie subcommittee jurisdiction over it as well.

To round out the Democratic membership of the Special Subcommittee on Air and Water Pollution McNamara appointed Jennings Randolph of West Virginia, Frank E. Moss of Utah, Lee Metcalf of Montana, Birch Bayh of Indiana, and Gaylord Nelson of Wisconsin. The ranking Republican member of the full committee, John Sherman Cooper of Kentucky, appointed three Republicans to the subcommittee: J. Caleb Boggs of Delaware, Jack Miller of Iowa, and James B. Pearson of Kansas. The subcommittee officially came into being on April 30, 1963.

In the field of air pollution five of the senators on the subcommittee were active: Muskie, Randolph, Boggs, Miller, and Pearson. The two most important, by reason of rank, were Muskie and Boggs. They were friends from their pre-Senate days, having known each other in the Governor's Conference. Muskie had served three terms in the Maine legislature. He was governor of Maine from 1955 until 1959 and was elected to a Senate term beginning in January 1959. Boggs served in the House from 1947 to 1953 and had been governor of Delaware from 1953 until 1961, when he entered the Senate.

The Senate Public Works Committee did not have separate staffs for the different subcommittees. Instead one central staff divided the work. The chief clerk and staff director, Ron M. Linton, spent well over half his time working with the Muskie subcommittee on both water and air pollution. Linton had been active in Michigan Democratic politics after being a newspaper reporter in several midwestern cities. In 1960 he worked on Senator Kennedy's personal staff during the campaign. Senator McNamara had hired him as chief clerk and staff director in February 1963, after he had spent two years in the Defense Department. The principal member of Linton's staff working on air pollution was John L. Mutz. In addition, members of the staffs of three of the senators on the subcommittee played leading parts in working out the final content of the air pollution bills. These were Muskie's administrative assistant, Donald E. Nicoll; Bogg's legislative assistant, William F. Hildenbrand; and Pearson's administrative assistant, Allen E. Pritchard, Jr.

In its work on water pollution through the summer of 1963 the group of senators and staff members exhibited a willingness to work together on a nonpartisan basis in order to produce widely accepted legislation. A feeling of friendliness developed among all of them. This same desire to work together and produce an acceptable bill also permeated the work of the subcommittee as a whole.

In the early spring McNamara had written Secretary Celebrezze asking for technical assistance "as needed" for his staff members working on air and water pollution. Dean Coston accordingly arranged with MacKenzie for this help to be supplied at the proper time. Thus in July and August, when it was clear the subcommittee would soon produce a water pollution bill and Linton's attention began to turn to air pollution, three employees of the Public Health Service—Sam Rogers, Tom Williams, and Charles Yaffe—began to work on a staff report on air pollution for the Public Works Committee. Such a report had been planned by Linton even before the creation of the special subcommittee. In the report, released a few days before the hearings on the bills began, the facts about air pollution were discussed. Both the problem and efforts to solve it were delineated. The report concluded that "It is obvious that current efforts are not on a scale adequate to contain air pollution even within its present unsatisfactory levels." It then pointed to the probable need for action in the main areas covered by the Roberts and Ribicoff bills: expansion of research, development of air quality criteria, strengthening of local control programs, financial assistance to state and local programs, and federal participation in enforcement.

*Consideration by Muskie's Subcommittee.* Muskie's subcommittee held its hearings September 9–11.[2] Three of the bills considered have already been described. These were the ones introduced by Senators Ribicoff and Engle and the one passed by the House. In addition, the subcommittee considered three other bills. The first of these had been introduced by Mrs. Neuberger and contained essentially the same provisions as the original Roberts bill plus two specific references to the necessity for reducing the sulfur compound content of the air. The second of the bills had been introduced by Republican Clifford P. Case of New Jersey. In February Mields and MacKenzie had made an effort to get Case to be one of the principal Republican sponsors of comprehensive legislation. They failed in these efforts. Case limited his interest to having the Public Health Service publish the criteria for clean air. The final bill considered by the subcommittee had been introduced by Republican John J. Williams of Delaware. This bill had essentially the same provisions as Engle's but also contained a fifty-fifty matching requirement in the grants program.

[2] The subcommittee had initially planned to hold field hearings in addition, before actually marking up the legislation. Partially because of White House insistence on speed Muskie decided to postpone the field hearings until after the legislation had been reported. These hearings were not held until the first few months of 1964.

The Senate subcommittee staff had, as usual, asked that the Department of Health, Education, and Welfare report only on the Senate bills and not on the House-passed bill. HEW expressed agreement with the objectives of all five measures bearing Senate numbers. It specifically asked that the grants program not be worded so as to provide aid merely for continuing existing programs. It also asked for an elimination of the allotment provision for apportioning money to the states. It preferred to have no time limit on the program but said five years would be acceptable. In the matter of enforcement HEW indicated preference for the Roberts approach to intrastate problems (as found in the Neuberger bill) over the Ribicoff approach. It also asked that the secretary have a choice of whether or not to call a conference on an intrastate problem rather than being forced to do so.

The Bureau of the Budget's report focused on the House bill. In doing so it agreed with the major points made by HEW. It also specifically opposed the "good faith" provision that the House had inserted in the interstate enforcement provisions. "To require further delay of a period of years to allow time for a 'good faith' effort to secure an interstate compact would seem to require unreasonable delay in affording the injured State some relief." It would be a bad precedent and administratively unsound, the bureau thought.

The Justice Department suggested a few words to add to the intrastate enforcement provisions of the Ribicoff bill in order to strengthen the constitutional basis for them. Whether the enforcement provisions were constitutional had been the subject of a debate between HEW and Justice, mediated by the Bureau of the Budget. The HEW lawyers still felt that the case was shaky. The Justice Department report gave some of the lines of reasoning that could be used to prove constitutionality.

Twenty-five persons appeared to testify at the fourteen hours of hearings. Secretary Celebrezze and MacKenzie appeared for the executive branch. Mayor Daley appeared for the Conference of Mayors and Mayor Joseph M. Barr of Pittsburgh for the Municipal Association. The County Officials had two representatives. Only Los Angeles sent a representative to speak for local health officials. Industrial groups were represented by spokesmen for the National Association of Manufacturers, the Manufacturing Chemists Association, the National Coal Association, and the American Iron and Steel Institute.

In addition to these men four senators supporting the legislation appeared in person and two others sent statements. Ribicoff, the sponsor of

S. 432, appeared as the first witness, making a long and forceful statement in favor of it.

Secretary Celebrezze said many of the same things that Undersecretary Nestingen had said in the House hearings. He again distinguished between control and enforcement. He reiterated the department's positions as stated in the formal report on the legislation. MacKenzie was more vigorous than Celebrezze in his support for enforcement powers. He stated that just because the technology was incomplete was not sufficient reason for hesitating to enforce abatement of pollution.

The Conference of Mayors specifically asked that the three-year program in the House bill be extended to five years. The other urban witnesses supported all of the legislation. Only one, a representative of the Association of Counties, thought the "good faith" provision with respect to interstate enforcement in the House bill was good and should be retained.

The industry spokesmen were much more vocal and more specific than they had been in the House hearings. The National Association of Manufacturers maintained its position of almost total opposition to the bills. But the three major groups representing specific industries were more selective in their opposition.

Two men, Myron Anthony and William Conner, appeared for the Manufacturing Chemists Association. They specifically endorsed the "good faith" provision, and requested that all power be taken from the secretary to call any conferences on his own initiative. They also objected to the requirement of reports as provided in H.R. 6518. They felt that the reports should be required only when it was clear that a public hearing would be held and that the reports should be supplied "to the hearing board as a basis for its action, not simply supplied to the Secretary." Mr. Conner said it was his "understanding" that "general health laws on the books of communities, our cities, our States, are sufficient to deal with air pollution to the degree that it affects health." He also again stressed that if no state or local officials invited the secretary of HEW to come into a local situation "we feel that the Secretary should not intrude himself." Muskie took strong exception to these positions.

Senator Neuberger, who had just finished testifying, remained in the room during the testimony of the Manufacturing Chemists' officials. She also questioned them and attacked their position in vigorous language:

> . . . to me you represent very special interests. . . . I am just amazed at the fact that you want the Federal Government to go ahead . . . and spend money

for research . . . but then it is supposed to stop. The Government is not supposed to do anything with the facts which it may uncover. . . .

Are you really concerned with the health of the people? This whole testimony indicates that you think that you as an organization have some closer boring-in process with the municipal or State government than you do with the vast Federal Government that represents all the people.

Muskie made it clear that he was aware of the Manufacturing Chemists' "sensitivity to the existence of the problem and its importance, and the need for some Federal participation." Conner summarized by reminding the senators that his organization was by no means opposing the bills. It merely desired some changes in specific language.

Senator Randolph was in the chair when Joseph Mullan of the National Coal Association testified. Mullan indicated that the only activity of the federal government in the air pollution field should be in research and that any other activity (presumably including grants as well as enforcement) should take place only upon the request of the governor or state air pollution agency.

Two men appeared on behalf of the American Iron and Steel Institute. Erwin Schulze, a Chicago lawyer, did most of the talking. Schulze contended that there was no "scientific basis" for the proposition that air pollution constituted "a mounting danger to our national health and welfare." He did not object to the grants program but favored a matching provision as contained in Senator Williams' bill. He recommended the complete elimination of the sections providing for enforcement and requiring reports from those polluting the air. Schulze also elaborated upon the necessity for distinguishing between "health" and "welfare" if the bill's justification was to be based on a threat to them. He insisted that most of the air pollution problems fell in the welfare category and that welfare should therefore be defined in the legislation.

The American Medical Association made its first public statement since its telegram of December 12, 1962 and its letter of January 9, 1963. It had not sent a statement for the Roberts hearings. During the winter and spring of 1963 the Medical Association's Council on Legislative Activities and its Board of Trustees reviewed the proposed legislation on air pollution. The Council on Legislative Activities heard formal presentations from both the Public Health Service and representatives of industry. Finally the council and the board voted to support legislation in the air pollution field but to oppose federal enforcement provisions. Thus Blasingame now wrote Muskie that "There appears to be no need to empower a Federal agency to seek from the court a remedy already available to the primary parties."

Throughout the exchanges with witnesses it had become clear that none of the senators on the subcommittee would oppose the legislation altogether. The Republican senators had probed into the legislation at several places to make sure it was reasonable. Senator Randolph had been solicitous about the effect of the bill on the coal industry. But Muskie, aided by Neuberger at one point, had kept up a running commentary on positions that he thought wrong. One of the big differences between the Senate and House hearings was that in the House all of the members had at least paid lip service to the necessity of emphasizing states' rights in the legislation. The Democratic senators were not convinced of this necessity. Muskie and Nelson were particularly insistent that the national interest submerged theoretical questions of states' rights. Mrs. Neuberger even suggested that the states' rights arguments were façades for specific economic interests.

*Lobby Efforts to Modify the Bill.* During the period between the end of the hearings on September 11 and the reporting of the bill to the full committee on October 31 the bulk of the lobbying involving the air pollution legislation took place. The industrial groups whose interests were affected by this legislation began to take the proceedings more seriously. At no point during the process had any group other than the Manufacturing Chemists attempted to discuss its position with the Public Health Service. Now the industrial groups that realized legislation could not be prevented but wanted it to be mild probed the Senate subcommittee for members who would agree with them.

A rudimentary form of industrial cooperation on this measure existed, primarily through the efforts of the Manufacturing Chemists and a consultant for Republic Steel. Hildenbrand and Pritchard asked the industrial groups to send their technical experts to a meeting with them in Pritchard's office. These people, knowledgeable about the special pollution problems in the chemical, coal, iron and steel, and oil industries, supplied only their views of technical problems. They did not comment on policy questions. The business of giving policy advice and suggesting amendments was still done primarily on a decentralized and uncoordinated basis, industry by industry, or even individual firm by individual firm. The two most active industries were chemicals and iron and steel.

The chemical producers, represented by the Manufacturing Chemists

Association, made the most concerted and organized effort to influence the actual writing of the legislation. The association's representatives realized that legislation, probably including enforcement powers for at least interstate problems, was inevitable. Therefore they began working within the realm of the possible. Senator Boggs and Bill Hildenbrand were their principal points of contact. One of them who had testified in the Senate hearings was an employee of Du Pont. Despite this tie-in with a Delaware firm, Boggs and Hildenbrand felt free to tell the association's representatives that they could not agree with them on a number of points. The association also contacted an assistant to Senator Randolph, whose state of West Virginia has a large chemical industry.

The Manufacturing Chemists prepared some suggested amending language as the basis of its discussions with the offices of Senators Boggs, Randolph, and Pearson. The thrust of this language was to put in the bill guarantees of consultation and cooperation between the federal and the state and local authorities. The association also wished to ensure that reports required of those emitting air pollutants be kept to a minimum. Specifically they requested that reports be limited to those situations where public hearings were already in prospect, a time at least six months later than the first stage of a conference.

The iron and steel effort on this bill was fragmented among individual companies. They continued supporting the suggestion made by the Iron and Steel Institute representative in the hearings that "welfare" should be defined. They also joined with the chemical producers in protesting the great discretion left the secretary with regard to reports on pollution. A representative of Wierton Steel had many discussions about specific language with Linton and Richard E. Royce of Senator Randolph's staff. He also presented to Muskie and Randolph themselves the steel industry's argument that "welfare" should be defined in order to prevent a rash of lawsuits.

Another steel representative provided some members of the subcommittee with suggested amending language. He wanted to change the findings section of the bill so that instead of talking about "mounting dangers to the public health and welfare" from air pollution it referred to "mounting public awareness of the possible dangers" of air pollution. He also restricted the grants program to "initiating fact finding which may ultimately be used" by local air pollution agencies.

The only other major trade association involved in this effort was the National Coal Association. It limited its attention primarily to Senator

Randolph, whose concern for the coal industry in West Virginia led the Coal Association to hope that he would be of great assistance.

The automobile manufacturers, not immediately threatened by the provisions of this legislation, limited their activity to a written reply to an allegation made by the Los Angeles air pollution officer in the hearings that all industries except the auto industry had cooperated with him. Their statement was received too late to be put into the printed hearings but it was circulated by McNamara to all members of the subcommittee.

Some efforts were made to lobby individual members of the subcommittee, but these attempts were few and ineffectual. For example, the Indiana Chamber of Commerce brought a delegation to see Senator Bayh. They even suggested new language. Their efforts, however, came on the last day of the mark-up sessions on the bill.

In general the industrial groups moderated their positions on the bill as the Senate subcommittee work on it progressed. After their initial proposals were rejected by the subcommittee they began to propose a series of more limited changes until finally they reached a point on which they and the subcommittee could agree. Several industrial representatives indicated that their real feelings would lead them to oppose any legislation on air pollution at this time. But they also indicated that they were aware some legislation would pass and so they were willing to talk about details in an effort to remove what they considered to be objectionable features. Their position was thus sifted through a series of filters—primarily rebuffs of a number of specific proposals—until it reached a point where it could have considerable effect on the language of certain parts of the bill.

Those favoring a strong bill did not, in general, feel the need to engage in a great deal of lobbying. They felt that the subcommittee would approve a bill at least as strong as that passed by the House and probably stronger. Thus Dean Coston kept in touch with Senate developments but did not urge particular positions on the senators. The White House kept abreast of the situation and insisted on a fair degree of speed, but also saw no need to push specific provisions.

The only group favoring a strong bill that made serious attempts to recommend specific language to the subcommittee was the Conference of Mayors. In their June meeting in Hawaii the mayors had adopted a resolution urging Congress to enact a comprehensive air pollution bill, including provisions for "action to abate interstate air pollution when state or local governments fail to do so." In late August Linton had initiated a meeting with the mayors in order to review with them the proposed legislation item by item. He wanted their views and also wanted some technical help from them. Those attending the meeting with Linton were a special counsel for the Conference of Mayors, a representative of Mayor Daley, and a representative of the Public Health Service. In addition to giving Linton information the meeting also served as a coordinating device for the forthcoming testimony of Mayor Daley in the Senate hearings. No specific agreements were reached at the meeting but Linton and the mayors' organization did come to some broad understandings about proposed amendments to the House bill.

A memorandum containing the Conference of Mayors' suggested changes in the House-passed bill was prepared September 17 and transmitted to Senator Muskie on the following day. An entirely new paragraph on the grants program removed any limits on expenditures and also removed the allotment provisions of the Roberts bill. Instead a flat 12.5 percent limit was placed on the funds that could go to any one state. Also the mayors suggested that instead of allowing the secretary to grant up to two-thirds of the cost of a local program, the grant be fixed at two-thirds, with no discretion given to the secretary. A similar proposal fixed the grants to interstate or intermunicipal programs at three-fourths of the total cost, with no discretion left to the secretary. The memo to Muskie made it clear that these provisions were meant to protect the nation's largest cities from discrimination in the operation of the program.

In the enforcement section the Conference of Mayors first suggested removing the language that would in effect prohibit cities from asking for enforcement assistance without the prior approval of the governor or air pollution agency of the state. The mayors argued that "A direct line must be established and maintained between the municipalities and the federal government since it is these two levels of government which are most actively involved and concerned and equipped to deal with air pollution control problems." They also suggested new language in the provisions for intrastate enforcement that would permit the secretary to provide to municipal officials, as well as to state officials, the findings of the public hearings and technical assistance with a view to local judicial action to achieve abatement. The memo did not suggest going as far as the Ribicoff bill, which permitted federal court action even in cases of intrastate pollution. In the section on interstate enforcement the mayors urged that the "good faith" provision be removed.

The final important suggestion by the Conference of Mayors involved the money amounts authorized. The mayors suggested a five-year program, increasing each year from $25 million in fiscal 1965 to $65 million in fiscal 1969. The total amount for the five years was $225 million.

*The Subcommittee Bill.* The senators themselves met in four informal executive sessions on the legislation. These lasted two to three hours each. Muskie and Boggs were present at all of these meetings although it was not possible to get a quorum of the subcommittee to attend any single meeting.

At the working sessions the senators stated their views on the intent of the legislation. Linton, Nicoll, Hildenbrand, and Pritchard—working within the framework of these views—drafted language and then cleared it with the senators. The subcommittee did its work quickly, never feeling the need for a formal vote on any amendment.

The only three areas of contention involved the "good faith" provision for interstate enforcement, the amount of money to be authorized, and the allotment formula. Senator Miller urged retention of the first provision, was for economy in the program, and urged an allotment formula designed to prevent the large cities and large states from getting all of the money. He was unsuccessful in convincing a majority of his colleagues of any of these positions. The subcommittee deleted the "good faith" provision. It compromised on a five-year program of $182 million, increasing from $25 million in fiscal 1965 to $50 million in fiscal 1969. Instead of any kind of an allotment formula the subcommittee accepted the mayors' suggestion of a flat 12.5 percent limit on the funds going to any one state.

The subcommittee kept both the Ribicoff number and the House number on the bill. It also used language and provisions from other bills before it. From Case's bill it adopted the stress on criteria to judge the purity of the air. Some of Mrs. Neuberger's concern with sulfur was added. The subcommittee added a section stressing the need for further work on automobile exhaust, and also a section requiring the secretary to issue permits to federal installations for the discharge of specific amounts of certain pollutants.

The subcommittee allowed the grant program 20 percent of the total authorization. It preserved the secretary's flexibility in determining what percentage of local and interstate or intermunicipal programs the federal government would finance, retaining the two-thirds and three-fourths limits respectively on such federal contributions. This section directed the secretary to pay attention to population, the extent of the problem, and financial need in apportioning the funds. It also specified that in order to be eligible the local agency could not reduce its nonfederal funds from the previous year.

In the enforcement section the Senate subcommittee retained the language requiring state approval of municipal requests for federal assistance, despite the contrary position of the Conference of Mayors. In the matter of intrastate pollution the subcommittee bill retained the original Ribicoff provisions, authorizing a federal suit with the written consent of the governor. This position was even stronger than that requested by the mayors.

In the reports section the subcommittee retained the language making reports possible at the conference stage. But it was responsive to the requests of industry by providing that the reports should be "based on existing data," thus obviating the necessity for expensive new surveys of individual stacks.

*Senate Approval.* The working sessions ended in late October and in ten minutes on October 31 the subcommittee formally sent its version of the bill (labeled both S. 432 and H.R. 6518) to the full Public Works Committee. The committee met for forty minutes on the bill and reported it to the Senate on November 7. Jack Miller submitted two language changes that were defeated by voice vote. The written report of the committee reviewed the need for the legislation and analyzed it section by section.

Before the bill came to the floor Republican Senator Jacob Javits of New York, through his staff, made clear to Linton, Nicoll, and Hildenbrand that he intended to introduce several amendments to the legislation on the floor. These involved state powers. Javits had sent copies of the bill to the New York State Department of Health at the time of the hearings and it had suggested language requiring state concurrence before a grant could be made to a locality. Gerard Manges, the chief Javits staff member involved, suggested that this be modified to require only consultation instead of concurrence. The amendment itself was worded that way and was cleared by Linton, Nicoll, and Hildenbrand.

The second Javits amendment, again stemming from the New York Department of Health, and again cleared through Nicoll, Linton, and Hildenbrand, allowed the governor of the state, in cases of intrastate pollution, to request either technical assistance from the federal government in bringing state judicial action or to request the secretary to have the attorney general bring a federal suit. On the floor Javits and Muskie made it clear that the purpose of this amendment was to give the governor a choice, thus retaining state control in situations involving intrastate pollution. They also made it clear they meant federal-state cooperation to foster action, not inaction.

The New York Department of Health also asked for a third amendment to make clear that in administering the grants program the extent of the problem was to be a more important criterion than either population or financial need. Javits preferred the use of a colloquy on the floor, rather than an amendment, to establish the legislative intent that the extent of the problem was the primary criterion. Nicoll drafted the short colloquy for the floor debate. In response to Javits' question on the floor, Muskie replied that "the Committee intends that in evaluating the three factors the Secretary give primary consideration to the extent of the actual or potential air pollution problem."

The Senate considered the air pollution bill on November 19. Senator Ribicoff presided. S. 432—with Senator Ribicoff's name on it—was called up from the calendar and was given a first and second reading and was amended. Before the third reading H.R. 6518, now containing the text of S. 432, was called up and passed. Thus the Senate could go to conference on the House bill.

The floor debate was short. No important amendments were offered except the two by Javits, which were accepted unanimously. Muskie, Boggs, Randolph, and Neuberger all congratulated and thanked one another.

Minority Leader Everett McKinley Dirksen of Illinois expressed some concern over the extent of the federal enforcement power. Muskie replied that it had been "the intention of the committee to protect the primary areas of the States and local governments in this field." He then cited a letter from the Manufacturing Chemists Association, dated November 6, "endorsing the bill in its present form." The letter was printed in the *Congressional Record.*

The existence of this letter suggests the unanimity of purpose of the subcommittee members and staff members, and it also suggests the nature of the subcommittee's relations with the concerned industries. Bill Hildenbrand had felt at the conclusion of the executive sessions of the subcommittee that the Manufacturing Chemists had left themselves in a bad light. He felt that the debate between their representatives and Muskie and Neuberger in the hearings made it appear as if they were unreasonable in their demands. Therefore, in order both to leave a better impression of the association and to attest to the reasonableness of the discussions its representatives had had with staff members and senators working on the bill, Hildenbrand suggested to the Manufacturing Chemists that they write a letter to Muskie expressing their appreciation for his consideration even if they could not approve the bill as a whole.

The Manufacturing Chemists, after reading the letter to representatives of iron and steel, pulp and paper, coal, and oil, read it to Hildenbrand on the phone and then delivered it to Muskie. The letter itself commended the subcommittee for "the highly significant improvements" it had made in the bill. The letter concluded that while the organization's position that state invitation should precede any federal enforcement action "is not fully reflected in the bill as reported by the subcommittee, we wish to express our deep appreciation for the careful consideration accorded our recommendations by the subcommittee and staff assistants concerned."

Muskie had clearly overstated the contents of the letter when he referred to it as an endorsement. The Manufacturing Chemists were unhappy with this slip and immediately called it to Muskie's attention. Muskie corrected himself in the *Record* the following day by changing his language describing the letter as "endorsing the bill in its present form" to "commending the committee's work on the bill."

The Senate floor debate concluded without any further suggestion of opposition to any part of the bill and it passed by unanimous voice vote.

## Passage of the Act

Prior to the single meeting of the conferees the industrial representatives stressed to the House staff the necessity of adopting the Senate provision on reports. This was the one area of the bill that, if improperly drawn, could cost many of the industries money. MacKenzie told Coston that the Public Health Service had no objection to most of the new Senate language.

The Senate conferees were Muskie, Randolph, Moss, Metcalf, Boggs, and Pearson. The House conferees were the seven members of the subcommittee, and Chairman Harris and ranking Republican John B. Bennett of Michigan from the full committee. Staff members from the two

committees met once before the conference to see if any technical problems were present. Muskie and Roberts had maintained contact throughout the late summer and fall on air pollution. Shortly before the conference they talked on the telephone to identify any technical problems that
might be present. It became evident that both agreed that the Senate bill
should be changed only slightly at conference. Hildenbrand called
Schenck's office and told him of the automobile section in the Senate
bill. Schenck raised no objections in conference.

Thus, when the conference met on December 4 there was little to discuss. The House accepted the Senate version of virtually all of the important sections. The one major Senate concession to the House version was
on the amount of money to be authorized. The Senate had called for
$182 million over five years. The House had called for $90 million over
three years (including $5 million additional for fiscal 1964). The con-
ference agreed on $95 million for three years (including the additional
$5 million for fiscal 1964). This compromise was based on the Senate
figures for the first three years and the House refusal to authorize money
for a fourth and fifth year. The conference members informally agreed,
however, that the program would be extended past the initial three-year
period.

The conferees took their report back to both houses on December 10.
In the Senate there was no debate at all on the bill. Muskie summarized
the conference agreements and the Senate adopted the conference report
by voice vote. In the House Roberts stressed the bipartisan aspects of the
bill and indicated that the money figures in it represented a House victory. Schenck testified to the friendly spirit of the conference and the high
quality of the product of that conference. Chairman Harris lauded Roberts and Schenck for their work on the bill and in the health field in
general. In reporting on the enforcement provisions Roberts stressed that
the governor remained in control of the intrastate procedures and had to
request the secretary of HEW to take action. Four Republicans attacked
the bill, especially the sections giving the secretary discretionary power,
providing for enforcement, and authorizing a grants-in-aid program and
$95 million of spending. After this short debate the House passed the
conference report by a roll call of 273 to 109. Ninety-three percent of
the voting Democrats and 42 percent of the voting Republicans voted
aye.

All of the agencies involved with the legislation recommended approval to the President. Both the Bureau of the Budget and HEW sub-

mitted drafts for the signing statement. On December 17 President Johnson signed the Clean Air Act into law. Roberts, Coston, Muskie, Boggs, Ribicoff, and Mields were present. In his brief signing statement the President said:

> I am glad to approve this legislation . . . under this legislation we can halt the trend towards greater contamination of our atmosphere. We can seek to control industrial waste discharged into the air. We can find the ways to eliminate dangerous haze and smog. All of us are very grateful to Congressman Roberts, to Senator Ribicoff, Senator Muskie, to the Chairmen of the Senate and House Committees, Senator McNamara and Congressman Harris, and to all of their colleagues in both the House and Senate who developed and guided this important bill through Congress. They truly can be proud of the efforts they made and the achievements that resulted.

## Concluding Comments

Everyone but a few industrial representatives seemed to be pleased with the new act. All saw some imperfections but virtually all felt these were outweighed by the good points of the legislation. The Department of Health, Education, and Welfare and the Public Health Service indicated satisfaction, although HEW immediately became embroiled in a bitter controversy over how best to administer the new program. Mields and the urban representatives were happy with the results, although apprehensive about the ability of the PHS to administer the law vigorously enough. Most industry representatives admitted they could "live with it," although they would have preferred some different wording. Only a few industrial lobbyists voiced disgust with the whole process.

Most content were Congressman Roberts and Senator Muskie. They had produced, without divisive partisan warfare, a major piece of legislation. The members of their subcommittees had worked together well and had agreed on specific language with astonishingly little difficulty. Muskie's special subcommittee maintained its interest in the subject by holding field hearings early in 1964. Roberts' standing subcommittee remained available to consider new legislative moves in the field of air pollution.

The Clean Air Act was aimed almost exclusively at the urban areas of the United States. Its primary impact was directed at those urban areas with serious air pollution problems that had not yet started to solve the problems themselves. Everyone involved in this legislative process realized that this was an urban issue. Virtually all felt that federal-city relations, as well as federal-state relations, should be preserved and guaranteed in the legislation. At least on the matters of aid for research and for local air pollution programs, an incipient urban community of interests became evident.

But the process leading to the Clean Air Act also involved substantial conflict, aroused by the question of whether to give the federal government enforcement powers in the air pollution field. The question of enforcement was a relevant urban concern, since without this last step—either at the local or at the national level—it would be unlikely that pollution could be sufficiently curtailed.

The conflict over federal enforcement exhibited many unusual patterns. These patterns are not fully explained by a standard theory of legislative politics as a process of coalition building. This theory expects that two coalitions—opposing one another—will be built. In the case of the Clean Air Act only one coalition—that favoring an enforcement section in the bill—was built; the opponents did not coalesce. Furthermore, the standard theory does not leave adequate room for the varying relations between the individuals involved and the institutions they worked for or represented.

Who were the primary figures in the coalition favoring enforcement, and what were the relationships between them and their institutions?

Certainly one of the principal figures was Hugh Mields. It did not matter so much which urban group he represented. The political influence of the Conference of Mayors was never a major factor; this influence is difficult to use in the executive branch and it was not needed in Congress. Mields's contribution was not that of an organization but was largely personal. He worked consistently for a strong bill and followed through by presenting specific proposed language. He provided a crucial element of continuity in the process.

Another important source of action was Dean Coston. His commitment to a strong bill eventually resulted in the commitment of the President. Again his contribution was personal and not institutional. The institution in which he was working—the Department of Health, Education, and Welfare—was neither particularly hostile nor particularly friendly. Those immediately involved with the program—members of the Public Health Service—were opposed to enforcement prior to the presidential commitment. Their opposition was based on a variety of reasons. This helps explain why Coston could maneuver successfully on behalf of his position. If either HEW or the PHS had been united on the grounds of its opposition it probably could have stopped Coston and his few allies.

A third figure of importance was Ken Roberts. Within his realm, the Subcommittee on Public Health and Safety, Roberts could take a variety of positions. In February 1963 he changed his mind and supported a bill with federal enforcement provisions. By changing his own mind he at once changed the mind of the subcommittee, the primary institution with which he was working. Roberts was working within an institutional framework, part of which he could control. He was also blessed with cooperative co-workers—particularly Chairman Harris and ranking Republican Paul Schenck.

Still another key figure was Senator Ribicoff. Although operating in the process as an outsider because he was not on the committee handling the legislation, he played an important role at an early stage in the process by introducing a bill including enforcement. His proposal became one of the primary points of discussion in the executive and the House as well as in the Senate. In fact, since the Senate subcommittee consideration came late in the legislative process, when there were several important alternatives to consider, Ribicoff's main contribution to the discussion may have been in the executive and in the House.

Finally, Senator Muskie was certainly a major source of action on the pro-enforcement side. He too was an individual operating within a specific institutional framework. The institutions themselves had changed in a way that allowed him to be effective. The major change was the death of Senator Kerr. Without this event it is doubtful if Muskie's will would have prevailed. But with a sympathetic chairman of the full committee, and with the aid of ranking Republican Senator Boggs, Muskie had ample leeway to produce the kind of legislation he favored. On the question of enforcement the subcommittee was not the scene of conflict but was instead the scene of unusually close cooperation.

There were also several sources of opposition to federal enforcement in the air pollution field. Before the President endorsed enforcement the most serious opposition came from within the executive, particularly from the Public Health Service and the Bureau of the Budget. Opposition also came from representatives of industries affected by the proposed legislation. Yet none of this dissent was effective. There were three central reasons for this ineffectiveness.

First, although proponents tended to view their opponents as monolithic, uncompromisingly conservative organizations dedicated to defeating federal enforcement power, this was true of none of them. The Public Health Service was conservative on the question of enforcement. But it was neither single-minded nor unreasonable. Rogers and Edelman met with Mields and helped draft stronger alternatives. And once the President took a position on enforcement those in the PHS directly involved supported him loyally. The Bureau of the Budget was also conservative on the question of enforcement power. But it was content to raise questions and made no strong attempt to prevent the President from endorsing enforcement in his health message. The industrial representatives took a range of different positions. Some opposed the legislation almost in its entirety but they had little effect. Others were willing to see legislation passed and worked closely with staff members in Congress to get the most acceptable language. Furthermore, the problems of the chemical industry are substantially different from those of iron and steel or coal or petroleum. These differences appeared larger than the similarities and there was no natural drive to seek common ground and launch a common effort. Also, the direct financial interest of most of the industries, despite some of the rhetoric and a few isolated threats of plant closings, was only in the reports section, and the most reasonable representatives were successful in getting that section amended.

Second, the opponents were in some instances outmaneuvered by the proponents in such a way that their opposition was rendered ineffectual. Coston bypassed the Public Health Service by getting the President committed to a strong bill. Confronted with a *fait accompli* the PHS supported the President rather than attempting to undermine his position by "end-runs" to Congress. Coston also outflanked the Bureau of the Budget, first by getting the President committed, and second by refusing to sponsor an administration bill that would have to be cleared by the bureau. He was content to supply Roberts with draft language.

Third, the industrial groups failed to adopt tactics that would lead to the achievement of their ends. What little effort they made to gain support was directed to the wrong places. They made no attempt to exploit differences of opinion in the executive branch. Instead of probing for points of access in the Roberts subcommittee they attempted to gain allies in the Senate subcommittee—precisely the spot where they had the least chance of success.

This case should give pause to those who contend that the only hope for urban areas resides with the executive. Here, without Congress, the executive would have produced legislation less far-reaching in its provisions than what was produced with the help of Congress. Also, the effective strength of Mields in this contest, in relation to the strength of the combined industrial groups, points to less sweeping conclusions than are usually made about the ineffective representation of the urban areas in Washington. In this case one urban lobbyist, working with subcommittee chairmen from the rural states of Alabama and Maine, represented the urban areas of the country with observable effect.

At the signing ceremony President Johnson gave primary credit for the legislation to specific congressmen. This is customary at such ceremonies even when the executive is primarily responsible for the legislation. In the case of the Clean Air Act, however, the President was accurate in apportioning the credit. Congress, even in the absence of a fully operative community of urban interests, showed that it could legislate for the benefit of urban areas in the 1960's.

RANDALL B. RIPLEY

# Legislative Bargaining
# and the Food Stamp Act, 1964

THE FOOD STAMP ACT was signed by President Lyndon B. Johnson on August 31, 1964, climaxing more than twenty years of agitation for such a law. And because of events attending its passage it appeared as a triumph for urban-oriented members of Congress.

It may seem puzzling to consider a food stamp bill as legislation for urban areas alone. Many rural areas would benefit. But for nine weeks and one day in early 1964 a series of events in the House of Representatives posed the question in such a way that food stamps seemed to epitomize urban legislative needs and demands. These events, coupled with the ten-year record of active support on the part of Representative Leonor K. Sullivan, Democrat from St. Louis, Missouri, demonstrated that in the House the political muscle behind food stamps was urban.

This case will focus on the progress of the food stamp bill through the House from mid-1963 until April 1964. The rest of the story is covered in less detail since the urban interest emerged almost exclusively in the House. Furthermore, the concern throughout will be less with the substance of the proposals than with the strategies used and the bargains made to facilitate passage. The strategies were urban-oriented even if the impact of the program was only partially urban.

## Congressional Support for a New Stamp Plan, 1944–63

In 1935 Congress passed and the President signed some amendments to the Agricultural Adjustment Act. Section 32 of these amendments pro-

279

vided that 30 percent of the tariff receipts on agricultural products be put into a separate fund that the secretary of agriculture could use for a number of purposes including encouraging the domestic consumption of surplus commodities or products "by diverting them, by the payment of benefits or indemnities *or by other means,* from the normal channels of trade and commerce." [Italics added.] The secretary used this authority in 1939 to begin a food stamp program that was designed both to supplement the diets of the poor and to rid the country of certain agricultural surpluses. The scheme was an invention of New Deal economists that embodied the principle of a two-price system. The story of its origin and trial would make an interesting case study, irrelevant here, in the processes of administrative innovation. As the Department of Agriculture summarized it almost twenty years later:

> The plan was designed to insure that the Federal contribution represented a net increase in food expenditures among participating families through the use of a two-color stamp system. Participating families were required to exchange an amount of money representing estimated normal food expenditures for orange stamps of the same monetary value. With these orange stamps, participants were provided—without cost—additional blue stamps which could be used to buy designated surplus foods.

Although the mechanics changed, throughout the subsequent two decades the basic idea of the participant buying some stamps and being given additional stamps remained a necessity in any food stamp proposal if it was to be at all acceptable to the Department of Agriculture.

At its peak, in May 1941, the food stamp plan had about four million participants. In terms of areas covered the peak of the program came in August 1942, when 1,741 counties and 88 cities were included in the program. The Department of Agriculture explains the demise of this first food stamp program simply: "The plan was discontinued in early 1943 when wartime conditions had greatly reduced unemployment and greatly increased demand upon United States food supplies." The department's summary in 1957 of the experience of the 1939–43 plan pointed out that it had increased food consumption levels among participating families but it had not guaranteed that they would buy all of the surplus foods on the list approved by the secretary. Instead, their purchases with the blue stamps tended to concentrate on a few foods and did not significantly diminish the surpluses of other foods. In addition, the two-color stamp plan was complex in its operations at the retail store level.

In 1944 Senators George D. Aiken, Republican from Vermont, and Robert M. LaFollette, Jr., Progressive from Wisconsin, introduced a bill calling for the reestablishment of a food stamp program. The Senate Agriculture Committee appointed a subcommittee to consider this bill. In the hearings on the proposal Aiken supported it as "a better solution of the problem of how to maintain the health and efficiency of our low-income citizens than any other plan that has so far been suggested." He made it clear that he expected both urban and farm families to benefit from the proposed program. The subcommittee took no action.

In the following years Senator Aiken and others periodically reintroduced food stamp bills. But no more hearings were held and there was no legislation.

Proposals for a food stamp plan created little interest and got little support in part because of the shifting policy position of the Department of Agriculture. Many of those associated with the initial program in 1939–43 were convinced of its merit and eager to see it reinstituted after the end of the war. The department explored the possibility during the immediate postwar period. But in 1949 the secretary of agriculture, Charles F. Brannan, proposed a general subsidy for farmers that would lower food prices. He specifically indicated that this would make a food stamp program unnecessary.

As it became clear that Congress would not pass the Brannan plan, the possibility of Department of Agriculture support for a food stamp plan again became more likely. This time another period of high employment, caused by the Korean War, intervened and lessened the need for such a program.

During the presidency of Dwight D. Eisenhower, with Ezra Taft Benson as secretary of agriculture, the department adopted new policies. After the defeat of the Brannan plan the relatively rigid and high price supports saddled the department with ever-increasing stocks of surplus foods. Benson opposed high price supports. He also desired to get rid of the mounting surpluses. Thus he expanded the direct distribution program for giving federally owned surpluses to the needy. State and local agencies had primary control over actual distribution with little or no cost to themselves. This combination of policies left no room for a food stamp program and the department consistently opposed the creation of one during the eight years under Eisenhower.

In short, after 1953 initiative for a new program, if it appeared, would be most likely to come from Congress.

*Mrs. Sullivan and Failure in the House, 1954–58.* In the 1952 congressional elections the Third District of Missouri, located in the city of St. Louis, sent to the House Leonor K. Sullivan, the widow of a six-term Democratic congressman from the same district, John B. Sullivan. A Republican had been elected at a special election following the congressman's death in early 1951 and had served for most of the Eighty-second Congress. Mrs. Sullivan defeated this Republican by more than 50,000 votes.

In 1954, her second year in the House, Mrs. Sullivan introduced a bill establishing a food stamp program, although she was not a member of the Agriculture Committee. She testified in favor of the bill before the House Agriculture Committee, which was conducting a broad-scale inquiry into the long-range farm program. Her proposal would have made all surplus foods—including fruits, vegetables, and meats that may be in surplus seasonally—eligible commodities for purchase by the use of food stamps. She reintroduced this proposal during all of the Congresses while Eisenhower was President.

A few years later she explained the reasons for her interest in a food stamp program. "Late in 1953 and early in 1954, when we were already in a recession . . . I became deeply concerned by the accounts of undernourishment among needy school children and others in St. Louis at about the same time the main concern on agricultural matters here in Washington seemed to be the unmanageable surpluses of food. The more I thought about this contradiction, the more indignant I became." A food stamp program was Mrs. Sullivan's answer to the contradiction. She had seen the direct distribution program at work in St. Louis and felt that it was humiliating, wasteful, and inefficient.

In 1956 Mrs. Sullivan helped to get a pledge on food stamps inserted into the Democratic platform. The Democrats promised to "inaugurate a food stamp or other supplemental food program administered by appropriate state or local agencies to insure that no needy family shall be denied an adequate and wholesome diet because of low income."

Also in 1956 Congress, in the Agricultural Act of 1956, required the secretary of agriculture to submit "detailed programs, with recommendations for any additional legislation needed to carry out such programs . . . for a food stamp plan or similar program for distribution through States . . . and local units of Government of future surplus production to needy persons in the United States, its Territories, and possessions, so as to prevent the accumulation of commodities in the hands of the Commodity Credit Corporation." Democrat Harold D. Cooley of North Carolina, the chairman of the House Agriculture Committee, was instrumental in obtaining this provision in the House-Senate conference on the farm bill. From this time forward Cooley was a loyal ally of Mrs. Sullivan in her attempts to get food stamp legislation. He was, however, hampered by a committee membership not much in sympathy with what it considered an urban-oriented welfare program.

On January 3, 1957 the Department of Agriculture submitted the required report. Its tone implied that the program of direct distribution of surpluses run by the department was promoting both disposal of surpluses and improved diets for the needy better than a food stamp plan could. It also suggested that a food stamp plan would be extremely expensive.

Specifically, the report argued that current dietary statistics and the 1939–43 experience had shown that the food needs of the poor did not overlap significantly with the surplus holdings of the government. Furthermore, the report stressed the administrative shortcomings of the 1939–43 program. If a new food stamp program were inaugurated the department felt that a greater effort should be made to promote the consumption of foods "experiencing marketing difficulty." It estimated the cost of a "minimum scope" program (six million people) at $600 million annually, and the cost of a "maximum scope" program (twenty-five million people) at $2.5 billion annually. Even with this scale of expenditure the department concluded that a food stamp program would not be effective in dealing with the "surplus in the hands of the Commodity Credit Corporation" or in "dealing with seasonal, temporary, or localized surplus situations."

In 1957 Mrs. Sullivan, as she had in every year since 1954, again introduced her food stamp proposal. The Agriculture Committee, to which it was submitted, felt that the proposal was not worked out in sufficient detail to be reported to the floor. Nevertheless, Mrs. Sullivan brought the proposal to the floor by herself in the form of an amendment to the extension of P.L. 480, the law dealing with agricultural surplus disposal abroad. In advocating the amendment she appealed particularly to urban representatives: "Let those Members who know of no needy persons in their districts . . . vote against this amendment if they like. But those of us who come from urban areas particularly know that the need exists and is not being met."

Chairman Cooley of the Agriculture Committee said that he could not

accept the amendment for the committee. He indicated he was sympathetic with the purposes of the amendment but he doubted "the pro-
priety of it in this bill." He suggested that she might take out the language that made the establishment of the program mandatory, and leave it
to the discretion of the secretary of agriculture. Mrs. Sullivan did not
agree to this change. After a short debate the House rejected the food
stamp amendment by a teller vote of 128 to 89.

In 1958 the Subcommittee on Consumers Study of the House Agriculture Committee held hearings on proposed food stamp programs. Mrs.
Sullivan said at the hearings that as a result of the 1957 floor discussion
and rejection of her amendment she had "obtained the promise of Chairman Cooley that the committee would take up the food-stamp proposal
separately this year and that he personally would support it."

The chief reasons for supporting a food stamp program according to
Mrs. Sullivan were that need existed and that the direct distribution plan
was failing to meet the need. She attacked direct distribution as she had
observed it working in St. Louis. She also pointed out that although the
department still had the 1935 authority and could start a food stamp
program administratively, in reality Congress would have to force Secretary Benson to move: ". . . it is up to us to build a hot fire under the
Department of Agriculture."

Mrs. Sullivan's chief opponent in these hearings was Don Paarlberg, an
assistant secretary of agriculture. He stated the department's position:
"As we now see developments ahead, we do not favor the adoption of a
stamp plan. That is, we do not believe the present program of making
Federal surplus foods available to needy people should be replaced by a
food stamp plan. The present arrangement . . . is a highly flexible program. . . . It accomplishes the job with a minimum of additional financial outlay." Paarlberg felt that the principal effect of the proposed
stamp plans (other congressmen besides Mrs. Sullivan had introduced
somewhat varying versions) would be "to shift to the Federal Government the entire cost of the physical distribution of surplus foods to needy
persons—a cost that is now shared with States and local communities."
More specifically, ". . . we are opposed to any system that would shift to
the Department of Agriculture the full cost and responsibility for direct
distribution." He also opposed the bills that would put the food stamp
program under the Department of Health, Education, and Welfare.
Paarlberg summarized the concerns of the Eisenhower Department of
Agriculture: a food stamp program would be too costly in general; it
would represent unfair charges on the department's—and hence, politi-

cally, the farmers'—budget; and the direct distribution program fed more people and, crucially, got rid of more surplus foods.

At the conclusion of the hearings the Agriculture Committee gave no evidence of being willing to vote a food stamp bill out of committee. Mrs. Sullivan immediately made it clear that she would object to all agricultural legislation that required unanimous consent for passage. The speaker of the House, Texas Democrat Sam Rayburn, talked with her and then with some members of the committee in order to facilitate the reporting of a bill. In early August 1958 a food stamp bill was reported out favorably. There was no minority report. The Rules Committee could not be induced to grant a rule on short notice and therefore Cooley decided to bring the bill to the floor on August 18 under suspension of the rules. This procedure requires a two-thirds majority for passage.

Debate was short and along party lines. Cooley stressed that the proposed program would be an additional outlet for surplus foods. Other Democrats stressed more humanitarian aspects of the proposal. The Republican position was succinctly stated by William S. Hill of Colorado: "We have had a good relief program. We have one working at this very time. Why this House should take this action this afternoon when our hearings disclose the fact that State after State has been doing an excellent job in providing surplus food for those who are out of employment and need extra surplus food, I do not know."

A majority of the members of the House supported the bill but it did not get the required two-thirds. Thus the bill was killed by a vote of 196 to 187. Eighty-two percent of the voting Democrats voted for the bill. Eighty-five percent of the voting Republicans voted against it. The following table shows what percentage of the urban, suburban, and rural representatives[1] of each party supported the food stamp bill.

|  | *Number of Representatives* | *Percent Pro-Food Stamp* |
|---|---|---|
| Democrats |  |  |
| Urban | 74 | 94.6 |
| Suburban | 22 | 95.5 |
| Rural | 110 | 70.9 |
| Republicans |  |  |
| Urban | 46 | 13.0 |
| Suburban | 34 | 23.5 |
| Rural | 95 | 13.7 |

[1] These categories are defined in the *Congressional Quarterly Weekly Report,* February 2, 1962, pp. 153 ff.

This table suggests that rural Democrats were less likely to support the bill than urban and suburban Democrats, and that suburban Republicans were more likely to support it than either urban or rural Republicans. Clearly party was more important than constituency in determining how any single representative was likely to vote.

*Legislative Success and an Unresponsive Administration, 1959.* In 1959, with the opening of a heavily Democratic Congress, members of both houses again introduced food stamp bills. The Subcommittee on Agricultural Production, Marketing, and Stabilization of Prices of the Senate Agriculture and Forestry Committee held three days of hearings. Senator Aiken again made it clear that he hoped that a food stamp plan would be used to benefit both urban and rural populations.

The full House Agriculture Committee held two days of hearings in late July. As in the Senate not many testified. Only a few from outside of government appeared, and they took predictable positions. The Farm Bureau opposed a food stamp program and labor unions supported it. As was expected, the Department of Agriculture opposed the proposals. There was general support for the program from representatives of needy areas—both urban and rural.

On August 11, 1959 the Senate committee reported a food stamp bill favorably. This bill provided for demonstration food stamp programs in from three to six areas only. One of the areas had to be rural. The committee authorized $20 million to carry out these demonstration projects, which were to terminate by January 1, 1962. The Senate considered the substance of this food stamp bill as an amendment to P.L. 480 in early September. On September 4, by a 46 to 41 roll call, it rejected an amendment by Hubert H. Humphrey, Minnesota Democrat, that would have established a $20 million program on a demonstration basis. On September 7 it accepted a $15 million demonstration program amendment, again offered by Humphrey, by a roll call of 44 to 38.

The House committee reported a food stamp bill favorably on August 15. This provided for the distribution of up to $1 billion worth of food each year. The total cost of the program could not be predicted by the committee majority. They said that the figures submitted by the Department of Agriculture were totally unrealistic and could not be relied on at all.

Twelve Republicans, the total Republican representation on the committee, signed a minority report in which they opposed the bill because:

(1) It represents the inexcusable invasion of State and local rights and responsibilities in the administration of their welfare programs; (2) It would not help farmers, taxpayers, or the needy. It would not alleviate our major surpluses while tremendously increasing the cost and decreasing the efficiency of the present distribution system. It places the Department of Agriculture directly into the welfare field, an area more related to the Department of Health, Education, and Welfare.

Prospects for bringing the large-scale bill to the House floor late in the session were not bright. Neither were the prospects for presidential approval. The House Rules Committee tabled it on August 19. Cooley therefore decided to offer the substance of the bill as an amendment to the 1959 P.L. 480 extension, which had wide support. Thus, on August 20 Mrs. Sullivan introduced her bill once again as an amendment to P.L. 480. The debate that followed was along party lines with dissident southern Democrats keeping quiet.

On the floor Mrs. Sullivan indicated that Cooley had supported a move within the committee to attach the food stamp bill to P.L. 480 but that this had been rejected. Now she attempted to make the broadest appeal to her fellow Democrats:

> Standing by itself, my bill might be vetoed. The Republican members of the Committee on Agriculture solidly oppose it—every one. Mr. Benson says he does not want it. He already has the authority to institute a food stamp plan such as called for in this amendment, but he won't initiate it on his own authority. He has told Congress . . . that if the Congress wants him to run a food stamp program, it must enact legislation calling for such a program. Placing such legislation on this bill is the best way to comply with that demand, and establish a more intelligent system of distributing surplus food to our needy.

The House responded to Mrs. Sullivan's appeal and passed the food stamp amendment by a teller vote of 156 to 96. The House language was permissive and did not make the establishment of the program mandatory.

In the conference on the P.L. 480 extension the Senate and House conferees reconciled their differing viewpoints by limiting the duration of the authority to two years (ending January 31, 1962); limiting the federal government's expenses in acquiring, handling, and storing the food involved to no more than $250 million annually; and making the language permissive rather than mandatory. On this last point the House managers stated:

> The conferees note that although the language of the amendment agreed

upon is permissive as in the House bill, legislation authorizing and directing food-stamp programs was passed by the Senate. It is the expectation of the conferees that the Secretary at his discretion will undertake such a program along the lines laid down in the conference report.

Both houses adopted the conference report.

The language of Congress, however, had no impact on the Eisenhower Department of Agriculture. The department never used the authority. President Eisenhower stated his views on food stamps when he signed the P.L. 480 extension:

> The food stamp plan it authorizes carries the implication that more surplus foods would be made available to the needy people of the United States. Actually the bill would not do this. Needy people received Federal surplus foods last year by direct distribution through State and local facilities. If implemented, this authority would simply replace the existing distributory system with a Federally financed system, further increasing the already disproportionate Federal share of welfare expenses. The food stamp administrative mechanism would be much more complex and it is extremely doubtful that it would provide any greater benefit to needy people than the present direct method.

Once again the Democratic party heightened the partisan nature of the argument over food stamp proposals by including a statement in its 1960 platform: "We will use the food stamp program authorized to feed needy children, aged and unemployed."

*Kennedy and Food Stamps, 1961–63.* After John F. Kennedy was elected President in November 1960 a task force in the Department of Agriculture began to work on a food stamp proposal. The employees in the Food Distribution Division of the department's Agricultural Marketing Service knew the most about the 1939–43 food stamp experience and also had kept abreast of subsequent developments. During the Eisenhower years the division had worked with the food distribution programs that the top policy makers in the department had decided upon. The members of the division had little or no influence on policy themselves. Some of them were favorably disposed toward a food stamp program. However, they felt that Mrs. Sullivan's proposal for use of surplus foods only would not work, and therefore they went along with departmental policy at the time in opposing the program before Congress, resting their objections on specifics, not on principle.

The task force that began work after the election did not consult with Mrs. Sullivan about its plans. Instead it developed the idea that a food stamp program should allow almost all foods found on the shelves of a grocery to be eligible for purchase with stamps. It also felt strongly that the program should begin on a pilot basis. The members of the task force felt that the pilot program would succeed and would thus set the stage for a broader legislative request within a few years.

After the inauguration of President Kennedy Mrs. Sullivan wrote both the President and the new secretary of agriculture, Orville L. Freeman, and asked that a food stamp plan be started. Mrs. Sullivan realized that her original conception would probably be changed by the Department of Agriculture officials working with the program but she was anxious that she not be shut out of the planning completely. Kennedy had been interested in food stamps since at least 1959 when he sponsored one of the many Senate bills on the subject. His first executive order was to expand the direct distribution system. Now he responded to Mrs. Sullivan by announcing at his second news conference, held on February 1, 1961, that "there are going to be set up five pilot projects for food stamp distribution, and that these will be in areas of maximum chronic unemployment."

In his "Program for Economic Recovery and Growth," sent to Congress on February 2, the President indicated the new plan would be based on the authority contained in the 1959 Act of Congress:

> I have instructed the Secretary of Agriculture, consistent with the bill enacted by the Congress last year authorizing establishment of pilot Food-Stamp programs, to proceed as rapidly as possible to establish pilot programs for needy families in localities in West Virginia, Pennsylvania, Eastern Kentucky, Northern Minnesota, Southern Illinois, and the Detroit area. It is my hope that this pilot program while providing additional nutrition to those now in need, will pave the way for substantial improvement in our present method of distributing surplus food.

The Department of Agriculture quickly convinced the President that it would be better not to rely on the 1959 legislation since it was going to expire in less than a year. It stressed that the President had ample authority in the 1935 act to institute a pilot program administratively. This the President readily agreed to. The department opened the first pilot projects in May, June, and July 1961. In his March 16, 1961 special message on agriculture Kennedy made it clear that a request for a new legislative base for food stamps would be forthcoming if the pilot program was successful. "These pilot plans will furnish operating experience necessary for our determination of the most effective kind of food allotment program." Both the President and the department agreed that a few years' experience in the pilot program would be necessary before asking for new food stamp legislation.

During the first two years that the pilot program operated—roughly from mid-1961 to mid-1963—Mrs. Sullivan kept close watch over it. She felt that the Agriculture Department had put too many rigid requirements in the program that would discourage poor people from participating. She made several suggestions on how to relax these requirements. She also had to initiate a major effort in order to get the department to put a pilot project in her home city of St. Louis. She asked the speaker of the house, the secretary of agriculture, and even the President for support on this request. At one of its rare meetings the Democratic Steering Committee in the House, at the insistence of Speaker John McCormack of Massachusetts, passed a resolution specifically requesting the Department of Agriculture to put a pilot food stamp project in St. Louis.

After the department acquiesced and a food stamp program was established in St. Louis, Mrs. Sullivan saw even more clearly what she considered to be mistakes in administration—which she felt led to less participation in St. Louis than could have been expected. She was in constant contact with the Food Distribution Division attempting to get the shortcomings rectified.

She also tried to mute Republican criticism of the program. The Republicans insisted the program was purely partisan because practically all of the pilot projects were being established in Democratic districts. Mrs. Sullivan sought to silence these critics by working to get a pilot program for John P. Saylor of Pennsylvania, who had been the only Republican to support her efforts on food stamps consistently and vocally since 1957.

On January 17, 1963, in his budget message to the Eighty-eighth Congress, Kennedy asked for "Legislation . . . to continue the food stamp program and funds . . . to operate the program in 1964 at the same level as in 1963." At this stage the situation looked bright for the administration. Within the executive branch there was no disagreement over the necessity of a legislatively based food stamp program. Those operating the program in the Food Distribution Division, Secretary of Agriculture Freeman, Agriculture's congressional liaison chief Kenneth M. Birkhead and his staff, and the President and his staff were working harmoniously on this issue—although it was not, of course, a program calling for a large-scale effort. The operations of the pilot program had occasioned no splits within the department or between the department and any other part of the executive branch.

In Congress the Senate appeared ready to pass food stamps. In the

House Chairman Cooley was strongly behind a food stamp effort. Mrs. Sullivan had disseminated information on food stamp programs to all House members through the years. She also played the vital role of evoking support for it from Democratic liberals, who by nature were suspicious of anything issuing from the conservative, crop-oriented Agriculture Committee. Cooley and Sullivan were aided by John J. Heimburger, counsel for the Agriculture Committee, and Charles Holstein, a staff member of the Banking and Currency Committee who had been appointed on Mrs. Sullivan's recommendation. She and Holstein had worked independently of the Department of Agriculture for a number of years but now trusted the department's support at the policy level and were ready to work with its representatives. Even some Republican support for a food stamp bill was expected.

But during 1963 and 1964 a series of events made the future of food stamps uncertain.

## Trading in the House, 1964

In 1963 the Senate Appropriations Committee asked that the Department of Agriculture include a specific budget request for the pilot food stamp program. In acting on the President's request to finance the pilot program in 1964 at the same level as in 1963 ($51.5 million) Congress balked a little. The House version of the agricultural appropriations bill called for only $40 million. The Senate version allowed the full amount. The conference finally agreed on $45 million. The reluctance of the Appropriations Committee in the House to continue supporting the pilot program at a level acceptable to the administration was an additional reason for seeking a separate legislative base.

*Agriculture Committee Consideration of an Administration Bill.* On April 22, 1963 Mrs. Sullivan introduced the administration's food stamp bill. Chairman Cooley had insisted that she be allowed to sponsor the request, rather than sponsoring it himself. She explained why separate legislation was needed, even under an administration willing to use the section 32 authority of the 1935 Act:

> . . . to extend the plan nationally would take all of the money now provided for each year under section 32—money used now for a variety of surplus removal programs. There would then be no section 32 funds left over for school lunch purposes, or removal of surplus perishables on an emergency basis. . . . Thus, new enabling legislation is necessary to authorize appropri-

ation of the full amount of funds needed to extend the food stamp plan nationally. This is estimated to cost about $360 million a year, although much of this cost would be offset by savings elsewhere in the Department budget.

The full Agriculture Committee held hearings on Mrs. Sullivan's bill (H.R. 5733) on June 10, 11, and 12, 1963. She had written to the members of the House soliciting their support in the hearings. The bill had been drafted in the Department of Agriculture, with the Justice Department working on the legal technicalities. At the hearings departmental representatives and several members of the House testified. Some interest groups sent statements but none sent witnesses.

The department report from Secretary Freeman indicated that the program would grow within five years to a stable cost of about $360 million annually. The pilot program had been operating since 1961 and by early 1963 included thirty-one different areas of the country. Freeman stressed that the pilot program had been deliberately designed to include both urban and rural areas. Naturally, all of the districts chosen for the test were poor, the level of poverty usually judged on the basis of unemployment. By May 1963 about 328,000 people were participating. On the average these people were receiving $10 worth of coupons (and, hence, $10 worth of food at retail prices) for an average cost of $6.10. Once the person bought the coupons he could then spend them in any store for any food item (excluding liquor and tobacco). The store would get its money back from the local bank, acting as agent for the government. Local and state welfare agencies set the standards for participants and also decided how many stamps a person could get for what cost. The central principle was that a family would continue to spend an average proportion of its income on food but would be given stamps to make up diet deficiencies.

In the hearings the major support for the proposed legislation came from Agriculture officials and from Mrs. Sullivan and several representatives of districts participating in the pilot program. They made it clear that the bill would protect the integrity of the local units of government involved. They favored the flexibility by which a state or local official could take into account local needs and practices in setting the ratio of money needed to stamps provided.

The proponents were hoping for three main sources of support for the bill: food processors, packers, wholesalers, and retailers; those unhappy with surplus distribution to the poor; and urban representatives wanting at least something to show their constituents besides programs aimed at the farmer. Economically, the stamps were designed to increase the aggregate effective demand for foods purchased through ordinary retail channels, on which the retailer made his normal margin of profit. The government therefore paid the trade distribution costs—packaging, wholesale, and retail margins—for whatever foods were selected by customers, rather than limiting its payments to the wholesale cost and transportation of selected commodities it could designate as surplus and ship in bulk. The stamp plan offered the promise of increased dignity, choice, and convenience for the needy. Instead of being forced to line up on a specified date and at a specified place for possibly unwieldy packages or unusable amounts of only a few food items, the poor could now shop as and when they pleased and for what they pleased in their own neighborhood stores. Finally, the stamp plan was the one food program that had even a partial urban orientation to it. Urban members skeptical about billions for farm programs could receive at least mild comfort from the prospect of millions for the urban needy.

No one appeared in person at the hearings to oppose the food stamp proposal. The opponents on the committee used several lines of argument to state their disagreement. A few simply did not view this program as a legitimate action on the part of the federal government. Others felt it would be pampering the lazy. Democratic Representative E. C. Gathings of Arkansas said that those on the relief rolls in his state were so lazy that Mexicans had to be imported to harvest the agricultural crops.

The Republicans, led by their ranking member, Charles B. Hoeven of Iowa, attacked the Agriculture Department for administering the pilot program in a totally partisan fashion. As Hoeven put it in questioning Secretary Freeman, "How do you explain that the first 26 pilot plans were all placed in the districts of Democratic Members of Congress?" John Saylor indicated that a good deal of criticism from him had been necessary before the secretary had agreed to establish a pilot program in his district—one of those suffering most from unemployment.

Hoeven chastised Mrs. Sullivan for bringing the name of Don Paarlberg, the former Republican assistant secretary of agriculture, into her testimony. "In your statement you voice criticism of members of the Eisenhower administration which, in my judgment, is completely out of order. Is there any need for you to attack the previous administration?" When Mrs. Sullivan answered that she wanted to leave the testimony on the record, Hoeven commented that "You apparently have not learned how to win friends and influence people."

A further thrust by the Republican opponents was to inject the race issue in order to woo away southern Democratic support. Paul Findley of Illinois hinted that he would later try to amend the bill in order to prohibit discrimination. "The President has been giving a lot of attention to segregation recently. I was wondering whether in the operation of the pilot food stamp program you limited it to stores which are racially nondiscriminatory?" When Freeman answered no, Findley eventually asked: "Would you object to language which would limit this to stores which operate on a nondiscriminatory basis?" Freeman answered, "I think that language is unnecessary." In questioning Howard P. Davis, Director of the Food Distribution Division, Republican Representative Delbert L. Latta of Ohio asked if "the way this bill is written and if it is passed the way it is written, would it not be possible to enforce civil rights legislation by withholding foods from needy areas until they did whatever was directed by the Justice Department?" Democrat George M. Grant of Alabama immediately got the hint and asked, referring to one specific section of the bill: "Is that not civil rights legislation?"

Both friends and foes made clear their intention of protecting what they conceived to be the farmers' interests in this legislation. Hoeven in part based his opposition to the program on its failure to deplete surplus food stocks. He also asked the question: "Why should this program be charged to the Department of Agriculture? . . . Would it not be more proper that this program be charged to the Department of Health, Education, and Welfare—it is more of a welfare program than it is in the field of disposing of surplus agricultural commodities, is it not?" Chairman Cooley agreed that he wished "that some way could be found to charge this up to welfare and not the farmer. With a $6 billion budget, the city people criticize us and complain that the farmers are a bunch of parasites, bloodsuckers and many other unwarranted epithets. As a matter of fact, more of this goes to the cities than it does to the country people. The benefits are more for the city people."

Republican Clifford G. McIntire of Maine stressed that the relation "between this program and the disposal of surplus commodities is incidental. . . ." Republican Charles Teague of California made sure that fresh fruits and vegetables, important in his district, would be included in the items eligible for purchase by food stamps.

The Agriculture Committee agreed that further deliberations were necessary before it could make up its mind on the food stamp proposal. Cooley therefore appointed a special subcommittee to study the legislation more closely. This consisted of Democrats Harlan Hagen of California, D. R. (Billy) Matthews of Florida, Benjamin S. Rosenthal of New York, and Frank A. Stubblefield of Kentucky; and Republicans Clifford McIntire, Catherine May of Washington, and Albert H. Quie of Minnesota. The subcommittee met in executive session on August 7, 8, and 15. These meetings included a trip to Uniontown, Pennsylvania, to inspect the workings of one of the pilot projects. At its final meeting the subcommittee approved legislation gradually expanding the food stamp program, but could not reach agreement on how the program should be financed. Despite the lack of complete agreement a clean bill incorporating the subcommittee amendments was introduced.

Between August and October 30 the Department of Agriculture was active in talking to the members of the committee to see if various individual objections could not be removed with specific amendments. At one point in mid-October it appeared that Democrat W. R. Poage of Texas, the vice-chairman of the committee, might move to put the appropriation in the Department of Health, Education, and Welfare. The Department of Agriculture feared that if he made this motion it would pass. The motion was forestalled, however. On October 30, 1963 the full committee met in executive session, only to find out that it still could reach no agreement on what a food stamp bill should contain.

During this period several issues were emerging as bars to favorable committee action. First, the Republicans and a number of the Democrats felt that this was a public welfare program aimed at establishing a minimum nutritional base for the poor people of the country. This kind of program, they insisted, should not be labeled agricultural just because it dealt with food; everybody has to eat. They felt that programs for the poor that were labeled agricultural should use only surplus foods—and thus aid the farmer.

Second, the Republicans and some of the Democrats felt that the federal government—and particularly the secretary of agriculture—had too large a part to play in the program as proposed. They were anxious that the discretionary power given to the secretary be quite limited—especially in the matter of licensing retail outlets for the program.

Third, the southern Democrats were afraid that the program would be administered in such a way as to discriminate against the South because of existing segregation. The Republicans quickly affirmed that this would have to be the administrative pattern—a pattern that would be reinforced by pending civil rights legislation.

Fourth, the Republicans—again supported by some conservative southern Democrats—felt that the states should be required to share the cost of the program.

During the last half of 1963 John Heimburger, the committee counsel, sought to make changes in the bill that would satisfy some of the objections without making the bill unacceptable to either the department or Mrs. Sullivan. To this end he discussed all of his proposed changes with Mrs. Sullivan and Charles Holstein and with Howard Davis of the Food Distribution Division. Mrs. Sullivan was even invited by the Agriculture Committee to sit in on three of its executive sessions on the food stamp bill.

On January 31, 1964 President Johnson sent to Congress his message on agriculture. In this message he said: "Under the pilot food stamp program, initiated administratively in 1961, needy people in 43 areas can increase their food purchases through regular commercial channels. I recommend legislation to place this program on a permanent basis and to make it more widely available."

The committee's answer to the President was quick in coming. On February 4 it voted 19 to 14 to table the bill.

*Tobacco Research for Food Stamps.* In December 1963, when the administration had been struggling desperately to win President Johnson's first test in the House, a cotton bill, the House Democratic leaders had talked to Chairman Cooley and had made it clear that as a token of appreciation for their labors in behalf of this bill, which was not highly regarded by many, his committee should report out the food stamp bill early in 1964. Cooley agreed to do what he could. His committee, however, was not willing to go along and the February 4 tabling action resulted.

Liberal Democrats thought the committee had, in effect, promised favorable action, and were angry at what they considered a double-cross. The tabling motion had been made by Virginia Democrat Watkins M. Abbitt. All of the fourteen Republicans on the committee plus Democrats Abbitt, Gathings, Grant, Thomas G. Abernethy of Mississippi, and Paul Jones of Missouri had voted to table. Fourteen Democrats had voted against the tabling motion and two Democrats had not voted.

The Agriculture Department had been taken by surprise on this vote. Its own headcount, substantiated by a poll taken by a staff member of the

Agriculture Committee, showed that only Abbitt and Abernethy would vote against the bill. Thus, even with solid Republican opposition, the administration expected to win 19 to 16. Furthermore, the department was optimistic about getting one or maybe two Republican votes. The Republican members caucused, however, and agreed on united opposition.

Three Democrats had surprised the department: Jones, Grant, and Gathings. Gathings apparently had been angered by the civil rights implications of the bill: that is, that programs in the South might be cut off by administrative fiat. The biggest problem for the department, however, was Paul Jones. He was worried that this bill would give the secretary of agriculture too much administrative power in a number of ways, not just in relation to civil rights. Thus the department representatives concentrated their persuasive power on Congressman Jones.

Cooley himself was infuriated by the action of his committee. Liberals in the House were angry not only at the committee but especially at Cooley, whom many did not trust. Mrs. Sullivan did trust Cooley and had been working closely with him. Nevertheless, she let it be known to him and other senior Democrats on the committee, as well as to Speaker McCormack, that she would again be forced to object to all unanimous consent agreements involving farm legislation unless the Agriculture Committee reported the food stamp bill.

In looking for another lever to persuade the committee to reconsider the tabling motion, liberal Democrats hit on a bill the committee had reported that would authorize public funds (also from section 32 of the 1935 law) for the support of a study of tobacco and health. Cooley, coming from a large tobacco-growing district, had a special stake in the tobacco research bill and was anxious for its approval.

Cooley led the witnesses who were to testify before the House Rules Committee on February 27 to ask for a rule permitting floor action on the tobacco research bill. Prior to this meeting it had become clear to Cooley that B. F. Sisk, a liberal Democrat from California, would try to prevent the granting of a rule until the food stamp bill had received favorable treatment in the committee. Sisk had cleared this maneuver with Speaker McCormack and Mrs. Sullivan but not with the chairman of the Rules Committee, Democrat Howard W. Smith of Virginia. Smith was so confident that a rule would be granted as a matter of routine that he interrupted the hearings on the request for a rule on the interest equalization bill—a tough political issue—to hear the request for a rule on the tobacco research bill. Smith indicated to the chairman of the Ways and Means Committee, appearing on the interest bill, that the interruption should only take a matter of minutes, and that there would be no problem. Sisk, a junior member of the Rules Committee who often spoke for the House leadership, said that he had a great many questions but that he would not take time to ask them now since it would delay the interest equalization hearings too long. The Rules Committee voted 6 to 5 not to grant a rule on the tobacco bill. Cooley reportedly expressed himself to Abbitt: "See, Wat, I told you that you shouldn't have voted against food stamps." Sisk reserved a motion to reconsider the tobacco bill, implying that it could be saved given favorable Agriculture Committee action on the food stamp bill.

On March 3 Mrs. Sullivan introduced another clean bill—H.R. 10222. This was the third clean bill she had introduced since first introducing the administration bill in April 1963. The next day the Agriculture Committee considered it. This bill represented all of the numerous changes in the legislation that Heimburger had written since the previous summer. Throughout the entire seven-month period from August 1963 to March 1964 he had been the chief communicator and compromiser in the attempt to get the Department of Agriculture, Mrs. Sullivan, and conservative Democrats on the committee to agree on specific language. He had tried to serve the members of the committee and yet to write a bill acceptable to the department and Mrs. Sullivan.

One of the final amendments that Heimburger wrote was designed to placate those committee members who felt that it was wrong to charge a welfare program to the farmer. This amendment provided that for budgetary purposes the line item for food stamps would be listed under the rubric "welfare." The requests for appropriations would still go to the Agricultural Appropriations Subcommittee, however.

At its final executive session the committee amended the bill in three ways. In the section on the administration of the program it added language making clear its intent that one of the major purposes of the program was to help the farmer by reducing food surpluses. Second, it reduced the amount of money authorized for the program. The Sullivan bill had called for $25 million in fiscal 1964, $100 million in fiscal 1965, $175 million in fiscal 1966, and $250 million in fiscal 1967—a total of $550 million. The committee cut the last three years to $75 million, $100 million, and $200 million respectively—making a total of $400 million over the four years. Third, by a vote of 18 to 17 the committee adopted an amendment offered by Albert Quie to make the states

pay half of the cost of the "free" coupons given the individual participants.

Finally, the committee voted 18 to 16 to report the bill to the floor
favorably. Abbitt and Abernethy remained adamant in their opposition
but three of the Democrats who had voted earlier to table (Jones, Grant,
and Gathings) were persuaded by the impending defeat of the tobacco
bill to join Cooley and the other Democrats in voting to report the bill.
No Republican voted to report it.

The committee majority (all Democrats) issued its report on the bill
on March 9. The report stressed that the purpose of the bill "is to bring
under congressional control and enact into law the rules under which
food stamp programs are to be conducted in local areas throughout the
country." It also stated the support of the committee majority for the bill
as "an essential instrument in the war on poverty." It praised the working of the pilot program and said it was now time to extend and expand
the program.

In a separate statement Cooley indicated his total opposition to the
amendment requiring state matching of federal funds: "This provision
would make the program inoperative. . . . State legislatures would not be
willing to appropriate funds for a food program to help needy people
when they are now unable to appropriate sufficient funds for adequate
welfare programs for these same people which cover many needs in addition to food. . . . Finally, this matching provision would endanger the
integrity of the stamp program as a food and agriculture program."

Thirteen of the fourteen Republicans on the committee signed a
lengthy minority report.

> We oppose the enactment of H.R. 10222 because the establishment of a
> nationwide food stamp plan is not needed; it would be extremely expensive
> and inefficient; it would destroy the rights and usurp the responsibilities of
> local and State governments; it would aggravate the problems of commodi-
> ties now held in surplus stocks by the Government; it would add hundreds
> of new employees in the Department of Agriculture; it would give the Sec-
> retary of Agriculture new broad and sweeping powers; it would be adverse
> to the needy people it is designed to help; and it would be of little benefit
> to U.S. farmers.

The Republicans also raised the civil rights spectre by claiming that Title
VI of the House-passed civil rights bill would be used to bar aid to areas
where discrimination prevailed.

Quie stated his own opinion separately. He made it clear that he
viewed the food stamp program as a welfare program and not as an agricultural measure. He felt that national welfare programs had come to

rest on the principle of state participation and matching of federal funds. If his amendment guaranteeing the matching principle in this program were adopted he, unlike his Republican colleagues on the committee, felt that "the food stamp plan will not get out of hand."

*Wheat-Cotton for Food Stamps.* On March 6 the Senate had added a wheat program to the cotton program passed by the House in December. The cotton bill with the wheat amendment was returned to the House. Both the administration and the Democratic members of the Agriculture Committee had a large stake in favorable House action on this bill. But it was evident at an early date that there was a sizeable number of potential nay votes among urban Democrats. These votes, coupled with a solid Republican front against the bill, could defeat it. Therefore Ken Birkhead, Agriculture's congressional liaison chief, and the House Democratic leadership conceived the strategy of tying the wheat-cotton bill to some bill that would appeal to urban Democrats. In short, they wanted to arrange a trade.

As indicated earlier, the food stamp bill had already been linked with the cotton bill in December and with the tobacco research bill in the Rules Committee in February. Until the House on March 12 defeated a pay raise bill for government employees (including members of Congress) there had been talk that the pay raise and wheat-cotton might be linked. However, farm votes helped kill the pay raise, which increased the antagonism of the urban Democrats toward agriculture bills.

Gradually during March it became clear that the trade would involve the food stamp bill and the wheat-cotton bill. No formal announcement was made of such a trade. Indeed, no formal meeting was held at which leaders of urban and rural blocs agreed on it. Instead, and this is typical of the operations of the House, it was a matter of a favorable psychological climate. The more the individual members and the press talked about a specific trade of rural votes on food stamp for urban votes on wheat-cotton the more firmly the exchange became implanted in the minds of the members. It was, in short, based on shared perceptions of a legislative situation in the House. This was bolstered by individual lobbying efforts relying on it as a persuasive point. Thus, Birkhead and Freeman from the Department of Agriculture, lobbyists for various parts of the cotton industry, and Democratic Senator James O. Eastland of Mississippi all made extensive contacts and used this argument.

The House Rules Committee granted a rule to the food stamp bill on

March 19. Chairman Smith, who was opposed to the bill, used his powers as chairman to delay filing the rule for ten days. This meant that the bill could come to the floor only after the Easter vacation—scheduled for March 27–April 6. Thus, since the House never considers important legislation on Mondays, the first opportunity for floor action would be on Tuesday April 7 and Wednesday April 8. The rule was open (allowing amendments) and provided for four hours of debate.

The Rules Committee granted a rule to the other half of the exchange package—the wheat-cotton bill—on March 25, by a 9 to 4 vote. The rule provided that the House would debate the Senate amendment to the cotton bill passed in December for only one hour and then be allowed one vote—up or down.

The President made clear his interest in the food stamp bill again on March 16 in his message on poverty. He clearly identified the food stamp program as part of the "war on poverty."

During the last few weeks before Easter vacation it became evident that the wheat-cotton bill was in much more danger of defeat than the food stamp program. The House leadership took a poll on both bills through the Democratic whip organization. This poll showed that 212 Democrats should vote for the food stamp bill—enough to win even if no Republicans voted for it (if there were the usual number of absentees). On the other hand, the poll on the wheat-cotton bill showed only 197 Democrats likely to vote aye—clearly not enough if Republican lines held solid. Thus, in the closing hours the main efforts of the speaker, the majority leader, and the whip, as well as of the department and the President, were aimed at getting more Democratic votes for the wheat-cotton bill. The appeals were directed especially at urban Democrats and stressed that passage of the food stamp legislation could be assured if they would help to get the wheat-cotton bill through.

At this point almost all of the participants, as well as the press, viewed the struggle in terms of the trade. That food stamps should be so clearly identified as a "gut" urban issue was somewhat incongruous. The Agriculture Department had made evident its intent to help rural areas with the program too. And, in theory at least, one major purpose of the program was to get rid of farm surpluses and strengthen farm prices by increasing food sales. The pilot program had included a mixture of urban and rural areas. Of the forty-three areas (forty counties and three cities) participating in it in early 1964 only seventeen (slightly less than 40 percent) had contained a population more than 50 percent urban—even using the Census Bureau's definition of urban as towns of 2,500 and more. A little over two-thirds of the total participants lived in the seventeen urban areas, however. Forty-one congressmen were representing districts directly involved in the pilot program. Twenty of these came from what *Congressional Quarterly* called urban or suburban districts, or mixed districts with a majority of the population urban and suburban. Only two members of the Agriculture Committee—Cooley and Republican Bob Dole of Kansas—had counties participating. Of the forty-one House members affected, thirty-three were Democrats and eight were Republicans.

The debate on April 7 and 8 was heated. All knew that the wheat-cotton bill was scheduled to follow the final action on food stamps immediately, and there were many references to the upcoming—and more costly and controversial—legislation. In debating the rule on the floor on April 7 Republican Clarence J. Brown of Ohio made the relationship explicit: "I am not unmindful of the fact that the chairman of the great Committee on Agriculture is alleged to have said that H.R. 10222, the food stamp bill, was designed as a sweetener for the purpose of getting support from the Members of Congress from the larger populated areas of the country, the big cities, and so forth, in return for their support of the so-called administration-sponsored cotton-wheat farm bill. . . ." Brown also said that the food stamp bill was "purely a welfare bill and not a piece of farm legislation."

After the rule was adopted by voice vote Chairman Cooley opened the debate for the proponents of the bill. Cooley regretted that the matter had become tied up in partisan politics and added that there was no reason to take the full four hours to discuss a program that had been approved, in principle, by the House in 1959. Republican Delbert Latta raised the question of why most of the pilot projects were in Democratic districts. One of his own counties had requested a pilot program but had been turned down. He expressed his fear that the department would administer an expanded program in a political way—giving benefits only to Democratic districts. Mrs. Sullivan spoke at length for the bill. She introduced a strong dose of partisanship by indicating that the Republican members of the Agriculture Committee "are still sticking with Mr. Benson and they can have him, as the John Birch Society already does." John Saylor, one of the few Republican supporters of the bill, argued that there was nothing wrong with arranging a trade on this bill. Harlan Hagen gave special praise to Saylor, along with Mrs. Sullivan, for their long association with this project. Catherine May indicated that she did not "oppose the food stamp plan per se" but that she wanted "to express the voice of caution before we take too many irrevocable steps in embarking on such a far-reaching and costly program on which there are still so many unanswered questions." Republicans McIntire and Quie led another part of the attack by insisting that this was a welfare program that should retain the matching provision.

The ranking Republican on the Agriculture Committee, Charles Hoeven, reviewed the history of the food stamp, tobacco research, and wheat-cotton bills. He summarized his view of things by saying that "It is the same old situation of you tickle me and I will tickle you and we will both tickle the third fellow. Then we will all smile and we will put one over on the taxpayers." In responding Cooley denied that he was "a party to any sort of dealing or wheeling or any other type of transaction that involves any more than a vote on this bill today and a vote on the other bills as they are scheduled by the leadership to come before the House."

The House adjourned after finishing general debate and reading the first section for amendment under the five-minute rule.

On Wednesday April 8 the House met an hour earlier than usual and resumed the amending process as a Committee of the Whole. During this process the Republicans raised the general civil rights question with regard to the program. In an attempt to woo away the southern Democrats they stressed that with a few exceptions no pilot programs had been located in the South, and that Title VI of the civil rights bill would prevent much of the South from benefiting from the program.

Despite this, however, the Democratic ranks held together during teller votes. Five Republican amendments objectionable to the leadership were defeated, including the Quie amendment on matching funds that had been adopted by the Agriculture Committee. The other amendments defeated included one to transfer the program to the Department of Health, Education, and Welfare; one to eliminate all imported foods, including coffee and tea; and one to cut the program off in 1967 rather than make it permanent. The only close vote was on the Quie amendment, which was rejected by a teller vote of 168 to 155. The Committee of the Whole adopted only two minor amendments in addition to those offered by the Agriculture Committee, and Cooley accepted both of them.

In the midst of the amending process the House recessed for two hours to pay respects to the body of General Douglas MacArthur, which was lying in state in the rotunda. Later in the day the Republicans moved adjournment as a further mark of respect. This motion failed. Republican Minority Leader Charles A. Halleck of Indiana registered a general protest on behalf of the minority at the procedure being used and the undue haste in insisting that both bills be voted on that day. Carl Albert of Oklahoma, the majority leader, replied:

> I am going to advise the minority leader that we are going to stay here and finish these bills and that the leadership of the committee has endeavored from 11 o'clock this morning to expedite the consideration of this matter so that the Members on both sides of the aisle could attend to important social functions. Every objection made to our considering this bill as having been read and every point of no quorum that was made has been made from the other side of the aisle. We do not apologize for going on with the consideration of this matter.

Chairman Cooley moved to cut debate off at 6 p.m. and this motion passed. The Committee of the Whole rose. The speaker resumed the chair and prepared to order a final roll call. However, the Republicans had one more delaying tactic to which they could resort. Charles S. Gubser of California demanded an engrossed copy (that is, printed, with all amendments) of the bill. The Democrats were ready for this demand and the printer was ready to accomplish the task within a few hours. In the interim the speaker let debate on the rule for the wheat-cotton bill open. Within a few minutes liberal Democrats, including Mrs. Sullivan, realized that this might mean that the final vote on wheat-cotton would come before the final vote on food stamps. Mrs. Sullivan quickly let the speaker know that this would be totally unacceptable to her because she was afraid that, having voted aye on wheat-cotton, southern Democrats would then either leave the chamber or actually vote nay on food stamps. The speaker then interrupted the debate and declared a recess, acting under the agreement that was thought to involve only the recess for MacArthur.

The House printer had the engrossed copy of the bill back in time for the House to reconvene at 9:05 p.m. The Republicans made known their unhappiness that a request designed to cover MacArthur had in fact given the speaker a power they had not foreseen. The speaker remained firm, however.

The Republicans now offered a motion to adjourn and demanded a roll call on the motion. This was defeated 239 to 173. The Republicans then exercised their right of offering a recommittal motion. This motion provided that the Quie amendment on state matching be put into the bill again. It was defeated 223 to 195. The House then passed the food stamp bill by a roll call vote of 229 to 189.

To complete the day the hour-long debate on the wheat-cotton bill was held and the House passed the bill 211 to 203. The House adjourned at 12:44 a.m.

*The Nature of the Votes.* Analysis of the three roll calls—on food stamp recommittal and final passage and on wheat-cotton—suggests several things. First, it suggests that these votes were all essentially party line votes:

|  | Food Stamps | | Wheat-Cotton |
|  | Recommittal | Final Passage | Final Passage |
|---|---|---|---|
| Democrats | 90% nay | 89% aye | 85% aye |
| Republicans | 3% nay | 7% aye | 6% aye |

Second, it suggests that within each party rural representatives were less likely than urban or suburban representatives[2] to support the administration on the food stamp issue:

|  | Number of Representatives | Percent Pro-Food Stamps (Final Passage) |
|---|---|---|
| Democrats |  |  |
| Urban[2] | 94 | 90.4 |
| Suburban | 28 | 96.4 |
| Rural | 120 | 86.7 |
| Republicans |  |  |
| Urban | 34 | 11.8 |
| Suburban | 35 | 11.4 |
| Rural | 107 | 4.7 |

Partisan activity and persuasion explain the different results on this vote compared to the 1958 vote (analyzed on page 285) when a major party fight did not occur. In 1964 party pressure greatly increased support for food stamps on the part of rural Democrats and greatly decreased support for food stamps on the part of suburban and rural Republicans.

Third, voting analysis indicates that those representatives whose districts were participating in the pilot program favored it more strongly than their fellow party members. Thirty-three Democrats had districts participating. Of these, thirty-one voted for the administration position on both roll calls involving food stamps. The other two did not vote. Three

[2] The categories used are defined in the *Congressional Quarterly Weekly Report*, February 2, 1962, pp. 153 ff.

of the eight Republicans whose districts benefited voted with the administration on both roll calls.

Finally, an analysis of all three roll calls taken together indicates the degree of success of the trade of food stamps for wheat-cotton among Democrats. Twelve Democrats were absent for all three votes. Six more were absent for one or more of the three roll calls but supported the administration when they voted. One hundred eighty Democrats supported the administration on all three roll calls and might best be labeled as "reliable traders." Twenty-six members were "greedy liberals," voting with the administration twice on the food stamp bill and against the wheat-cotton bill. Twelve members were "greedy conservatives," voting against the food stamp bill twice and for the wheat-cotton bill. Eight members were "half-hearted traders," voting with the administration on one food stamp roll call and against it on the other and voting for the wheat-cotton bill. Eight Democrats were against both programs on all three roll calls. Three members voted in wholly unique patterns.

In short, the trade was 82 percent successful in that only the "greedy liberals," "greedy conservatives," and "half-hearted traders" refused to participate in the bargain. Even if only the "reliable traders" are counted the trade was 71 percent successful.

On the following day, April 9, the House Republicans retaliated for the late session on food stamps and wheat-cotton by tying up the House for four and a half hours, making the conduct of legislative business impossible. Carl Albert, objecting to the Republican moves, said: "We had a job to do yesterday and we did it."

Also on April 9 the President issued a short statement praising the action of the House in passing both the food stamp and wheat-cotton bills.


Ratification of House Action


In late April the staff of the Senate Committee on Agriculture and Forestry prepared an explanation of what was contained in H.R. 10222 for the use of the senators on the committee. Hearings were held on June 18 and 19. The first day was devoted entirely to the testimony of Secretary Freeman, accompanied by Howard Davis of the Food Distribution Division. On the second day representatives from the National Grange, the National Farmers Union, and the Appalachian Committee for Full Employment appeared. All supported the House-passed bill.

In opening the hearings Chairman Allen J. Ellender, Democrat from Louisiana, stressed the long record of bipartisan support for the food stamp bill. He especially praised Senator Aiken, who had introduced at least one food stamp proposal in every Congress beginning with the Seventy-ninth. In turn Aiken in his testimony stressed his continued support for the bill and highlighted how it would help the agricultural economy.

Freeman in his testimony basically supported the House-passed bill. However, he asked that the prohibition on "luxury foods and luxury frozen foods" be removed. He felt this would be too difficult to administer as it would involve checking on thousands of grocery stores.

The only opposition came from Republican Senator Bourke B. Hickenlooper of Iowa: "As I look at this bill and your statement it seems to me that it is an utterly open-ended no-control bill. There are no guidelines in this bill except the local discretion and manipulation of local authorities in making available these food stamps." He also raised the question of civil rights in administering the program.

Shortly after the hearings, on June 23, the President at a press conference indicated that the food stamp bill was one of the thirty "must" bills that he wanted passed before Congress adjourned.

Six days later the Senate committee voted 14 to 2 to report out H.R. 10222 with seven minor amendments. The minority did not issue a report. The amendments eliminated the prohibition of soft drinks, luxury foods, and luxury frozen foods from the program, and provided that where a food stamp program was in effect the direct distribution program could not also be used. The wording on "eligible households" was rewritten. Language requiring the secretary to "provide for an equitable and orderly expansion among the several States in accordance with their relative need and readiness to meet their requested effective dates of participation" was added. The amount of money was left unchanged except that the committee eliminated the supplementary authorization of $25 million for fiscal 1964.

The Senate considered the bill on the floor on June 30, the day after the report was issued. There was no real debate. Ellender and Aiken set the tone of the few remarks by praising the longstanding and widespread bipartisan support for the bill. The only amendment accepted, by voice vote, was one offered by Republican Jack Miller of Iowa to bar the use of stamps for imported meat. Republican J. Caleb Boggs of Delaware, a member of the committee, offered an amendment providing that the states contribute 10 percent of the cost of bonus or "free" food stamps to persons not on public assistance. Ellender said that the committee had rejected the same amendment almost unanimously and hoped that the Senate would too. It did. It also rejected two minor amendments. The Senate then passed the food stamp bill by voice vote.

On July 23 Cooley requested unanimous consent for the House to agree to the Senate amendments without going to conference. Hoeven agreed with the request because he feared that if a conference were held the prohibition of imported meat would be removed. However, another Iowa Republican, H. R. Gross, objected. Cooley then asked the House Rules Committee to grant a rule allowing the House by majority vote to concur in the Senate amendments without going to conference. The Rules Committee granted the rule on August 11 and the House passed the Senate version of the food stamp bill on the same day by voice vote.

The only possible problem at this late date was removed when Heimburger prepared for Cooley's use on the floor some language designed to make the legislative history cover a final objection by Paul Jones. The department and Cooley both approved of the language, which related to the possibility that some people might not be eligible for food stamps, local relief, or direct distribution. These persons would be included in an emergency category.

On August 31 President Johnson signed the bill into law. In a short statement made at the time of signing he called the Food Stamp Act of 1964 "a realistic and responsible step forward toward the fuller and wiser use of our agricultural abundance. . . . As a permanent program, the Food Stamp Plan will be one of our most valuable weapons for the war on poverty. It will enable low income families to increase their food expenditures, using their own dollars."

## Concluding Comments

Thus, in 1964 a program was made permanent. It began expanding toward the goal of spending $360 million annually. By July 1, 1965 the number of participants was expected to be about one million. In early 1965 a reorganization in the Agriculture Department put the food stamp program in a division of its own, under a new deputy administrator for consumer food programs in the Agricultural Marketing Service.

The program was not exclusively urban in character at any time during its twenty-five-year history except for a few weeks in the House of

Representatives in the late winter and early spring of 1964. At that time the program appeared to be urban because urban Democrats were the most concerned about it. A close examination of the events that took place then suggests some generalizations about the winning strategy for urban liberals in the House, and also about their little-used bargaining power.

It appears from this case that urban liberals can increase their voting strength in two ways. First, they need to get the bill for which they are fighting identified as a party issue. Since the preponderance of the urban liberals are Democrats and are likely to continue to be so, if recent party ratios continue this tactic will immediately mobilize on their side the party with the greater chance of winning. Of course, this is not always enough. Democratic majorities may look large on paper but melt on issues that awaken the feeling and energies of those not disposed to aid urban areas. Thus, the second part of the winning strategy involves arranging a broadly understood trade or bargain between the urban and rural segments of the Democratic party in the House. If the trade is largely successful, as it was in this case, then Republican votes will be unnecessary, although the chances of victory shrink with the size of the Democratic margin. Involving Republicans in such a trade is difficult, in part because Republican party unity on spending issues has been high in the past few Congresses.

This case is unusual in that the device of a trade was needed to get the food stamp bill out of committee, as well as to get it passed in the House. Much urban legislation goes through committees that in the past few years have been liberally oriented—such as Education and Labor and the Housing Subcommittee of the Banking and Currency Committee. Some urban legislation goes through Interstate and Foreign Commerce, which is generally conservative. Here the bill was in the Agriculture Committee, which is composed almost entirely of rural members chosen on the basis of the commodity interest they represent. This unfavorable situation was overcome, however, because the liberals and the House leadership were aggressive in holding a bill dear to some farm members —tobacco research—hostage for favorable action on the food stamp bill. This was immediately and dramatically successful. Such trades are hard to plan far in advance but in this case urban forces were alert and seized an opportunity when they saw it.

All of this suggests that the urban liberals in the Congress can have substantial weight. Here a program that had been a more or less dormant issue in Congress for twenty years and was about to be scuttled again in the House Agriculture Committee was saved and passed when the urban-oriented members of the House came to life and, with the crucial backing of a Democratic administration, took skillful advantage of the power resources available to them. The agricultural forces themselves then used food stamps as a crutch to help them pass the much larger and more costly wheat-cotton program. They, too, were aided by the President's desire to see their bill enacted.

In a sense the urban Democrats had more bargaining weight than they were willing to use. It is likely that the food stamp bill could have passed the floor without being attached to any rurally oriented bill. Yet the urban Democrats acceded to a wheat-cotton for food stamp trade. Perhaps they felt bound by the actions of the President and the House leadership, who were devoting much more time to wheat-cotton than to food stamps. At any rate, the southern Democrats from cotton districts benefited from the trade far more than the urban northerners.

Obviously, no group of members can always demand the better of a trade. But this case, along with general literature on recent Congresses, indicates that the rurally oriented, moderate-conservative southern Democrats get a preponderant share of better bargains. This can be accounted for partly by such factors as seniority and the greater time and effort they put into a legislative career as compared with their northern liberal counterparts. Even with the necessary qualifications, however, the passage of the food stamp bill in the House in 1964 should indicate two things to urban-oriented liberals (at least among the Democrats) : their potential bargaining power is greater than they perhaps have realized, and skill is necessary in using this power or they will still be on the short end of most bargains.

ROYCE HANSON

# Congress Copes
# with Mass Transit, 1960–64

CULMINATING A FOUR-YEAR STRUGGLE to win a
federal commitment to the solution of the mass transportation problems
of America's major cities, President Lyndon B. Johnson on July 9, 1964
signed the Urban Mass Transportation Act (P.L. 365). Transportation
had long been a federal concern; urban transportation had not. The federal government's transportation policy traditionally focused on the
movement of commerce, national security needs, and railroad employment. The United States did not begin to feel the full impact of the automobile until after World War II. Even then, it was only after attempting to deal with the automobile, particularly through the 1956 federal
highway program, that the country began to recognize the existence of
urban transportation problems of national significance.

The Development of the Issue

Although federal aid for farm roads and for highways had been established in the infancy of the auto age, highway building was neglected
during the Second World War. Afterwards, some states embarked on
ambitious construction programs, including the establishment of freeway
and turnpike systems, but such efforts were sporadic, and inadequate;
they could not keep up with the advances in automobile technology, production, and use. By 1956 auto users, state roads agencies, the automo-
tive industry, and the road builders had built a powerful coalition to produce the most generous federal grants-in-aid program ever devised—the

Federal-Aid Highway Act with its provision of 90 percent federal assistance for the construction of an extensive and truly magnificent interstate highway system.

As the highway program came into effect, however, it became clear that its impact on the country's burgeoning cities had not been fully comprehended. Traffic increased as highways were built. The suburbs expanded at low densities made possible by roads and autos, but the price of two cars in every garage was bumper-to-bumper traffic on the new freeways and massive congestion in the streets downtown. Highways were replacing rails in moving passengers, and on the roads the cars were replacing buses. As the interstate program begin to move from the open country into the metropolitan areas and into the core cities themselves, the costs of construction increased with land values. And while freeways offered expedient means of displacing parts of the slums in some cities, there was increasing anguish on the part of planners, architects, and other city leaders that the highways might destroy the city. One critic of the auto age, after viewing the effect of the freeway system on Los Angeles, exclaimed: "I have seen the future and it doesn't work."

Critics were occasionally dismissed as romantics by heady highway engineers rejoicing in new power and new technology. But increasing costs, technical problems of fitting highways into the cityscape, rising political opposition to the obliteration of communities by freeways, and pressures for housing construction resulting from dislocation—all these and more —underscored the need to reconcile the highway with the city in a better fashion than had been found. In 1957 six eastern governors concluded at an Arden House conference that "at the heart of the problems of most metropolitan areas is the problem of mass transit." In 1958, at a symposium on urban transportation sponsored by the Connecticut General Life Insurance Company, the participants—planners, architects, engineers, and other specialists in urban problems—concluded that rapid mass transit systems were essential to the livability of cities. "The answer to the transportation problems of our densely built up urban centers does not lie in the private car alone," wrote Wilfred Owen in *Cities in the Motor Age*,[1] a summary of the Connecticut General Conference, ". . . an adequate public transit system is essential. Without it the motorist in today's big city may strangle in his own congestion. . . ."

But the same year at Sagamore, New York, a national conference on

[1] Wilfred Owen, *Cities in the Motor Age* (Viking, 1959).

highways and urban development maintained the emphasis on a highway solution to the urban transportation problem. Conferees pointed out that from 1950 to 1955 transit patronage in major cities had dropped more than 26 percent and in smaller cities by 50 percent. However, the loss of transit patronage to automobiles that appeared to some to make a case for more highways created severe economic problems in the transit industry and in railroad commuter service.

The financial crisis of the railroad industry became the subject of extensive congressional hearings in 1958. James M. Symes, president of the Pennsylvania Railroad, the nation's largest system, told the House Interstate and Foreign Commerce Committee that his company's passenger deficit in the previous decade amounted to almost half of its net freight income. The Pennsylvania Railroad, he reported, had abandoned almost 50 percent of its annual passenger mileage from 1945 to 1956. In New York the New Haven Railroad was tottering toward bankruptcy.

After Congress passed the Transportation Act of 1958, which was designed to strengthen the competitive position of railroads *vis-à-vis* other carriers, railroads began to petition for abandonment of commuter and other passenger service. Within a few months the Interstate Commerce Commission had received petitions to discontinue 110 trains. Many other applications were filed with state agencies. At Senate Interstate and Foreign Commerce Committee hearings on bills dealing with the train discontinuance problem, Democratic Senator Harrison A. Williams, Jr., of New Jersey testified that 493 trains had been discontinued in New Jersey alone in the nine months following passage of the 1958 Transportation Act.

As the commuter crisis became apparent, big-city mayors and urban state governors began to react. Philadelphia's Mayor Richardson C. Dilworth negotiated an agreement with the commuter lines in his city to increase service and cut rates on experimental routes with the help of a city subsidy. Governor Robert B. Meyner of New Jersey proposed using turnpike revenues to subsidize commuter service. A number of major cities undertook extensive transportation studies. In Philadelphia, Chicago, San Francisco, Washington, and other cities, the studies recommended improvement or creation of extensive mass transit facilities and programs.

In early 1959 Mayor Dilworth called a meeting of chief executives of a dozen large cities and seventeen railroads. They met in Chicago and later in Philadelphia to discuss means by which the commuter crisis might be met. At the Philadelphia meeting they decided to ask the

American Municipal Association to prepare an analysis of transit problems in five major cities that relied heavily on commuter rail service.

The Municipal Association report, "The Collapse of Commuter Service," was published in the fall of 1959. It estimated that if the five cities surveyed—New York, Chicago, Boston, Philadelphia, and Cleveland— were to lose their rail commuter service, then a highway program great enough to replace that rail service would cost $31 billion. For New York alone the report estimated that if only half the mass transit commuters switched to cars, ten square miles of additional parking space would be required.

In December 1959 the Dilworth committee issued its report. It called for long-term, low-interest loans to public bodies for transportation improvement; a study of the desirability of federal grants to improve mass transit; reform of federal, state, and local tax policies; and "rationalization" of federal transportation policies regarding regulation of the industry and its promotional activities.

*The Beginning of Political Action.* Thus, by late 1959 the basis for a new political coalition was beginning to emerge. Big-city mayors, commuter groups, major commuter railroads, the transit industry and its suppliers all needed relief. To these "hard" interests could be added urban planners and architects and those concerned with urban housing, amenities, and the habitability of cities. Two elements were lacking: a political catalyst, and a clear and persuasive technical explanation of the problem.

The latter deficiency was harder to remedy than the former. Normally, the federal bureaucracy contains an impressive assortment of specialists in a public policy area. But urban transportation was a new area of focus. Heretofore, federal transportation policy had been concerned with the national, or at least the regional, requirements of the major carriers. Also, it was heavily biased toward regulation of carriers and development of a national highway system, rather than toward urban development and urban transportation problems. The three agencies of the federal government where some expertise existed were the Interstate Commerce Commission (ICC), the Bureau of Public Roads in the Department of Commerce, and the urban planning components of the Housing and Home Finance Agency (HHFA). Under the 1952 reorganization acts the Department of Commerce had gained an undersecretary for transportation with major responsibility for transportation policy. However, this responsibility had never been fully or positively exercised. In fact, in the years following establishment of the undersecretaryship the trend was toward decentralization of policy making and bureaucratic autonomy in transportation policy. The Bureau of Public Roads evinced little interest in assuming a role in mass transit. Its responsibility was administration of the Highway Trust Fund, a responsibility that might be conceived to involve a proprietary interest in keeping the highway program free from encumbrances. The bureau's staff was not equipped to deal with either rail or bus transit problems. The ICC was concerned with the fate of commuter service, but it lacked any experts on the broader issues of urban transit and had no proprietary interest in gaining knowledge of, or in devising, a program for the intrastate bus and rail systems. In general, the administration of Dwight D. Eisenhower was unresponsive to the urban mass transit problem, appearing to consider it a "local" aspect of transportation policy.

The mayors and their new allies, the railroad and transit interests, initially also conceived of the issue in terms of transportation policy rather than urban policy. Therefore, when Dilworth's committee succeeded in obtaining the support of the American Municipal Association and the United States Conference of Mayors for its objectives, and work was begun to produce legislation, the first efforts were based on a strategy of working through the Commerce Committees of Congress. In February 1960 the mayors of New York, Philadelphia, Cleveland, and St. Louis, together with Governor David L. Lawrence of Pennsylvania and the presidents of the Pennsylvania and the New Haven railroads, presented the program of the Dilworth committee to the Subcommittee on Transportation of the Senate Commerce Committee. They requested immediate help in the form of a long-term, low-interest loan program for maintenance and extension of all types of mass transportation systems, and asked for a study exploring a grants-in-aid program. The Transportation Subcommittee showed little interest in the loan program, which would benefit only a few railroads; after all, the subcommittee's focus was the rail industry, and not cities or nonrail mass transit systems.

The mass transportation supporters especially wanted to interest the Senate Commerce Committee chairman, Democrat Warren G. Magnuson of Washington, in their proposals. The principal lobbyist for mass transit was Patrick McLaughlin. He was the staff member of the American Municipal Association who had conducted the association's study of commuter service, and he was also the Washington lobbyist for the city of Philadelphia. Early in 1960 McLaughlin had drafted legislation that the group hoped Senator Magnuson would introduce. This proposed bill, the "Mass Transit Financing Corporation Act," would have created a corporation in the Department of Commerce authorized to purchase bonds or to make loans at one percent interest to public bodies to acquire, maintain, and improve mass transit facilities and equipment in metropolitan areas. It would have operated a revolving loan fund of a half billion dollars. A number of representatives from urban areas introduced the bill in the House. Senator Magnuson, however, remained uninterested.

### The Williams Bill, 1960

Harrison Williams, a New Jersey Democrat, was serving his initial term as a United States senator. He was a member of the Banking and Currency Committee and its Housing Subcommittee. First elected in 1958, he had at once interested himself in the commuter crisis, testifying before the Commerce Committee on the problem of discontinuing commuter trains. He had also sponsored amendments to the 1958 Transportation Act designed to alleviate the discontinuance problem. But his proposed amendments died in the Transportation Subcommittee in 1959.

Williams' legislative assistant, Ardee Ames, a former journalist, was intensely interested in urban problems, especially the mass transportation issue. He urged Williams to take up the cause of the cities in meeting their transit problems. New Jersey was the nation's most urbanized state and Ames thought Williams needed an issue with which he could achieve popular identification. Both the senator and his assistant were acutely aware that New Jersey had not reelected a Democratic senator in many years. Ames talked with McLaughlin about Williams sponsoring his legislation, but McLaughlin, of course, was trying to interest Magnuson, a senior senator and the chairman of the crucial committee.

In reviewing bills that had been introduced on mass transportation, Ames spotted a House bill by Representative Donald J. Irwin, a freshman Democrat from Connecticut. The aspect of Irwin's bill that most interested Ames was its provision for placing jurisdiction over a federal mass transportation program in the Housing and Home Finance Agency. HHFA operations were under the jurisdiction of the Housing Subcommittee. Williams could play a major role in development of the legislation if the program were reconceived as *urban* legislation rather than *transportation* legislation. Moreover, as they examined the problem, consulting with the office of the legal counsel in the Senate, with Commerce Department officials, and with McLaughlin, Williams and Ames became convinced that transit legislation required a closer relationship to urban planning programs than to the national highway program administered by the Bureau of Public Roads. They reasoned that transit should be considered an urban development problem because of the impact of mass transportation on land uses and the urban economy, and because rail lines do not serve low density development. Fear of the domination of "highway interests" in the Bureau of Public Roads added to their resolve to lodge the new program in the Housing Agency.

Ames and Williams drafted a bill, then, that changed jurisdiction over the program to the Community Facilities Administration, an HHFA component. Williams' bill also amended section 701 of the Housing Act to allow use of planning assistance funds in developing mass transit programs in the context of comprehensive plans for metropolitan areas. Williams scaled down the cost of the program from $500 million to $100 million in long-term, low-interest loans, choosing the $100 million figure on the basis of his judgment of what size program might pass Congress. He anticipated administration opposition to his bill and feared that a large expenditure proposal would excite strong opposition, but he wanted a figure big enough to indicate that the program was respectable. The lack of reliable technical data on the magnitude of the need made the assignment of any cost figures difficult at best.

*Support and Opposition.* By now McLaughlin was sure he could not obtain Magnuson's help. Without a sponsor he readily embraced Williams, his bill, the scaled-down authorization, and the strategy of moving the legislation through the Housing Subcommittee. Accordingly, the Municipal Association dropped McLaughlin's draft and backed Williams' bill.

On March 24 Williams introduced his bill (S. 3278); he was joined by twelve cosponsors including a number of Republicans. Since the bill was festooned with amendments to existing housing laws it was routinely referred to the Banking and Currency Committee. Democrat John J. Sparkman of Alabama, chairman of the Housing Subcommittee, initially showed little interest in the bill, but he was most cooperative in accommodating Williams' desire to expedite hearings on it. Sparkman and Williams agreed that S. 3278 should be considered as separate legislation from other housing measures, but hearings were held in conjunction with all other bills related to housing.

The approach of the legislation, from its incubation in the Dilworth committee to the Williams draft, was designed to obtain as much railroad industry support as possible and to avoid any railroad opposition. Thus, while railroad groups were not altogether of one mind, the industry did support the bill. As a concomitant of this support the Interstate Commerce Commission endorsed the legislation in early May, before hearings commenced. The ICC commented that the legislation would "provide Federal assistance to State and local governments in attempting to solve what is essentially a local problem, but one in which the Federal Government has a real concern."

The attitude of the Eisenhower administration generally was less helpful. Norman P. Mason, the HHFA administrator, wrote Banking and Currency Chairman A. Willis Robertson, Democrat from Virginia, that his agency had serious objections to S. 3278. The HHFA objected to the interest rate formula in the bill, arguing that it amounted to a subsidy that would "result in a program far exceeding any proper Federal responsibilities in this field." Also, the agency—in accord with the general position of the Eisenhower administration—objected to the "back door" financing aspect of the bill. This procedure entailed financing the program through direct borrowing from the Treasury without the need for periodic appropriations of funds by the congressional Appropriations Committees. (This issue reappeared and is discussed at a later point in the story.)

The acting secretary of the treasury, Laurence B. Robbins, was even more emphatic in expressing opposition:

> The Department would be opposed to the enactment of the bill. The Department believes that Federal financial assistance should be limited to situations where such assistance is considered necessary to achieve impelling national policy objectives and Federal participation in programs which are more appropriately the responsibility of States and local authorities must be held to an absolute minimum if budget expenditures are to be kept within reasonable limits in the years ahead.

Treasury emphasized its feeling that urban mass transit was a local and private industry responsibility. It also objected to the interest rate formula of the Williams bill.

Given administration opposition to his bill, Williams carefully prepared for the hearings in order to show the need for the legislation and to demonstrate the extent of his support. With McLaughlin's collaboration an impressive array of favorable witnesses was assembled. The hearings began on May 23 and lasted for three days. After the first session Williams presided. Only those members of the subcommittee who supported the bill attended.

The witnesses came from three primary groups: mayors and governors, the rail and transit industries, and experts on urbanism or mass transit. While the regional concentration was eastern, major cities from other parts of the country were also represented, as were national organizations of city officials. Williams, as the lead-off witness, built the case for his bill and refuted the administration's objections. He drew a picture of a failing but essential urban service with no place to turn for assistance but to the federal government. And he tried to show that the transit problem affected many cities and a great majority of the nation's people. After Williams the mayors and governors discussed the plight of their cities and the railroad transit experts documented the need for federal assistance. No hostile witnesses appeared. Only two statements in opposition were submitted: by the United States Chamber of Commerce and the Investment Bankers' Association of America. HHFA officials had opposed the bill in earlier general testimony covering all housing legislation, but did not appear during these hearings.

*Senate Action.* The Housing Subcommittee and the full committee approved S. 3278 without recorded objections, and on June 15 the Banking and Currency Committee reported it out. Sparkman said that he felt the hearings showed an impressive need for the legislation. The majority leader, Texas Democrat Lyndon B. Johnson, indicated his support for the Williams bill. The Democrats were driving to establish an image of concern for cities, and Johnson himself was shortly to announce his candidacy for the Democratic party's presidential nomination.

Only one material change was made in the bill as reported by the committee. The community facilities revolving loan fund, from which the mass transportation loans would be made, was increased from $100 million to $300 million, with $100 million reserved for transit loans. Thus, the effect was to double the available funds for other public facility loans. Sponsors of the legislation felt this "sweetener" would make the program more salable to representatives of small cities without transit needs.

The committee report, prepared by Williams, documented the case for the bill in considerable detail, using the record established at the hearings. The case for a minimum program of $100 million was reasserted, and it was pointed out that a larger sum was probably justified.

On June 27 the bill came before the Senate. Williams made a brief speech endorsing it. He was supported by Republicans Prescott Bush of Connecticut, Thomas H. Kuchel of California, Kenneth B. Keating and Jacob K. Javits of New York, and by Democrats Sparkman and Joseph S. Clark of Pennsylvania. Williams accepted an amendment by Kuchel to make San Francisco eligible for assistance for some actions already taken. Only Senator J. Strom Thurmond, Democrat from South Carolina, opposed the bill in the floor discussion. Thurmond stated constitutional and financial objections. He argued that the transit problem was essentially local and that the federal government should not become involved in it.

The Williams bill was passed by a voice vote. The next day it was referred to the House Banking and Currency Committee. Although several House members had introduced companion bills after the Senate committee had acted favorably, the bill appeared to have no strong patron on the House subcommittee. No one really took it seriously on the House side. The administration was opposed to it, dimming any hope that action by the House would lead to a signed law. Ames, as Williams' major legislative missionary for the bill, did not have the time to cultivate House support in 1960. Thus, no action was taken on the bill during the remainder of the Eighty-sixth Congress; it simply died in the House committee.

While no legislation was enacted in 1960, the Williams bill stirred considerable interest in urban mass transportation. The mayors and their congressional allies succeeded in having a strong urban mass transportation plank that called for federal assistance inserted in the Democratic platform. The party's presidential nominee, Senator John F. Kennedy, endorsed unified planning of all forms of urban transportation in a major campaign speech in Pittsburgh in October 1960. After his election, President-elect Kennedy established a special task force on housing and urban development. This group endorsed the Senate-passed bill and urged the incoming President to establish a study commission to determine future mass transit needs.

In January 1961 the Senate Commerce Committee published *National*

*Transportation Policy,*[2] a staff study report known as the Doyle report for the staff director. The study gave some attention to the particular plight of the commuter railroads, but it also argued for assistance to urban transportation generally and for a new program of economic and technical research on urban transportation. While its recommendations were quite cautious, essentially urging more study, the value of the Doyle report to advocates of transit aid was its documentation of the severe problem.

For these reasons the 1961 prospects for urban mass transportation legislation looked bright.

## Mass Transit in the Housing Bill, 1961

*The Second Williams Bill.* In late December of 1960 Senator Williams resolved not to wait for the new administration to take office before introducing a new version of his bill. First, he was unsure what the new administration would recommend or when it would ask for it. He wanted to capitalize on the support already established in the Senate and push for early action. Second, he wanted to maintain control of the legislation and his own clear identification with the transit issue.

When the Eighty-seventh Congress convened in January Williams began to line up cosponsors for an expanded and somewhat bolder version of the 1960 Senate bill. Where that measure had provided $100 million in loans his new version provided a $250 million loan fund, but with only $100 million to be obligated the first year. In addition to keeping the provision allowing use of federal planning assistance funds for urban transportation planning, Williams now provided for a $75 million mass transportation demonstration grant program. Finally, the new version created a new office in the HHFA to administer the program instead of making it part of a broadened community facilities program. On January 11 Williams introduced the bill as S. 345 for himself and eighteen other senators: Republicans J. Glenn Beall of Maryland, Styles Bridges of New Hampshire, Bush, Javits, Keating, and Kuchel; and Democrats Clark, Alan Bible of Nevada, Thomas J. Dodd of Connecticut, Paul H. Douglas of Illinois, Clair Engle of California, Ernest Gruening of

[2] *National Transportation Policy,* Report of the Senate Interstate and Foreign Commerce Committee Special Study Group on Transportation Policies in the United States, S. Rept. 445, 87 Cong. 1 sess. (1961).

Alaska, Vance Hartke of Indiana, Hubert H. Humphrey of Minnesota, Edward V. Long of Missouri, Wayne Morse of Oregon, Stuart Symington of Missouri, and Steven M. Young of Ohio. The cosponsors included six of the fifteen members of the Banking and Currency Committee and four of the nine members of the Housing Subcommittee. Sponsorship was also well distributed geographically, except for the South, and strong Republican support seemed likely, especially from Bridges and Kuchel.

Williams now tried to muster administration support for his legislation. Early in 1961 he participated along with a group of mayors in a White House session with President Kennedy and key advisers such as Secretary of Commerce Luther H. Hodges, Special Counsel Theodore C. Sorensen, Assistant Special Counsel Lee C. White, and Elmer B. Staats, deputy director of the Bureau of the Budget.

The Kennedy administration, while at least theoretically committed to federal aid for mass transit, had some difficult problems of its own. The Bureau of the Budget's analysts had little data of a technical nature on which to base financial recommendations. There was no assurance that either a demonstration grant or a loan program, especially one as small as that proposed by Williams, would have much impact on the mass transit problem. Yet the legislation had considerable symbolic value for an administration determined to take some significant action in urban affairs.

Now that passage of urban transit legislation was more than an academic question the bureaucracies with potential stakes in the issue began to awaken to its implications. The new administration, unlike its predecessor, could not actually oppose the program. If it were created, someone had to administer it. The Bureau of Public Roads and the Department of Commerce both claimed a strong interest. Some HHFA officials of the new administration evinced a proprietary interest in the legislation as drawn by Williams. The new HHFA administrator, Robert C. Weaver, seemed doubtful about the program, however, and open-minded on who should administer it. Clearly the mayors were now committed to administration by the Housing Agency.

The President was almost totally preoccupied with the Cuban situation during the early weeks of 1961. Efforts of the White House staff in the domestic policy arena were devoted primarily to legislation such as medicare that had been hanging fire for several years and to new proposals such as the Peace Corps to which the President had strong personal or political commitments. While President Kennedy had established a number of task forces on national problems, none dealt specifically with the mass transportation problems of cities. There was nothing, then, in either the White House or the Bureau of the Budget to trigger an automatic presidential response. These factors, coupled with the potential jurisdictional conflict between the Department of Commerce and the HHFA, and with the Budget Bureau's doubts about the efficacy of the Williams program and concern about its impact on the total budget, led the Budget Bureau to equivocate on the subject. Further, the President and the bureau were considering plans for the reorganization of executive agencies dealing with both urban affairs and transportation. Where should the mass transportation program be placed if the administration succeeded in getting both a Department of Urban Affairs *and* a Department of Transportation?

Confronted with such uncertainties and bureaucratic disagreement, the President's political instinct was to wait and see. The administration remained silent for two months on the subject.

On March 9 President Kennedy sent his housing message to Congress. It was a severe disappointment to Williams, who had hoped for an endorsement of his bill, but it clearly reflected the uncertainties about the program within the administration. Proposing a package of new or expanded housing programs, Kennedy made only scant mention of urban transportation. He urged improvement of rapid transit services and reiterated his instructions to the HHFA administrator and the secretary of commerce to coordinate their planning programs. When he came to treat the transportation problem directly, he acknowledged that "Nothing is more dramatically apparent than the inadequacy of transportation in our large urban areas." However, his proposal was mild:

> But to solve the problem of urban transportation will test our ingenuity and put a heavy drain on our resources. While the responsibility for working out these solutions rests primarily with local government and private enterprise, the Federal Government must provide leadership and technical assistance.
>
> Accordingly, I have asked the Administrator of the Housing and Home Finance Agency and the Secretary of Commerce to undertake an immediate and extensive study of urban transportation problems and the proper role of the Federal Government in their solution.

Essentially the strategy of the administration was to play for time. The Institute of Public Administration was retained by Commerce and the HHFA to conduct the study. It would not report until late in 1961.

*A Transit Amendment for Omnibus Housing.* On March 20 the

Housing Subcommittee began hearings on S. 345. Again Williams invited a series of witnesses to make the case for his bill. No representatives of the administration appeared. No material opposition was expressed except by O. Roy Chalk, president of D.C. Transit in Washington, D.C. Chalk labeled the bill as "critically deficient" in its protection of private transit companies. He recommended a "private enterprise" amendment to authorize federally guaranteed loans to private companies for the acquisition of modern equipment.

On April 4 the Housing Subcommittee began its extensive hearings on the omnibus housing bill of 1961. Pro-transit senators asked each friendly witness questions about the relationship of mass transportation to the metropolitan programs of the HHFA contained in the bill. During the examination of administration witnesses Sparkman asked Urban Renewal Commissioner William L. Slayton if the proposed mass transit program "does . . . not tie right in with your programs?" Slayton readily agreed. Sparkman then asked HHFA Administrator Weaver ". . . if such legislation is passed you would be perfectly willing to take over administration of it? And, Dr. Weaver, do you agree with what has been said as to its being inherently a part of our urban renewal and community development problems?" Weaver agreed.

Williams continued to draw forth support for placing a mass transportation program in the HHFA. Mayor Dilworth placed the Conference of Mayors and the American Municipal Association in support of such action. Mayor Richard Daley of Chicago was likewise led by Sparkman and Williams into a series of responses linking mass transportation with housing and renewal programs.

After the hearings were completed on housing legislation the Banking and Currency Committee began work in executive session to develop a clean bill to bring to the floor of the Senate. Williams moved to amend the urban planning and the community facilities titles of the omnibus bill to incorporate the program he had proposed in S. 345. In order to assure committee support he scaled down the loan authorization to $100 million and reduced the demonstration grants from $75 million to $50 million. Urban planning funds were made specifically available for mass transportation planning, and comprehensive planning requirements were established as conditions for assistance. Sparkman was somewhat cautious, not quite certain about the wisdom of incorporating the mass transportation program into the omnibus bill; but once the committee acted he strongly supported the amendment.

On May 19 the mass transportation program came to the Senate floor as a part of the clean bill on housing (S. 1922). While a number of committee members filed dissents from the majority report, none directly attacked the transportation program. Chairman Robertson opposed most, if not all, of the loan programs, including that for mass transportation.

The omnibus bill was debated in the Senate during the first two weeks of June. Democrat Frank J. Lausche of Ohio strongly opposed the mass transportation demonstration grants and moved to delete them. His motion was narrowly defeated, 46 to 44. Only eight Republicans opposed Lausche's amendment: three were members of the Banking and Currency Committee—Beall, Bush, and Javits; the others were Keating, Clifford P. Case of New Jersey, Hugh Scott of Pennsylvania, John Sherman Cooper of Kentucky, and Margaret Chase Smith of Maine. Democratic support for the mass transit demonstration grants came largely from northern states, with only a few southerners voting against Lausche. On June 12 the Senate passed the omnibus housing bill by a vote of 64 to 25.

The House Banking and Currency Committee had reported its version of the housing bill on June 1 (H.R. 6028). Respectful of the administration's uneasiness on the mass transportation question, the House bill made no mention of the subject. Williams and the mayors, however, intensified their pressure on the White House to endorse the Senate amendments.

On June 19 the White House gave a weak response. Instead of urging that the Senate amendments be accepted, President Kennedy sent a letter to Speaker of the House Sam Rayburn of Texas recommending an administration mass transportation bill. The administration bill made no provision for loans. It provided only $15 million in demonstration grants and allowed use of planning assistance grants for mass transportation planning. The program was to be administered by the HHFA and the administrator of that agency was required to submit a full mass transportation program to Congress in January of 1962. To Williams the bill appeared to be an obvious stall for time until the Commerce-HHFA study could be completed.

Democratic Congressman Abraham J. Multer of New York introduced the President's bill and scheduled hearings for late June before his Banking and Currency subcommittee. In the meantime the housing bill came to the floor of the House for action. Republican William T. Cahill of New Jersey offered a mass transportation amendment, but was defeated on a voice vote. The vote was clearly influenced by the prospect of separate hearings by the Multer subcommittee on the President's proposals. The housing bill passed the House of Representatives without any provision for federal assistance to mass transit.

The House and Senate omnibus housing bills now went to conference. Williams, along with other senators and several big city mayors, again urged the President to back the Senate amendments on mass transportation.

The administration was now substantially boxed in. In its own bill it had conceded the point of HHFA administration. The only remaining problem was to develop a compromise on financing with which the Bureau of the Budget felt it could live. Once this was accomplished the President was ready to agree to the supplications of the mayors. At the final meeting of the conference the administration's liaison men gave presidential support to the Senate amendments. Multer, who was also a House conferee, had scheduled two days of hearings on the administration bill. The administration was now in the embarrassing position of having to rescue Multer from his advocacy of a program about to be scrapped. On the first day of hearings Dr. Weaver presented the administration's terms for capitulation. Loans for mass transportation would be supported by the administration, but only to the level of $50 million instead of $100 million, as in the Senate bill. Demonstration grants would be set at $25 million, instead of $15 million as in the administration bill or $50 million as in the Senate bill. In other words, the administration agreed to half the Senate authorizations. And this is what the conference committee recommended. Multer's subcommittee took no further action, and both the House and Senate accepted their conferees' recommendations.

On June 20 President Kennedy signed Public Law 87–70, the Housing Act of 1961. The mass transportation program became a legal reality.

*The Battle over Funding.* The battle for a program was far from won, however. The Housing Act authorized loans and grants for mass transportation, but funds had to be provided in the supplemental appropriations bill (H.R. 9169) to carry on the program. The administration requested $60,000 in administrative funds. The Deficiencies Subcommittee of the House Appropriations Committee was chaired by Democrat Albert Thomas of Texas, long a foe of contract authority and Treasury borrowing that allowed programs to be financed without annual direct appropriations—so-called "backdoor" financing. When Weaver appeared for the administration to support the request for administrative funds, Thomas and other subcommittee members questioned him intensively on both the backdoor issue and the amount needed for administration. Where direct appropriations are made for a program the Appropriations subcommittees frequently examine the need for the full amount authorized, and may, of course, establish any figure below the authorization. Where contract authority or Treasury borrowing is authorized, the Appropriations Committee normally cannot reduce funds for the programs so financed, for it lacks power to alter the substance of legislation. During the years Democrat Clarence Cannon of Missouri headed the Appropriations Committee there was a running battle between Appropriations and the legislative committees for control of programs. Thomas, with Cannon's approval, resolved to bring the conflict to a head with the supplemental bill for 1962.

The Thomas subcommittee proceeded accordingly. In violation of the rules of the House of Representatives against legislating in appropriations bills, the subcommittee proposed to amend the Housing Act of 1961 to provide that the loans and grants for mass transportation (and other programs) should be subject entirely to the appropriations process. The Appropriations Committee accepted this proposal, and then approved a total appropriation of only $42,500,000, including up to $130,000 for administrative expenses. Thus, the demonstration grant program was cut from $25 million to $12,500,000 and a maximum of $30 million was allowed for loans. In its report the Appropriations Committee said: "The justifications were very vague and indefinite about the amount of money needed for loans and grants."

When Thomas brought his bill to the floor, Democrat Albert Rains of Alabama, chairman of the Housing Subcommittee of the House Banking and Currency Committee, raised a point of order against Thomas' amendments converting the financing of the program from contract authority to direct appropriations. In anticipation of the Rains motion Thomas had worded his bill in such a manner that when the point of order was sustained, as it had to be, the entire mass transportation program would be killed because he had made the administrative funds an integral part of the total appropriation. Without administrative funds a program legally cannot be conducted, regardless of the contract authority it may possess. Thus, the House of Representatives passed the supplemental appropriations bill on September 15 after completely eliminating any administrative funds for the mass transit program.

Senator Williams and other transit partisans attacked the House action and succeeded in persuading the Senate Appropriations Committee to restore the $60,000 requested by the administration. The Senate passed the supplemental bill on September 26 and sent it to conference with the House.

Congress at this point was on the brink of adjournment. Also, a simmering feud between the House and Senate Appropriations Committees was beginning to strain the abilities of the conferees to reach agreement on crucial items of difference in the supplemental bill. The House conferees were led by three ardent Democratic opponents of backdoor spending—Cannon, Thomas, and Michael J. Kirwan of Ohio. Their Republican colleagues, Ben F. Jensen of Iowa and John Taber of New York, were in full accord with the Appropriations Committee view on the backdoor spending issue. The House conferees refused to reach any agreement with the senators on the mass transportation program. They reported the item in disagreement and recommended that, instead of the Senate provision restoring administrative funds, the House enact language similar to that originally proposed by the House Appropriations Committee and stricken by Rains's point of order. Direct appropriations of $42,500,000 were provided. The hour was late and end-of-session fever was rampant. Hostility toward the Senate was high. A conference report may not be amended. So the House approved the report of their conferees by a voice vote and then, without requesting a further conference, adjourned for 1961. The Senate was left with no choice but to concur in the House action if the supplemental bill was to be enacted at all. The bill passed the Senate a few hours later and was signed by President Kennedy on September 30.

Thus Congress wrote the mass transportation program of 1961. On October 31 HHFA Administrator Weaver announced the creation of the Office of Transportation, and the next day appointed John J. Kohl, a professor from the University of Wisconsin, to the post of assistant administrator in charge of the mass transportation program.

Consideration of an Administration Bill, 1962

*The Administration's Proposals.* In December 1961 the Institute of Public Administration completed its study of the mass transportation problem for the HHFA and the Department of Commerce. Its report contained an extensive analysis of both the financial and the organizational aspects of the problem. Although this report was never published by the government, its findings and recommendations became widely known. It was later published by the institute in modified form.

The Institute of Public Administration estimated foreseeable investment needs in mass transportation facilities at $9.8 billion during the 1960's. The report recommended a ten-year direct federal grant program of $2.5 billion to match a similar local public contribution, thereby providing for half the need, which could not be financed without federal assistance. As a possible alternative to direct grants, the institute suggested grants to pay 50 percent of debt and service costs on mass transportation improvements for ten years. The cost of such a program was estimated at $135 million per year. If 70 percent grants were given, as incentives to development of effective regional planning and development agencies, the program would cost $185 million annually.

In addition to its financial recommendations the institute urged that grants be made conditional on establishment of continuing regional planning processes; that aid be given only to public agencies; and that before highway plans were approved by the secretary of commerce, they be reviewed by a regional planning agency representative of local governments. Perhaps the most controversial recommendation was that some moneys from the federal highway trust fund (which provides the 90 percent federal grants for the interstate highway system) be used for "transit and other urban transportation improvements which are designed to relieve transit pressures and promote more efficient operation of federal-aid highways."

Following receipt of the institute's report the administration formulated its position. On March 28 HHFA Administrator Weaver and Commerce Secretary Hodges made public their recommendations to the President. Essentially they advocated expansion of the 1961 program, but placed emphasis on direct grants instead of loans. They recommended a $500 million, three-year grants program, a continuation of the $50 million loan fund, and an increase of the $25 million demonstration grants program by $10 million per year for three years. Federal grants would pay two-thirds of net project costs. The HHFA-Commerce proposals urged comprehensive planning requirements but did not address themselves to the regional organization issues raised in the institute's report. Discussion of diversion of highway trust funds was also avoided. (One recommendation, however, dealing with establishment of a comprehensive planning process as a requirement for highway aid became a separate 1962 amendment, in a diluted form, to the Federal-Aid High-way Act.) The officials also recommended advance congressional approval for interstate compacts dealing with mass transportation.

On April 4 President Kennedy sent his transportation message to Congress. The section on urban transportation focused on the need for "comprehensive" and "balanced" transportation planning. He asked Congress to enact the $500 million program his secretary of commerce and HHFA administrator had recommended. The $50 million loan fund was to remain available for three years, to meet "emergency" problems where the comprehensive planning requirements could not be met. The demonstration grants program was to be increased by reserving up to $30 million from the new $500 million grants program. The President also asked for advance approval of interstate compacts.

Certain features of the bill, introduced by Senator Williams and eighteen other senators as S. 3126, were important reflections of prior experience with mass transportation legislation. The bill was designed to aid small as well as large cities. The HHFA administrator was given jurisdiction of the program, as had been the case in Williams' earliest bill. Relocation of families displaced by projects was required. Most importantly, the administration bill provided for financing the program through direct appropriations.

*Hearings.* Once again the Banking and Currency Committee of each House held hearings—the Senate in April and the House in May—and once again there was virtually a unanimous chorus of approval from witnesses. Only the Farm Bureau and the United States Chamber of Commerce presented hostile testimony.

Two new problems arose in the hearings, however. California's Senator Clair Engle introduced legislation to provide federal guarantees for revenue bonds of local transit agencies (S. 2390). Engle pressed his bill as an additional program to be included in the administration bill. It was particularly designed to meet problems in Los Angeles and San Francisco, which were proceeding to develop systems to be financed from fare-box revenues. Since they would have no deficit they would not be eligible for grants, but the sale of bonds would, of course, be expedited if the bonds were federally guaranteed, allowing acceleration of programs.

The other new element was the request by organized labor for protection of union rights that might be affected by the mass transportation

program. At the Senate hearings Andrew F. Biemiller, director of legislation for the American Federation of Labor-Congress of Industrial Organizations (AFL-CIO), endorsed both the administration and the Engle
bills, but urged stringent protections against the use of federal funds for
the acquisition of private transit companies by public bodies that might
subsequently refuse to honor preexisting union contracts and such union
rights as collective bargaining. At the House hearings Biemiller repeated
his request for amendments specifically protecting union rights: "We ask
that provisions be added to . . . protect public utility workers in the right
to union recognition, the right to collective bargaining, the right to ne-
gotiate with management, and the right of access to channels for griev-
ance and dispute settlement." Labor's concern was stimulated by the action of Dade County, Florida, which took over a private transit company
already unionized. The county then refused to recognize the union.

The Senate hearings ended in late April. The House finished hearings
on May 11. A compelling case had again been made for federal aid—
probably for more aid than the bills authorized—and massive support
had been demonstrated ranging from the AFL-CIO to the American
Bankers Association.

*Stalemate in the House.* The House committee approved the administration bill by a vote of 16 to 7 and reported it with amendments on
July 3. The committee deleted advance approval for interstate compacts.
Only four members, all Republicans, registered a written dissent from
the committee report. Their principal objections were to a new spending
program that was bound to increase and to subsidization of what was essentially a program for only a few metropolitan areas.

Significant Republican support developed in the committee, however.
Representative William B. Widnall of New Jersey had developed an increasing interest in mass transportation legislation since the 1961 action
in Congress. Widnall was the ranking Republican on the Multer subcommittee and the second-ranking Republican on the Housing Subcommittee. He had shown a long and constructive interest in urban legislation. The Pennsylvania Railroad's representatives urged him to play a
larger role in transit legislation. Widnall was not hard to convince. His
concern was further stimulated by the fact that as a New Jersey Republican he had more than an academic interest in Senator Williams' almost
exclusive identification with legislation to relieve commuter problems.
Widnall also was a leading member of the group of House Republicans

who sought to improve the image of their party through development of constructive legislation. He was now to become a key member in determining the fate of the bill. He sought to obtain sufficient Republican support to ensure its passage in the House.

In spite of its impressive support in the Banking and Currency Committee, the mass transit bill languished in the House Rules Committee. Although the President and the House leadership listed the bill (H.R. 11158) as one of the top ten "must" items in the administration program, the Rules Committee, chaired by Democrat Howard W. Smith of Virginia, refused to grant a rule. In spite of Smith's opposition, it was generally understood that the leadership could muster enough votes to bring the bill to the floor. This was not done because the speaker and the majority leader did not feel they had the votes to enact the bill. It would appear that the leadership was using the Rules Committee as an excuse to forestall a probable defeat.

On September 19 a group of urban Democrats, primarily members of the Democratic Study Group, tried to bring the mass transportation bill to the floor for debate under the Calendar Wednesday rule. They finally abandoned the effort after two and a half hours were consumed by two procedural roll calls, two quorum calls, and demands that the clerk read the previous day's journal. The opposition to the bill was led by Democrats Howard Smith, John Bell Williams of Mississippi, and Joe D. Waggonner, Jr., of Louisiana, and Republican H. R. Gross of Iowa. The House took no further action in 1962.

*Senate Referral to the Commerce Committee.* The Senate committee reported on August 7, after a 10 to 4 vote in favor of the bill. Senators Robertson, Bush, and Homer E. Capehart, Republican from Indiana, signed individual statements of opposition. The significant dissenter was Bush, who had supported the 1961 Housing Act amendments. Bush argued: "A desirable program of limited application has been perverted into a $500 million 'pork barrel' into which the Administrator of Housing and Home Finance Agency may dip his hands for largesse to be bestowed on favored communities in his sole discretion." Bush also objected to a key committee amendment that once again reflected the institutional interest of the Senate and of a legislative committee. As reported from committee the bill provided financing through contract authority instead of by direct appropriations as proposed by the administration.

On September 14 the bill came to the floor of the Senate. Senator

Lausche, who had opposed the mass transportation grant provisions of the 1961 Housing amendments, demanded that the bill be referred to the Commerce Committee before it was debated on the floor. Lausche argued that the bill involved issues that gave the Commerce Committee jurisdiction. He had enlisted the support of his chairman, Warren Magnuson, who in turn intervened with Democratic Majority Leader Mike Mansfield of Montana to urge the referral. Williams, as the floor manager of the bill, took a hasty count of his strength. The result of the count made him fear he would lose any attempt to defeat Lausche on the issue of jurisdiction over the bill. If he lost on such a vote, and the bill was re-referred, the Commerce Committee would then have had jurisdiction instead of Banking and Currency. To avoid such an outcome Williams permitted a unanimous consent agreement to be worked out that gave the Commerce Committee a "look" at the bill. The agreement referred the bill with instructions that it be reported back to the Senate by September 24.

Lausche, as the ranking Democrat on the Surface Transportation Subcommittee, held three days of hearings. The tenor of testimony was hostile, either to the bill in its totality or to specific parts of it. Because of the short deadline for reporting back to the Senate, the Commerce Committee returned the bill without recommendations. No further effort was made to bring it to the floor, however, because of the inability to obtain a vote in the House even if it passed the Senate. Instead, on October 4 and 5 Congress enacted a joint resolution (S.J. Res. 235) that extended the life of the program enacted in 1961 from December 31, 1962 to June 30, 1963. Then Congress went home to campaign.

The Lausche hearings raised two basic issues in fairly sharp perspective: the possible impact of the legislation on private transit industries; and the problem of guaranteeing bonds, raised first by Senator Engle. Other questions were also injected, including the feasibility of other forms of assistance to transit companies such as tax relief or even making private companies eligible for direct assistance.


## Engineering the Urban Mass Transportation Bill, 1963–64

Before the Eighty-eighth Congress convened in January 1963 Senator Williams, in consultation with the supporters of mass transportation legislation, decided to introduce a bill immediately rather than wait until after the administration made proposals to Congress. Williams wanted to obtain early action and gain some prestige for the bill by having a low number on it. On January 9 Williams and Congressman Multer introduced companion bills in the Senate (S. 6) and House (H.R. 649). This time Williams had twenty cosponsors. The bill was the same as the one that had been reported by the Senate Banking and Currency Committee in 1962.

On February 18 President Kennedy submitted the administration's new bill to Congress. It was introduced in the Senate by Williams (S. 917) and in the House by Albert Rains (H.R. 3881). The administration bill differed from S. 6 in only a few particulars. Financing was to be provided by direct appropriations and the administration bill omitted the provision of S. 6 that limited an expenditure in any state to 12.5 percent of the grants funds—the provision intended as a "sweetener" for those who feared the bill would be a bonanza for a few large cities.

The committees in both houses held hearings at the end of February and through the first two weeks of March. While almost all witnesses were emphatically favorable, a major issue did arise: the question of the preservation of union and labor rights.

*The Labor Issue.* In the fall of 1962, after Congress had adjourned without acting on mass transit legislation, Bernard Cushman, general counsel of the Amalgamated Association of Street, Electric Railway and Motor Coach Employees of America, returned to his duties after recuperating from a heart attack. On his desk he found a copy of the 1962 Senate-passed bill, which he examined in routine fashion. In light of the recent incident in Miami to which Biemiller had alluded in his 1962 testimony, Cushman became deeply concerned that federal funds might be used to assist communities in purchasing companies with which the Amalgamated, the largest transit union, or the railway brotherhoods had contracts and collective bargaining agreements. Without explicit restrictions in the bill, Cushman feared that the public agencies might not honor these prior agreements. He was also concerned that the new technology in transit not become a means of laying off workers without retraining and reemployment opportunities.

In late 1962 Cushman prepared a memorandum on municipal takeovers of transit operations and discussed the matter with union officials, members of the administration, and Senator Williams. Cushman found that the administration was not inclined to "rock the boat" on the legislation. Senator Williams, who had counted on organized labor's support for the bill, promised to look into the problem.

When Williams let it be known he would introduce S. 6 in January, Biemiller strongly opposed its introduction before working out language to meet the newly defined interest of the unions. Williams had already made plans for his floor speech and decided to go ahead as planned. Cushman also "raised Cain" with Williams and saw to it that Amalgamated locals in New Jersey also contacted him. Williams and Ames took the position that an extensive union rights amendment such as Cushman advocated might impair the bill's chances in committee or on the Senate floor. Cushman replied, "I don't think it'll pass without it."

As a result of the union's concern Williams inserted into his speech introducing the bill a paragraph on the labor issue:

> I introduce this legislation in full recognition that in its present form it may not take due cognizance of matters brought to my attention only last week. . . . I am particularly concerned that every effort be made in this legislation to provide safeguards for collective bargaining and arbitration, to protect employees displaced by adverse effects of new transit facilities, to protect rights of employees displaced through automation, and to review the impact of advance consent to transit compacts.

Prior to the hearings Williams and Cushman held extensive discussions on possible labor amendments. In early February, before the hearings, Cushman went to Miami to meet with Labor Secretary W. Willard Wirtz who was there to confer with the AFL-CIO executive committee. Cushman, Biemiller, and George Harrison, representing the railroad brotherhoods, spent an evening with Wirtz and the following morning with his staff. They presented the secretary with draft language for an amendment. Wirtz felt the unions' language, which dealt with specific protections, would have to be generalized, but promised to recommend an amendment that would retain the substance of the draft.

The next development came on March 7 when Wirtz called a meeting to tell the union representatives that the White House had rejected the Miami draft. He then made some suggestions for a labor amendment that Cushman felt gutted the purposes of a labor protection amendment. Wirtz argued that while his proposals were general, a legislative history could be built to indicate its intent, and that further protection should be given by requiring that the secretary of labor participate in approval of grants. The union leaders felt these ideas were inadequate, and therefore unacceptable.

Wirtz did not reveal his specific language until the next day when he testified first before the Senate committee and then the House committee. There he presented an amendment that made grants conditional on establishment of "fair and equitable" arrangements to protect the interests of employees. The amendment protected contract privileges and benefits, collective bargaining recognition, individual employees against a worsening of their positions, priority of employment or reemployment for employees temporarily laid off, and paid training or retraining programs.

Biemiller and Cushman were still not satisfied. They decided to place labor in opposition to the bill unless their requirements were met. The unions wanted specific language to require: the employment of employees of any system acquired through a federal grant; preservation of all employees' rights, privileges, and benefits, and assumption of any existing collective bargaining agreements; guarantees to protect the right of collective bargaining and authority for enforceable arbitration agreements; protection against worsening of positions; paid retraining programs; and priority of employment. The attitude of the union spokesmen was reflected in Cushman's statement that "If you do not write in safeguards in this legislation along these lines, what you will be doing, in effect, is subsidizing union busting." In addition, the unions opposed the advance approval for interstate compacts, which might abrogate union rights.

Cushman and Biemiller, along with representatives of transit and railroad locals, talked to Banking and Currency Committee members. The committee adopted, at Williams' suggestion, a labor amendment close to the lines suggested by Secretary Wirtz. This amendment "encouraged" collective bargaining, whereas the unions wanted to require it. Williams, Ames, and other committee sponsors felt the bill would be endangered if the union amendments were added. The administration would not budge from the position expressed by Secretary Wirtz.

Williams gambled that the unions would not oppose the bill if some language could be obtained that addressed itself to their problem. Cushman, however, after talking with Biemiller and other union representatives, decided to try to obtain his objectives through an amendment offered on the Senate floor. His preliminary vote count suggested that the entire bill could be defeated if such an amendment were not added.

With the help of the AFL-CIO, the railway brotherhoods, and the international officers of the Amalgamated, Cushman now set in motion an extensive effort to contact senators through the local unions and labor councils. Another sounding indicated enough votes could be mustered to pass the amendment. Cushman also sought the help of Senator Wayne Morse, a labor law expert, and Michigan's Democratic Senator Pat McNamara, a former union officer, in perfecting language for the amendment, which Morse and McNamara agreed to sponsor. Between March 14, when the Banking and Currency Committee approved the bill, and April 1, when it finally came up for Senate debate, the Cushman campaign had been effective. The Senate Democratic leaders were convinced that a labor amendment was required if the bill were to pass. The day prior to Senate debate Williams contacted Cushman to confirm the prognosis on labor amendments. Staff members were assigned to work out a mutually acceptable amendment for Williams to cosponsor. Ames was not involved in the discussions since he had represented Williams in the early stages of the negotiations, and had advised against the amendment. Cushman and the Senate staff members worked until about 3:00 a.m. the eve of the debate, finally developing the amendment sponsored by Morse, McNamara, and Williams.

The amendment, which still had some ambiguities, met the problem in two parts. The labor standards section of the bill was made more specific. "Continuation" was substituted for "encouragement of the continuation" of collective bargaining rights. Equally significant was the insertion of a clause into Section 3 of the bill, which ostensibly protected private enterprise, prohibiting use of federal funds to purchase facilities or develop projects unless the HHFA administrator and the secretary of labor jointly found that the assisted project complied with the labor standards section of the act. Thus, the recipients of federal funds were precluded from acquiring private companies and then abrogating union agreements, and it was made mandatory that collective bargaining be protected where it existed.

*Senate Action.* The Banking and Currency Committee had reported S. 6 on March 14 by a 9 to 6 vote. The opposition had come from four western Republicans—Wallace F. Bennett of Utah, John G. Tower of Texas, Milward L. Simpson of Wyoming, and Peter H. Dominick of Colorado. Chairman Robertson registered his usual objections, and Democratic Senator William Proxmire of Wisconsin opposed the bill on the grounds that the program would grow too large and the problem could be handled locally. Democrat Edmund S. Muskie of Maine voted to report the bill, but stated that it was not justified in the face of other national priorities.

On the pattern established in 1962, the bill was then referred to the

Commerce Committee under a unanimous consent agreement. Senator Lausche, who had conducted the 1962 hearings by the Surface Transportation Subcommittee, had abandoned his earlier tactic of outright opposition in favor of introducing his own bill (S. 807). Lausche's bill proposed to stimulate investment in transit operations through federal guarantees of local revenue bonds. Only new systems and extensions of old systems would be eligible. Fares must be set at levels that would cover costs of operation and financing. The Lausche bill also provided for federal income tax exemption for profits resulting from state and local tax reductions. Finally, the bill established a Division of Urban Transportation in the Department of Commerce to administer the program.

The Lausche bill was considered along with S. 6 by the Subcommittee on Surface Transportation. The hearings were held on four days in mid-March and presided over by Senator Strom Thurmond, originally the only opponent of mass transportation legislation. Administration witnesses opposed S. 807. The Treasury Department opposed allowing tax exemption of profits from state or local tax reductions and also opposed supporting tax-exempt local and state revenue bonds. Lausche's bill had been warmly endorsed by the U.S. Chamber of Commerce in its earlier testimony before the Banking and Currency Committee.

The Commerce Committee did not approve the Lausche bill. Despite the opposition of Lausche, Thurmond, and Republicans Norris Cotton of New Hampshire, Thruston B. Morton of Kentucky, and Winston C. Prouty of Vermont, it did approve S. 6, but with some substantial amendments. The Banking and Currency Committee had again approved financing through contract authority. The Commerce Committee recommended direct appropriations. It recommended a reduction in the grants program from $500 million to $375 million. The most important substantive amendment recast the entire bill by adding a section establishing a guaranteed bond program for local public bodies. Under this new program a determination would have to be made of whether guaranteed revenue bonds would meet the needs of the applicant. Only if bond guarantees would not meet the needs could grants or loans be given. The Commerce Committee's amendments were accepted by Williams in another unanimous consent agreement. It was clear he did not think he could produce the votes to defeat them.

Debate ensued for three days in the Senate. On the first day, April 2, Republicans Tower and Barry Goldwater of Arizona offered amendments to the worker protection section of the bill. Goldwater was defeated 63 to 27 on his amendment to delete the clause, and Tower lost 52 to 36 in his attempt to require worker protection rules to follow state laws. None of the twenty-seven senators who voted for Goldwater's amendment supported the bill on final passage.

On the following day Lausche attacked the bill on two fronts. First he raised the issue of jurisdiction and offered the amendment that had been rejected by the Commerce Committee to create a Division of Urban Transportation in the Department of Commerce to administer the mass transportation program. His amendment lost 62 to 33. The main effect of the vote was to demonstrate that, so far as the Senate was concerned, the HHFA had won the jurisdictional battle.

Then more crucial amendments were offered by opponents of the bill. Lausche attempted to delete the entire grants program, making the bill essentially a bond guarantee program. The amendment lost 57 to 41. Shortly after, Tower offered an amendment to reduce the federal contributions from 50 percent to one-third for emergency programs and from two-thirds to 50 percent for projects meeting the comprehensive planning requirements of the bill. Tower's amendment came within three votes of being adopted—it was defeated 47 to 44. Of the senators who had supported the Lausche amendment, all but one, Senator Muskie, voted for Tower's proposal. Tower also picked up four senators who favored the bill and had voted against Lausche. Thus, Tower's amendment, posing the simple "more or less aid" question, cut deeply into the strength of the supporters of the bill.

The final test for the bill came on the amendment by Morse, McNamara, and Williams to add the section on worker protection demanded by the unions. Tower had earlier provided a test of strength on the collective bargaining issue by offering an amendment to require application of state rules on collective bargaining to local agencies obtaining federal aid under the bill. His amendment had been defeated by 56 to 41. Morse's amendment carried by a vote of 52 to 41.

On the vote on final passage the supporters of the bill won 52 to 41. Of the absentees, Democrat George A. Smathers of Florida had not voted on any of the preliminary amendments and had not announced a position; three others were for the bill and three were against it. Six southern Democrats, plus Republican Kuchel and Democrat Frank Church of Idaho who had voted with Tower to cut the percentage of federal aid, supported the bill. Five Democrats who opposed the aid cut voted against the bill.

*Analysis of the Senate Vote.* Eight major votes, including final passage, indicate the pattern and depth of support for the bill. Support for the bill was remarkably solid throughout the voting. Thirty-six senators (thirty-three Democrats and three Republicans) who supported final passage voted against every amendment. Four more defected only on the attempt by Lausche to place the program in the Commerce Department. Two of these were members of the Commerce Committee. Of the remaining twelve senators who made up the majority, most, if not all, were certain to vote for final passage. Nine of them, however, apparently had reservations about the magnitude of the program and supported Tower's amendment to limit the federal grants percentage. Six of the eight southerners in this group voted for Tower's states' rights-collective bargaining amendment and against the Morse amendment. Two others voted for the Tower labor amendment and one other voted against Morse. Only three of the twelve voted for either the Lausche or Dominick jurisdictional amendments.

The hard core of opposition came from the Republican party. Only six Republicans—five easterners and Kuchel—voted for passage of the bill. Fourteen Republicans and two Democrats voted for every crippling amendment and against final passage. Another seventeen senators could be considered hard core opponents even though they voted with the bill's sponsors to defeat one, two, or three amendments. Four of these senators, from Virginia and Mississippi, voted against Lausche's attempt to place the program in the Department of Commerce. Two other southern Democrats voted against the Dominick amendment to reduce HHFA power in administering the program. Three Republicans opposed Tower's amendment to impose state rules regarding collective bargaining agreements. Massachusetts Republican Leverett Saltonstall and Vermont Republican Prouty were the only two of the opposition core to vote for the Morse amendment providing for worker and union protection. Beyond the solid opposition, Democrats Proxmire and Muskie were publicly committed ultimately to oppose the bill.

The opponents exceeded forty-one votes—their final strength—only on Tower's amendment to reduce the federal contribution to total cost in the grants program. Their basic core of thirty-five solidly supported Tower. Proxmire voted with the opponents, but Muskie did not. Eight senators who ultimately voted for the bill defected on this issue, however. Had not Muskie and four other Democrats—Birch Bayh of Indiana, J. Howard Edmondson of Oklahoma, Gale W. McGee of Wyoming, and Thomas J. McIntyre of New Hampshire—who later voted against final passage joined the Williams forces to beat the Tower amendment, it would have carried.

Basically the opposition relied on three substantive issues: the question of jurisdiction over the program, on which they were badly defeated; the labor issue, which Tower succeeded in mixing with the states' rights issue to win a few southerners who later voted for the bill; and the issue of the extent of federal participation in meeting the mass transit problem. The latter issue was the most telling against the bill. The narrow vote by which the bill's supporters defeated the Tower amendment cutting the percentage of the grants suggests the wisdom of Williams' acceptance of the reduction of the authorization from $500 million to $375 million.

On final passage twenty-seven of the opposition votes came from the twenty-five least urban states. Only seven opposition votes were produced in the thirteen most urban states. It is difficult to argue, however, that the vote in the Senate was based on a cleavage between urban and rural constituencies. Table 1 shows the votes for and against final passage of S. 6 compared with the extent of urbanization in the states whose senators voted. Senators from the most urban states overwhelmingly voted for the bill (14 to 7), but the senators from the least urban states split more closely—eleven voting for the bill and fifteen against it.

Another index of urbanism is the existence of major metropolitan centers. Only four senators from states containing a metropolitan area with a million or more people voted against S. 6 on final passage. The fifteen states containing these largest metropolitan areas provided twenty-five votes for the bill. Enthusiasm for the bill was less, however, in the thir-

Table 1: *Relation of Votes on Final Passage of S. 6 to Urbanization of Constituencies*

| Urban percentage of state population[a] | Number of aye votes | | | Number of nay votes | | |
|---|---|---|---|---|---|---|
| | Dem. | Rep. | Total | Dem. | Rep. | Total |
| 89–74 (13 states) | 10 | 4 | 14 | 1 | 6 | 7 |
| 73–63 (12 states) | 15 | 2 | 17 | 4 | 3 | 7 |
| 62–52 (12 states) | 10 | 0 | 10 | 5 | 7 | 12 |
| 51–35 (13 states) | 11 | 0 | 11 | 7 | 8 | 15 |
| Total | 46 | 6 | 52 | 17 | 24 | 41 |

[a] U.S. Bureau of the Census, *United States Census of Population, 1960,* United States Summary—Number of Inhabitants, p. XVII.

teen states containing maximum metropolitan areas of 500,000 to a million people. These states provided twelve votes for S. 6 and twelve votes against it. It would appear that in spite of numerous attempts to make the bill more palatable to nonmetropolitan senators, it remained basically a big-city measure, with the additional votes accruing largely on party, factional, and regional lines.

*House Inaction.* The administration bill (H.R. 3881) that had been introduced by Housing Subcommittee Chairman Rains was reported from committee on April 9, 1963, five days after passage of the Senate measure. Except that it provided for direct appropriations instead of contract authority and eliminated advance approval of interstate compacts, H.R. 3881 differed little from the House companion bill to S. 6. The administration's version of the labor amendments was retained. The Rains subcommittee approved the bill by a vote of 8 to 2 and the full Banking and Currency Committee by 16 to 7. All seven opponents were Republicans. Five Republicans, all from eastern urban districts, joined William Widnall, the key Republican proponent, in support of the bill.

The House bill now went to the Rules Committee. While it appeared to supporters of the legislation that a rule could be obtained for floor consideration, the Democratic leadership was once again wary of bringing the bill out of the committee for fear of failing to muster a majority on the floor. Also, civil rights and income tax revision were currently occupying much congressional time and administration attention.

Although Democratic leaders had hoped to make mass transit legislation a distinct Democratic victory, it appeared that the bill could not be passed without Republican votes. Representative Widnall therefore became an increasingly important figure in its passage. Speaker of the House John W. McCormack of Massachusetts told him that thirty Republican votes would be required, and the New Jersey Republican set out to round them up. Since the leadership was occupied with other legislation, however, no hard count was made for the remainder of 1963. The Rules Committee did not act, nor was it asked to act by the speaker or the leadership. Thus, the measure made no further progress in the House in 1963.

*Mobilizing Republican Support.* The interest groups that had initiated the earlier legislative proposals and had provided the substantiating testimony for the mass transportation bills now began a concerted effort to procure a favorable vote in the House. The American Municipal

Association, the United States Conference of Mayors, and railroad and transit companies jointly financed the creation of the Urban Passenger Transportation Association. Lawrence Henderson was retained as lobbyist for the group. Henderson was an old hand with urban legislation, having served on the staff of Senator Sparkman. He was also an exceptionally skilled and highly respected lobbyist with excellent contacts in the House of Representatives. Henderson assumed his position in February 1964. By the first of April he was confident that he had the votes to pass the bill.

The key to passage was the extent of Republican support. To assist Widnall, Henderson mobilized the industrial members of the Urban Passenger Transportation Association such as the American Transit Association and the railroads. Representatives of carriers and supplier industries contacted House members and obtained information on their positions. All information was coordinated by Henderson. City officials checked their congressional delegations and confirmed their support of the bill. Where congressmen might waver, industrial groups such as the Rapid Transit Institute or the American Transit Association circulated memoranda on the number of jobs that the legislation could be expected to stimulate in specific congressional districts.

Once Henderson and Widnall were sure they had enough votes, their problem was to get the bill onto the floor. The poll they had taken showed that there were enough votes in the Rules Committee to report a rule for the bill. The roadblock was the leadership, which, in spite of protestations of support for mass transportation, did not seem inclined to act on the measure. This reluctance was explainable in part by the tough floor fights on other administration bills. Also, in late 1963 a mass transit bill for the District of Columbia was recommitted by an overwhelming vote. As a result the speaker was quite dubious of the survival capacity of the national bill.

Henderson telephoned Mayor John Shelley of San Francisco, a former member of the House and a close friend of Democrat Hale Boggs of Louisiana, the majority whip. Henderson urged Shelley to call Boggs and ask that the leadership bring the bill out of the Rules Committee. Shelley called, as suggested. Boggs, however, told the mayor that he simply did not have enough Republican votes to assure passage. Shelley, who was irked by this response, called Henderson to complain of his embarrassment at having to back down when Boggs maintained he could not risk defeat of the measure by bringing it to the floor.

Henderson, highly displeased by Boggs's position, suggested that Shelley talk to Widnall and check the vote. After Shelley and Widnall discussed the vote count, Henderson and Widnall determined to bring the matter to a head. Widnall felt the leadership and the administration were not in earnest about the bill, and feared the Republicans would be blamed for its failure. He went to see Speaker McCormack and asked how many Republican votes were needed. McCormack still estimated a need for at least thirty. He seemed skeptical of Widnall's claim of thirty-five or thirty-six votes.

In the meantime, Henderson tried to talk with Boggs, but the majority whip was unwilling or unable to find time to go over the vote lists with him. Widnall then made preparations to call a news conference where he planned to blast the Democratic leadership for refusing to call up the bill, and to name the Republican members who were ready to vote for it. When he found he could not talk to Boggs, Henderson informed Albert Rains of what had occurred and what Widnall planned. Rains, in turn, saw Speaker McCormack at a party and relayed the information. The speaker was alarmed and promised to see Widnall as soon as he returned from a short trip to Boston. Widnall agreed to hold his fire until the conference with the speaker. When the two met, Widnall presented his ultimatum: bring the bill to the floor or he would talk to the press. The speaker agreed to request a rule immediately. The bill was reported from the Rules Committee by an 8 to 4 vote on May 20.

*The House Vote.* The House debate took place on June 24 and 25. Although Widnall had pleaded with the Republican leadership not to make the bill a party-line vote, his plea was rejected. This meant that the pressure was on him to hold his Republicans in line. While both Widnall and Henderson were concerned by the Republican leadership's position, it proved to have little impact, draining off only a few votes. In part this resulted from Minority Leader Charles A. Halleck's fairly accommodating posture toward Widnall's Republican allies.

Rains, as manager of the bill, offered only one amendment, substantially identical to the worker protection language contained in the Morse-McNamara-Williams amendment in the Senate. The amendment was adopted by a vote of 234 to 170. Twenty-eight Republicans supported the labor amendment.

The crucial vote was on the minority's motion to recommit the bill, made by Representative Frances P. Bolton of Ohio. Recommittal was defeated 215 to 190, with thirty-three Republicans voting against their leadership's motion. The motion was worded so as to appear positive in intent. Thus it had the potential of attracting votes from members of both parties who favored some action but did not feel that large-scale spending was as yet justified. The recommittal motion provided:

> That the Committees on Banking and Currency of the House and Senate shall conduct an intensive continuing review of—(1) the results derived from the mass transportation demonstration and research projects authorized . . . [by] the Housing Act of 1961, and (2) the status of the planning processes . . . in order to insure that such processes and projects have been sufficiently carried forward to provide the engineering data and other information necessary for an effective mass transportation program before further action on such a program is undertaken by Congress.

The bill then was enacted as a substitute for S. 6, the Senate bill, by a vote of 212 to 189. Widnall suffered a net loss of only one of the thirty-nine Republicans he had counted in support of the bill. All thirty-three Republicans who voted against recommittal voted for the bill's passage.

An analysis of the crucial recommittal vote reveals the sources of its support and opposition. Table 2 shows that of the 214 pro-transit (against recommittal) votes, cities provided 75, suburbs 32, and mixed districts—primarily containing urban and suburban areas—provided 39 votes. The revealing element, however, is that 68 representatives of rural districts—almost as many as from cities—voted to save the bill. If the urban, suburban, and mixed district anti-transit votes are combined, metropolitan area congressmen cast 76 votes against mass transit on the recommittal vote. This metropolitan defection was almost entirely offset by rural votes.

A shift of 13 votes would have killed the bill on the recommittal mo-

Table 2: *House Votes on the Motion To Recommit the Mass Transit Bill in Relation to Type of Constituency*[a]

| Constituency | Number of pro-transit votes (against recommittal) | | | Number of anti-transit votes (for recommittal) | | |
|---|---|---|---|---|---|---|
| | Dem. | Rep. | Total | Dem. | Rep. | Total |
| Urban | 70 | 5 | 75 | 9 | 14 | 23 |
| Suburban | 17 | 15 | 32 | 1 | 15 | 16 |
| Mixed (urban-suburban) | 31 | 8 | 39 | 5 | 32 | 37 |
| Rural | 63 | 5 | 68 | 40 | 74 | 114 |
| Total | 181 | 33 | 214 | 55 | 135 | 190 |

[a] Classifications derived from data and maps in the Census Bureau's 1963 *Congressional District Data Book* (Districts of the 88th Congress).

Table 3: *State and Constituency*[a] *Distribution of House Republican Votes Against the Motion To Recommit the Mass Transit Bill*

| State | Urban | Suburban | Rural | Urban-suburban | Suburban-rural | Urban-suburban-rural | Total |
|---|---|---|---|---|---|---|---|
| California | 1 | 0 | 0 | 0 | 0 | 0 | 1 |
| Connecticut | 0 | 0 | 0 | 1 | 0 | 0 | 1 |
| Massachusetts | 0 | 1 | 0 | 0 | 3 | 0 | 4 |
| Nebraska | 1 | 0 | 0 | 0 | 0 | 0 | 1 |
| New Jersey | 0 | 6 | 1 | 0 | 0 | 0 | 7 |
| New York | 3 | 4 | 0 | 1 | 0 | 0 | 8 |
| Pennsylvania | 0 | 4 | 3 | 0 | 1 | 1 | 9 |
| Washington | 0 | 0 | 0 | 0 | 1 | 0 | 1 |
| Wisconsin | 0 | 0 | 1 | 0 | 0 | 0 | 1 |
| Total | 5 | 15 | 5 | 2 | 5 | 1 | 33 |

[a] Classifications derived from data and maps in the Census Bureau's 1963 *Congressional District Data Book* (Districts of the 88th Congress).

tion, which surely would have been successful had Widnall's Republicans not voted against their party. A detailed analysis of the Republican vote in Table 3 indicates that as many as 11 of the crucial votes came from 5 rural districts (3 of them in Pennsylvania, 1 in New Jersey, and 1 in Wisconsin) and from 6 mixed districts containing substantial rural populations (3 in Massachusetts, 2 in Pennsylvania, and 1 in Washington). Only 5 of the 33 Republican votes came from cities, but 14 urban Republicans voted anti-transit. The strongest Republican support came from the suburbs. Of the 30 suburban Republicans in the House, half voted their "commuter interests."

*Enactment.* On June 30 the Senate accepted the House version of the mass transit bill rather than send the two bills to conference. An amendment by Senator Javits to substitute the language of the Buy America Act for the requirement that U.S. materials be used for work done under contracts pursuant to federal grants or loans was easily defeated, 65 to 14.

As passed, the bill provided for a three-year, $375 million grants program, financed by direct appropriations. Seventy-five million dollars were authorized for expenditure the first year, and $150 million for each of the next two years. Grants could be given for two-thirds of net project costs where all planning requirements had been met. Fifty percent grants were authorized for urgent situations. Fifty million dollars of the total program fund could be used for research, development, and demonstration projects. Provision was made for relocation of families displaced by projects, and the private industry and labor rights protections were included. President Johnson signed the bill into law on July 9.

## The Case in Perspective

The urban mass transportation legislation would seem at first glance to be almost "pure" urban legislation. Its objective was to improve the character of cities. It certainly had the support of the organized mayors. In spite of the adoption of the formula limiting expenditures in any one state to 12.5 percent of the grants funds, and the open-ended definition of urban area as almost any place the HHFA administrator decided to give a grant, it was correctly perceived as a bill designed primarily to aid large metropolitan areas. Nonetheless, it was both more and less than a purely urban bill. Its clients were not just cities, but specific railroads and transit companies. The demonstration and research program was most attractive to the suppliers and manufacturers of transit equipment. Of the railroads, the western lines were, for the most part, indifferent to it, but a number of eastern lines—especially the Pennsylvania—showed much concern. The coalition that assured passage of the 1964 act was built on a combination of metropolitan interests and industry interests. If one looks at the critical votes required to pass a bill as the index of the effectiveness of a legislative bloc, it would seem fair to accept the judgment of one Senate staff member who concluded that rather than a triumph for urban forces, the bill's passage can be attributed to the legislative lobbying skill of Henderson and the pressure of the transit industry.

The urban mass transportation bills also suggest that urban pressure groups are selective in what they support, or at least in what they support intensely. Generally, organized labor is conceived of as an urban interest group. On transit legislation the unions initially gave their endorsement. When their own institutional interests appeared to be endangered, however, they were willing to jeopardize the entire measure for the sake of safeguarding collective bargaining and worker rights. With the unions it was clear that whatever new employment and urban convenience might result from the bill, the number one issue was the protection of the existing members of the union. While this kind of behavior is only natural for membership organizations, it does suggest that the forging of a legis-

lative coalition on urban legislation may not proceed on the assumption
that unions or other groups with clientele interests will automatically fall
into line and lend solid support to the effort. There is little to indicate
that labor worked assiduously for the bill once its interests were as-
suaged. Labor's representatives did, however, "pull out the stops" to secure adoption of the amendments they felt were required to protect
union members.

One of the most intriguing aspects of this case is the extent to which
the legislation was both initiated and shaped by members of Congress
and by the institutional politics of the Congress. The role of the administration in the entire process was marginal. The Eisenhower administration was openly hostile to the idea of federal assistance. The Kennedy
administration was undecided and equivocal about the program throughout 1961. Vacillation by the White House contributed materially to the
evisceration of the funding of the bill, first in the conference committee,
and later by the Thomas Appropriations subcommittee. When the administration finally produced a program, its major contribution was to
change the emphasis from loans to grants, a decision that, whatever its
merits, conceivably cost the program votes in the Senate. At no time did
the administration exercise forceful leadership.

Williams and the mayors, aided by Sparkman, engineered the early
Senate actions and finally moved President Kennedy to save the program
in the conference committee. Widnall, Henderson, and the industry were
the catalysts in the House, where the leadership was lethargic in its efforts to find the votes needed for passage. There was little administration
pressure for a vote until Widnall "blew the whistle" on the leadership.
Clearly, it cannot be said that the administration championed the cause
of urban areas and was frustrated by an uninterested or anti-urban Congress.

Williams, in particular, was reponsible for the initial concepts of the
legislation. It deviated little from the pattern he set. His decisions were
based largely on a political, as distinct from a technical, assessment of
the problem. He proposed a modest program and it remained modest, as
an inducement to passage. The cost of this stratagem and of the paucity
of hard data was the reduction of the final grants program to $375 mil-
lion from the proposed half billion.

The senator's political interests were also a prime determinant in giving jurisdiction to the HHFA instead of the Commerce Department.
While a good case was made for this decision, it illustrates the extent to

which congressionally initiated programs may produce administrative consequences, not on the basis of the program's requirements, but rather on the basis of the political requirements of their sponsors.

It is doubtful that the legislation could have survived the Commerce Committee, where it had no ardent supporters, at least two bitter foes in the subcommittee with jurisdiction—the chairman, Thurmond, and the ranking Democrat, Lausche—and where the chairman of the full committee, Magnuson, was not interested enough to introduce the legislation when asked to do so by the American Municipal Association. The fate of urban legislation, like that of most legislation, depends heavily on the choice of the arena into which it is cast.

One of the major influences on the final shape of the legislation was the institutional politics of the Congress itself—the conflict between the substantive and the Appropriations Committees over contract authority and direct appropriations. Although Williams doggedly insisted on the former, he was deserted by the administration and completely outmaneuvered by Representative Thomas. Senator Lausche's flanking effort in behalf of the Commerce Committee also resulted in considerable substantive alteration of S. 6 through the insertion of the bond guarantee title as the new heart of the bill. Both incidents of internecine conflict in the Congress suggest that one of the effective weapons against urban programs may be the substitution of procedural questions for substantive ones.

Finally, the history of urban mass transportation legislation emphasizes the difficulty that both Congress and the executive branch have in coming to grips with complex urban problems. Technical data are not available. Conventional federal financial or appropriations practices are not easily adaptable to meet the need, even if it can be precisely defined. For new problems involving such variables as impact on land use, employment, and the development of new technology, neither branch of government is adequately staffed to define the problem, much less solve it. And the Congress is not organized to review legislation in an "urban" perspective.

In spite of all this, Congress produced a mass transit program of sorts before the administration decided what it wanted. And Congress set the program's pattern, albeit a familiar one. It may not have innovated. It did act.

FREDERIC N. CLEAVELAND

# Legislating for Urban Areas: An Overview

THE INDIVIDUAL LEGISLATIVE problem cases have portrayed Congress and congressmen at work in analyzing complex public issues, balancing networks of pressures and influences, and hammering out policy and program ideas designed to cope with acute problems of urban living. It now remains in this closing section to try to fashion some kind of "big picture" out of the case studies. This overview seeks to examine the cases collectively, searching for insights and perhaps tentative generalizations bearing upon three areas of central concern in the project: the politics of congressional policy making for urban areas; urban affairs as a field of national policy; and the nature of urban interests and their representation. The organization of the overview is based on the analytical themes sketched out in the Introduction. The pages that follow contain in part findings and interpretations, in part conclusion and recommendation, and in part hunches about the future and about some of the sensitive indicators that may be worth further study and analysis.

## The Politics of Congressional Policy Making for Urban Areas

This inquiry focuses on three major aspects of the subject: First, legislative initiatives in dealing with urban problems—what do the cases suggest about the sources of policy ideas and of tactical and parliamentary skills in guiding bills through Congress? Second, the problem of issue context—how do congressmen and senators view urban problems legislation? And third, congressional voting on urban affairs bills—what patterns and influences do the legislative problem studies reveal in congressional voting behavior?

*Legislative Initiatives.* Much can be learned about the way Congress legislates in particular fields of public policy by examining the sources of policy ideas and of tactical judgments. Such legislative initiatives are difficult to pinpoint since they typically involve a complex mix of contributions from senators and representatives, congressional staff members, and specialists in the executive branch and the interest groups. These case studies illustrate the normal patterns and the variety in the mix.

When strong legislative initiatives came from Congress itself—either on substance or on strategy—the key generators tended to be members acknowledged by their colleagues as legislative experts in the field; often they were subcommittee chairmen with staff resources at their disposal. Democrat John A. Blatnik of Minnesota illustrates this standard pattern. Becoming chairman of the Subcommittee on Rivers and Harbors of the House Committee on Public Works in 1955, within six years he built a reputation as the principal architect of water pollution control legislation. M. Kent Jennings explained why this reputation was justified: "Not only did [Blatnik] perform the major legislative roles of sponsorship, marshalling of support, negotiating and bargaining with others, and planning of overall strategy, he also played an innovative and initiatory role." (p. 108) Two illustrations from Jennings' account of Blatnik at work reveal the chairman's competence in managing his subcommittee and in bargaining with his senatorial counterpart. During the 1956 markup sessions on his bill Blatnik skillfully disarmed the opposition to the enforcement provisions: "The chairman called for a vote on each major section, but saved the grants-in-aid provisions until the end, rather than presenting them in proper order, and the Republicans, holding their fire until the grants section was introduced, allowed the enforcement provisions to slip by without much objection." (pp. 76–77) Again, in shepherding the 1959 water pollution control bill through Congress Mr. Blatnik deliberately omitted from the bill, as reported by his committee and passed by the House, any provision for use of "low flow augmentation" to help control pollution. Blatnik knew that Democratic Senator Robert S. Kerr of Oklahoma, manager of the comparable bill in the Senate, had championed this approach for some time. As Jennings described it, "[Blatnik] and his aides felt that it would be wise to leave it [the provision for low flow augmentation] out of H.R. 6441 because this would give them something to bargain with at the conference table. As it turned out, their expectations proved sound." (p. 100)

While legislative leadership from within Congress usually comes from members with some seniority who have established themselves as experts on the committee with legislative jurisdiction over a field, there are exceptions. An aggressive freshman member (particularly in the Senate) looking for a major cause to enhance his reputation both within Congress and at home can also provide initiative and decisive leadership. The problem studies furnish two illustrations: Democratic Senator Harrison Williams of New Jersey in his handling of the urban mass transit legislation, and Democratic Senator Edmund S. Muskie of Maine in his role in the passage of the Clean Air Act of 1963. Moreover, in the food stamp case the prime generator in the House of Representatives was not even a member of the Agriculture Committee that managed the bill. Thus, ideas can be generated and sold by an aggressive initiator with little prior congressional experience, and even by a member who is outside the committee responsible for the legislation in question.

The fluidity in patterns of legislative leadership is further demonstrated by evidence of how sources of initiative can change over time when Congress is dealing with issues that have been before it for several sessions. The replacement of a veteran committee chairman by a younger member intent on winning recognition for legislative accomplishment can be decisive. This factor was at work in altering the mix of initiatives for legislation controlling water and air pollution. The elevation of Democratic Senator Pat McNamara of Michigan to the chairmanship of the Senate Public Works Committee, following the deaths in rapid succession of Senators Kerr and Dennis Chavez, Democrat from New Mexico, opened new possibilities. When, in addition, first-term Senator Muskie—actively seeking to build a reputation as an effective legislator —was appointed to head the key subcommittee, the stage was set for passage of major programs for water and air pollution control. New centers of initiative in the Senate committee made a crucial difference.

Interest group professionals, House and Senate staff, and executive agency legal and technical experts are also potential sources of legislative initiatives, at times playing significant roles in developing creative program ideas, in bargaining to compromise differences, and in mobilizing and maintaining support among members of Congress. Their contribution is likely to become especially important when bills involve complex technology and intricate problems of regulation, as, for example, in the Clean Air Act of 1963. At two different stages in the legislative history of this statute congressional staff, interest group professionals, and executive agency specialists made decisive contributions.

Randall B. Ripley considered in some detail the roles of Hugh Mields, Jr., of the American Municipal Association (later with the United States Conference of Mayors), and Dean Coston, special assistant to Health, Education, and Welfare's assistant secretary for legislation, in winning support for the inclusion of federal enforcement in the proposed legislation. Both were key centers of personal strength and influence in the coalition favoring federal enforcement. Mields "worked consistently for a strong bill and followed through by presenting specific proposed language. He provided a crucial element of continuity in the process." Coston's enthusiastic support for a strong bill, in Ripley's judgment, "eventually resulted in the commitment of the President. Again his contribution [like that of Mields] was personal and not institutional." (p. 275)

Creative participation by interest group professionals, this time in collaboration with Capitol Hill staff, also came during the drafting of the enforcement section of the air pollution bill in the Senate's Special Subcommittee on Air and Water Pollution. The parent committee's staff director, legislative assistants from three senators' offices, and a small group of representatives from the industries most directly affected by the proposed legislation met in frequent and extended sessions for more than a month to produce a viable bill. The technical specialists from the chemical, coal, iron and steel, and oil industries were basically opposed to any legislation. But they were aware that some bill was going to be enacted and, knowing intimately the special pollution problems of their own industries, were prepared to work "within the realm of the possible." This meant a willingness "to talk about details in an effort to remove what they considered to be objectionable features of the bill." Ripley described the give-and-take process through which acceptable compromises were attained:

> In general the industrial groups moderated their positions on the bill as the Senate subcommittee work on it progressed. After their initial proposals were rejected by the subcommittee they began to propose a series of more limited changes until finally they reached a point on which they and the subcommittee could agree. . . . Their position was thus sifted through a

series of filters—primarily rebuffs of a number of specific proposals—until it reached a point where it could have considerable effect on the language of certain parts of the bill (p. 267)

This process produced a bill that won wide bipartisan acclaim; it embodied federal enforcement, yet the most deeply affected industries felt "they could live with it."

Informed judgment on tactics and access to a key congressional decision maker at the critical moment are other important contributions that may come from outside Congress as well as from within. Two cases in the series provide illustration. Robert F. Kennedy, then attorney general, rescued the juvenile delinquency bill late in the 1961 session. His direct approach to Democrat Howard W. Smith of Virginia, chairman of the House Rules Committee, helped to bring the bill out of the Rules Committee and to the floor for final passage. (pp. 132–33) The urban mass transit bill had languished in the Rules Committee for more than a year because House Democratic leaders feared that they lacked the votes to pass it. The urban lobby groups—the Municipal Association and the Conference of Mayors—teamed up with railroad and transit companies to establish the Urban Passenger Transportation Association with the mission of getting the legislation passed. The paid lobbyist for this group, Lawrence Henderson, working closely with the ranking Republican member of the Housing Subcommittee, William B. Widnall of New Jersey, finally threatened and cajoled the Democratic leadership into risking a floor vote on the bill. Then, to ensure its passage, the association and Congressman Widnall worked hard to hold in line the thirty-nine favorable Republican votes. They succeeded. (pp. 342–45)

Of course, legislative initiatives that are ill-conceived and inept can contribute directly to the defeat of legislation. Judith Heimlich Parris developed this point in describing the failure of the Kennedy administration and its Senate leaders to win congressional approval for the reorganization plan to establish a Department of Urban Affairs and Housing: "the White House failed to get either a department or clear cut votes on the merits. . . . The immediate cause of this failure lay in the realm of legislative tactics." (p. 209) Such bungling initiatives may, like the successful ones, come both from inside and outside the Congress.

The most important finding regarding legislative initiatives that emerges from these seven studies concerns the vitality of Congress itself as a source of initiative in legislating on urban problems.[1] In five cases

[1] Lawrence H. Chamberlain in *The President, Congress and Legislation* (Columbia

—aid to airports, air and water pollution, food stamps, and urban mass transit—Congress provided the leadership, the continuity, the persistence in formulating new policies and programs and guiding them through the political thicket of the legislative process to final decision.[2] In most of these cases, it is true, there were important assists from interest group representatives or executive agency professionals. In contrast, however, these same cases reveal executive department leaders, the White House, and the Bureau of the Budget for the most part either hesitant and divided, resulting in halting and sporadic initiative, or frankly opposed, resulting in outright obstructionism.

This finding must of course be examined in the light of the changing political environment that marked the period from the mid-1950's to the mid-1960's. When one party controls the White House and the executive branch while the opposition party dominates both House and Senate, the political situation stimulates the majority leadership in Congress to exercise policy initiatives. Such was the case during the Eighty-fifth and Eighty-sixth Congresses when many of the events reported in these studies actually occurred. The shift to one-party control of both executive and legislative branches came with the election of 1960. In the Eighty-seventh Congress, with the Democrats holding both the White House and Capitol Hill, measures that had been developed and refined, often in futility, by the Democratic majority leadership during the latter years of Dwight D. Eisenhower's presidency had reasonable prospects of presidential and executive branch support. This was true for water pollution control and the food stamps program. Initiative in juvenile delinquency legislation and in efforts to establish a Department of Urban Affairs actually shifted from Congress to the President with the advent of John F. Kennedy to the White House.

---

University Press, 1946) reached a similar conclusion after examining systematically and in some detail the legislative history of ninety major bills passed by Congress over a fifty-year period from 1890 to 1940. He classified these bills as follows: 19 (approximately 20%) involved preponderant presidential influence, 35 (approximately 40%) preponderant congressional influence, 29 (approximately 30%) joint presidential-congressional influence, 7 (less than 10%) preponderant pressure group influence. (Pp. 450–53.) Chamberlain concludes: "These figures do not support the thesis that Congress is unimportant in the formulation of major legislation. Rather, they indicate not that the President is less important than generally supposed but that Congress is more important." (P. 454.)

[2] In the two remaining cases, involving juvenile delinquency legislation and the bill to establish a Department of Urban Affairs, the principal initiative came from the White House.

In two other cases—urban mass transportation and air pollution control—legislative initiative remained significantly with Congress despite a young, vigorous President who was the acknowledged leader of the majority party in both House and Senate. Royce Hanson characterized the dominance of congressional initiative in the passage of urban mass transit legislation as "one of the most intriguing aspects of this case." He continued:

> The role of the administration in the entire process was marginal. . . . At no time did the administration exercise forceful leadership.
>
> [Senator] Williams and the mayors, aided by [Senator] Sparkman, engineered the early Senate actions and finally moved President Kennedy to save the program in the conference committee. [Congressman] Widnall, [lobbyist] Henderson, and the industry were the catalysts in the House, where the leadership was lethargic in its efforts to find the votes needed for passage. There was little administration pressure for a vote until Widnall "blew the whistle" on the leadership. Clearly, it cannot be said that the administration championed the cause of urban areas and was frustrated by an uninterested or anti-urban Congress. (p. 348)

Randall Ripley reached much the same conclusion in his study of the Clean Air Act of 1963: "This case should give pause to those who contend that the only hope for urban areas resides with the executive. Here, without Congress, the executive would have produced legislation less far-reaching in its provisions than what was produced with the help of Congress." (pp. 277–78)

The case studies, then, cast considerable doubt on the stereotype of a passive legislature simply responding to presidential initiatives. When opposing parties control the presidency and the Congress, the political environment for policy making invites and positively encourages the exercise of congressional initiative. Moreover, even when the political environment would tend to dampen congressional initiative—for example, when a young, aggressive President occupies the White House and his party is in full command of both House and Senate—even then Congress may prove to be the dominant force in advancing new program ideas in some policy fields, in shaping certain bills and guiding them through to enactment. Champions of urban causes, therefore, can look to Congress as well as to the President for leadership in initiating new policies and programs and in pressing for their enactment into law.

*The Importance of Issue Context.* Issue context refers to the way members of Congress perceive a policy proposal that comes before them, how they consciously or unconsciously classify it for study and analysis, what specified policy setting or group of policies they believe it is related to. These frames of reference go a long way toward providing a structure to guide consideration of the proposal in the legislative process. They help to determine what kind of approach is taken in analyzing it, whose advice enjoys privileged access, whose knowledge is considered expert, and how much attention is given to the urban dimensions. Indeed, they directly influence outcomes: whether legislation is adopted, what its nature will be, and—equally important for these studies—what happens to the urban interest involved.

Many of the bills to which Congress devotes a large proportion of its time in every session fall easily into well-established issue contexts. The policy questions involved have been considered frequently in the past; the same committees handle the legislation each time; representatives of the same executive agencies and interest groups that testified pro and con in past years usually appear again in much the same roles; sources of support and opposition within Congress tend to be substantially the same; even the issues debated may change very little. Whatever changes do occur are likely to be marginal. In other words the issue context, which is known and anticipated, is in effect a conservative influence no matter how much the facts giving rise to the immediate problem may vary from one session to another. This is the pattern for appropriations bills, for rivers and harbors bills, for labor legislation, for agricultural bills—indeed for most major legislation. The fact that issue contexts are well known and commonly accepted does not lessen controversy or rigidly predetermine outcome. Rather, the point is that in many fields of public policy Congress over time has established well-defined patterns for decision making.

Not so, however, with many urban problems when they enter the congressional arena. Urban concerns are easily sidetracked or subsumed under more salient political issues. Policy for urban areas often emerges indirectly as a result of the pursuit of another objective. Or the urban dimension—the implication of a policy idea for urban development—is passed over entirely. Often the urban interest appears to be too fragile or too new to survive as a major issue in its own right. Federal aid to airports was adopted to promote civil aviation; its contribution to metropolitan development was a by-product. The Department of Urban Affairs bill failed to pass in 1962 in part because it became submerged in a civil rights issue.

The history of the Federal Housing Administration (FHA) program, which was discussed briefly in Mrs. Parris' study of the Urban Department bill (p. 175), is another case in point. When the first FHA bill was adopted by Congress in 1934, congressmen, senators, and other policy makers viewed it as economic recovery legislation designed to create new jobs in the sagging building construction industry, to stimulate home building, and to help support and encourage real estate investment. The potential, long-range impact of the program upon urban development—the fuel it would furnish for the great migration of city dwellers to the suburbs to become home owners, with the consequent blighting of the core city—was scarcely, if at all, perceived. The absence of well-structured issue contexts for urban-related problems helped to mask the significance of this legislation for metropolitan development, delaying a confrontation until after World War II. By that time the complex of problems associated with central city blight had become infinitely more severe. Even so, the immediate post-war legislation on housing and slum removal was viewed as a major means to the goal of full employment. Expanding the labor force in the construction industries was a way to absorb extensive manpower released from military service, and at the same time meet the pent-up demand for housing created by the rigid restrictions upon home building during the war years. Federal policy concerning urban development was still evolving indirectly as a latent function of programs to promote recovery and expansion of home construction. Only with the progression of new laws from the Housing Act of 1949 through urban renewal legislation to the Demonstration Cities Act of 1966 did the federal government finally begin to build a deliberate policy on urban development. The costly failure of Congress in the 1930's and 40's to recognize the significance for metropolitan development of its urban-related legislation—a failure occasioned by the absence of established frames of reference emphasizing the urban dimension—caused severe aggravation of already serious problems of city life.

A careful reading of the seven legislative cases confirms the central importance of issue contexts in congressional efforts to cope with urban problems. But, as the seven studies also suggest, there is little evidence that Congress has developed regular patterns of decision making where urban problems are concerned.[3] To put it another way, Congress has

[3] Certain urban problems—for example, housing, slum clearance, and urban renewal—have occupied congressional attention over a long enough period of time to have achieved status as relatively routine areas of congressional decision making. Although there are still highly controversial policy issues involved, such as the rent supplement issue in

not yet developed stable issue contexts organized around the notion of "urban affairs policy." When a bill related to urban concerns is introduced there is little to go on in trying to predict how legislators will perceive it or what frames of reference they will employ to inform and direct their problem analysis and formulation of a solution. The situation is revealed clearly by a comparison of the water and air pollution studies. While Jennings in his case study concluded that water pollution was not considered essentially an urban problem (pp. 106–07), Ripley observed that "everyone who was concerned about air pollution, both in Congress and in the executive, made it clear that the problem was centrally urban in character." (p. 225) Obviously, two quite different issue contexts were present.

The frames of reference congressmen bring to bear on particular legislative proposals are built up over time under the subtle influence of many factors, in part institutional, in part political, and in part derived from the nature of the substantive policy itself. The seven case studies afford some insight into how issue contexts tend to be fashioned in the urban policy field and how unstable they can be.

*The Impact of Institutional Factors on Issue Context.* The committee to which a bill is assigned in the House or Senate helps at the very start to define the frame of reference members will employ in viewing this policy proposal. It also helps to structure the way interest group leaders, executive agency representatives, and the informed public view the issue. Legislative proposals in well-established policy fields like agriculture, taxation, immigration, and the like will be referred to the same standing congressional committees that have considered bills in that policy field for generations. The committee system is reasonably well designed to encourage rational and comprehensive policy making in these fields. For bills concerned with urban problems, however, the situation is quite different. Assignment to a committee is as likely to mask as to make clear the urban dimension of the legislative proposal. Committees of the national legislature are organized largely on the basis of governmental functions, cutting across the concerns of geographic areas around which local governments are organized. Not one of the committees in either house demonstrates broad concern for urban dimensions of the issues be-

---

the Eighty-ninth Congress, the issue contexts for housing bills and urban renewal tend to follow standardized patterns. (The emergence of federal policy on urban development is described briefly on pp. 13–16 of the Introduction.)

fore it. The groups that most nearly approximate this broad concern are probably the Housing Subcommittees of the House and Senate Banking and Currency Committees, or perhaps the District of Columbia Committees, but even here each pair of committees has its own special orientation, the former functional and the latter geographic. The seven legislative cases reveal six different House committees and six different Senate committees playing a central role in managing bills about urban problems. No wonder Congress has not yet developed reasonably stable issue contexts to guide the approach taken to urban affairs!

The effect is obvious when bills significantly related to urban matters come before committees and subcommittees organized around other interests. The Senate Commerce Committee's Aviation Subcommittee, which considered aid to airports, is designed to be more concerned with the governmental function of promoting civil aviation than with solving problems of urban areas. The House Agriculture Committee is discharging its responsibilities properly when it looks upon food stamp legislation as an aspect of surplus crop disposal, and not as an urban welfare program. The committee of origin helped to determine the issue context in which these two legislative proposals were considered.

Yet committee jurisdiction in both House and Senate is not rigid, and the situation sometimes permits maneuvering. For example, although transportation bills are normally assigned to the Commerce Committees of the two houses, the urban mass transportation bill was introduced by Senator Williams, a member of the Housing Subcommittee of the Banking and Currency Committee. The Williams bill was written so as to stress the identification of the urban transit problem with other urban concerns rather than as an addition to national transportation policy. The bill, for instance, assigned responsibility for administration of the program to the Housing and Home Finance Agency (HHFA), not to the Commerce Department or the Interstate Commerce Commission. Also, it was full of amendments to existing housing laws. When it was referred to the Banking and Currency Committee instead of the Senate Commerce Committee, the chairman of the Commerce Committee made no objection.[4] The urban mass transit bill was perceived by most members of

---

[4] Royce Hanson in discussing the background of the Williams bill, first introduced in 1960, noted that "the [big-city] mayors and their new allies, the railroad and transit interests, initially also conceived of the issue [of urban mass transit] in terms of transportation policy rather than urban policy." Accordingly, the group began its legislative work "based on a strategy of working through the Commerce Committees of Congress. . . . The Transportation Subcommittee [of the Senate Commerce Committee] showed

Congress in the issue context of urban problems legislation and not as a part of transportation policy. This first assignment created a precedent that will lead in time to a pattern.

Assignment of the Williams bill to the Housing Subcommittee helped to ensure serious attention to the urban dimensions of the legislation. A leading Democrat on the Surface Transportation Subcommittee of the Commerce Committee, Senator Frank J. Lausche of Ohio, later led floor opposition to the bill; it is interesting to speculate on what might have happened to the urban interest embodied in this bill had it been managed by the Commerce Committee under his influence. Clearly, in that event the policy setting for the legislation would have been defined differently.

The functional orientation of congressional committees conforms roughly to the organizational patterns of the executive branch. These similarities help to reinforce the interdependence and mutual interests that bring together the agency officials, congressional committee members, and interest group leaders concerned with the same area of governmental function.[5] Given these patterned relationships of mutual support, the origin of a legislative proposal in a particular agency or assignment of a bill to a particular committee has much to do with determining who will administer the program. It is also likely to determine the organized interests that will enjoy favored access. To continue the illustration cited above, the urban mass transportation program was established by Congress as an additional function of the Housing and Home Finance Agency and not assigned to the predictably more hostile Commerce Department. Big-city interests had close ties with the HHFA (now the Department of Housing and Urban Development), while highway and transportation interests with privileged access to the Commerce Department could only look on from the outside.

Another aspect of the congressional committee structure that may at times alter the frame of reference within which urban problems are considered is the long-standing jurisdictional rivalry between the substantive committees and the Appropriations Committees. On several occasions in

---

little interest . . . ; after all, the subcommittee's focus was the rail industry, and not cities or nonrail mass transit systems." (p. 315)

[5] See J. Leiper Freeman, *The Political Process: Executive Bureau-Legislative Committee Relations* (rev. ed., Random House, 1965) for a detailed analysis of how a "policy-making subsystem" can emerge from the interactions among these three components— congressional committee members, executive bureau officials, and interest group leaders.

recent years this rivalry has complicated congressional efforts to assist in the resolution of urban problems. The mass transit story is again a case in point. Here the traditional conflict was aroused when the committees writing the legislation proposed "back-door" spending—that is, giving the administering agency contract authority enabling it to borrow from the Treasury rather than depend on annual appropriations to finance its grant-in-aid operations. This "back-door" approach strikes at the roots of the power vested in the two Appropriations Committees. When this issue is raised it can lead to a significant restructuring of the way members view the urban policy under consideration. Instead of a debate over alternative ways to cope with the actual problem, the debate revolves around a defense or attack on the annual appropriations process, often with little regard for the substantive policy issues involved. When this occurs congressional institutional factors have succeeded in distorting the issue context for formulating federal policy for urban areas and in undermining the integrity of the policy-making process.

Congressional procedures are at times another important institutional influence on the way a proposed bill is viewed. Skilled legislative tacticians can on occasion force a major test of strength over a procedural question and in the process completely evade a direct confrontation on the substantive issue. This, too, can lead to a drastic redefinition of the issue context. The ill-fated efforts of the Kennedy administration to achieve approval from the Eighty-seventh Congress for converting the Housing and Home Finance Agency into a new Department of Urban Affairs illustrate this point. The administration's legislative goal could have been achieved either through passage of a conventional bill or through congressional defeat of a resolution disapproving a reorganization plan submitted by the President. The administration first tried the route of the conventional bill, only to have the bill bottled up in the House Rules Committee without ever coming to a floor vote in either chamber. Determined to make a second effort, the President submitted a reorganization plan, believing that if it failed he would at least gain a partisan election issue. To achieve his ends it was important to obtain a record vote in both houses on the resolution expressing disapproval, preferably with the floor vote occurring first in the Senate where administration support was more dependable. When the resolution to reject the reorganization plan was unexpectedly called up in the House before the Senate Government Operations Committee had completed its study of the plan, there was no recourse but to try for a Senate vote to discharge this committee. This was the only floor vote secured in the Senate on the issue of the proposed Department of Urban Affairs and Housing; it was not a vote on substance but on whether to discharge a committee from further work on the reorganization plan. Judith Parris captured the sentiment of the vote, highlighting how the urban issue before the Senate was obscured by the redefinition of its context through procedural tactics:

> Congress is jealous of its prerogatives; the administration's reorganization plan had touched upon some of them. This issue reached its zenith in the Senate, as the key vote was taken on whether the Government Operations Committee should be discharged. [Democratic Majority Leader] Mansfield's remarks were patently defensive. . . . He noted that "the President's hand was forced" by the House Rules Committee veto and that the reorganization plan had been the only recourse of the White House. (pp. 210–11)

Thirteen of the sixteen standing committee chairmen in the Senate joined in voting against the doomed discharge petition. An important urban issue was here sidetracked into a procedural contest for power between the new administration and the congressional oligarchy of committee chairmen. Institutional factors sharply skewed the issue context of this legislative proposal.

*The Impact of Political Factors on Issue Context.* The way congressmen perceive an urban issue, or any issue for that matter, is often significantly conditioned by political considerations. In the more highly structured fields of public policy, the influence of politics upon the frames of reference is likely to be stable and predictable. Such is hardly the case with policy issues involving urban affairs.

One recurring concern of the sponsors of urban legislation is how to avoid having their bill labeled a "big-city bill." Given the rural tradition and the small-town orientation of many members of the Congress, champions of urban legislation in a number of the case studies worked strenuously to define the issue context for their proposals so as to allay the opposition of and attract support from those representing non-metropolitan constituencies. Jennings reported that the grants program in the water pollution control legislation was carefully designed "to give relatively more aid to the smaller urban locales" in order to attract "the support of congressmen and state officials representing the smaller to medium size municipalities." (p. 106) Similar efforts in two other instances brought little or no results. Mrs. Parris observed in regard to the bill to establish a new Department of Urban Affairs that "the stigma of a 'big-city' bill dogged the proposal throughout its days," despite "direct reference to smaller localities [which] was intended to combat this argument of opponents." (p. 196) John E. Moore observed that "advocates of juvenile delinquency legislation were sensitive to the potentially crippling impact of its association with urban problems, and took pains to point up the rural aspects of juvenile delinquency." (p. 122)

On several occasions, as the studies show, politics intervened with telling effect in the form of high partisanship. President Eisenhower's veto of the airport aid bill in 1958 and the unsuccessful efforts to override his veto turned the substantive issue (with its urban development overtones) into a straight partisan issue of Republican "economizers" versus Democratic "reckless spenders." The study of the Food Stamp Act of 1964 affords a particularly interesting example. In this case partisanship actually transformed into urban legislation a bill that in the twenty-five years it had been before Congress in one form or another had never been thought of in this way. Randall Ripley noted the anomaly: "That food stamps should be so clearly identified as a 'gut' urban issue was somewhat incongruous. The Agriculture Department had made evident its intent to help rural areas with the program too. And, in theory at least, one major purpose of the program was to get rid of farm surpluses. . . ." (p. 301) The key to this paradox was the efforts of House Democratic leaders, the White House, and the Agriculture Department to get urban Democratic votes for the administration's wheat-cotton bill by trading rural Democratic votes for the food stamp bill. Ripley described the way the stage was set:

> Gradually during March it became clear that the trade would involve the food stamp bill and the wheat-cotton bill. No formal announcement was made of such a trade. Indeed, no formal meeting was held at which leaders of urban and rural blocs agreed on it. Instead, and this is typical of the operations of the House, it was a matter of a favorable psychological climate. The more the individual members and the press talked about a specific trade of rural votes on food stamps for urban votes on wheat-cotton the more firmly the exchange became implanted in the minds of members. It was, in short, based on shared perceptions of a legislative situation in the House. This was bolstered by individual lobbying efforts relying on it as a persuasive point. (p. 300)

Three issues familiar in contemporary politics ran through several of the legislative cases, and without exception served to alter the issue context and divert attention from the urban concerns involved. These are the issues of economy, of federalism (or states' rights), and of civil rights. In each of the cases involving some form of loan or grant provision to enable state and local governments to cope more effectively with an urban problem, states' rights were invoked in the debate and advocates of the balanced budget inveighed against federal spending. Royce Hanson, in describing the response of the Eisenhower administration to the original Williams bill to support urban mass transportation, noted that the Treasury Department "emphasized its feeling that urban mass transit was a local and private industry responsibility." He quoted President Eisenhower's acting secretary of the treasury, Laurence B. Robbins, in a statement combining the themes of states' rights and economy in attacking the bill:

> The Department believes that Federal financial assistance should be limited to situations where such assistance is considered necessary to achieve impelling national policy objectives and Federal participation in programs which are more appropriately the responsibility of States and local authorities must be held to an absolute minimum if budget expenditures are to be kept within reasonable limits in the years ahead. (p. 318)

Democratic Senator Strom Thurmond of South Carolina sounded the federalism theme in threatening to filibuster the juvenile delinquency bill on the last day of the session in 1959: ". . . the Federal Government has no jurisdiction in the field [juvenile delinquency] under the Constitution; and . . . even if it did . . . it would be more advisable to leave this field in the places where it more rightly belongs—in the home, the school, the community, and, if necessary, action by the State." (p. 119)

Perhaps the most dramatic illustration of how a sharply divisive issue can transform the way many members of the Congress view an urban problem occurred when the Urban Affairs Department bill in 1962 became ensnared in a civil rights controversy. President Kennedy had appointed the talented Negro economist and housing expert, Robert C. Weaver, to be administrator of the Housing and Home Finance Agency. The bill before Congress proposed to elevate this organization to full department status. Judith Parris pointed up the dilemma:

> . . . Weaver increasingly became an issue. The President, hoping to avoid the controversy as much as possible, still had made no commitment to name the HHFA Administrator as the secretary-designate. Yet Mr. Kennedy had also refused to assure Democratic Senator John J. Sparkman of Alabama,

chairman of the Senate Banking and Currency Subcommittee on Housing and ordinarily an administration ally, that he would not appoint Weaver. By now most of those close to the scene thought that Weaver was slated for the job, and few southern legislators could face with equanimity the prospect of helping a Negro into the cabinet. Sparkman, liberal on every issue except civil rights, champion of the HHFA, and one-time advocate of the [new] department, refused to support the bill. If Sparkman did not support the measure, it was clear to the White House that few southern senators would.

In the House, where the administration's working majority was still narrower, the outlook for votes from the southern bloc was even more bleak. (p. 199–200)

These illustrations indicate clearly the conditioning effect politics can have in shaping the way Congress approaches a proposed policy. In these cases the effect was to obscure the central urban questions involved, sometimes forcing important decisions to be made on totally irrelevant grounds.

Presidential politics can have similar distorting effects on the issue context. It was in part the concerns of presidential politics that involved the Department of Urban Affairs bill in the civil rights controversy noted above. As Judith Parris brought out, the White House made the strategy decisions on this bill. Why, then, with the bill still before the House Rules Committee, did the President choose to force Congress to take a stand rather than bide his time for a more favorable situation? Mrs. Parris characterized the White House assessment of the situation:

> The political support of the urban North, including the Negroes, was of greater importance to him [President Kennedy] than the voting support of the South in Congress. Indeed, if the matter came to a simple choice, a public posture as champion of the big cities and a Negro cabinet member was far more valuable than the housekeeping advantages of promoting the HHFA to cabinet status.
>
> A push for the department, whatever its outcome, would publicize the President's stance and redound to his political advantage. (p. 201)

The requirements of presidential politics, as assessed by the President and his advisers, called for pressing the Rules Committee to act. When that showdown killed the bill, the next decision was to resort to the alternative approach, the reorganization plan. Mrs. Parris also put this strategy in the context of presidential politics:

> By the time the Senate hearings on the reorganization plan ended, the White House no longer expected to win the battle to create the new cabinet

agency. Nearly all the urban Republicans whose support the administration had hoped to gain, particularly because of the civil rights issue, were refusing to rise to the bait. The South appeared to be lost. . . .

Nonetheless, the President wanted every member to stand up and be counted in response to an official roll call. If he won Republican votes after all, he might possibly get the department. If he lost them, he had a ready-made campaign issue to take to the urban and Negro voters who were the core of his electoral strength. (p. 209)

The urban issue here involved had become a pawn in another game, the game of presidential politics, and strategy and tactics were designed according to the rules of that game. Whether the legislative outcome would have been any different with a different approach is beside the point. The frame of reference within which congressmen viewed the bill had been transformed when the President decided to make use of the department proposal for partisan ends. The frame of reference had first been redefined by the intrusion of the civil rights issue and then further redefined to meet the demands of presidential politics.

*The Impact of Policy Content on Issue Context.* In addition to institutional and political factors influencing the way congressmen view a legislative issue, the nature of the substantive policy is also a significant influence. A field of public policy usually has its own distinctive character that helps to shape the issue context of legislative prospects in its area. Tax policy, for example, is inherently more sensitive politically than many policy fields, for bills in this area are likely to affect powerful economic interests and significantly large numbers of voters.

As a field of national policy, urban affairs encompasses highly varied substantive content, since urban problems in fact span the gamut of requirements for living in that most complex creation of modern society, the metropolis. The conceptual and definitional confusion that results was discussed briefly in the Introduction. (pp. 3–5) The intermingling in urban policy issues of areal concerns with functional concerns is likely to pose perplexing problems for legislators. They are more inclined to think of governmental policy and program as organized solely around governmental functions. This conforms to the familiar jurisdictional patterns of executive departments and agencies and of congressional committees. Major legislative proposals before Congress are typically couched in the language of governmental function and addressed to existing programs established on a functional base.

There may be an underlying, perhaps subconscious, reason for this bias. Since the members of Congress themselves represent geographic areas, there may be a concern that legislative proposals reflecting areal interests directly might polarize members along irreconcilable lines related to the kinds of constituencies they represent. As long as legislators can fit urban problems into the more familiar patterns of governmental function, they may be able to avoid, or at least mute, such polarization.

The difficulties of trying to define an appropriate issue context for a particular legislative proposal in the urban affairs area is clearly indicated in Royce Hanson's analysis of federal efforts to define the urban transportation problem:

> Normally, the federal bureaucracy contains an impressive assortment of specialists in a public policy area. But urban transportation was a new area of focus. Heretofore, federal transportation policy had been concerned with the national, or at least the regional, requirements of the major carriers. Also, it was heavily biased toward regulation of carriers and development of a national highway system, rather than toward urban development and urban transportation problems. (p. 314)

Three agencies of the federal government possessed some expertise—the Interstate Commerce Commission, the Bureau of Public Roads in the Department of Commerce, and the urban planning components of the Housing and Home Finance Agency. Yet the three were widely separated. Each saw only a segment of the urban transportation situation, possessed only a portion of the essential data, and viewed the problem through the highly distorting lenses of its own program concerns. For largely political reasons, and not from a technical assessment of the problem, the solution developed in the Urban Mass Transportation Act of 1964 viewed mass transit as an urban development problem, with its roots in "the impact of mass transportation on land uses and the urban economy. . . ." (p. 317) In his concluding comments Hanson generalized from the experience with urban transit legislation to the broader problem of developing national policy for urban affairs:

> Finally, the history of urban mass transportation legislation emphasizes the difficulty that both Congress and the executive branch have in coming to grips with complex urban problems. Technical data are not available. Conventional federal financial or appropriations practices are not easily adaptable to meet the need, even if it can be precisely defined. For new problems involving such variables as impact on land use, employment, and the development of new technology, neither branch of government is adequately staffed to define the problem, much less solve it. And the Congress is

not organized to review legislation in an "urban" perspective. (p. 349)

Hanson's analysis indicates that in this instance the formulation of effective policy required that Congress adapt the complex technology of rapid, mass transportation to the special needs of the urban setting—concern for land use and the potential impact of a rapid transit system upon patterns of physical, economic, and social development in the urban area. Inherent in urban affairs as a policy area is this special requirement of reconciling and synthesizing the technical requirements for performing a particular governmental function or service, such as providing public transportation or controlling delinquency, with the technical requirements for maintaining balanced and "liveable" urban centers.

The difficulties facing legislators in trying to develop such a synthesis are further compounded by the gap that sometimes exists between the perspectives of professional specialists and of informed laymen. Furthermore, not infrequently there will be sharp differences of doctrine and opinion dividing various groups of specialists in their approaches to some urban problem. The controversy over implementing the juvenile delinquency legislation passed in 1961 is a case in point. John Moore has recounted the bitter conflict between congressional sponsors of the act and those in the executive branch responsible for directing the program. This disagreement was viewed by Democratic Congresswoman Edith Green of Oregon and her colleagues on the House Special Education Subcommittee as an instance of willful departure from the legislative intent expressed in the act. They had visualized the act as supporting "action projects," providing "federal aid for research and demonstration projects designed to develop and test a number of specific approaches to juvenile delinquency control" such as "the early identification of potential delinquents, the use of former delinquents to reach the unrepentant, the impact of school dropouts, and the laws affecting the employment of minors." President Kennedy's Committee on Juvenile Delinquency and Youth Crime, on the other hand, had endorsed "the comprehensive community-oriented attack on juvenile delinquency" and contemplated "integrated programs in a few communities" with the primary emphasis upon "intensive and coordinated efforts on the part of private and governmental interests." As Moore observed, "although the two approaches were not mutually exclusive, there was a significant difference in emphasis." (pp. 141, 128) When the modest appropriation ($10 million annually for three years) was devoted largely to comprehensive integrated projects requiring advance planning of nine to twenty-four months,

Mrs. Green and many of the other original sponsors became increasingly disenchanted. Moore commented: "So long as the professional enjoys the layman's confidence, the communications gap between laymen in Congress and experts in the executive branch is not especially important. Once that confidence has been lost, however, the layman is unwilling to let the expert proceed independently, and is frequently unable to specify alternative approaches." (pp. 152–53)

As a policy field, then, urban affairs poses some difficult problems handicapping efforts to build reasonably stable issue contexts. Judging from these seven legislative case studies, the policy content of urban affairs is often concerned with new technologies and with innovation in approaches to social and human, as well as physical, problems. Often solutions will call for an interdisciplinary approach, perhaps involving complex intergovernmental relations. Frequently the federal government has little or no past experience in this area. Always the demand is for new and creative solutions; and some of the problems may in fact be insoluble. When policy proposals of this nature are before Congress, it is safe to predict that the task of developing relevant frames of reference will be extremely perplexing and frustrating. In addition, frames of reference to be adequate in this field must provide some basis for synthesizing the concerns of geographic area and of governmental function. Despite these difficulties, however, the building of reasonably stable issue contexts within which to examine urban affairs policy proposals is essential for congressional understanding and constructive action.

*Congressional Voting on Urban Affairs Legislation.* In the legislative problem cases record votes were examined wherever possible to identify predominant voting patterns, and especially to test the pull of urban and rural constituencies upon the voting behavior of congressmen and senators. In five cases the roll call votes demonstrated a dominant pattern of party voting.[6] The evidence was clear: all five cases involved legislation sponsored by the Democratic congressional leadership, and in every instance rural and small-town Democratic members voted in much larger

[6] These cases involved voting on the Federal Airport Act of 1959, the Water Pollution Control Act of 1961, the Juvenile Delinquency and Youth Offenses Control Act of 1961, the Food Stamp Act of 1964, and the Urban Mass Transportation Act of 1964. Voting on the Clean Air Act of 1963 deviated from the pattern, showing substantial support from both sides of the aisle; indeed, in the Senate the vote for the bill was unanimous. Voting in the seventh case, on a Department of Urban Affairs, is discussed separately below.

proportions to support these urban bills than did Republicans from urban and suburban districts. This predominance of party influence over constituency influence strikingly confirms the finding of much research on Congress that political party is most likely to be the decisive factor in congressional voting.[7]

Within this general pattern in the cases, however, some minor deviations occurred, reflecting the pull of constituency factors. In almost every vote examined, the Democratic majority lost a significant minority of its members to the opposition. The deserters tended to share certain characteristics: they represented rural–small-town constituencies, largely in the South, and their voting records reflected fairly consistent opposition to an expanding role for the federal government. On the other side of the aisle the reverse occurred: Republicans voted heavily against the legislation, but generally a few broke party traces to join the Democratic majority for the bill. These Republican deviants, too, shared certain characteristics: they represented urban-suburban constituencies, largely in the Northeast and Far West, and they tended somewhat more than most Republicans to favor expansion in the role of the federal government. This finding that constituency factors explain, or help to explain, the variations from the standard practice of party voting is also supported by much prior research on congressional voting behavior. Political scientist Lewis A. Froman, in reviewing the principal findings of such research, noted: "These studies [of congressional roll call voting] indicate that party is the single most important predictor of roll-call behavior, and that constituency factors explain most of the deviation from party votes."[8]

The one exception to this pattern occurred in the voting on the ill-fated bill for a Department of Urban Affairs, defeated in 1962. In the House the voting was badly skewed by a civil rights twist that solidified southern opposition. Only one vote was taken in the Senate; it came on a procedural issue bringing forth indignant opposition from all defenders of Senate prerogatives.

In addition to supporting the simple conclusion that both party and

---

[7] See n. 7, p. 8, in the Introduction.

[8] Lewis A. Froman, Jr., "Inter-Party Constituency Differences and Congressional Voting Behavior," *American Political Science Review,* Vol. 57 (March 1963), p. 57. Also see Julius Turner, *Party and Constituency: Pressures on Congress* (The Johns Hopkins Press, 1951); Duncan MacRae, Jr., *Dimensions of Congressional Voting* (University of California Press, 1958); and David B. Truman, *The Congressional Party* (John Wiley, 1959).

constituency influences are salient, the cases also suggest the presence of an ideological element that usually reinforces the effectiveness of both party and constituency pressures. Every one of the five case studies that showed the standard voting pattern concerned passage of legislation involving an expansion of federal government activities in urban affairs and an increase in federal spending. On both these issues it is safe to predict a cleavage within Congress along liberal-conservative lines; floor debate on the bills and the patterns of interest group support generally reflected this underlying ideological division. The subtle interaction of ideology, political party, and type of constituency, and their combined impact upon congressional behavior are suggested by Randall Ripley in his study of party leadership in the House of Representatives. In exploring the significance of party loyalty—the willingness of congressmen to follow the policy positions taken by their party leaders—Ripley discovered among members of the House of Representatives that degree of party loyalty and general ideological predispositions tend to vary within each major party according to the urban or rural nature of the members' constituencies:

> Loyalty [of congressional party members to their party leaders] varied according to the urban, suburban, or rural nature of the district. In the case of Democrats, the rank order of most loyal to least loyal was suburban . . . , urban . . . , rural. . . . Among Republicans, rural members were most loyal. The urban members were the next most loyal. . . , and the suburban members were the least loyal. . . . The ideological stances of these three groups tended to be the same within both parties: suburban members the most liberal (hence the most loyal Democrats and the least loyal Republicans) and rural members the most conservative (least loyal Democrats and most loyal Republicans).[9]

Lewis Froman also explored the relationships among constituency, party, and congressional voting. He was interested in discovering whether voting differences between Democratic and Republican congressmen can be explained by differences in the kinds of constituencies they come from. Accordingly he compared the voting behavior and constituency characteristics of northern Democratic congressmen and northern Republican congressmen in the Eighty-seventh Congress, first session. Measuring constituency differences in terms of gross socio-economic indicators, Froman found that

[9] Randall B. Ripley, *Party Leaders in the House of Representatives* (Brookings Institution, 1967), pp. 155–56.

congressmen from each party tend to represent different kinds of constituencies. Northern Democratic constituencies are more urban, more racially mixed, have a lower percentage of owner-occupied dwelling units, and have more people per square mile than Northern Republican constituencies. In other words, factors usually associated with "liberalism" (urban, lower socio-economic status, non-white, and densely populated areas) are the factors actually associated with the more liberal party.

Froman concluded modestly: "It seems a fair inference that Democrats have more liberal voting records partially, at least, because they come from more liberal constituencies." He later reinforced this conclusion when he looked at the more marginal cases and found that "Democrats from conservative-type districts and Republicans from liberal-type districts do tend to vote more conservatively and liberally, respectively, than their party cohorts."[10]

These are not dramatic findings, or startling conclusions. They do not fly in the face of conventional wisdom. But they do underline the difficulties of trying to isolate and analyze with any precision the determinants of congressional voting behavior in legislating for urban areas. The simple analyses of roll call votes employed in the legislative problem studies offer confirming evidence that voting on urban affairs bills, like voting on other kinds of legislation, tends to follow a dominant pattern of party voting. But the votes may also be taken as evidence of potentially important constituency influences and perhaps of the effect of ideological predispositions. Are there other factors that can help to explain the dynamics of congressional voting on urban problems legislation during this period?

Perhaps significant as causal factors are the subtle changes occurring in the power systems of both House and Senate. In the House of Representatives the Democratic Study Group (DSG), a relatively cohesive bloc made up largely of liberal northern and western Democrats, many representing urban and suburban constituencies, came on the scene during the Eighty-fourth Congress. This informal group grew in size until it included about half of the 257 Democrats in the House during the Eighty-eighth Congress and almost three-fifths of the 295 House Democrats in the Eighty-ninth Congress. It had an influence on legislative outcomes during much of the period covered by the studies reported in this volume. During this time the group maintained its own whip organization and a small professional staff that prepared background analyses of certain proposed and pending legislation. Its effectiveness was hard to mea-

[10] Froman, "Inter-Party Constituency Differences," pp. 58–59, 60.

sure except in isolated cases of highly visible activity, like the DSG whip operation during floor consideration of the 1964 Civil Rights Act. Throughout that long debate DSG efforts helped to ensure that ample liberal majorities were on hand at a moment's notice to frustrate the legendary parliamentary skills of the old-guard southern leadership. In the late 1950's and early 1960's many DSG members in a very real sense served as spokemen for urban causes, reflecting in their committee work and on the floor of the House broad concern for employing federal power and resources boldly to solve human problems.[11]

Urban lobbyists have frankly asserted for some time that in the Senate they can count on substantial support for most urban causes; it is the House of Representatives they have to worry about. The sheer size of the Democratic majority in the Senate from the Eighty-sixth Congress through the Eighty-ninth Congress has been one obvious factor. Another has been the Senate's amazing Democratic Class of 1958, which survived almost intact when its members faced reelection in 1964. In the more loosely structured Senate several of these able young Democrats progressed rapidly to subcommittee chairmanships. In two instances members of the Class of 1958 achieved positions of dominant influence over issues especially important to urban areas: Senator Edmund Muskie while in his first term became chairman of the Subcommittee on Air and Water Pollution of the Public Works Committee; Senator Harrison Williams, also in his first term, emerged as the expert on urban transportation in the Housing Subcommittee of the Banking and Currency Committee, and managed the mass transit bill on the floor.

Finally, the significance of vigorous White House leadership must be noted—leadership that is attuned to the problems of urban life and prepared to bring federal resources to bear upon their solution. In both the Kennedy and Johnson administrations the thrust from the White House to Capitol Hill was directed toward positive action on legislation for urban affairs. This single fact may well have been decisive in producing legislative success in several of the cases examined here.

Forceful presidential influence and new sources of leadership in the majority party in both House and Senate have served to reinforce the tendency toward party voting on urban issues. While influences of constituency and ideology have occasionally worked to produce variant be-

[11] See Ripley, *Party Leaders*, pp. 176–77; Richard Bolling, *House Out of Order* (Dutton, 1965), pp. 54–58; Kenneth Kofmehl, "The Institutionalization of a Voting Bloc," *Western Political Quarterly*, Vol. 17 (June 1964), pp. 256–72.

havior, for the most part these factors also seem to have reinforced the pull of party. Not surprisingly, House and Senate majorities for passing these urban affairs bills have tended to be Democratic party majorities. This raises the interesting possibility that what is occurring is a settling of political debts, that urban voters are cashing in their political notes with the national Democratic party in the White House and on Capitol Hill. To put it another way, perhaps the apparent dependence of urban dwellers upon the Democratic party for action to solve urban problems is the reverse side of that party's historic reliance on big-city political organizations and voter turnout as the heart of its electoral coalition in national politics. The same cities that have voted substantially for Democratic presidential candidates have increasingly been forced to seek solutions to their growing problems by turning first to state capitols and then to Washington. Issues salient to urban dwellers thus become more and more "nationalized," more often determined by decisions taken in Congress and in the White House. As this occurs the participation of urban dwellers in national politics becomes more important, not just in determining election outcomes but perhaps also in influencing legislative outcomes. If this is a reasonably accurate assessment of currents in contemporary American politics, then political parties are destined to play an ever more crucial role in representing metropolitan interests, and there is likely to be an increasing nationalization not only of urban issues, but also of big-city politics.[12]

## Urban Affairs as a Field of National Policy

The legislative problem studies reveal no widespread recognition and acceptance of urban affairs as a field of national policy. Members of Congress typically have not yet developed stable frames of reference through which to approach the analysis of urban problems. Not infrequently, important urban dimensions are shunted aside as a congressional committee pursues some other aspect of the policy proposal before it. Definitional and conceptual confusion surrounds the idea of urban problems as a policy sector. In comparison to established policy fields like agricultural policy, labor policy, or foreign trade policy, urban affairs policy appears vague and hopelessly diffuse.

[12] See Charles E. Gilbert, "National Political Alignments and the Politics of Large Cities," *Political Science Quarterly*, Vol. 79 (March 1964), pp. 25–51.

Yet at the same time the legislative cases do contain bits of evidence suggesting that some recurring patterns of urban affairs politics are beginning to emerge. Certain spokesmen for urban causes appear in a number of the case studies. Some of the more interested pressure groups have taken stands often enough to make their position on proposals for new programs reasonably predictable. Skilled urban government officials and local political leaders are developing stable relationships with certain executive agency personnel in Washington. Local leaders are maintaining channels of access to sympathetic members of Congress, to certain congressional committees, and to committee staff specialists. Some junior members of the House and Senate now look upon urban affairs as a potential field for legislative specialization, a field in which to build a legislative career. Congressional district reapportionment is beginning to have its effect in redressing the balance of power between urban and rural areas in the House of Representatives; and reapportionment is also beginning to change the faces of state legislatures across the country.[13] At the least, urban affairs can be described as an incipient field of national policy making, with a structure of politics beginning to emerge around some urban issues.

*An Urban Affairs Policy Spectrum.* What light do the case studies shed on the problem of defining an urban affairs policy sector? Indeed, they pose the conceptual problem neatly, for the issues serving as the focus of these studies do differ in the extent to which the urban dimension is dominant. The policy continuum, suggested in the Introduction (p. 9), can at this point help to relate the urban issues analyzed in the problem studies to the whole range of policies that concern urban dwellers and urban areas. How do the issues fit into this continuum constructed along the dimension of "urban-relatedness"? None of these issues would be located near the "low urban-relatedness" end of the spectrum. This part of the continuum is reserved for such fields as tax policy and foreign trade policy, for example—matters of concern to all members of a mass society, including urban dwellers, but with no special relevance to urban areas or to people living in cities. In these fields the causes of the problems to be remedied, their incidence, and the direction

[13] Perhaps the most persuasive evidence that reapportionment is in fact increasing the legislative power of urban-suburban areas is the determined efforts of congressmen and senators representing rural and conservative interests to change or delay the application of the Supreme Court's "one man, one vote" doctrine by every possible constitutional and legal means.

of efforts to cope with them do not appear in any significant way urban-based or urban-related.[14]

Policies for urban mass transit and air pollution control would clearly belong at the "high urban-relatedness" end of the continuum. Solutions to these problems are intimately involved in the governmental function of urban development; problem analysis and the design of appropriate remedial action are in both cases peculiarly urban-related. Where the problems in question are exclusively urban problems, the policies to cope with them are distinctively urban affairs policies. Other programs and policies located at this end of the spectrum would include those for urban and community renewal, housing and building code enforcement, urban open space, and local planning assistance.

The center portion of the spectrum claims the great variety of public policies concerned with issues that are significantly urban-related without being distinctively and exclusively urban. Such problems become more severe within areas of greater population density; their solution is complicated by the presence of the city. Issues in four of the legislative studies—aid to airport development, water pollution control, the food stamp program, and control of juvenile delinquency—are all properly located in this part of the continuum. Policies to cope with juvenile delinquency, for example, would fit into this central portion of the spectrum closer to the exclusively urban end than, say, education policy or policies to promote employment and economic growth. Obviously the incidence of delinquency is greater in densely populated areas of metropolitan cities. Underlying causes and proximate causes are both likely to be urban-related, growing out of congested living in racial ghettos, overcrowded schools, inadequate recreational facilities, and the anomic existence associated with impersonal life in the big city. Moreover, remedies for the complex problems of delinquency may well involve important urban components, or be closely tied to new programs and responsibilities that become the charge of the city government. Yet juvenile delinquency is not solely an urban issue, for it occurs in sparsely settled areas as well, nor are its causes necessarily or solely urban-based. Policies to cope with juvenile delinquency are as appropriately included in an urban affairs policy sector as are urban renewal policies, but there is a difference:

[14] It is, of course, possible to conceive of certain specific tax policies that would be highly urban-related; for example, land taxes designed to stimulate certain kinds of development and discourage other less socially desirable land uses in urban areas. Such policies would be a part of the urban affairs policy sector as well as part of the field of tax policy.

urban renewal is part of the governmental function of urban development; control of juvenile delinquency warrants inclusion in urban affairs policy because of areal considerations, the presence of the city. Efforts to formulate and implement policies to deal with juvenile delinquency must recognize and build on this factor, the urban environment.

The urban policy continuum does not in itself provide a clear definition of the appropriate scope for urban affairs as a field of national policy. It does, however, point the way to developing definitional criteria for such a policy sector. It suggests three broad categories into which domestic policy can be classified: policies with no significant urban dimension, those concerned with problems that are distinctively and exclusively urban, and all those policies in between that are directed to problems not exclusively urban but having an important urban component. The latter two groups make up the field of urban affairs policy.

It is now possible to sketch in broad outline the nature of urban affairs as an identifiable field of national policy making. First, it contains a nucleus composed of policies designed to cope with distinctively and exclusively urban problems. This core group of policies is associated with performance of the governmental function of promoting urban development. Secondly, the policy sector embodies a broader group of policies designed to remedy problems that have important urban components without being exclusively or peculiarly urban. These problems and the policies to cope with them are significantly urban-related because they occur and are intensified in cities and because their solution is severely conditioned by the presence of the urban environment. These policies constitute the areal dimension of the field. Since the problems involved are not exclusively urban, this part of the policy sector may intersect or overlap with other policy fields at any number of points.

Defining the scope of urban affairs policy making in this flexible fashion fits well with the dynamic character of the field. As the function of urban development itself expands, generating more complex technology and placing new demands on government for additional policies and programs, the core of the policy sector can expand too. The broader category of urban-related policies can also readily accommodate new policies and programs designed to treat newly emerging problems. As urban growth continues, problems and policies now considered insufficiently urban-related to be a part of this sector may develop such significant urban dimensions as rightfully to claim inclusion. The conception of the urban affairs policy sector proposed here will tolerate such additions.

The field of urban policies defined in this manner cannot claim exclusive boundaries, separating it from other policy sectors. Policies and programs addressed to issues like poverty, air and highway transportation, crime, racial and ethnic conflict are part of urban affairs policy but they are also part of welfare policy, or transportation policy, or economic development programs, or law enforcement programs. One might wish for a more tidy system of classifying major public policies into self-contained categories; but such a system would depart from the realities of modern living, especially living in great metropolitan areas. Lasting solutions to many of the problems associated with urban living can come only through comprehensive analyses of problems and the development of coordinated attacks upon them. Emphasis upon the overlap between, say, civil rights programs and urban affairs policy is much more likely to bring progress toward remedies for destructive rioting in the slums than an artificial abstraction of civil rights policy making from the context of the decaying urban environment in which racial tensions fester and grow. The interrelationships of causes and the coordination of remedial efforts require direct attention. To view racial tensions as a concern of urban affairs policy makers and the slum conditions of the ghetto as a concern of civil rights policy makers is constructive. An honest and realistic conception of the urban affairs policy field must call attention to these overlaps and focus upon the need for more coordination in the search for remedies.[15]

While this broad definition of the urban affairs policy sector does enlarge the field, it does not destroy its integrity. As long as the problems and policies included must meet the test of a considerable degree of urban-relatedness, then the field can be held to manageable proportions. Its scope defined in this fashion is not coextensive with all national domestic

[15] The approach to policy analysis proposed by political scientist Theodore Lowi (see n. 6, p. 6, in the Introduction) might prove especially useful in exploring these overlaps among policy fields. Lowi's categories for public policies—distributive, regulatory, and redistributive—are intended to cut across traditional, subject-matter policy sectors and focus upon distinctive elements of decision-making style, patterns of coalition building, and uniformities in the structure of politics as the basis for associating policies. Accordingly, this approach might yield a kind of cross-sectional analysis, perhaps revealing new dimensions of affinity and conflict among groups of public policies. Even a superficial examination of the policy issues involved in the seven case studies in this volume suggests that each of these issues could properly be classified in one or another of Lowi's three categories.

policy. Still it is broad enough to contain both the functional dimension (urban development policies and programs) and the areal dimension (urban-related policies and programs).

*Implications for Congressional Structure and Procedure.* The executive branch has already recognized the field of urban affairs policy as it is defined here, and reflects the nature of the field, at least in part, in its organization for formulating policy and administering programs concerned with urban areas. Under clear presidential leadership, and with the support of Congress, the executive branch took the major step in this direction in 1965 by establishing the Department of Housing and Urban Development. As its name implies, this department is concerned with issues in the core of the urban affairs policy sector: its central role is administering national policy to guide the direction of urban growth. Seeking a more comprehensive approach in the administration of urban programs, the department from the beginning has served to bring more coherence to federal policies and programs for aiding cities.[16] Perhaps it can also furnish a better channel for the expression of urban concerns in the legislative process. Certainly it brings into the arena of national policy making another, and higher status, actor with a commitment to the central importance of urban problems.

The more serious structural problems for urban affairs policy making lie in the legislative branch, for, as noted earlier, the structure and process of the House and Senate are not well suited to giving comprehensive consideration to the needs of cities. Institutional adaptations in the executive branch can undoubtedly help, but they are not an adequate substitute for some modification in the organization of Congress itself

[16] In 1963, two years before the establishment of the Department of Housing and Urban Development, Norman Beckman, then assistant director for metropolitan areas on the staff of the Advisory Commission on Intergovernmental Relations, expressed bluntly the need for coordination in developing and implementing urban policies and programs: "Present organization and staff for development and coordination of urban policies and implementation are at best minimal, probably less than for any other major area of federal activity involving a comparable number of agencies. It can be said with some truth that we have an agricultural policy, a foreign policy, even a housing policy, but there is little to point to in the way of an urban development policy." Norman Beckman, "Our Federal System and Urban Development: The Adaptation of Form to Function," *Journal of the American Institute of Planners,* Vol. 29 (August 1963) pp. 157–58. Mr. Beckman left the Advisory Commission in 1966 to become director of the Office of Intergovernmental Relations and Urban Program Coordination in the Department of Housing and Urban Development.

to facilitate effective policy making in this field. Ideally the structural arrangements should reflect something of the nature of urban affairs as a field containing both functional and areal dimensions. The task is to formulate arrangements that will reconcile both functional and areal considerations, and also provide a focus for expressing congressional concern with urban problems.[17]

The National League of Cities, experienced in working on urban-related bills with many congressional committees reflecting widely varying jurisdictions and interests, has proposed the establishment of a joint congressional committee on urban affairs.[18] The league's proposed committee would be modeled after the Joint Economic Committee, with broad research responsibility but no legislative mandate. The joint committee idea is admittedly a modest suggestion, for it could be accomplished without disturbing the present jurisdiction of any committees in either house. It would represent a start, however, and a start with some symbolic value. Sparked by a few powerful and aggressive members of the House and Senate ready to champion urban interests, and skillfully guided in a strategy of building close relationships with key legislative committees responsible for managing bills, such a joint committee could make a useful contribution. By assembling an able professional staff, conducting imaginative studies, and holding public hearings, the committee could become a leavening influence and an important additional source of legislative initiative.

[17] See James Fesler, *Area and Administration* (University of Alabama Press, 1949), for an informative discussion of the problems of reconciling functional concerns and areal concerns in the administration of federal programs. His analysis highlights in another setting the difficulties faced by cities—areal governments—in adapting their needs and demands for assistance to a federal legislature and executive branch organized to develop policy and provide aid largely on the basis of governmental function.

[18] Mr. J. Kinney O'Rourke, general counsel of the National League of Cities, set forth the proposal in testimony before the Joint Committee on the Organization of the Congress in June 1965: "It would be impossible, from a practical standpoint, to sort out all of the Federal activities and programs affecting urban areas and place them within the jurisdiction of one committee in each House, as is intimated by the provision of the national municipal policy [a comprehensive declaration of policy adopted by the National League of Cities each year at its national convention]. We suggest, therefore, that you consider the establishment of a Joint Committee on Urban Affairs. We suggest that the committee be charged with undertaking broad studies of urban problems and Federal-aid urban programs. The committee should study the problems these programs are designed to solve and make recommendations to the appropriate legislative committees regarding the implementation of Federal-aid programs and the creation of new ones." *The Organization of Congress*, Hearings before the Joint Committee on the Organization of the Congress, 89 Cong. 1 sess. (1965), Part 7, p. 1058.

The essential importance of issue context, however, suggests that there is probably no satisfactory substitute for the establishment of a legislative committee on urban affairs in each house of Congress. As long as the House and Senate conduct vital legislative business through a system of highly specialized committees, any field of public policy for which no legislative committee feels or expresses proprietary concern is doomed to remain dependent on the vagaries of legislative politics. A joint committee with no legislative jurisdiction might help somewhat, but it cannot meet the more serious need for a concerned committee in each chamber with full authority to manage urban affairs bills on the floor. Without such committees, urban interests—as the legislative problem cases reflect—win recognition only when they are in a coalition with interests politically more viable.

But establishing a standing legislative committee on urban problems in each house represents a much more difficult objective. To give such new committees adequate scope would require collecting bits and pieces of jurisdiction from many other standing committees in the House and Senate. Each established committee threatened with a loss of power and jurisdiction would represent a potential rival, ready to contest the new competitors on every bill they sponsored. There are, however, recent precedents for the transfer of jurisdiction to new legislative committees—the Science Committees—and also for the establishment of new legislative committees through the consolidation of old committees—the two Armed Services Committees. These may be looked upon as general precedents, but they do not offer direct analogies to the case at hand.

The Eighty-ninth Congress' Joint Committee on the Organization of the Congress suggested another approach that is likely to prove more acceptable than carving up the jurisdictions of many existing committees to create new legislative committees on urban affairs. The joint committee proposed adding jurisdiction over urban affairs legislation to the responsibilities of an already existing legislative committee in each house. Specifically, it contemplated that the Senate and House Banking and Currency Committees would be redesignated committees on banking, housing and urban affairs. In support of this recommendation the *Final Report* of the joint committee stated:

> The phenomenal growth of urban areas, the enormous problems this growth has spawned, and the current and probable future expansion of Federal programs to deal with these problems, signified in part by the creation of a new Department of Housing and Urban Development, point to the need

for specialized congressional recognition of this increasingly significant area of public policy. The present concern of the Banking and Currency Committees in each House with housing problems, coupled with the membership and staff expertise in this general area, make these committees the logical instruments for the evaluation of proposals dealing with new matters affecting urban areas. The Joint Committee does not feel, particularly in view of the relatively light workload of these committees as they now exist as well as their expertise in the area of housing, that a separate urban affairs committee in each House is needed.[19]

Positive action on this recommendation would create two legislative committees serving as congressional counterparts to the Department of Housing and Urban Development. Since the Banking and Currency Committees already possess legislative jurisdiction over many of the programs carried on by the department, the transfer of jurisdiction from other legislative committees would be minimal. These newly constituted committees of Congress and the Department of Housing and Urban Development would then become the principal policy-making agents for the core area of the field of urban affairs, that is, for policies and programs exclusively urban and concerned with the governmental function of guiding urban development.

But there would still be an important place for a nonlegislative joint committee on urban problems. It would symbolize and give expression to congressional concern for the significant areal (city) dimensions of issues not exclusively urban—issues like water pollution control, crime and delinquency prevention, antipoverty programs, and others that are located in the broad middle sector of the urban policies spectrum. In many cases such issues would clearly be outside the legislative jurisdiction of the committees on banking, housing and urban affairs, and also outside the mandate of the Department of Housing and Urban Development. Responsibility for managing bills on these matters would remain with the same functionally organized legislative committees in the House and Senate that have handled them in the past. Thus the Public Works Committees would continue to manage water pollution control legislation; antipoverty legislation and juvenile delinquency bills would still come before the House Education and Labor Committee and the Senate Committee on Labor and Welfare. But when such bills contained a significant urban component the members of the joint committee on urban problems would have special access and would speak with special author-

---

[19] *The Organization of Congress,* Final Report of the Joint Committee on the Organization of the Congress, S. Rept. 1414, 89 Cong. 2 sess. (1966), p. 17.

ity. The joint committee should be composed largely of congressmen and senators who represent highly urbanized districts and states. To ensure effective coordination, its members should also include some who hold seats on the principal committees and appropriations subcommittees having jurisdiction over legislation with important, though nonexclusive, urban relevance.

The proposed joint committee would perform a "watch-dog" role, ensuring that Congress would give adequate attention to the urban dimension of *all* relevant bills under consideration. Through staff studies and well-planned public hearings on significant problems and issues, the committee could help to establish a foundation of urban affairs policy upon which the legislative committees could build when formulating specific bills. Imaginative legislative leaders on this joint committee and a skilled research staff would have full opportunity to explore new urban concerns, anticipating emerging problems before they became acute, and seeking out ways to coordinate better and make more comprehensive the main body of policies for the urban component of national life.

Standing legislative committees on banking, housing and urban affairs and a nonlegislative, joint committee on urban problems could contribute much to developing more stable frames of reference to guide congressional consideration of urban problems. Assignment to these committees would be attractive to many House and Senate members because of their obvious constituency relevance. Urban interest groups, finding a central source of urban affairs competence in Congress would be encouraged to develop continuing relationships with those committees and their staffs; this in turn might contribute more stability and cohesiveness to the interest groups themselves. Finally, such structural and procedural developments would match the rising importance of urban affairs in national politics and serve the interests of both national political parties by developing legislative specialists capable of giving constructive leadership in the shaping of party positions on urban issues.

## The Nature of Urban Interest and Their Representation

The legislative problem studies are for the most part inconclusive when examined for clues about the nature of urban interests and the patterns of interest representation. Indeed, the most significant findings are negative: no traditional, comprehensively defined and well-organized urban interests appear; nor have the case studies revealed any identifiable, conscious, and broad urban constituencies. Though disappointing, this is not surprising when one recalls the diffuse nature of metropolitan politics. The interests of urbanites tend to be organized around a host of special concerns of particular groups. Moreover, efforts to develop a broader urban political constituency are very likely to be frustrated by the complexity of overlapping jurisdictions at the local level: congressional district lines, county lines, municipal divisions, and special district lines crisscross the city map. State boundaries often intervene to complicate further any approach to urban interests on an area-wide basis. Political scientist Norton E. Long, in a provocative essay on "The Local Community as an Ecology of Games," has pinpointed the consequences for city government of the many interacting groups pursuing their own specialized ends:

> The lack of over-all institutions in the territorial system [the city] and the weakness of those that exist insure that co-ordination is largely ecological rather than a matter of conscious rational contriving. . . . [But] even in a city where the municipal corporation provides an apparent over-all government, the appearance is deceptive. The politicians who hold the offices do not regard themselves as governors of the municipal territory but largely as mediators or players in a particular game that makes use of other inhabitants. . . . They play politics and politics is vastly different from government if the latter is conceived as the rational, responsible, ordering of the community.[20]

The problem is compounded by the difficulty of mobilizing the natural constituency or clientele of important new urban-related programs. Despite growing experience in the "war on poverty," little is yet known about how, or indeed if, the poor and underprivileged can be organized, or potential and actual delinquents can be mobilized for constructive activity. But these groups obviously require representation in some form. Can reliance be placed on the fiction of "virtual representation" through social workers, parole and probation officers, housing and urban renewal specialists, and so on? The Office of Economic Opportunity is trying through its community action programs to bring representatives of the poor into effective participation in planning and implementing local antipoverty programs. Success or failure in these efforts may possibly provide guidelines for coping with the alienation of such "unorganizable" groups. Yet the pressure group pattern affords little promise of provid-

[20] Norton E. Long, "The Local Community as an Ecology of Games," *The American Journal of Sociology,* Vol. 64 (November 1958), p. 255.

ing representation for these kinds of interests. One long-time student of interest groups, E. E. Schattschneider, made the point pungently: "the heavenly chorus [of pressure groups] sings with a strong upper class accent. Probably about 90 percent of the people cannot get into the pressure system."[21]

Is it perhaps chasing a will-o'-the-wisp to search for urban constituencies that are more than a temporary collection of special interests coming together around a particular issue? Some argue that the distinction "urban" is no longer meaningful. "There are no longer urban problems and rural problems," they say, "only human problems." In some philosophical sense this is clearly true; yet political debate is still structured around these distinctions. Members of Congress, agency bureaucrats, and politicians at all levels still respond to cues expressed in these terms. And interest group spokesmen, local officials, and members of urban-based professions still give the cues.

As urban affairs gains recognition as an identifiable field of public policy, what effect is this likely to have upon urban interests and the way they are represented in the political process? An urban affairs policy sector, defined as suggested above, could provide a number of organizing themes around which presently segmented interests might coalesce. The nucleus of the sector, those policies and issues distinctively urban and related to the governmental function of urban development, could be one such unifying theme. A grouping of physical planning and development interests can be readily conceived, focused on programs of the Department of Housing and Urban Development and identified with the function of guiding urban growth. The remainder of the policy sector, consisting of urban-related problems and policies, can be visualized as falling into clusters, each centrally concerned with the urban *areal* dimension of another governmental function, such as education, welfare, economic development, and so on. Some of these clusters could also serve as organizing themes for urban interests, each cluster functioning as a magnet to attract a loose coalition extending over a number of related issues and programs. One coalition might emerge around the theme of economic development, for instance, its policy centered on the federal programs of the Economic Development Administration and certain activities of the Office of Economic Opportunity. Such urban-interest coalitions, loosely organized around identifiable sets of problems, issues, and pro-

[21] E. E. Schattschneider, *The Semi-Sovereign People* (Holt, Rinehart & Winston, 1960), p. 35.

grams, each set associated with a different governmental function, might in time evolve into relatively coherent urban constituencies. The "pressure politics map" of urban areas would then contain a number of urban constituencies, each an aggregation of interests sharing involvement in some governmental function with important urban dimensions, and each able to focus governmental and political attention upon meeting defined problems. This would be moving closer to broad-based urban constituencies and away from the chaotic situation of a jungle of special urban interests symbolized in the description of the city as an "ecology of games."[22]

Development along such lines would be a modest adaptation of established patterns of pressure politics to meet the special needs of urban interests and their representation. While such an adaptation is theoretically possible, the evidence provided by the legislative problem studies is too fragmentary to establish that this kind of development is in fact occurring, or that it is likely to occur. Indeed, in some ways the pluralistic character of urban interests appears to be incompatible with typical patterns of pressure group politics. Perhaps an alternative model of representation through more inclusive political organizations like political parties is more appropriate and congenial to urban interests.

*Urban Interests and Political Parties.* Is it possible that urban interests, in their essential nature, are like consumer interests? And is it possible

[22] Robert H. Connery and Richard H. Leach, in their book *The Federal Government and Metropolitan Areas* (Harvard University Press, 1960), contrast urban interests to the essentially unified agricultural interest and conclude that the absence of a unified metropolitan interest has much to do with the haphazard and disconnected way Congress deals with urban problems: "Although Congress has paid considerable attention to a number of individual urban problems over the past twenty years, it has done so only haphazardly. It has ignored the problems of metropolitan areas as such . . . there is a fundamental difference between the kind of one-interest situation that exists in the case of agriculture and the many-interest situation that exists in metropolitan areas. The political power of the farmers is, to be sure, the result of their overrepresentation in legislative halls and their effective political organization, but even more, it is the result of the fundamental unity of their particular interest. In metropolitan areas, there are a great many interests, many of which are opposed to one another." (P. 94.) In trying to draw conclusions from this kind of comparison between urban interests and agricultural interests, it should perhaps be recalled that organized agricultural interests also were slow to emerge. Despite the overwhelmingly rural character of the population when the Constitution was adopted—with some 90 percent of the people dependent upon farming for their livelihood—it still required almost a century to aggregate agricultural interests and to evolve self-conscious, stable, and continuing group organizations to represent these interests.

that as the United States becomes more and more urban in the midst of affluence, new patterns are beginning to emerge in American politics, patterns giving a much larger role to consumer values? In this country consumer interests have always posed difficult problems for politicians —and for political scientists. They are essentially residual or latent interests, for everyone is something else first and a consumer second. The "something else" has typically been "producer"—merchant, or farmer, or machine operator, or teacher. Through much of American history one of the dominant political patterns has been bargaining among these producer interests for a greater share of the national income. Today, however, for many people living in metropolitan areas (and two-thirds of Americans now do), the ability to live better already depends more on opportunities to *spend* with greater intelligence—that is, on "consumer bargaining"—than it does on ability to earn more—that is, on "producer bargaining." The spurt in public sector spending during the 1950's and 60's can be viewed in large part as a governmental response to the rising demands of urban consumers. Every day federal, state, and local governments devote more energies and more resources to providing public services and facilities, most of which are for urban dwellers. This is the dynamic, expanding area of government at all levels—more and better education, health services, highways, recreational facilities, and so on. Concomitantly, except for national defense and foreign relations, the traditional governmental functions, while still important, have become relatively more stable, with levels of operation and support apparently growing far more slowly. The increasing power of consumer values is apparent in the political controversies revolving around the extent and quality of governmental services and their distribution, whether concerning medical care, clean air, or the expansion of public universities to accommodate the youth of a mass urban society. Perhaps a transition is already under way toward a more balanced politics reflecting a larger role for consumer bargaining and ample recognition of both consumer and producer values.

Conceiving urban interests as consumer-like or residual helps to explain the difficulty, even perhaps the futility, of trying to organize city dwellers for pressure politics. Pressure politics are most effective when built around the exclusive concerns of well-defined and relatively small groups of articulate, single-minded people. But this pattern of organization and representation may be ill suited to the needs of larger groups with multiple and diffuse interests, interrelated in part yet lacking cohesion, and at times in open conflict.[23] This is clearly the nature of urban interests. Mobilizing and giving effective expression to such groups of interests—inclusive rather than exclusive in kind—is a job for the large-scale political organization, in short, for the political party. Within the party urban constituencies can capitalize on their size and find a mechanism for mediating and reconciling internal differences. Urban interests, then, can best find representation and expression by moving into the national arena of party politics.

The emergence of metropolitan problems as high-priority issues in national politics is already well under way. Walter Lippmann saw the trend in 1965 when he observed, "The edifice of the Great Society will have to be built, if it is to be built at all, in the great cities."[24] This trend means an increasing voice for urban voters in congressional politics and, with it, further pressures on the Congress to adapt its structure and process to the needs of legislating for urban areas. The two major political parties already recognize that presidential elections are decided in the nation's highly urbanized states and especially in the metropolitan cities. Their presidential campaigns have increasingly become a national competition for the support of urban voters. The time is fast approaching, perhaps is now here, when the parties will base their appeal to those voters on proposed national solutions to urban problems, and on the party's performance record in governing metropolitan communities. City dwellers will then achieve full representation for urban interests through the political process—representation in the Congress of the United States and representation in national politics. At that point urban affairs will have attained full status as a distinct and important area of national policy.

[23] As Schattschneider has observed, "Pressure politics is a selective process, ill designed to serve diffuse interests." *The Semi-Sovereign People,* p. 35.
[24] Walter Lippmann, "The Dog That Didn't Bark," *Washington Post,* Nov. 2, 1965.

# Index

391